JFK Assassi

Shades From The Fence

Jerry T. Dealey

JFK Assassination: Shades From The Fence

JFK Assassination: Shades From The Fence

Foreword

With the modern age of writing a book/eBook, there are things that will happen. So, let me get this out of the way, first:

JFK was probably killed as the result of a shooter named Lee Harvey Oswald.

Do you hear the virtual 'Slamming' sound? That is the sound of every extremist that believes that there was a Conspiracy in the Assassination of JFK, and Oswald was an innocent "patsy". Some of them have just slammed this book shut! They will probably go into Social

Media such as Facebook, Twitter, etc. and start proclaiming that this is a Warren Commission / "Lone Nut" viewpoint and should never be read. Some of the more extreme will claim that I am a Warren Commission apologist (or worse names), and should never be listened to. Some may even want to "string me up". I expect it. I have been doing this far too long, to expect anything else.

So, let's also go the other way:

There was very likely a Conspiracy to Assassinate John F. Kennedy.

Do you hear more 'slamming' sounds? This is the sound of the believers of "Lee Oswald acted alone". It is probably a lesser noise. But it is equally stubbornness to a mind made up, whether accurate or not. People will jump to the idea that this is just another "Conspiracy Theory", and should simply be disregarded. OK. I just lost a number of those that believe that Lee Harvey Oswald acted completely alone

I have gone out of my way to make these 2 statements up front. I want these 2 statements to show up in the early part, so that the 'extremists' of either group, will stop "wasting their time"! I can live with them disappearing, and immediately criticizing this work, based on their own 'slant' on the JFK case.

Let me eliminate a 3rd group:

JFK Assassination: Shades From The Fence

I will NOT tell you who killed JFK!

If you bought this book thinking I will tell you who killed JFK, you should also stop reading now. (If you did not yet buy the book/eBook, now is the time to return it to the shelf or click out.) Again, let's give 'them' a chance to move on....

This book is about the Research involving the JFK Assassination. If you already know what you believe, then do NOT buy or read this book. I will not convince you in any fashion whatsoever. I don't expect to. There are some that simply have not made up their minds about who was behind the Assassination. This book is dedicated to them.

Sure. I will present information about the case, including an overview of what happened that day. I will also touch on many theories of the case. This includes the Warren Commission 'theory' (that is what it is....not a 'fact') of the case.

If my writing is an eBook, I want them to see these statement on the first page, so that they do not 'buy' a book that is opposite of their viewpoint. I am tired of dealing with those that limit their viewpoint, and refuse to look at other opinions. That includes BOTH sides of the JFK case. If your mind is made up, and you are set in your view of what happened: stop reading.

Give it a few seconds.... Some will stop now. Many will start 'slamming me' in the next few minutes on Social Media.

Still here? Ok. Now that they are gone... let's get started...

I can almost promise to bore you, and not fulfill your desire to know what happened. In addition, if you were looking for the chance to express your opinion about how stupid I am, and how my opinion is completely unsupportable.... you also will likely be very disappointed. Not that I can swear I am not really stupid, or that I can support my opinion. It is because I will not be giving any hard opinion! (But look for me on Facebook...we might engage there.)

Acknowledgements

There are 3 groups that I wish to Thank and Acknowledge.

As always, Diana, Ali and Jessie. My lovely wife and our two equally lovely daughters.

I especially want to thank Debra Conway and Jim Hess.

Debra was the owner and creator of JFK Lancer. It was a group of Researchers whose members were out to seek the truth. It was also founded with former co-owner Tom Jones, to allow the publication of books and other materials on the Assassination. In the early days only the largest and most sensational books were taken by the other Publishers, so Lancer became an outlet for the less known authors. (Before eBooks, where almost everyone can publish.)

Debra also allowed me to Moderate her JFKLancer.com Forum. I learned a lot from that Forum, even if it did tend toward the Conspiracy Theory side.

Jim Hess created the "Fair Play 4 JFK" Facebook group, which he still trusts me to Administer for him. This one tends to have more Lone Nut believers, but the majority of its 2500+ members poll as believing in a Conspiracy. I still feel it is one of the more balanced groups out there.

I hope I did, and continue to do a good job for both of these individuals.

Lastly, I seriously want to think every members of the JFK Assassination "Research Community" that I have debated, discussed, cussed, and dealt with. The interchange has been a great hobby for years, and even those that I disagree with I learn from. The group is too large for me to start listing names, but if you and I have civil discussion today, or had them in the past, you are part of that list.

My deepest thanks to all of you!

JFK Assassination: Shades From The Fence

Table of Contents

1. Why Bother?

Ok. Why am I bothering to write another JFK Assassination book? I swore I would never write one. There were thousands, and certainly no need for me to add to that overwhelming volume of information and opinion. I have no new information to contribute. There will be no 'smoking gun' here.

I was 8 years old in 1963, and did not even live in Dallas, Texas, at the time. However, I have been 'involved' in the JFK Assassination since the day it occurred. Mostly, it was because of my family name and heritage. Dealey is my real name. So it was a matter of having your family name being presented and dragged "through the mud" about the JFK Assassination. So…I have been involved for over 58 years, whether I wanted to be or not.

I am known in the "Research Community" (Community being a very 'loose' term) as being a Fence Sitter (FS). On some pages, that is called "Undecided". There are many flavors of Fence Sitter. That is what the title of the book implies as there are many "shades" of theories between the extremes. There are a lot of variations between the Black (Government/LBJ killed JFK and set up Oswald as a 'patsy') and White (WC – Oswald acted completely alone, without influence).

In my mind, what does "Fence Sitter" mean? It means that I am uncertain that JFK was killed as a result of a Conspiracy. In my opinion, there were certainly 'Conspiracies' to kill JFK (details later). But, I am uncertain that he was actually killed as a result of any of these Conspiracies. They may have simply existed, but Oswald could have acted without their influence or involvement, on his own. Or, he could also have acted while being involved with or influenced by others.

If you believe in either extreme, and have not already slammed the book shut, then I hope you will join us in the rest of the writing. I will not likely sway you away from your opinion. However, I hope to show you how every opinion matters, as well as those that are "on the Fence" about what happened. I cannot promise that I will convince you of any viewpoint; nor that I will dissuade you of any leaning that you already have. However, I will try to present both sides of any debate, and hope you will join us in an open discussion of both sides of the JFK Assassination.

I do not have the answers. I only wish I did....

So? Why write.....?

I have dealt with the JFK Researchers for many years. I have also read, and followed, many books on the subject. I debate with and know many of the Authors of these books. We have had spirited debates on the subject over the years.

Most of the books are based on one side of the other. There have been almost no writings on the 'Middle of the Road' viewpoint. For years, I never even saw the need. I still am uncertain if "need" is the right word? I will give you almost nothing new in the information of the JFK case. I will only discuss many, many questions, as well as talk about the many theories I have been subjected to over the years. Of course, I cannot guarantee that you have already been exposed to this information, as I do not know the reader's experience in studying the case. Perhaps you might get some new information, but no guarantees.

The last thing I wanted to do was to contribute to the thousands of books on the JFK Assassination. I had nothing new to contribute. I still don't.... But I have been dealing with every side of the Assassination debate for several years.

This writing will likely not be about the details and physics of the case. If that is what you want, I can suggest many excellent books on the subject. I will, of course, provide at least one short chapter on the "Events of the Day" as they occurred. This is the least I can do for the Newcomer to the case, who may have purchased this writing, thinking it would give them the details that they have not yet extensively researched, or read about. Those of you who have followed the case for years (if you are still reading this!), can certainly skip that, and any other chapter.

JFK Assassination: Shades From The Fence

Additionally, I will try not to name names, and get into the various "Researchers" of the case. I have dealt with almost all of them. However, I will try not to point the finger at any of them, whether I agree with them or not. I may allude to many viewpoints in the case. If that viewpoint is the reader's viewpoint....then you might identify with it. "If the shoe fits...wear it", as they say. However, I am not getting into individuals, or their viewpoints. I will spend a lot of time in this book talking about the various theories, proofs, facts and questions that I have heard from Researchers over my 35+ years dealing with the case.

However, (IMO- In My Opinion), there is actually a very large segment of the Research Community that are "on the fence" about what happened that day. There are no major writings that address this side of the debate. Most of the books are one extreme, or the other. Hopefully, this one is an honest question about the many aspects of the case, without the bombastic: "you must believe in what I believe", which many Assassination books present.

Please follow me. If I lose you, because you have already decided what happened, I have no problem with that. I fully expect it.

I am hoping that I can present an open discussion of the case, without 'brow beating' you into believing any opinion of the case. I am really not sure that I have one (although I may talk about many aspects of the case)....

Most of all, I hope the reader will try to look at both sides of the case. Too often someone hears a piece of information they like, and then do not think through the logistics and logic of the information they are hearing. For many others, it is that the WC came up with a 'valid' scenario, and that is good enough for them that they do not look carefully at the legitimate questions which may have been ignored by the WC. Or, they insist that Oswald was in the 2nd floor lunchroom at the time, and then do not consider the planning and logistics involved with getting others into the building, setting up a

3

JFK Assassination: Shades From The Fence

sniper's nest, and exiting the building without being discovered by any of the 73 employees of the building, or Oswald himself.

My slogan throughout the book will be that I really hope the reader "Thinks for themselves"!

The hardest part of writing a "book".

This is my 2nd book. The first one was easy, because I presented the history of Dealey Plaza, Dallas Morning News and the Dealey family. It was a matter of looking up information, and compiling it in one place. The purpose was to simply supply information to the JFK Research Community at large. This was information that most had not really researched. It was a rather simple effort, as all I had to do was collect factual information that was not disputed, and present it.

Even back in 2001-2002, I was aware of the many limitations to writing a book. Now, that I am no longer still simply compiling and supplying information that many do not have, I am even more aware of the limitations of writing a book. There have been thousands of books written on the subject of the JFK Assassination! Probably overkill. The last thing the world needs is another on the subject: hence, I was reluctant to "dive into" those waters.

So...what is this book really about?

This book is about the many theories, questions, doubts and information presented since the JFK Assassination. In my 4 decades of being involved in the JFK Assassination, I have literally heard it "all".

I cannot, and will not tell you that these opinions are right, or wrong. I do not know… However, I hope that if you believe in one "extreme" or another ("Black" or "White") that you do so because you have investigated and analyzed the case as an independent thinker. Independent thinker is the biggest attribute that I give to any student of the Assassination. That

4

JFK Assassination: Shades From The Fence

applies to every subject you might consider. Do not let anyone's opinion, or motive to sell books, films, YouTube, forum, etc. influence you in any way. Certainly, you can take all of it as input into what you decide. But if you simply echo someone else's view point (including mine), then you need to dig deeper.

I respect anyone who has come to a conclusion about what happened in November 1963, the time leading up to it, and the debate that has happened since. You are ahead of me in the game, because after 58 years, I am simply unsure that Kennedy was assassinated by a "Lone Nut", named Lee Harvey Oswald, or as a result of a Conspiracy.

This book will likely cover the many Theories of the JFK Assassination. I will not tell you which one is more valid, or less valid, than any other. I will not cover every "theory" that has been presented over the many decades since the Assassination. You are certainly invited to dig deeper, as a Researcher/Student. I really encourage you to, if you are that interested in what happened almost 60 years ago.

I will never tell you what to believe. I will never tell you that you are wrong, in any belief that you may hold. I do not have omnipotence, nor complete knowledge in what happened. I cannot tell you who the guilty parties are.

Many will be quick to call me naïve, in that I might even consider the Warren

Commission version of what happened. (I don't simply accept it.) On the other side, those that accept the WC version of these events, are seemingly not concerned about the many legitimate doubts about who killed JFK.

Those doubts have always been there. Many can be explained, as I have done in many instances over the years. However, the sheer volume of doubts cannot (IMO) be ignored.

Coincidences? Possibly. Many adherents of the "Lone Nut" viewpoint, are simply too quick to reject the number of doubts.

I am not certain that anyone is wrong. I really do not know.

JFK Assassination: Shades From The Fence

What IS in this book?

This book is about theories, speculation and information that has been shared between the Research Community over the 25+ years I have been involved with them over the Internet. I have heard every theory, more than once. Many are die hard supporters of their particular theory.

I fully respect every one of them. Of course, that does not mean that I agree with them, or even like some of them! At the same time, I do not pick my friends based on agreeing with everything they say, write or think. That would be incredibly boring.

I respect any theory, on both sides of my Fence, that they can debate and support in a civil manner. Unfortunately, many cannot support their own theories logically, or with full consideration of alternate information. These, I cannot respect. (You know who you are, I hope. However, some are "too stupid to even be embarrassed", as the old saying goes.) If you are merely echoing what someone else said, what you read in some book, or YouTube video, etc. then you are NOT thinking for yourself.

The biggest thing I can tell anyone, is "think for yourself". Do not accept whatever you have seen on-line, in a YouTube video, on a web site, in a publication, or any other source! This includes whatever I may write in both this writing, or on the many on-line groups and forums, I may Moderate or participate in.

In this writing, I promise to try to cover many theories and conclusions. I will also offer doubts and other information that might cause you to re-evaluate what you believe. That is all that I am asking! I simply want the reader to look at both sides of every argument, instead of accepting what the latest author, or "on-line guru" has to say.

So... those of you who have hung with me, so far, I hope you enjoy this book...

JFK Assassination: Shades From The Fence

I really want to present the various theories of the JFK Assassination. The 'middle of the road' view of the Assassination. Or, as some have called it on the Internet, the "Fence Sitter" or "Undecided" side of the Assassination. This book is written to illustrate this middle of the road view of what happened.

I really believe that a large number of America is stuck in some form of shades of gray on what happened in the JFK Assassination. They are simply not on the extreme viewpoints of the Kennedy Assassination. Unfortunately, many are simply not fully informed on the subject. They have settled on their "opinion" because of a casual overview. They might simply want to trust their government and its conclusions. Others may be more interested in the latest "who-dunnit", which we all enjoy. Still others, may have legitimate questions about the Assassination that they cannot answer.

I can certainly be wrong about this! I am not an expert about what happened that day. Nobody really is. If they tell you they are, put your hand on your wallet and hold tightly! Do NOT buy the bridge they are trying to sell you, or the swampland that goes beneath it.

Question EVERYTHING! Including me.....

2. The Name Game?

"This was the name I was assigned, and told to use, by my first Handlers!" – Jerry Dealey

The above quote is the tongue-in-cheek response I have used over the years. Many Researchers accuse me of using a false name, and taking my last name from Dealey Plaza. The above is tongue-in-cheek because a "Handler" in the spy game, is usually a paid contact or actual employee of the spy Agency, who 'handles' various assets and people used by the spies. These assets may be informants, couriers, actual spies, etc. who are not in the direct pay/employment of the agency involved. This protects these assets from being discovered as being a part of the agency, in the view of the opposing group. The Handler may also receive discreet or indirect payments, or other compensation, from the Agency involved, or an employee. The purpose is to prevent a direct link to any intelligence that could compromise the asset. It certainly would not do to have a direct financial link, or any other link, to the Enemy!

In my case, my "first Handlers" were Mom and Dad. Since I could not walk, talk, or take care of my feeding/toilet needs when I was first born, they Handled me early on. This is the name I was given when I was born. I even have documentation. ("Birthers" take note.) They gave me my name. They documented it with a birth certificate, here in Dallas, Texas, where I was born. I guess they could have lied to me....

They always told me to use the name, and I have hardly ever deviated from that.

Actually, when my birth parents got their final divorce in 1962, my mother had a habit of trying to change my last name to my step-father's. I was not old enough to originally resist. Therefore, I did spend some of my elementary school under an alias. So, in November of 1963, I was in 3rd grade under an

8

JFK Assassination: Shades From The Fence

'alias'! Subsequently, I cannot absolutely prove that I was not a shooter in Dealey Plaza in November of 1963... But being 8 years old and in school, is an alibi I will stick with!

Dealey Plaza did not spring up from the dirt, or drop from heaven, with the name carved on a stone or written in the sky above. It was named after somebody. (Would you believe?) It was named after my Great Grand Uncle, George Bannerman Dealey (G. B. as he was usually called.) There is a statue of him on the south side of the Plaza. It was named in his honor, although he never owned the land that the Plaza is built upon. There were 2 city blocks of businesses, which the City of Dallas purchased and tore down in order to build the Plaza.

It was built as an entrance to Dallas, from Fort Worth and other parts west. It was part of the main highway, U. S. 80. It was created was from 1934 to 1936, intended to be in time for the 1936 Texas Centennial, celebrating the 100th year of Texas' formation as a Republic. (Note: Texas seldom celebrates Statehood.) Many such projects were done in 1936, in many of the major cities in Texas.

The actual location of the Texas Centennial, was in Dallas' Fair Park. 1936 has been called, "The year America discovered Texas." The Texas Centennial has been referred to as a World's Fair. However, it was not. A World's Fair must include multiple countries being invited to participate, even if many times it is only the host country which supplies most of the events and exhibits. This was an Exposition, approved by the Bureau International des Expositions, in Paris. This is the same organization that selects and approves actual World's Fairs.

An Exposition is normally not an International undertaking, but is often as large and grand as a World's Fair. In fact, Dallas hosted the Texas Centennial Exposition in 1936, plus the Greater Texas & Pan-American Exposition, in 1937, both on the State Fair grounds. (Having invested in the buildings, why not?)

G. B. Dealey was the publisher and major stock holder (owner of majority shares) of the Dallas Morning News. He was instrumental in the planning and designing of the layout of the City of Dallas, and all improvements. This included the planning and overhauling in 1936 of the Texas State Fair grounds (270 acres), and other city improvements. When they built Dealey Plaza as a grand entrance into the city, they named it Dealey Plaza in his honor. He attended the opening ceremony, and was in the 1st car to travel under the "sub-way" (Triple Underpass).

After his death, in 1946, a statue was ordered and dedicated. It sits on the south side of the Plaza, by the reflecting pools on Houston Street. My Grandfather always said it was shocking to show G. B. outdoors, without a hat on. Being a good Englishman, G. B. would never go outdoors without his hat. So...if some day you hear that someone has been arrested for putting a hat on a statue in Dealey Plaza, it might be me. (Anyone have a size 40 Fedora?)

There were 5 boys and 3 girls that were siblings in the generation of G. B. They were born in Manchester, England, in the mid 1800's. The father, George Dealey Sr., put the family on a sailing berk, and sailed the Atlantic in 1870's, landing on Galveston Island after many weeks at sea. They lived in a small lean-to structure on the deck of the ship. They were even becalmed at sea for several days during the transit. Can you imagine having to take care of a large family, including infants, for several weeks in such conditions? (Slave ships were much more incredibly horrible, so by comparison to those poor souls, they had it made.)

Three of the oldest boys, would work for the Newspapers over the years. The oldest, Thomas William Dealey (T. W.), started working for the Galveston News, at the age of 15.

When he was promoted to a higher level a few years later, G. B. was hired to take his place in the Mailroom. James Quayle Dealey, would also work for the Newspapers in his later years. He was also a Sociology Professor for Brown University, and helped establish North Texas State University – now UNT.

JFK Assassination: Shades From The Fence

The two youngest brothers, Samuel D. Dealey Sr., and Charles L. Dealey (my Great Grandfather), assisted the father, George Dealey Sr, in running a Tea and Spice import business, never working for the Newspapers.

When the Telegraph and the railroads came to north Texas in the early 1880's, The Galveston News sent young G. B. to scout out a good location for a sister newspaper that could share information and reporting by telegraph. G. B. selected Dallas, because it was becoming the major railroad crossroads for the major north-south, and east-west lines. He was appointed reporter in 1883 to the Galveston News, and stayed in the Dallas area. In October 1885, the Dallas Morning News officially opened, and G. B. was promoted to Office Manager. Eventually, the family that owned the DMN sold their ownership to G. B. Dealey, and he sold shares to raise the funds. He retain controlling stock in the new corporation: Belo Corp. (A. H. Belo was the founder of the Galveston News, back when Texas was still a Republic. 1836-1846)

Around 1890, George Dealey Sr. moved most of the family from Galveston, up to Dallas.

Here they opened a Real Estate company, and struggled for many years. Charles L. and Samuel D. assisted with that family business. T. W. Dealey continued to work as Manager for the Galveston News, until his health failed him. Belo Corporation sold the Galveston News about 1923, during a 'war' with the Klu Klux Klan that G. B. and his newspaper fought.

Kidnappers, take note, I am from the poor side of the family. Charles L. Dealey was a 'circuit rider' preacher at one point during his youth in the Galveston area. I am almost certain he took an oath of poverty, that has stuck to my branch of the family ever since. (If you kidnap one of my 2 daughters, take note that they are 'high maintenance' and very opinionated.....)

G. B. Dealey married a girl in 1884, from Kansas City. While there, he noted how well planned and laid out the city's civic improvements were. He continued to promote improvements to Dallas' city leaders, and was instrumental in

JFK Assassination: Shades From The Fence

hiring a city engineer named Kessler, based on Kessler's designs for Kansas City. The Kessler Plan was proposed in 1910-11, and included a park on the downtown's western end to be a "grand entrance" into the city. When the Dallas' Citizen's Council (of which G. B. was a member) adopted such a proposal leading up to the Texas Centennial, they named it Dealey Plaza. Dealey himself never owned any of the property, although he did own 13-17 acres of land immediately west of the Triple Underpass/railroad lines.

That area was historically called the Dealey Annex. However, it has recently been changed to "Martyr's Park". (Not sure exactly who the 'Martyrs' were...)

G. B. had seemingly groomed the oldest of his 2 sons, Walter Dealey, to work in the newspaper business, as well as establishing one of the country's first commercial radio stations. His younger son, Edward "Ted" Dealey, also worked for the newspaper, but seemingly was not as interested in journalism. The three daughters of G. B. also married newspaper men. Walter suddenly died during the Great Depression, from over-exertion. Ted reluctantly took the heir apparent mantle, after Walter's death. When G. B. Dealey died in 1946, his appeared to be the political opposite of G. B. Dealey, who was considered by many US newspapers as the "Dean of American Journalism". While G. B. was considered very liberal and socialistic, Ted was extremely right-wing, radical conservative. JFK and Ted Dealey had a number of run-ins, and Ted attended a White House brunch in September of 1961, in which he lectured and insulted Kennedy. It was because of this, that Kennedy allegedly told Jackie they were headed into "nut country" the morning of November 22nd, before they left the Hotel Texas, in Fort Worth, to head to Dallas.

There was an infamous, "black border ad" in the Dallas Morning News on the morning of Nov. 22nd, 1963. (A full page advertisement surrounded by a black border.) Supposedly none of the Dealeys saw the ad, or approved the ad, before it was published by the advertising department. Allegedly, when

12

JFK Assassination: Shades From The Fence

Publisher Joe Dealey (Ted's son) found out about the ad, he was embarrassed and mortified. He supposedly showed it to his father, after the assassination. Ted allegedly said he did not see the ad ahead of time, but if he had, there was nothing in there that he would have rejected or not allowed. Ted Dealey was IMO, the main 'stinker' of the family. I do not justify him in any way! He just happens to be someone I am related to.

If you do want to connect me to the fore bearers, there are many better Dealeys to which I would prefer to be connected. George Dealey Sr., and T. W. Dealey were instrumental in establishing the Galveston Texas orphan's home. G. B. Dealey did many civic improvements, plus a sustained fight with the Klu Klux Klan in the 1920's, which almost bankrupted him and the Belo Corporation. Again, my own Great Grandfather, Charles L. Dealey, was a 'lay' minister, and did a lot for charity.

Samuel D. Dealey Jr. was the most decorated USN sailor in World War II. He was the skipper of the U.S.S. Harder, and was known by the nickname "The Destroyer Killer" (book title by Edwin P. Hoyt). Of the total 35 Japanese destroyers sunk by the United States Navy submarines in the Pacific War, Dealey and the Harder was responsible for sinking 7. Two of these were sunk in the Harder's fifth patrol, for which Dealey was given the Congressional Medal of Honor. I maintain a site about Sam Dealey at "navy.togetherweserved.com", for those interested. There is also the above book, as well as a later book, "Death at a Distance: Loss of the USS Harder", by Michael Sturma. If you are interested in the Pacific theater's use of submarines and history, I strongly recommend this latter book. The previous book focuses on Sam Dealey's biography too much, but the second book is more about the submarine tactics and other boats.

But, if you insist on vilifying me because of my relatives, go ahead. I can probably find something evil to say about your last name also.....

13

JFK Assassination: Shades From The Fence

3. JFK Research Involvement

(Reader, this chapter is mainly about me. You can certainly skip it, as it only gives my background, credentials and areas of specialization in the JFK Assassination case. I will not be offended, as this is the part that will probably bore you to death.)

"I know everything about the Kennedy Assassination... except what the Hell happened!" – Jerry Dealey

I guess I should apologize to journalist Larry J. Sabato. The statement above was one of the first I said to him in the lobby of the Adolphus hotel. JFKLancer's November in Dallas conference was going on, and Deb Conway sent Larry over to see me to discuss Researching the JFK case. (He also took my tour that day.) He immediately said it was a great quote, and asked if he could use it in his book, "The Kennedy Half Century" (2013). I agreed, but asked if he could replace the mild expletive with the word "really". He did. Now I feel guilty that I used the actual quote in my book, but asked him to change it. Sorry, Larry!

Naturally, since the Plaza was tied to my name and family, I have always been a student of the Assassination. Initially I was a casual student, but later became a very active Researcher/Student.

Of course, as a child of 8 during 1963, and living most of the year in the Denver, Colorado area, my initial research was limited. I did try to read many of the books being written, if I could find them in the libraries of my area. Did not buy many, although I did purchase a paperback copy of "They've Killed the President: The Search for the Murderers of John F. Kennedy" by Robert Sam, Anson. I remember reading a number of other books, at a fairly early age. I also managed to acquire a copy of the Warren Report, but not the 26 volumes.

15

JFK Assassination: Shades From The Fence

Naturally, I saw the 1967 CBS News Inquiry show, and other news programs and documentaries. In the 60's, these were few and far between. Also, being before video tape, you could not collect and view as you can today.

I did come down and stay the summers in Texas, with my grandmother and my father. We would often drive through Dealey Plaza, on our way somewhere, and I was fascinated about doing so. Like many, my reaction was that it is incredibly smaller than you think about it when seeing the news and films.

Once I could drive, and borrow the family car, when in Dallas I could go down and spend time in the Plaza. I also looked for other Assassination related sites, when I could find addresses and locations in the newspaper archives at the libraries.

About 1979, I purchased my first computer. It was a Radio Shack/Tandy TRS-80. I trained myself to use it, and write BASIC programs. Eventually, in 1980-83, I attended college, and became a Computer Programmer. For many years, the TRS-80s were my only personal computer, as IBM did not introduce the IBM-PC until 1981.

Of course, these were the MODEM days (ringing buzz...?). Dial-up between computers was the only way to network in those days. But there were limited server networks that you could dial-in to access. Telenet/Tymnet (1975) and Sprintnet, were some of the first.

Most networking, was simply dialing into someone else's computer. I used my TRS-80 to run a BBS (Bulletin Board System) in the early 80's, allowing co-workers to access "rooms" were they could message each other. One of these rooms was a JFK room, to discuss the case.

However, co-workers were not very interested in the case, and after a few weeks, I closed that room, so I might have space for other rooms. (The BBS ran on high-density 'floppy' drives.) In the mid-80's, networking improved somewhat. Newsgroups started appearing on networks such as Compuserve and AOL. Some of these Newsgroups were about

JFK Assassination: Shades From The Fence

JFK. (alt.assassination.jfk, for instance) But there was no Internet, so information was still hard to come by. It was still dial-up, and slow and 'clunky'.

After moving back to Dallas in 1984, I was able to do more in researching the case, and seeing the sites related to the assassination. I remember that I used to bore my visiting family to death about the sites, and did my first family tours in the late 80's. But again, most information was from used and new books that you could find at the library, or purchase at a used book store. Slow progress.

Once living in Dallas, I started showing up in Dealey Plaza for the November anniversaries. Although not knowing anyone, and nobody knew me, I enjoyed listening to the various speakers/witnesses that would attend. This was often as they were being interviewed by the press and news media, where I could stand close by and listen. (Basically, a 'lurker'.)

From these people, I learned about the A. S. K. Conferences. I attended some of the sessions, starting in 1992. This is about when I really got hooked on the topic. They spent most of the time asking pointed questions about the Assassination, Oswald, etc. I found them highly interesting, but was never convinced one way or the other about their being a conspiracy that caused the death of JFK. But did they raise some very valid questions? Yes..

In 1995-6, I came across "Dealey Plaza UK". This is a British group of Researchers, led by Ian Griggs. I contacted Ian, and we started an email exchange. In 1996, when he attended the first November in Dallas conference in Dallas, I met up with Ian, and attended the Conference. Being a Dallas native, with transportation, we joined up for several days to drive the sites related to the Assassination. (Plus meals, and many, many drinking sessions.)

This was also when I met Debra Conway and Tom Jones, who were the founders of JFK Lancer. ("Lancer" was the Secret Service code name for JFK.) I also met other local and out of town Researchers and Authors. Having not contributed to Research at this early date, they did not know me very well.

JFK Assassination: Shades From The Fence

Naturally, many were fascinated to meet a Dealey, since that name and family had been an integral part of the events.

JFK Lancer initially had a dial-up internet presence on StarText. StarText was a information exchange service sponsored by the Fort Worth Star-Telegram newspaper. It was very limited, allowing you to read downloaded text. It did not have an ability to post, comment or exchange information. With the ability to access the "WWW" (World Wide Web) Internet, Debra subscribed to a Forum service. Here there was the ability to post, read, search and exchange information, including graphics, photos, etc.

Many Forums were now available to the average Researcher, possessing an Internet connection. JFKLancer, Education Forum, DeepPolitics and other Forums, some of which are still active today. I became a minor presence on almost all I could find.

Around 1998-99, I became the prime Moderator of the JFKLancer.com Forum, as well as a couple of my own "FreeForums" history and JFK forums. I did this for several years, until JFKLancer Forum was taken down in summer of 2003.

Facebook, and other (un)Social media was the virtual demise on most of the on-line Forums. It became easier to simply post on Facebook, instead of applying for access on the old Forums. Forums had more stringent rules you had to agree to abide by. I have been on Facebook since the beginning, and am a member of dozens of Kennedy related Groups. I still Moderate my own group, and the Fair Play for JFK group, set up and owned by Jim Hess.

I have always tried to be balanced in my Moderation. As long as the person is civil and respectful, I have always tried to allow almost any theory or opinion to be talked about. I feel that people are "what they post", and are known based on that. In your personal life you may be another "Mother Teresa", and steeped in love and kindness. However, if you act like a complete troll online, that is how most of us will know and remember you. But you are expected to be able to support and discuss your theory, opinion, etc. Nobody cares what you think, just because you think it. If you cannot discuss and support it, you are wasting everyone's time.

Of course, on my own Forums or FB Groups, I can allow anything. However, on occasion, Deb Conway or Jim Hess, may decide some topics or opinions are off limits. They have therefore asked me to 'boot' some people who are obnoxious, offensive and sometimes repeating the same old stuff over and over, without discussing and supporting it. I have had to do this on occasion, but mostly the Forums and Groups I have Moderated have never deleted or limited someone based on which side of the Fence they are coming from. Obscenity, racism, unrelated topics, and persistent insults are still likely to cause deletions and banning.

In 1996 JFKLancer conference I met Ken Holmes Jr. Ken would give tours, professionally. He specialized in Bonnie and Clyde, JFK and Dallas History tours. We hit it off pretty well, and he became a very good friend of mine. So, I started also doing Tours. Initially, it would be as a hobby, or if Ken was otherwise busy and needed me to step in for him to do a bus, or private party, tour. By 2000, I started doing paid tours myself, and continued to do so, until the COVID-19 pandemic hit in 2020. I gave about 50-100 tours a year, mostly focused on the JFK Assassination (although I have done a few Bonnie and Clyde, Fort Worth Stockyards, and Dallas history tours).

Some of my tours would be for people only casually interested in the JFK Assassination, but some would be Researchers well versed in the case. I have also done tours for National Geographic, History Channel and other movie and documentary makers, as well as school groups, traveling soccer teams, and about every other travel group you can think of.

Of these, the casually interested are the hardest to do, because you have to talk like crazy to get all of the information out, without missing something. (Had to do a few, through an 'interpreter', which really makes it challenging.) I actually enjoy some of the experienced Researchers who have taken my tour, as we can debate and discuss in much more detail that the newcomer can not.

In about the turn of this last century, a Researcher in the case was complaining about the Sixth Floor Museum. (Can you imagine.....? LOL) Some thought the Museum was making plans on closing down Dealey Plaza, and charging admission. They mistakenly asserted that the Dealey family gave the property under the condition that it remain a public park, and that we should take control of it back if the Museum tried to dominate it in such a fashion.

I realized that many of the Researchers had no idea of the history of Dealeys, Dallas and the property now called Dealey Plaza. Additionally, they seemed to have little idea on how a city takes property from private citizens, if they need it. This got me into Active Research, instead of the passive research I had been doing to that time. I did a lot of digging into the Plaza, the buildings, and the history and politics of Dallas. The result was my first book, "D in the Heart of Texas" in 2002. This was a small and self-published (500 copies) about these subjects. (I still have a couple of boxes of books left.)

Anyone interested in the history of the Plaza, Dallas, Morning News, and the Dealey family can look for the book. This little book, written in large type (Mom was legally blind, although she could read large type), dealt extensively into these subjects, and touches only very briefly on the Assassination itself. I will not include it in this book, as I am certain I will bore you enough with the various 'Shades of Gray', details, opinions, logistics and interpretation of the JFK assassination.

In addition to my Tours, I have done extensive public speaking on the Assassination. I have done JFKLancer conference presentations for multiple years, as well as provide Tours during the conference for those interested. Also, I have appeared in multiple documentaries, and films. (At least one was a French Canadian documentary, where my words were dubbed in by someone else. Since I don't speak French, I could not be certain if what they were saying was what I actually meant to say. Hard to watch.) I have spoken to a number of groups at libraries, schools, and other speaking engagements.

I have also done a number of debates with other Researchers. In 2013, a traveling stage play "Oswald: The Interrogation" was to appear at Fort Worth's Casa Manana Playhouse in Fort Worth. They contacted me, and asked if I could suggest a public Debate after a performance of the play. I initially thought I could get Hugh Aynesworth (Dallas Morning News reporter in 1963) and Robert Groden ("JFK" researcher and consultant), to do it. But in talking to some fellow Researchers, I was told it would not be a good idea to have these individuals in the "same room" together! I therefore debated the Lone Nut side of the debate, although I told everyone I was "on the fence", and not a believer in the Lone Nut version. Jim Marrs, and other Researchers were in the audience that night. (It was NOT recorded.) I used the event to promote my tours, while Robert had the first release of his extensive book: "JFK: Absolute Proof, The Killing of a President". It was ruled a draw by those there, but it was fun, and we both came out ahead.

In my opinion, there is too many topics in the JFK Assassination for anyone to be considered an "expert" on all of them. I therefore focused my study to the history of the Plaza, the buildings in the Plaza, as well as the history of the place and Dallas in general. Almost all of my published work has been about the sewers and the Texas School Book Depository. These were also the focus of my conference presentations, over the years. I often supplied even experienced Researchers information they were unaware of, or had not considered. I am still often contacted by other Researchers and authors to do some 'legwork' on topics they cannot easily research, and I can because I live in Dallas area.

Of course, even in my articles and other published works, I touch on many other subjects. For instance, as far as I know I am the only person who has done a shadow study in Dealey Plaza during November (at least Gary Mack said I was). This is to help time-stamp some of the photos taken that day. I am also about the only person who has asked for photos of the freight elevators, which Gary and Steven Fagin (current Archivist) took and allowed me to use in one of my presentations.

I have also done some work on police/security assignments, logistics about photo/film "alterations" that many Researchers claim happened, and other subjects. I mainly have extensively focused on the interior of the TSBD and the reported movements inside of the building.

These will be included in subsequent chapters of this book, which will compile much of my work, in addition to the overview of the many "shades of gray" of theories about what happened.

So....enough about my name and public speaking experience...

4. The Research Community

The word "Community" sounds much more friendly than it actually is. But since we share a common "interest", regardless of location, I still use it. It will include almost everyone who has shown more than a passing interest in the JFK Assassination. Throughout the book, I use the word Researcher to include all members of this community. But the group encompasses many levels, from the person who has a passing interest and posts as a hobby, to the Pioneers who wrote books, presented, discussed, made movies, etc. before Social Media, Forums or the Internet in general.

Because of my decades of experience in the case, I have dealt with almost every major Researcher. I know many of the authors, speakers at conferences, and dedicated Researcher that has been doing this more than casually on the internet. Of course, there are hundreds of them. I know a few well, but most only casually. Many of the old printed page authors, and a few of the modern e-book authors still contact me on occasion for reference help, etc. Much of this is because I live in Dallas, and can more easily access the library, city directories, and other research information.

However, over the years I have focused my own research on the old Texas School Book Depository (TSBD), the history and politics of Dallas, and of course the history of the Dealey family, Dealey Plaza, Dallas Morning News, and other local subjects. Like anyone else, I have dabbled in all aspects of the case, but nobody can focus on everything. (If they say they know everything, hold onto your wallet...)

It is very safe to say that this is likely the most studied crime in the 20th century! It is so much easier now, because of the computer and social media, to get involved. Almost anyone can post their opinion and join the Research community. This is good, but also bad, because there are Trolls. Some simply are looking for a good fight, or to stimulate argument, instead of civil debate and discussion. (On the Facebook groups I moderate, we try never to call someone a Troll….. but they really do exist.)

But many will see a documentary, film, TV show, take a tour, read a magazine or book, or simply stumble onto the case on the internet. They will take a strong interest in the case, and attempt to study and learn more. The internet, and social media, make this much easier than it used to be. I did my first modem BBS (Bulletin Board System - for you younger persons) in 1980, including a "room" for JFK. Since then, I have done Startext, NewsGroups, Forums, Blogs, and Social Media (FB, Instagram, Twitter, MySpace, etc.). The internet is a great information tool, if you can ignore and tolerate the Trolls.

Social Media (Facebook, Twitter, etc.)

I have been doing this a long time, and prefer the old Forums, to the modern Social Media platforms. These use to require a little more vetting before you could join (like being referred by someone else). They also were easily broken up by Topics, so you could easily post within a Topic or subject that interest you. They were easily searchable, and the topics were always available under a header that you could find. FB and Twitter post simply scroll off the screen, because it was not designed for topics, searches and (In My Opinion – IMO) for serious research. It was designed to have social exchange and fun, with your 'friends'.

Facebook and Twitter are much more popular, and almost anyone has access to these platforms. That means that more people interested in a group or subject can read and post about it. (In fact, the onslaught of Facebook practically rendered the old JFKLancer Forum inactive, until Deb Conway finally shut it down.) This makes the information more readily available to anyone. That triggers more interest in the subject, with even the most casual student/passing interest. There are groups out there for almost any subject you are interested in.

But these comments come with a warning. You are posting on THEIR Group (or page) and they have the right to control the content in any way they choose. This is in addition to any rules the company that runs the Media (Facebook, Twitter, etc.) feels is appropriate. For many years I have heard from some who believe this is an infringement of their First Amendment right of "Freedom of Speech". Guys, that is a misread of the First Amendment. The amendment simply states that the Congress will not pass any law to limit your speech. That does not give you the right to say anything you want, anywhere you want. If a company owns the Media (newspaper, TV show, platform, etc.) they have the right to control its content.

Many Groups (FB) or Forums are very intolerant of opinions that do not match the Administrators/Moderators and the most common posters in that group. Some of these will actually warn you up front, by saying something like "LN (Lone Nut believers) are not welcome here." Others will want CT (Conspiracy Theorists) to stay away. Unfortunately, many Groups will NOT warn you up front. They will wait until you post an opinion they do not agree with, and often "ban" you from their group, and delete your posts. But expect to be ridiculed and attacked for any strong opinion, either way.

However, some groups will simply ban you because they believe you are a LN or CT. They will often do this without explanation, comment or notification of any kind. You will simply be "gone" and unable to access the Group any longer. Of course, they have the option to delete anything you posted.

Some of the less honest Admin/Mods will simply delete your comment, as if you never posted it. It will simply disappear. Of course, with Facebook, it might simply be that it scroll off the screen, and you are having trouble finding it. But some will simply delete it. This often happens when they feel they are losing the debate, or simply do not like your post.

The Groups I now Moderate, I try to focus on Civil discussion. I hope it means that any opinion/theory can be openly discussed and debated. But I "own" (creator) one group: "November 1963: JFK Balanced" (search) where I would like any theory to be discussed and debated, as long as it is Civil and not offensive to others. However, I do not own the other Groups, and they are subject to other people's decisions (vote by Moderators, mainly).

YouTube, e-Books, Blogs and other Internet media

The other drawback of the Information Age, is that we are often flooded with too much. The reader/viewer needs to be careful about what they watch. Everything should be evaluated and considered, before you accept anything as truth or fact. There is a lot of disinformation and misinformation that we are constantly exposed to. The same is true about films, documentaries, e-books and blogs. Just because someone can create it, and it looks like it is well polished and researched, it may simply be garbage. There are also very sophisticated parties that are trying to instigate and control what people think and do. This has created much too much division/hate in the world.

Blogs tend to only be what the owner has posted. That means they pre-approve the posts you see (some FB groups also use this technique). If you post something they do not approve, it will never be seen on their Blog (or Group). It may look like a honest exchange of ideas and opinions, but it may not be. It had to be approved for you to see it.

As mentioned, I am not a very big fan of e-books. Sure, they make a writing more available to many more readers, but the often contain information that was not approved by a neutral editor/publisher. Much of it is not even "peer reviewed", which allows your peers to let you know their opinion of a body of work. The advantage of both a publisher and peer review, is it makes the work more palatable for consumers. If it is a waste of time, in the eyes of publisher(s), or even your peers, it probably should not be released.

JFK Assassination: Shades From The Fence

But too many Researchers are too casual about their sources. If they can quote a book, or YouTube, etc. they think it means something! They post it with a "look what I found" type of attitude. It is simply someone else's opinion, no matter how polished it may look.

This is especially true of books and stories about what a witness 'said'. Often this conversation is at a much later date, and is subject to memory and misinterpretation. This can be accidental, or intentional, depending on the nature of the witness or the interviewer. A statement years later could very easily been manipulated out of the witness by a clever interviewer, or simply meaning something to the interviewer very different than what the witness believes or intended to convey.

The Research Community (IMO)

Several months ago, I posted in a few Facebook groups what I consider makes up the Research Community. It is presented below.

First of all, this is my OPINION as is almost anything you encounter. Opinions are like belly buttons (I cleaned it up): everyone has one, and very few are interested in somebody else's. But I have been doing this for more than 2 decades. What follows is a general Categorization of the Research Community, in my opinion...

PIONEER RESEARCHER: These are the people who first stepped forth and criticize the WC, HSCA, and even each other before the Internet. They published a book, in documentaries, or public speakers, BEFORE the Internet (where everyone can put in their "two bits".) They did the digging into the case, when it was not very easy. Some believed in the Lone Nut version of the case, some believed in a Conspiracy, but most simply called out the questions that the official investigations skipped over, or refused to address.

JFK Assassination: Shades From The Fence

The early Authors used old fashion techniques of books, phone, contact and snail-mail, to do their research. Many wrote books criticizing the Warren Commission, without presenting an actual theory themselves. It has gotten much easier in modern times, because of the computer and the internet. I highly respect those that came before, in the pre-computer "horse and buggy" days.

RESEARCHER: (Most today put themselves into this category, but you cannot place YOURSELF in a category, but the opinion of OTHERS is the deciding factor.) These are the people who have specialized into areas of the case. (Nobody can know every subject.) Most importantly, they have been paid to speak on the case, been published by others (I do not count self-publishing, as anyone can do that today), or appeared in a serious commercial Documentary based on their apparent expertise and knowledge. (Again, a self made "documentary", like YouTube, does NOT count.) They could even have made a presentation at any of the major Conferences about the case, where someone else values their opinion and specialization enough to ask them. Many have a set opinion on the case, but even lacking that, they are asked their Opinion by someone else.

STUDENT: This is actually the category that 90% of the self-proclaimed "researchers" belong. Naturally, there are good students and bad students. The good students may have a set opinion, but they can DISCUSS AND SUPPORT that opinion. The bad students have a tendency to have an opinion, but be unwilling and unable to discuss and support. This category also includes those that have a passing interest in the case, including the "hobbyists". Some have done extensive research in a few topics of the case and specialize in those topics, but have never been asked to speak on those topics by someone else in a commercial, or published, venue. Some know a lot about the case, but are extremely shallow in their ability to discuss and support. Some are still "searching" for the "Truth".

JFK Assassination: Shades From The Fence

That you can find a question that has not been answered, or raise doubts about anything in this case (see my Seeds of Doubt chapters), does not mean that you cracked the case. All information needs to be evaluated, discussed and corroborated by other information. We can all ask questions, even the poorest Student.

FACILITATORS: This includes those that are willing to put together any open discussion of the case. That could be in Conferences, or an Internet page or group. If your page or group allows only those with opinions similar to yours, then you are NOT part of this group. You simply have a blog, page or group, where your opinion, or those that echo your opinion, can continually state their case, and reject those that have an opposing view. This is little more than a self-serving group, and is not a truly open site. I can think of nothing more boring than those who sit and support each other, and pat each other on the back.

The remaining categories may very well be Students, but subject to lesser esteem (again, in my opinion).

DISCIPLES, ACOLYTES and PROPONENTS: These are the people who seem to be constantly promoting and praising a particular Researcher, and his works and opinions. They seem to think if they can quote Researcher/Student "John Doe", it somehow proves their case. Additionally, many will quote multiple Authors, Researchers and Witnesses, and somehow think the ability to quote them actually proves something. It does not. They might even think of themselves as Facilitators, in that they provide a group, page or blog. But if these sites are only discussing or promoting a particular viewpoint by a particular individual, they are simply a mirror image of that person, and therefore worthless. Most common are "Blogs", where all input is screened by the Admin, and only those that agree are approved.

GROUPIES: These are people that try to quote as many people as possible, as if that means something. They often flit to legitimate Researchers, and try to get their photos taken with them, as if that also means something. They play the "name game" and try to list the number of people that 'follow' them, or that they have met (if the Researcher does not know you, it does not count). I guess, legitimate Researchers 'need' Groupies, to give them entertainment, and some ego boost.

INSTIGATORS and TROLLS: These are people who are on the Internet, or Social Media, simply because it is fun to argue. They often use one-liners, and insults, to otherwise legitimate discussion. They stir things up, and there is a lot to be said for that because a site without controversy can be very boring indeed. But many are just looking for a fight, and simply cannot support their opinions, questions and views in a fair, balance and open discussion of the case. They simply like to argue, and cause problems. However, unlike the following category, they are good at it, and can successfully get multiple responses and arguments on the garbage they put out. The more others respond, the more important the Troll becomes.

HOUSEFLIES: The least respected category of the Research Community, I refer to as a Housefly. They find some manure somewhere, land on it, coat themselves in it, and then their weak intellect believes they have found something incredible! So, they fly off to "spread the word" and show their findings to others.

Of course, their limited intelligence does not understand what they have found. They certainly cannot explain or support where it came from, or what it means to the Research. They will not discuss it. They will simply repeat it over, and over. They will be extremely proud of the information and question they have found. They think that they are clever, smart, and helping others by what they have found. Worst of all when you swipe at them to chase them away, they will claim that you are unintelligent, because you do not understand the value of this manure. They may even try to tell other flies how stupid you are, and claim their own reputation and credibility is so much above others.

But, like a fly, they are just annoying. They will continue to be annoying, but are not intelligent enough to realize that everything they say actually contributes to their own worthless

JFK Assassination: Shades From The Fence

reputation. Even if it is a complaint/insult of others, it is only strengthening everyone's opinion of their own ignorance.

When Moderating, I try to leave them alone. I might give them an opportunity to discuss and debate the glorious information they feel they have found. But when they cannot (or will not), it says a lot more about them, than it does about the case, or the people they are trying to insult! I will not bother getting up and finding a 'fly swatter' and searching them out, nor will I 'ban' them. I will simply let them continue on, even though they are not "smart enough to know they should be embarrassed".

Again, all of the above is simply my opinion, based on 25 years of following the case. You can ignore it (as most of you will), or "plug" yourself into the category that truly fits!

But, it is NOT what category YOU think you belong to, but rather where OTHERS think you belong!

One additional comment about the Internet: You ARE whatever you write. Look, in 'real life', or to your family, neighbors or friends, you might be as loving and caring as Mother Teresa. But those of us on the internet only know you by the personality that you project on the internet. If you constantly point to offensive or hateful opinions and sites, that is how we know you. If you are always abusive and insulting, that is how we know you. If you are thoughtful and civil, that is how we know you. Basically, you ARE however you present yourself to others, not how those close to you think you are, and probably not your own self-image.

Summary
Throughout the book, I will be discussing many of the theories and opinions I have encountered over the years. However, I doubt I will be naming names. If you see your agreement on some of these theories and opinions, fine. But I have been doing this for some long, there are very, very few

opinions that I feel are unique, or even new. (Some do surprise me from time to time.) I certainly will not cover every opinion, nor branch out into every theory, or controversy.

The Research Community is now very vast. Because of the internet, it is becoming larger every day. It is composed of serious people, and those that only have a passing, mild interest in the case. It also contains "newbies", that are just now getting an interest in the case, and are searching for answers. But it also contains jerks, Trolls, and those that are willing to take advantage of others.

What I say, or others might say, might contribute to the study of the case, or might be misinformation or intentional disinformation. It is simply someone's opinion, or what they want you to think is their opinion. Take it with a "grain of salt".

If you are new to the Research Community, I have been plugged in and doing it long enough to feel qualified to speak for all of us, and say "Welcome!" If you have been a member for many years, thanks and please continue.

As I intend to put in the Acknowledgements part of this book: Thanks to ALL the members of the Research Community, whether we agree or not!

Of course, everything I write in this book is MY opinion.

Ignorance frequently begets confidence. Ignorance more frequently begets confidence than does knowledge: it is those who know little, and not those who know much, who so positively assert that this or that problem will never be solved by science.

Charles Darwin

5. Events of November 22nd - 24th, 1963

In the 1st chapter, "Why Bother?", I promised that I would at least list the events that happened that November, 1963, weekend. This is for the "newbie" to the Assassination. The least I can do for those (poor souls?) that may only have this book as their first exposure to the JFK Assassination, is to give them the events.

For most of the readers, I suggest you simply skip this chapter. (Sorry, no partial refunds...) There will be nothing really new here. I will not be putting down the results of any digging into the case by me, or any other Researcher. No new facts, no theories, no new information whatsoever. It has all been covered before, so if this is familiar ground for you, I suggest you skip the chapter. You will not have missed anything...

At first glance, you might think that this should be an easy chapter to write. I would simply have to list the events that we all agree happened that weekend. However, it is almost impossible to get the Research Community to agree on anything!

The additional difficulty is how much to include, or how little. Much of the information did not come out as it happened. If you lived in Dallas, and were capable of watching all 3 major networks, you were aware of much of this information. However, even then, much of the information came out later, by Researchers.

For example, I will likely include much of the information that happened on the Dallas Police radio. This information was available if you were a Policeman, or happened to be listening to the 2 police channels. But if you were an ordinary citizen, you certainly would not have heard any of it, until months or years later. The details of the police radio transmission were simply not available until published much later. For clarity, however, I will try to include some of it, especially the parts that pertained to J. D. Tippit. Tippit was the Dallas Police Officer shot and killed in Oak Cliff that afternoon. (Timeframe is still a subject of dispute in the Research Community.)

The flip side of the above coin is that I cannot possible list everything that happened, based on when it happened. There is simply too much minute detail to go into. If you really want a detailed account, there are books that I can recommend. "Death of a President", by William Manchester, immediately comes to mind. It was written under authorization of Jackie Kennedy, and reads much like a story. (However, it is strictly an Oswald-did-it viewpoint, so the book is panned and hated by many of the more conspiracy minded Researchers.)

Again, this is not going to be as easy as I originally thought, but here goes with a very broad overview…

The plans of the Texas trip

Some time in the spring of 1963, it was announced by the White House that Kennedy would likely make a trip to Texas in the fall. Even with Texas' own Lyndon Johnson on the ticket as Vice President in 1960, JFK had just barely won the state. It was felt that a trip to Texas would be required, to get votes for the 1964 election.

In addition, by the fall of 1963, there was a tremendous rift in the Texas Democratic party. This was between the Conservatives and the more Liberal side of the party, and the elected representatives. On one side, was Senator Ralph Yarborough. He was considered by many to be the "leader" of the Liberal side of the Democratic party. He simply did not get along well with Lyndon Johnson, and Texas Governor John Connally. Connally had been Lyndon Johnson's 1960 Campaign Manager, and the Cannallys were good friends with the Johnsons. Connally was elected Texas Governor in the 1962 mid-term elections.

JFK Assassination: Shades From The Fence

So, a 3-day five-city trip of Texas was decided upon. This would allow the Democratic Party to have several fund-raising appearances in all 5 cities. Although not originally planned, Jacqueline Kennedy accompanied JFK for this first campaign fund-raising trip. She allegedly hated campaigning, but agreed to come on this Texas trip. This greatly expanded the excitement for the many Texans who supported Kennedy and his glamorous wife. (Of course, many did NOT like Kennedy, especially in the ultra conservative Texans.) Vice President Lyndon Johnson, Governor John Connally, Senator Ralph Yarborough, and other national politicians were also part of the trip.

It started on Thursday, November 21, in San Antonio and Houston, with both motorcades and stops where the President would speak. In San Antonio they stopped at a luncheon in a hotel, while in Houston they went to the Space Center. Then on Thursday night, they traveled to Fort Worth, where Jackie and JFK stayed in the downtown Hotel Texas. Arriving late that night, no event was planned.

The remainder of the trip included a breakfast in the Hotel Texas, and a motorcade to Carswell Air Force base. From there they would take the short flight to Dallas' Love Field, followed by a motorcade through the city in the Presidential limo, and a luncheon at the Dallas Trade Mart. They planned to return to Love Field and fly to Austin, with another motorcade and a dinner. The plan then was to go LBJ's central Texas ranch for the night. This would be followed by a lavish barbecue on Saturday, making it a 3-day trip, and a return to Washington on Sunday evening. This would get them home for John Jr's 3rd birthday, Monday, November 25th. (Instead, it was a national day of mourning – a sad birthday present for little John.)

Morning of Nov. 22 – Fort Worth to Dallas

The motorcade in both Fort Worth and Dallas had been printed in the local papers. In Fort Worth, the Fort Worth Star-Telegram carried it, and in Dallas the Friday motorcade was published in both the Dallas Morning News, and the afternoon newspaper, the Dallas Times Herald. The Times Herald map showed the jog from Main St. to Elm St., as it had for several days. However, the Dallas Morning News map did not show the jog, as it was drawn by a different artist.

The Dallas Morning News also featured a "Black-Bordered Ad" (Researchers' reference) on a full page of the Dallas Morning News. That Friday morning a Hotel Texas maid brought the newspaper to the suite of rooms occupied by the Kennedy's and got JFK to autograph the newspaper. (This paper was auctioned a few years ago for a reported $50K.) Whether Kennedy had seen the black bordered ad that morning is unknown, however. He did allegedly say to Jackie that morning that today they were heading into "nut country". (Given his relationship with my cousin, and DMN publisher Ted Dealey, this was likely after he autographed the newspaper.) In addition to the newspaper, a flier also appeared on Dallas streets that morning, saying Kennedy was "Wanted for Treason".

John Kennedy came out of the Hotel Texas before the breakfast, and walked across the street. Here he spoke on a flatbed truck podium and greeted the crowd of onlookers who did not have seats at the Chamber of Commerce breakfast event. After a few words, he went into the breakfast. He was later joined by Jackie, with much fanfare. He was also presented a hat during the event, to "protect him from the rain". He did not wear it.

There was then a motorcade through the downtown Fort Worth area to Carswell Air Force Base. Large crowds were present on all sides. Air Force One then departed for the brief flight to Dallas' Love Field.

Dallas Motorcade

In the days leading up to the visit, Dallas Chief of Police Jesse Currie, had been quoted on radio and TV making the statement that any acts that could embarrass the City of Dallas would not be tolerated. This was because of an incident that had occurred earlier in the fall, where UN Ambassador Adlai Stevenson had been hit by a protestor's sign when leaving Memorial Coliseum, after making a speech where he was heavily heckled. Even so, Friday morning there were a number of protestors at Market Hall who had their mouths "taped closed", and these were 'run off' by Dallas Police before the Motorcade began.

Air Force One landed around 11:30 AM. Large crowds were in attendance behind a small chain-link fence, close to the staging area. (In 1964, people on the tarmac was considered normal, as you had to walk across the tarmac to board most airplanes.) Instead of simply getting into the limo, Kennedy walked up to the fence and shook hands with many of the large crowd who had come to see him. Jackie followed, delaying the departure of the motorcade.

Once the couple got into the limo, joining Governor John Connally, his wife Nellie, and the 2 Secret Service drive (Greer) and escort (Kellerman), the limo left the airport through a hole opened in the surrounding fencing. (They never went into the actual Terminal building.) They proceeded out of the airport on Cedar Springs, turned right on Mockingbird Ln. for a few blocks, and went south down Lemmon Ave. Both sides of Mockingbird Ln. and Lemmon Ave. were jammed with cheering crowd and spectators.

The limo only stopped twice, both on Lemmon Ave. At one time JFK asked Greer to stop the limo so that they could greet a couple of Catholic nuns on the side of the street. The other stop, teased the children by asking what they were doing out of school.

At the bottom of Lemmon Ave. they turned right onto Turtle Creek, which later turned into Cedar Springs. They followed this route surrounded by cheering crowds, until they again turned right (south) onto Harwood St. This brought them into the outskirts of downtown Dallas, with buildings exceeding 8 or more floors.

JFK Assassination: Shades From The Fence

At Main St., in the NW intersection, they turned right on Main St. and headed West towards the western end of downtown Dallas. From this point on, they will be surrounded by about 10-12 blocks of the largest buildings in the Dallas area. In many of these buildings there would be people hanging out of open windows. In 1963, many office buildings had windows that would open, as they were built before air conditioning became dominate in building design.

Additionally, huge crowds lined the sidewalks, as thick in places as 30 people deep. These crowds bled into the street, causing the limo to slow, and Greer to open his door so that he could use it to fend off anyone who pressed too close to the limo. Secret Service Agent Clint Hill, who was Jackie's protection, gets off of the follow up car many times to cling to the back of the limo. At one point, a young teenage male gets too close to the limo, requiring SS Agents to intervene and throw him back into the crowd.

The crowds were huge in this part of the motorcade. This is Dallas' traditional parade route for all of the major events and motorcades. Elm St. (1 block to the north) was a one-way street going west through the downtown area, and was the main route for the Dallas rapid transit bus system. Commerce St. (1 block to the south) was another one-way eastern street. Some Researchers have asked over the years why they could not go down Elm St. and thus avoid the 120 degree turn from Houston to Elm in Dealey Plaza. Such crowds, and a motorcade, would shut down Dallas' public transportation in the downtown area for about an hour, while the people gather, the motorcade drive through, and the crowds and traffic clears.

Police radio logs entries will be used for much of the remaining chapter, as live TV of many of these actions was not possible.

At about 12:10, Ambulance 606, with Aubrey Rike and his partner Dennis "Peanuts" McGuire were at Harwood and Cedar Springs watching the motorcade pass. At about 12:19 unit 289 of the DPD called for an ambulance to 100 N. Houston St. (Dealey Plaza), with a man apparently having an epileptic seizure. Ambulance 606 responded and reported they were code 3 (lights and siren) to Parkland hospital around 12:25.

At 12:26, unit 38 reports that people are walking across Stemmons Freeway (southbound), apparently to position along the northbound side where the President will be coming up to exit for Market Hall. That is the last transmission before a stuck microphone on Channel 1 will create a continuous carrier for over 5 minutes.

12:30 – all Hell breaks loose

The following is from Channel 2 of the Dallas Police radio. Channel 2 was usually the tactical channel the police used, while Channel 1 was the routine one used by the patrol and traffic units. They used Channel 2 for all vehicles associated with the Motorcade that day. The transcripts can be found as CD 705 (CD stands for Warren Commission Document).

12:30 p.m. KKB 364.

#1: (Curry) Go to the hospital - Parkland Hospital. Have them stand by.

#1: Get a man on top of that triple underpass and see what happened up there.

#1: Have Parkland stand by.

Dallas 1: (Decker: in Curry's car) I am sure it's going to take some time to get your man in there. Pull every one of my men in there.

Disp: Dallas 1, repeat, I didn't get all of it. I didn't quite understand all of it.

Dallas 1: Have my office move all available men out of my office into the railroad yard to try to determine what happened in there and hold everything secure until Homicide and other investigators should get there.

Disp: 10-4. Dallas 1 -Station 5 will be notified.

Disp: 1, any information whatsoever?

#1: Looks like the President has been hit. Have Parkland stand by.

Disp: 10-4. They have been notified.

#4:	We have those canine units in that vicinity, don't we?
#1:	Headed to Parkland. Something's wrong with Channel 1.
#5:	1, what do you want with these men out here with me?
#5:	Just go on to Parkland Hospital [with me].
#83:	Dispatcher on Channel 1 seems to have his mike stuck.
#1:	Get these trucks out of the way. Hold everything. Get out of the way.

Unknown: motorcycle up on Stemmons with his mike stuck open on Channel 1. Could you send someone up there to tell him to shut it off? (12:34 p.m.)

#190: Do you still want me to hold this traffic on Stemmons until we find out something?

According to his book, "At the Door of Memory", Aubrey Rike states that he had delivered the epileptic to Parkland and at 12:35 (or so). The man was sitting on a stretcher in the emergency room area hallway, recovering, and they had not yet even gotten his name. Aubrey states that suddenly a group of "suits" burst in and demanded the stretcher. He told them they would have to find another one, as his patient was using this one. They did, and within a minute or two they came rushing back in with Jackie running beside the stretcher. Kennedy's head was covered, but having just seen Jackie's pink suit moments before, Aubrey immediately realized it was the President. The stretcher was rushed into Trauma Room 1. The epileptic gentleman simply walked away, forgotten in all of the excitement.

Three motorcycle cops that were accompanying the motorcade stopped in Dealey Plaza in the seconds after the shooting.

1.   Marrion Baker had come up Houston St., turned onto Elm St., parked his motorcycle and immediately ran into the Texas School Book Depository building.

2.   Bobby Hargis, who had been left of the Limo and SS car, parked his bike on the southern side of Elm St., across from the sidewalk and stairs coming down the hill. Bobby crossed the street and ran up the hill to look over the wall and fence, to see if he could see a shooter. He did not go behind the wall or fence, but returned to his motorcycle, went through the triple underpass. (Said that he again parked and ran up that slope, then returned to his motorcycle and proceeded to Parkland Hospital.)

3.   Clyde Haygood, who had been towards the extreme rear of the motorcade, followed Curry's radio instructions and parked his bike right by the storm drain on the northern side of Elm St. He ran up the grassy knoll to the railroad yards (and can be seen doing so in multiple photos and film frames), climbed on top of the concrete wall.

Officer Marrion Baker's foot hit the bottom step of the TSBD (films and photos) about 22 seconds after the head shot to Kennedy. He had been traveling north on Houston St. when the shots sounded. He says he saw multiple birds flying off the roof of the building, and reasoned the shooter was on the roof, or a very high floor. He turned the corner onto Elm St. where he immediately parked his bike, and ran into the building. Once inside the double doors, he encountered Janitor Eddie Piper. He asked Piper where the roof was, and the startled Piper actually said he did not know. But on his way into the building Baker had passed Warehouse Manager Roy Truly, who thought he should follow Baker into the building to assist him. Piper pointed out Truly to Baker, as Truly came through the entrance. Truly had entered in time to hear that Baker wanted to go to the roof.

Truly led the way, with Baker following. After opening the half door of the Will-Call counter (latched, although that was rare), they went through the mainly open first floor to the freight elevators in the NW corner of the building. Truly looked up the rather open elevator shaft (slatted gates) and saw that both elevators were on the 5th floor. He pushed the call button for the automatic (west) elevator, and hollered up the shaft to "Release the elevator." (close the doors)" Truly said he hollered a 2nd time and pushed the call button repeatedly, but the elevators did not move. He told Baker they would have to take the stairs. Baker had spent the entire time looking for any movement or suspects, although he was certain they would have been coming down from a higher point. Baker allegedly had his pistol out.

Truly came up the 1st set of stairs, and crossed the 25 feet of the 2nd floor, so he could access the next set of stairs. However, when Baker started to cross this area, he saw movement in the 2nd floor lunchroom and diverted. Here he saw Oswald walking away from the lunchroom door, so Baker ordered Oswald to stop and come to him. Truly, who realized that Baker was no longer behind him, came back down to the 2nd floor, and found Baker in the lunchroom, with his pistol pointed at Oswald's stomach. Baker and Truly discussed that Oswald was an employee, and not seeing any obvious agitation of Oswald, let him go and they proceeded up the stairs towards the 3rd floor. The lunchroom encounter probably lasted about 20 seconds or so.

JFK Assassination: Shades From The Fence

In the initial few minutes, multiple police and citizens followed in climbing up to the railroad fence, or the grassy knoll parking lot. Some also headed towards the TSBD, while a few simply left the Plaza. TSBD Employee Mrs. Robert Reid immediately returned into the TSBD after the shots, to phone her husband. She went up the front stairs (which only go to the 2nd floor), walked across the secretary area towards her desk in the back of the large room. She saw Lee Oswald come from the lunchroom area, with a Coke in hand. He walked through the room to the front stairs area, and goes down.

At 12:34, Haygood reports that a man "up here" (railroad yards) says the shots came from the TSBD.

At 12:35-6 Sgt. D.V. Harkness has a witness (Amos Euins) stating the shots came from the 5th floor of the TSBD. (He also echoes this report on Channel 1, which has now cleared.) He puts Euins on the back of his 3-wheeler and moves to the TSBD, placing Euins into Captain Sawyer's car. Sawyer had arrived and gone into the building, taking the passenger elevator to the "top floor" (it only went to the 4th), walking through and then returning downstairs to set up a command post at Elm and Houston.

At 12:37 (or so) there is a report of a man that was injured by a ricochet off of the pavement, James Tague. There is also a report by E. D. Brewer of a man who saw a rifle being withdrawn from an upper floor window (Howard Brennan). The Dispatcher asks if the building has been sealed off yet? D. V. Harkness, seeing that the front of the building has multiple officers watching it, proceeds to the dock side of the building to seal off the back. He will later state that the building was sealed by 12:38.

Even employees, returning to the building, were initially stopped. At 1:46 a call is put out on Channel 1 for Charles Givens, as he is one of the warehouse workers missing from the building. He was initially denied entry, until Police realize he is waiting outside and let him enter. Other employees tell stories about having to identify as an employee to enter the building. Most Dallas Police and Dallas Deputy Sheriffs now

43

turn their attention to searching the TSBD, having seen nothing of import in the railroad yards or grassy knoll. Many will, of course, gather witness statements and search the Dealey Plaza grounds. This includes the 8 officers stationed in Dealey Plaza holding the crowd back while the motorcade passed through. Officer White will guard a disturbance in the grass, by the manhole cover on the south side of DP. At 12:45, the Dispatcher will issue a description allegedly provided by witness Howard

Brennan. Brennan had been sitting on the northern curve of the wall, across the street from the TSBD. He stated that he saw the man slowly withdrawing a rifle from the window, in the seconds after the last shot. Photographer Bob Jackson also saw a rifle being drawn back into the window, and pointed out the location to Tom Dillard, who was sitting next to Jackson in the convertible. Dillard immediately took a photo. Amos Euins also reports seeing the rifle.

WFAA film journalist Tom Alyea was sitting in a car on Commerce St. in Dealey Plaza when the motorcade came through. He had just returned from covering the Fort Worth breakfast at the Hotel Texas. He grabbed his borrowed camera and ran across the Plaza and entered the TSBD within a couple of minutes, before they sealed the building. The film he took was later thrown out the door to a fellow WFAA newsman, when Alyea could not get out of the sealed building. The co-worker took the film to the WFAA studios where it was developed, and shown on live TV within minutes. Much of the film was left on the cutting room floor and tossed out as too dark or exposed.

Radio Newsman Pierce Allman and CBS newsman Robert MacNeil also ran into the building within minutes of the shooting. Both later reported that a young man exiting the building was asked about a phone location, and he pointed them inside. They both believe this was Lee Harvey Oswald. We do have audio recording of Allman's radio report, with him sounding rushed and out of breath. MacNeil will also call in a report to CBS, which will be turned into bulletins. No other newsmen were able to get into the building, once the front door was sealed off (12:35 or so).

The WFAA/Alyea film shows the hectic search of the building. It was actually searched in 2 waves: the 1st looking for a shooter, and the 2nd looking for evidence and weapons.

The sniper's nest is found in the southeast corner of the 6th floor, around 1:05 PM. Three shell casings are discovered on the floor of the sniper's nest, surround by walls of boxes of books, and with 3 small boxes in the window which could have been used as a rifle rest. Alyea would later report that he filmed over the boxes making up the wall of the sniper's nest, hoping the get the position of the shells, and the pristine scene on film. Unfortunately for Alyea, he is using a borrowed camera, and it often loses its sprocket loop, causing him to find a dark place where he opens the camera (exposing the recent film) to restore the loop. This early shot of the sniper's nest does not survive, or ends up on the cutting room floor when processed (without Alyea being there) by WFAA.

A paper bag is also allegedly found near the SE corner, but never photographed in place. The rifle is found in the NW corner, close to the stairs, around 1:25 PM. Alyea's film shows Lt. Carl Day checking the rifle for fingerprints, and Fritz ejects a live round from the chamber after Day says it is ok to touch the bolt action.

Day would leave the TSBD about 2 PM, holding the rifle by its strap. The paper bag, a Dr. Pepper bottle found next to the sniper's nest, and other evidence would also leave at this time, to be taken back to the crime lab to be processed. Studebaker, the relative new crime lab assistant would remain behind to take photos of the sniper's nest, and to process the boxes for fingerprints. The shell casings would also remain with Studebaker.

Inside the hospital, all available doctors were working on Kennedy to save his life in trauma room 1, while Govenor John Connally was taken into emergency surgery to work on his back and chest would, which had also punctured and collapsed his right lung.

Initially the doctors thought they had a faint pulse from Kennedy, as well as ragged breathing. They removed his clothes and ace bandage/back brace, and connected plasma tubes to him. The emergency doctors cut through a small wound in the President's throat, to insert a tracheostomy breathing tube into his throat to assist his breathing. They also tried closed chest massage. While trying frantically to save his life, they did not turn him over and were completely unaware of the bullet wound in his back.

When the doctors discussed opening the chest to do open heart massage on Kennedy, the Neurologist who had been standing by the head watching parts of the brain come out with the compressions, stopped them. After looking briefly at the head wound, they felt there was nothing they could continue to do.

In consideration of Jackie, who had been present in the room, or just in the hall outside, through most of the efforts, they probably 'fudged' the time of death a little bit, to the time after the Catholic priests had administered the Last Rites. The official time of death was set at 1:00 PM, but actual death was likely a little before that time.

The first CBS bulletin interrupted the soap opera "As the World Turns" at 12:40. It took until 12:47 for Walter Cronkite to appear live from the newsroom, and update the public. It was not until about 1:24 that Cronkite announced that Father Huber had been one of the 2 priests let into the room, and he had administered the Last Rites to President Kennedy. At 1:38, Cronkite announced the official report that Kennedy had died, giving the official time of 1:00 PM CST.

Lyndon Johnson had been held in a small room close to the emergency area by the Secret Service. Once Kennedy had passed, he was informed, and it was decided he should return to Air Force One at Love Field as quickly as possible. He asked that they not announce Kennedy's death to the waiting Press, until after he had left the hospital. He, Lady Bird, other

JFK Assassination: Shades From The Fence

officials and several of the Secret Service got into Chief Curry's and other vehicles, and took back roads to Love Field. They kept a low profile, in case there were other attackers.

At the hospital, Aubrey Rike called Peg O'Neil's funeral home to have them deliver a Brittanica casket (O'Neil's best model). While waiting for the casket, the nurses and ambulance people wrapped Kennedy's head in a sheet and put a rubber fitted sheet under the body, to keep blood from soiling the casket. Once delivered, Rike and his partner McGuire lifted the body into the casket, and started to wheel it out.

A shoving match over the body then proceeded to take place. The Dallas County Coroner Earl Rose insisted that according to Texas state law, a homicide trial required that the autopsy be completed in Dallas. Murder, even of the President, was a state crime and not a federal one, at that time (this would change after the JFK assassination). The feds knew that Jackie would not leave the body, and they wanted to get both of the Kennedy's on Air Force One, and out of Dallas. An argument ensued with Rose and the local law enforcement on one side, and Kenny O'Donnell and the Feds on the other. Some reports even have the SS agents showing weapons at one time.

Finally, phone calls were made, and Dallas County Justice of the Peace Theron Ward was contacted. He allegedly released the body to Jackie (family) and feds, under the condition that Kennedy's physician Admiral Burkley accompany the body to an autopsy. The body was loaded into the waiting Hearse, Jackie got inside, and the Secret Service drove it to Love Field. It arrives and is loaded onto the plane (after some difficulty) at 2:14. O'Neil and Rike were shoved to the side, and the Feds took the Hearse, owned by O'Neil, to Love Field. The pair also scrambled to drive the Ambulance to Love Field so that O'Neil could pick up the Hearse, after the casket was loaded onto the plane. O'Neil will report years later that he never received any payment for that Britannica Casket.

They would wait at Love Field until Federal Judge Sara Hughes could come out and do the Oath of Office on the airplane. She finally arrives around 2:28, and the ceremony is

47

done on the airplane about 2:32. Only a Dictaphone recording of the event took place, while LBJ puts his hand on a Catholic missal, a book of prayers and devotions (no bible on board) at 2:34 PM. After the ceremony, Johnson orders the plane in the air, and Dallas Police Chief Jesse Curry, Judge Sara Hughes and any other local officials leave the plane. The plane departs at 2:41 to go back to Washington, D.C.

Oak Cliff related events

Dallas' ABC affiliate WFAA went live at about 12:45 PM, with Jay Watson interrupting live programming. Within about 10 minutes of the broadcast he is joined by witnesses Bill and Gail Newman, and their 2 young boys. They describe what they saw, and Bill states he heard only 2 shots, but Jay Watson and co-worker Jerry Haynes, who were in Dealey Plaza, both state they heard 3.

According to the Dallas Police version of the DPD radio transcripts, at 12:54, Patrolman JD Tippit (#78) is told to be "at large" in Oak Cliff for any emergency that comes in. This was his last actual exchange with the Dispatcher, although according to the same transcripts, #78 did call in two times at 1:08 PM, without a Dispatcher response. Tippit's normal patrol area was in central Oak Cliff, but this order allowed him to move into northern Oak Cliff, closer to the downtown Dallas area, just across the river.

The following is again from Channel 1 of the Dallas Police Radio logs. The last prior time marker given by the Dispatcher was at 1:16, so this use of the police radio by citizen T. F. Bowley occurred just after 1:16 PM.

Citizen: Hello, police operator?

Disp: Go ahead. Go ahead, citizen using the police radio.

Cit.: There's been a shooting out here.

JFK Assassination: Shades From The Fence

Disp: Where's it at? The citizen using the police radio . . .

Cit.: Tenth Street.

Disp: What location on Tenth Street?

Cit.: Between Marsalis and Beckley. It's a police officer. Somebody shot him. What -- what's . . . 404 Tenth Street. Can you hear me?
(Man and woman's voices in background)

Disp: 78. (trying to raise JD Tippit)

Cit: It's in a police car, number 10.

Disp: 78.

Disp: 78.

Cit: Got that?
Hello, police operator. Did you get that?

Another Dispatcher: Attention. Signal 19, police officer, 510 E. Jefferson.
(510 E Jefferson is actually the Warren Reynolds car sales office, who had phoned in a report.)

Cit: Thank you.

35:     35.

259:     259.

Disp: The citizen using the police radio: Remain off the radio now.

JFK Assassination: Shades From The Fence

Ambulance 602 is located just a block and a half from the 10th and Patton shooting site, at a Funeral Home at 400 E Jefferson. The log shows he dispatched at 1:17, and asked for clarification on the address.

Car salesman Ted Callaway, who works across Jefferson from the Warren Reynolds lot, also hears the shots and heads to the scene going north on Patton. He sees Oswald trotting towards Jefferson from 10th St. reloading his revolver as he goes. Callaway hollers at Oswald, who raises the pistol briefly, so Callaway lets Oswald pass.

When the ambulance arrives they find Tippit's pistol on the ground, and lay it on the hood of the #10 squad car. Callaway then assists in putting Tippit on the stretcher. After the ambulance leaves to take Tippit to Methodist Hospital, Callaway also gets on Tippit's radio;

#85:   85.

Disp: Suspect running west on Jefferson from the location.

#85:   10-4.

Disp: No physical description.

Callaway: Hello, hello, hello.

Disp: 602.

Callaway: Pardon, from out here on Tenth Street, 500 block. This officer just shot. I think he's dead.

Disp: 10-4. We have that information. The citizen using the radio: Remain off the radio now.

JFK Assassination: Shades From The Fence

The Ambulance will later go back into service after taking Tippit to Methodist Hospital, about 1:22. At 1:28 the police radio will report that Tippit is Dead On Arrival (DOA), on channel 2.

For the next several minutes Police show up at the 10th and Patton site. Many are patrolling and looking for the shooter of JD Tippit. At 1:22 Officer R. W. Walker radios in a description of the suspect of "He's a white male, about thirty, five eight, (siren) black hair, slender, wearing white jacket, a white shirt and dark slacks."

Multiple witnesses are at the 10th and Patton area when the shooting took place. A few of these 13 or so witnesses will later pick Oswald out of the many lineups, at police headquarters. The descriptions and color of his clothing will vary, however.

At 1:25, Officer 279 (unknown) will report that a white jacket was found on the ground behind a gas station at 400 Jefferson St.

For the next several minutes there are reports of the suspect being seen on Jefferson, 10th St. and many of the blocks in the area. This includes a church basement at 10th and Crawford. At 1:34, Patrolman C. T. Walker reports that he is seen running into the library at Marsalis and Jefferson. Many officers converge on the library. Employee Adrian Hamby was a little late to work at the library, and ran into the building. Seen running, the police surround the library, to the surprise of Hamby and the other librarian. The police report that it is the wrong person on the radio within a couple of minutes.

At 1:37, Chief Curry is en route to Love Field per Channel 2. He reminds the Dispatcher to not put that information on the air of the more public Channel 1.

At 1:44, in Dealey Plaza, railroad Lee Bowers holds up a freight train so that police can check it out. Around 2 PM, 3 "tramps" who had been pulled off the train are escorted to Dallas

County Sheriff's offices on Houston St.

JFK Assassination: Shades From The Fence

Also, at 1:44 the Tippit shooting suspect is reported to be in the Texas Theater. He had ducked into the entryway of the Hardy Shoes store as a police cruiser was u-turning behind him. Manager Johnny Brewer saw him acting suspiciously, and followed him to the Texas Theater. Box Office worker Julia Postal was standing on the street trying to see why all of the squad cars had been speeding up Jefferson. Oswald ducks into the Theater without paying. Brewer and Postal discuss it, and check inside with concession stand worker Butch Burrows, who had been busy and had not seen Oswald. Brewer tells them he had been acting suspicious anyway, so Postal phones the police while Burroughs and Brewer watch Oswald.

By 1:50, several police cars have surrounded the Texas Theater. N. M. McDonald and other officers enter the back door, which is opened by Johnny Brewer. Brewer points Oswald out to them, and they work their way to his location in a center section, 3 rows from the back of the theater. When McDonald tells Oswald to stand up, he allegedly shouts "This is it." and pulls his pistol. McDonald grabs the pistol and causes it to misfire when Oswald pulls the trigger, probably saving his own life. McDonald manages to wrest the pistol from Oswald, and many other officers surround him and scuffle with him.

At 1:52, Sgt. Gerald Hill reports that the suspect is arrested, and they are on their way downtown with him, to headquarters. Some members of the press had made their way to the Texas Theater, after hearing many of the police radio reports. They had made a connection between the shooter of Tippit, and the Kennedy shooting, although many in the Police reportedly had not yet thought about it.

Path of Oswald

For most of this chapter, I have been only talking about events witnessed by multiple people, or those on the police radio and therefore heard by multiple people. Oswald's movements that day are questioned by many. However, I will

52

fill in what various witnesses later said they saw of him, and the probable travels based on these witnesses.

Mrs. Robert Reid: At about 12:32/3 he is seen coming out of the 2nd floor lunch room, and crossing the 2nd floor to the front stairs of the building (which only go down to the 1st floor).

Pierce Allman (newsman): enters the front of the TSBD and encounters a man he later believes to be Oswald, give him directions to a phone in the TSBD.

Dallas Bus Driver Cecil McWatters: Says a man bangs on the door of the bus, while it was stopped in traffic between stops about at Murphy St., while going west on Elm, about 6 blocks east of the TSBD. Oswald's former landlady Mary Bledsoe was also on this bus, and hoped he would not say anything to her. Oswald was on the bus about 2 minutes, and got off when it was stuck in traffic at Lamar St., heading west. We do know that the Dallas bus Oswald got on had a time check point on Elm St. and St. Paul St. where a supervisor would hold the bus, if it was earlier than 12:35. Between that time, and the time the police dispatcher got the first report of Tippit being shot, at 1:16, all times are estimates.

Taxi driver William Whaley states that Oswald got into the front door of his cab, at Lamar and Commerce. He gets into the front street and asks to go to the 500 block of N. Beckley. He is let out at Beckley and Neeley (4 blocks past his rooming house).

Housekeeper Earlene Roberts is trying to tune her television set, "around 1 PM", when Oswald walks in. He is in his room a couple of minutes and comes out wearing a jacket. She last sees him just standing in front of the house, as if waiting for a northbound Beckley bus.

These times are highly disputed. Some quote Earlene Roberts as an exact time of 1 PM, instead of the approximation she gave. Many contend that Oswald could not possibly go the 9/10th of a mile to the 10th and Beckley site, in time to shoot Tippit. Many have done this fast walk on my tours, and it can be done without running in about 12 ½ minutes. The exact route is unknown, as nobody was really paying attention to people walking up and down the Oak Cliff streets.

Oswald is tied to both shootings

Warehouse manager Roy Truly naturally had Oswald on his mind. He had seen Baker stick his pistol into Oswald's stomach during the encounter in the 2nd floor lunchroom. Naturally, he wanted to talk to him, and spent several minutes asking if anyone had seen him. There was a quick check of all warehouse employees and until 1:44 both Givens and Oswald were the only warehouse workers missing. Truly felt the police should know about Oswald, so he gets his name and pulls his address (Ruth Paine house, in Irving) out of the file. He gives this information to Captain Will Fritz, who is in the building managing the JFK shooting investigation. Again, Givens name was given out on the police radio about this time. Givens had a police record, while Oswald did not except in New Orleans.

When Fritz returns to police headquarters a little after 2 PM, he tells Sgt. Gerald Hill that he was to go to an address in Irving to pick up a Lee Oswald. Hill asks why, and is told it is in connection with the JFK shooting. Hill tells Fritz that he could save the trip, because that man was already in his office waiting to be interrogated. At that moment, Oswald becomes the primary suspect in both killings.

Around 2:31 PM, WFAA's Jay Watson sat down with a Dallas dressmaker named Abraham Zapruder. The dressmaker had brought his 8 mm film camera into the studio to see if they would develop it. Watson interviewed him on the air, while WFAA discussed the film. WFAA did not have the proper processes to handle 8 mm film, which is actually 16 mm that must be split. Zapruder would later be driven to Eastman Kodak Company, who agreed to process the film right away, while Zapruder and the feds waited.

Throughout the live WFAA broadcast, they would show films of the motorcade, through Parkland Hospital, and the departure of LBJ and the Kennedys. They would also show the Alyea film that had been tossed out of the TSBD, and processed. All networks would have almost continuous coverage the remainder of the weekend, and in a lot of ways it was the 'graduation' of TV news! (refer to the TV News chapter later in the book)

Throughout the afternoon and into the evening there is much confusion and misinformation broadcast on all networks. When LBJ first goes into Parkland, some report he is holding his chest, and it is reported as a possible heart attack. At other times they discuss a shootout between the Secret Service (Agent Kenney had pulled out an automatic rifle in the follow-up car after the head shot), and the shooters. At one time, they reported a Secret Service agent had been shot on the hill in Dealey Plaza. Much of this was just based on the poor communications in 1963.

Throughout the afternoon, Oswald was fingerprinted and shown in multiple police lineups. In most of these, he stood out like a sore thumb, and often was raising witness attention to himself by yelling about how unfair they were. He moved between the jail elevator and Captain Fritz' Homicide office on the 5th floor, multiple times throughout the afternoon and evening. The press often shouted questions, and he would respond with declarations of his innocence, and his just being a "patsy". He was arraigned and officially charged in the evening for the Tippit shooting (the better case against him). It was late in the evening around midnight that he was allowed a "press conference". Actually, the Press were not supposed to ask questions, and the Dallas leaders simply wanted to show that Oswald had not been beaten or abused by the Police, and asked Curry to "show" Oswald. However, there were multiple microphones and a TV camera, so Oswald started speaking. The press shouted questions at him. He was informed by a journalist during the showing that he had been accused of shooting JFK, but in reality the arraignment on this charge did not occur until the early hours of Saturday morning. Weeks later, photos of that room show nightclub owner Jack Ruby in the back of the room. Ruby would also be photographed several times in DPD headquarters on Saturday.

Throughout the day, Oswald's wife Marina, her 2 children and mother Marguerite Oswald would also be taken to police headquarters to visit Oswald. Additionally his brother Robert Oswald would also appear, and speak to his brother.

It took the Press almost no time to find Oswald's background information, about his 1959 defection to the Soviet Union, his 62' return, and his summer of 63' arrest in New Orleans for a scuffle while he was handing out Fair Play for Cuba literature. In New Orleans he also appeared on a TV show, and radio debate with anti-Castro Cubans. This information was disseminated by the national press, leading many to believe there was a conspiracy with pro-Castro/Communist forces.

Co-worker Buell Wesley Frazier, who gave Oswald a ride to work that day, was also brought into police headquarters. He was extensively questioned, sometimes threatened (he says) and even given a polygraph test late that night. He was released, however.

The President(s)

Air Force One took off around 2:41 CST, and headed back to Washington DC. On the trip a number of calls were made to the White House to make arrangements for transport, an autopsy, and preparation of the body for burial. Since Kennedy was a former Navy officer, the decision was made by his Doctor Admiral Burkley and Jackie Kennedy, to have the procedures done at Naval Medical Center, Bethesda, MD.

The airplane was met by Bobby Kennedy, and a gray ambulance. Bobby rushed past LBJ to the back of the plane, and he and Jackie exited the plane by a lift truck. LBJ and Lady Bird came down the steps, and LBJ made a brief public statement, before leaving for the White House.

At Bethesda, Commander James J. Humes, Director of Laboratories at the facility, was the chief Pathologist for the autopsy. He was joined by Commander J. Thornton Boswell,

Chief of pathology. Both were qualified Pathologists, and administrators/instructors; but it is contended that neither had ever done a Court acceptable forensic autopsy. U. S. Army Lt. Colonel Pierre Finck, a Forensic Pathologist, also came in and participated later that evening, after the autopsy had already begun.

When Finck arrived, they had only taken X-rays of the head and skull. Finck had to ask for additional X-rays of the body. He states in his sworn testimony in the Clay Shaw trial, in Feb. 1969, that he was prevented from dissecting the back and neck by the Generals and other high ranking officers in the room. He only probed the back wound, but because of the difficulty of contracting muscles (which move after the shot), he was only able to get the probe in "the very first section of an inch".

Additionally, the autopsy doctors did not call the Parkland doctors that night, and were unaware that the tracheotomy incision had been made through a pre-existing wound. They were therefore very concerned that they could not find a bullet in the body, until they were told that a bullet was found on a stretcher in the hospital. In his 1969 testimony, Finck answers that it was not a "complete autopsy", in his opinion:

"Q: What you are telling me, Colonel, is as you didn't go into the other half of the brain and completely ascertain what may have or may not have been there then you did not do a complete autopsy, is that correct? Yes or no and then you can answer the question.

A: Yes. As regards the wounds on the external aspect of the body, what we found on the 24 November '63 was adequate as regards the external wounds of the brain. Q: Is this in your opinion a complete autopsy under the definition used by the

American Board of Pathology? Yes or no and then you can explain it.

A: On -- No. On the 24th of November because to my recollection we based our autopsy report on the 24th of November on the information obtained from people at the scene. We based it on our gross autopsy findings pertaining to the wounds as they were described on the body and the X-rays taken before and during the course of the autopsy.

Q: Am I correct, Colonel, did I hear your answer that it was "no" and then you explained it?

A: I explained it because there were supplemental reports, examinations of clothing that was made at a later date."

The Killing of Oswald

Saturday was pretty much a rush by the Press to get every detail about Oswald and his background into the news. Oswald was additionally processed in line-ups, visitations by family, and interrogations. He attempted to have Ruth Paine call an attorney by the name of John Abt, in New York. Because of a statement he made at the midnight "press conference" about not being given proper representation, a Louis Nichols from the Dallas Bar visited Oswald and offered an attorney. Oswald declined, trying to contact Abt (who was out of town, and never contacted).

By Saturday afternoon, it was decided by Dallas Police Chief Jesse Curry that they would let Oswald rest that evening. He informed the Press, many of whom had also been up 30 hours or more, that nothing else would happen that evening. He suggested they also go home, or to their hotels, and rest. Not wanting to miss any transfer to the more secure Dallas County Jail (normal procedure), they protested. Curry told them that if they returned by 10:00 AM on Sunday morning, they would not miss anything. This was not giving a schedule of when the transfer would actually happen, as many believe. It was simply a time before which no transfer would take place.

Reportedly, during the night, the Dallas authorities received a number of anonymous phone calls that threatened Oswald. This allegedly prompted Sheriff Bill Decker, and others, to suggest they move Oswald secretly during the night. Curry, who was under pressure from the City officials to do everything in full view, insisted on honoring his word to the Press and move Oswald Sunday morning. Decker would normally send a Deputy to pick up prisoners, but allegedly told his Deputies they were not to be involved with this transfer.

When Oswald was brought down the Jail elevator, handcuffed to Detective Jim Leavelle, and walked out into the basement, Jack Ruby stepped forward and fired a single shot into Oswald's abdomen. The 38 bullet entered Oswald's left front side, just under the lung, proceeded through every major stomach organ, and ended up just inside the skin on the right side of his back. The shooting occurred at 11:20 AM, just 4 minutes after Ruby telegrammed money to one of his dancers, at the Western Union station half a block away. Ruby was quickly arrested and taken up to the same prison cell that Oswald had just vacated.

Oswald was immediately taken back into the office he had just walked through and laid on the floor. An ambulance came down the ramp, and they loaded an unconscious Oswald, joined by Jim Leavelle, and he was rushed to Parkland Hospital. He was treated in Trauma Room 2 (across from where Kennedy was treated), but never regained consciousness. LBJ even called and told the Doctor that a Federal agent would be in the room, and he wanted a confession!

However, Oswald was pronounced dead at 1:07 PM.

Again, this is a greatly shortened version of that weekend, for those who have not readily studied the case yet. The reading list in the back of the book will include many books that go into much greater detail.

6. Dallas Police

This is the first chapter that will include an article I did for the Dealey Plaza Echo. This one was written in 2009. It is about the Dallas Police and their procedures, Motorcade, Security and the events of that weekend. It appeared in a Dealey Plaza Echo article, in 2009/10. That journal is the product of the group Dealey Plaza UK, of which I am an Honorary Lifetime Member.

The article is cut-and-pasted below:

Along with following the research of the assassination of President Kennedy, for many years I have given tours of Dallas, Dealey Plaza, and the related JFK Assassination sites, including where Lee Harvey Oswald and Jack Ruby worked and lived. During these tours, and from other researchers on the various JFK related forums, I have been asked many times about the Dallas Police procedures used in November, 1963. These questions often contain some major misinformation and myths about the assassination and the procedures, protection, and policies in place for that weekend events. I have therefore compiled the following information, to cover some of the more common questions and misconceptions. This information has been taken from a number of sources, such as reports by Dallas Police, Secret Service and FBI; therefore, it should be taken with a grain of salt, as all of these agencies were trying to "save face" after the events of that weekend, and their reports will naturally reflect that intent.

This article is not an attempt to make excuses for the Dallas Police, Dallas County Sheriff, or other law enforcement agencies. Many of the security put into place that weekend, for both the President and the suspect, were woefully insufficient. Much of it was standard law enforcement practice for that time, but these practices were very short on what was actually

JFK Assassination: Shades From The Fence

needed, and they were discovered as such. While there were reasons for many of these shortfalls, I certainly can't say they were all **good** reasons. It is simply my intent to list many of the reasons that were in place, and the reader should be able to see why many of these procedures were certainly changed after that weekend.

I am not in law enforcement, although I am licensed with the Texas Department of Public Safety as a Non-Commissioned (no gun) Security Officer. I am simply a Dallas historian, researcher, author and Docent for a number of Dallas museums. But because of these questions, I have spent a lot of time researching police procedures that were in effect in November of 1963. I also have run this paper by a number of current and former Dallas law enforcement officers, before publication, and I thank them for their assistance.

Purpose of the Texas Trip

For a better understanding of this article, the purpose of that November trip to Texas should be covered. The type of trip becomes a factor in what type of security would have been in place. For example, had it been a trip to a foreign country, such as Kennedy's trip to Berlin, it would have required completely different security. A good, and valid, comparison is most likely the trips to Houston, San Antonio and Ft Worth completed earlier in this Texas trip, since the purpose and intent of these visits were obviously the same as Dallas. Security should have been just as strict (or lax) in these cities. The purpose of the Texas Motorcade was to be seen by as many voters as possible. This meant large crowds, which naturally creates more security issues.

In 1960, Kennedy had been elected by the closest margin in history, just barely defeating Republican Vice President Richard Nixon. Although his actions in the 1962 Cuban Missile crisis bought Kennedy favor with much of the American people, it cost him votes in the anti-Castro Cubans of Florida, and other states. He was also concerned about loss of votes in the South, caused by his Civil Rights stance. Additionally, Kennedy needed to help mend a major split between leaders of the Democratic Party, centered on Lyndon B. Johnson, the former Senator from Texas and now Vice President, and other Texas politicians. Even with LBJ on the ticket, Kennedy had barely carried Texas in 1960, and there were rumors that LBJ would be dropped from the ticket in 1964.

Dallas Politics and Concerns

In September of 1963, United Nations Ambassador Adlai Stevenson was heckled in Dallas while giving his speech on United Nations Day at the Dallas Memorial Auditorium Theater. Upon leaving that venue, he was struck and stunned by a woman wielding a protest sign. Additionally, just before the November 1960 election Vice Presidential candidate Johnson had an encounter with protesters, as he and his wife, Lady Bird Johnson, attempted to have lunch at Dallas' Adolphus Hotel. These events and others, were covered by the national press, and helped give Dallas the unfortunate nickname of "City of Hate" among the press. In addition, Dallas has been the home to many extreme right-wing agitators, including Major General Edwin Walker, who the Kennedy administration forced to resign after he was found to be using his position to indoctrinate soldiers in his right-wing positions. Furthermore, many right-wing Oilmen, such as H.L Hunt, lived in the area, and many heavily criticized Kennedy and his policies on Communism. These included such outspoken critics as my cousin, Edward "Ted" Dealey, the publisher/editor of the Dallas Morning News, and a person who had exchanged heated words with John Kennedy in person. Kennedy reportedly referred to Dallas as "nut country," and many of his advisors, including Adlai Stevenson, suggested he avoid Dallas.

These episodes worried the Dallas city leaders and businessmen. Allegedly[1], they even discussed the option of

JFK Assassination: Shades From The Fence

"uninviting" Kennedy to Dallas, but could think of no graceful way to do so. According to some, even Dallas leader and businessman, Stanly Marcus (whom the Dallas Citizen's Council jokingly referred to as "our lonely liberal"), of the Neiman-Marcus department stores, encouraged Kennedy to stay away from Dallas.[2] Hoping to thwart potentially embarrassing incidents, Dallas passed a city ordinance making it illegal to interfere with any legal public gathering and the visit would go ahead as scheduled. Police Chief Jessie Curry went on television and radio urging the people of Dallas to be aware of any activity that could disrupt the presidential visit to the city and to report it to the Police as soon as they noticed anything[3]. Basically, the City of Dallas was afraid of any embarrassing incidents, and particularly worried about the right-wing extremists or their followers.

The shooting of the President and Governor by a left-wing pro-Communist was a major surprise to everyone in Dallas, and the nation. Although a shooting of the President could never be considered a good thing, in some ways the people of Dallas were actually relieved it was from a pro-Communist, instead of a right-wing Dallasite. As a suspect Oswald's background as a proCommunist / Marxist-Leninist would later be a major factor in his security.

Motorcade Route Selection and Security Assignments

The security of the President of the United States is the sole province of the US Secret Service. In addition to Counterfeiting (they were part of the US Treasury Department), this is their primary function. Everything that is required by the Secret Service, they must specify to the

---

[1] Leslie Warren, "Dallas: Public and Private"
[2] Stanley Marcus, "Minding the Store: A Memoir" pg 255
[3] Jesse Curry, "JFK Assassination File"

JFK Assassination: Shades From The Fence

Federal, State and local law enforcement agencies of the host city. It is not the job of the City of Dallas, or its law enforcement agencies to specify what security precautions should be made, nor change the security on its own. Of course, the local law enforcement agencies can make suggestions, but it is up to the Secret Service to specify what security precautions should be in place to protect the President. Much of these precautions, such as open windows on open floors, are influenced by the purpose of the Motorcade. In this case, where the purpose was to allow the maximum number of voters to see the President, these precautions may have been loosened, which in hindsight was obviously a mistake.

There are many sources for the reader to find descriptions of how the security arrangements were put together. One of these is the Warren Report, as one of its two primary purposes was to review the efforts of the Secret Service. In addition, the Dallas Police files have a number of summaries written, after the fact, documenting the meetings and discussions between the host city and the Secret Service. "Dallas: Public and Private" and many other books detail these discussions and arrangements.

Initially, the location of the luncheon was a choice between the Dallas World Trade Mart on Stemmons Freeway in northwest Dallas, and the Women's Building in Fair Park on the east side of Dallas.[4] The Women's Building might have been the more secure site, as Fair Park was surrounded by iron fences and gates, and was the site of the annual State Fair of Texas. However, it was the smaller facility, and the city leaders wanted to show off the new World Trade Mart, to indicate Dallas as a major international business center. (Dallas was the 8th largest city in the US.)

Either way, the Motorcade would have gone down Main St., through the center of downtown Dallas as that was the traditional parade route through the city, as well as being able

---

[4] Dallas Assistant Chief Charles Batchelor's event timeline memo to Chief Curry, Dallas' DPD files of evidence

64

JFK Assassination: Shades From The Fence

to expose the President to the maximum number of voters. If the Women's Building had been chosen, the most likely path would have been eastbound down Main St., as it was when Franklin D Roosevelt rode through Dallas to commemorate the 1936 Texas Centennial Exposition, also in Fair Park. Either way, the motorcade would pass through Dealey Plaza, the western "doorway" of Dallas.

The actual route of the motorcade was as follows:

"Motorcade proceeds southeast along airport apron past parking lot towards Continental Hangar; bearing right before Continental Hangar and proceed out onto airport entrance road *(Cedar Springs)*; left on airport entrance road to right of median strip; left on Mockingbird Lane; left *(right)* on Lemmon Avenue; right on Turtle Creek Boulevard; bear left onto Cedar Springs Road; left on Harwood; right on Main Street; right on Houston Street; left on Elm Street; bear right on access road to Stemmons Freeway (Interstate 35-E); continuing northwesterly on Freeway; exit at Wycliff-Industrial Boulevard Exit; right on Industrial Boulevard; right into side parking lot of Trade Mart (parking lot roped off); stop at side door near front of building. Distance of ten miles. Time 40-45 minutes.

Trade Mart to Dallas Love Field

Proceeds northwesterly out of parking lot; right on Industrial Boulevard; left on Harry Hines Boulevard; exit at Mockingbird Lane Exit; right on Mockingbird Lane; left on airport entrance road; right towards special entrance cut in fence west of Continental Hangar (same entrance used on inbound trip); continue north along airplane parking area; left along employee parking lot direct to AF #1 and AF #2 on airport apron. Distance four miles. Time 12-15 minutes.

JFK Assassination: Shades From The Fence

Note: The Parkland Hospital is located on the original route to the Trade Mart and Love Field. These routes were not varied." [5]

Occasionally, I am asked why the motorcade did not simply go down Elm St., so that it could avoid the 120-degree left turn that going Main-Houston-Elm required. This turn was allegedly against Secret Service guidelines; and if against guidelines in 1963, these guidelines were apparently ignored for this motorcade. Of course, after the assassination, all Secret Service guidelines were reviewed and heavily revised for the future.

Elm Street is (and was) a one-way street going westbound through all of downtown Dallas. Consequently it was the major public transportation throughway for the city buses, heading westbound, just as Commerce Street was the throughway for eastbound traffic and buses. To close this street down, wait for major crowds to gather, and then wait for those crowds to dwindle down, a major part of the city's public transportation system would have to shut down or be disrupted. This, in addition to Main Street being the traditional parade route the citizens were used to, made Main Street the choice. Both streets had major office buildings, with open windows on them; however, this allowed more voters to see the President, so these security concerns were overlooked. (Of course, if security were the major concern, a public motorcade would not have happened, just as it had been limited in Florida, earlier in the month, because of threats to the President.)

The other question that frequently comes up is why they did not simply cut over to Stemmons Freeway from Main Street, in the Dealey Plaza Annex (the area west of the Triple Underpass). The border between Main and Elm Streets is a curbed median, whose narrowest point is about 3 feet across. This median is raised with a 6-inch curb, as well as a sign that says no right turn, and it extends past the entrance to Stemmons Freeway. If a Motorcade had attempted to jump this hurdle, it

---

[5] Report of the US Secret Service on the Assassination of President Kennedy

would have had to slow down much more than the 120-degree turn required from Houston to Elm Streets. It just was not feasible with a motorcade involving dozens of cars, motorcycles and busses. (It is alleged that at one time the removal of this curbed median was offered, but declined as unnecessary by the Secret Service. I have been unable to confirm this.) Such a project would have disrupted city traffic, but may have been the best solution if that turn was to be avoided. The Secret Service did not call for this to be done, however.

Still another option would be to continue to Industrial Avenue on Main St. However, in those days Industrial Avenue was what the name implied. It had been built from the old Trinity River bottom, and only had a few sparse industrial businesses along it. Moreover, liquor stores, bail bondsmen, a few nightclubs and some homeless people also inhabited the area. It was never recommended as a route by Dallas law enforcement, nor did Dallas Secret Service Agent Sorrells suggest it. Instead, they planned to use the Stemmons Freeway, possibly because it was a fairly recent addition to the city, and the City leaders wanted to show Dallas as a modern, progressive city.

Many who ask me about going down Main Street point out that it would be almost as "quick", and would exclude the 120 degree turn from Houston to Elm Streets. However, it should be remembered that "quick" was not the purpose of the Motorcade, and being seen by as many people as possible was the purpose. By going down Stemmons Freeway, many Dallas residents could stop at the side of the Freeway, as well as the service roads, to see the President. It is true that Industrial Avenue ran between the Trade Mart and Market Hall, and the motorcade would turn on Industrial Avenue when close to the Trade Mart.

Washington Secret Service Agent Lawson, Dallas Agent Sorrells, Dallas Assistant Chief Charles Batchelor and Deputy Chief Lunday drove the entire motorcade route on Monday, November 18.[6] During this drive, Batchelor noted the number of Police Officers needed for every intersection or overpass, as dictated by Lawson and Sorrells. Additional manpower was requested where the Secret Service felt it was needed and other security requirements were discussed. Specifically, among those discussed was the need to keep the overpasses manned with law enforcement, and have those officers instructed not to allow anyone to stay over the immediate path of the Presidential party. (Officers Foster and White would later let some 20 or so railroad workers stand over the Triple Underpass, which would be the possible reason for later actions in Dealey Plaza.) Other security details were discussed, including the taking down of the fence at Love Field, so that the motorcade would not have to travel through the public driveways within the airport.

The law enforcement assigned to the event was some 493 men. Of these, 173 were for traffic and security along the 12-mile motorcade route, while some 56 men were assigned security at Love Field. There would be 190 men assigned for security within the Trade Mart, where Kennedy would pause for lunch and speeches, with 74 men for security and traffic in and around the Trade Mart.

The plan was to have the traffic officers leave the streets open, while monitoring progress of the motorcade on Channel 2. The pilot car, and the lead car, would then inform the officers of their progress, so that they could close the streets to traffic when the motorcade was close, and then re-open them after it had passed. This would disrupt traffic flow the least, except on Main Street where the gathering of huge crowds was expected (and normal for any parade).

Bill Decker and the Dallas County Sheriff's Department

Bill Decker had been Sheriff, or in the department, for decades, and was well respected even by the criminals. He was

---

[6] Dallas Assistant Chief Charles Batchelor's event timeline memo to Chief Curry, Dallas' DPD files of evidence

JFK Assassination: Shades From The Fence

part of the department during the Bonnie and Clyde ambush, in 1934 (although not directly involved). He knew many of the shadier characters in Dallas on a first name basis, as even to the bad guys, he was friendly. Often referred to as a "Decker Warrant," he simply stated he wanted to talk to someone and that person would just show up at his office. He had a reputation even among the criminals as being a fair man to deal with. He treated them well, and was respected by them. (Never heard any claim of corruption stick though, just a mutual respect.)

Of course, there are many myths about their relations, and I don't trust all of the stories. For example, when convicted murderer Ray Hamilton supposedly came out of a Fort Worth hideout without firing a shot, just because Decker hollered to him, "C'mon out, Ray. This is Bill." (Other versions say Decker snuck around behind him and got the drop on him.)

There was always cooperation when needed, but (like today) there is also a somewhat inter-agency competition as well. FBI and local law enforcement also have some competition whenever jurisdictions overlapped. The City of Dallas did not take up all of the County of Dallas in 1963. Even today, only parts of the City are outside the County lines. The Sheriff's office had jurisdiction within the city limits, but generally focused on the areas of the suburbs and county areas outside of the City of Dallas, leaving most law enforcement within the city to Dallas police.

Decker's department was involved in the November 1963 Presidential security, to the extent that the Secret Service asked for help. I agree that Decker did tell his plain clothes detectives that they had no involvement with the Motorcade security. I do not think this implies an ulterior motive on Decker's part, nor anything sinister. He simply was not asked to have his detectives involved in security by the Secret Service, and relayed to his men that they had no such duties. (This statement is probably not documented anywhere, though.) As Dallas County still had laws to enforce, those detectives were therefore available for other duties, since not everyone in

JFK Assassination: Shades From The Fence

Dallas could be assigned to the security route. The Sheriff was, however, included in the lead car, as one of the chief law enforcement persons in Dallas. In addition, Assistant Chief Batchelor's statement to Chief Curry specifies that at least 15 of Decker's deputies were at the Trade Mart for security.[7]

There were at least 46 men from the Texas Department of Public Safety (Highway Patrol) and a number of men from the Texas Rangers assigned to the motorcade and Trade Mart security. These Texas law enforcement officers provide security for the Texas Governor John Connally, and provided drivers for many of the cars in the motorcade for the entire Texas trip. As before, the Secret Service determined who, and how many people they needed.

Sharpshooters on the Roof of the County Courthouse

There has long been a story that Deputy Sheriff Harry Weatherford and another officer had been stationed on the roof of the Dallas County Courthouse (Decker's building) with a rifle, as a form of security. Dallas historian and author, Jim Gatewood, presents this story during his public speaking, and insists that Weatherford took a shot at Oswald, and caused him to miss his final shot. Even though Weatherford's affidavit, taken that weekend, quotes him as being down on Main St. with fellow officers, and no other officer is ever named as being on the roof with him, the story persists.

Fellow researcher, Denis Morissette, had an exchange in 1990 with Sheriff Jim Bowles that is still on his web site. That exchange is often quoted as confirmation of this event by Jim Bowles. Below is the quote.

---

[7] In Gary Savage's book "JFK First Day Evidence," former Sheriff Jim Bowles refutes the HSCA assertion that the stuck microphone was in the Motorcade, and mentions the stuck microphone picked up a broadcast from a Deputy Sheriff patrol car (pg 344), which implies that these Deputies appear to be from the uniformed patrol division, and not the plain clothes detectives.

JFK Assassination: Shades From The Fence

Quote: (from Denis' page) ------------------------------------
-----

Question : Do you know about Deputy Sheriff Harry Weatherford waiting on the roof a building near assassination site with a rifle?

BOWLES : Yes, Harry Weatherford was on the roof with a second deputy, and he had a rifle. They were assigned there for security. My first recollection of the suggestion that Weatherford might have been implicated was from the imagination of Penn Jones who, so far as I know, never worried about the other deputy. It would seem strange that a hit man would be stationed with a living witness. It does not fit reason.

Many will selectively include only the first sentence of Jim's response, which (by itself) appears to show he is confirming the event. However, I take the quote in the entire context of the full paragraph. My interpretation *(in italics)* is that Jim Bowles is saying, "Yes, *"I know the story." He then recounts how the story goes:* "Harry Weatherford was on the roof with a second deputy, and he had a rifle. They were assigned there for security." He then goes on to refute the story, using the words "suggestion" and "imagination of Penn Jones." He explains some of the holes in the story and that it "does not fit reason."[8]

I also know a former Dallas journalist that covered the Jack Ruby trial and the JFK assassination. In a break in the Ruby trial, he recalls Sheriff Bill Decker casually talking about having sharpshooters on the roof for security because it was the tallest building in the Dealey Plaza area. He specifically

---

[8] I covered this opinion with Jim Bowles at the November In Dallas conference in November of 2009, and he confirmed that the first line was sarcasm, and NOT a confirmation that Weatherford was on the roof. He agrees with my interpretation.

recalls Decker using the terms "two sharpshooters on the roof of the courts building" and "tallest building;" however, he is still uncertain he heard the word "motorcade." and may have just assumed it. I pointed out that this may have been security for the Jack Ruby transfer, or trial, since it was mentioned so much later, during Ruby's trial.[9]

Allegedly, researcher Larry Harris once asked Harry Weatherford this question of whether he was on top of the building to his face, and Weatherford called him "a little SOB" and told him he "killed lots of people." Some take this as confirmation, but I simply feel that Weatherford was tired of hearing this particular story. If Decker had overridden Secret Service requests and posted his own security without telling them, those men ran the risk of being spotted as a threat by Secret Service or other security personnel, which would be dangerous., Further, it could be only in hindsight that many researchers center their security concerns on Dealey Plaza, as Decker (and others) had to be concerned about the entire motorcade route, and not just the place where the shooting actually happened.

This "myth" simply refuses to go away. While I cannot say that it did not happen, I will let the reader decide the validity of the above statements that it did.

Sealing off the Crime Scene and Search

Another concern that I am often asked about is the apparent lack of sealing off Dealey Plaza, or the Texas School Book Depository (and even the Presidential limo) as a crime scene. The questions point out a 10-15 minute delay in sealing off the TSBD, and that Dealey Plaza and the limo were never sealed off as a crime scene. This allowed the hundreds of spectators, and traffic, in Dealey Plaza to tromp all over the Grassy Knoll

---

[9] After the events of November 22-24, 1963, security for high profile prisoners changed, and Ruby was given much more security than Oswald had been.

area, other Plaza areas and Elm Street, spoiling any evidence the grounds could give us.

First, the Presidential limo was considered the responsibility and province of the Secret Service, and was actually beyond the control of Dallas law enforcement. This also applies to the body of the President, although Dallas Coroner Earl Rose did try to fight for the legal requirement of the autopsy being done here in Dallas County. The partial cleaning of the limo at Parkland Hospital (probably just enough to get the roof on properly), and the removal of the limo and body was forced upon Dallas law enforcement by a Secret Service (and Jackie Kennedy) that simply wanted to get out of Dallas as quickly as possible. We will no longer consider the limo, or body, for this discussion.

Sealing off Dealey Plaza was simply impractical (if not impossible) for a number of reasons. The most pressing of these reasons is the size of the crowd and the number of Dallas Police officers in the Plaza. There were around 10 officers in the Plaza for security, traffic and crowd control. Three of these were stationed at Main and Houston Streets, three at Elm and Houston, and two more on the west side of Main Street. These officers were assigned to stop traffic when the motorcade got close, and allow the pedestrians to form a line across the cross streets to view the motorcade. After the last vehicle of the motorcade had passed, they were to get the pedestrians back on the sidewalks, and allow traffic to resume., As well, there were two officers (White and Foster) assigned to the railroad yards on top of the Triple Underpass, who were to keep the bridge clear.[10] By contrast, there were anywhere from 350 to 500 people in the Dealey Plaza area watching the motorcade. Most of these were on Houston Street, but soon swarmed all over Dealey Plaza. There simply was no way that 10 officers could hold back such crowds.

---

[10] They claimed their instructions were to "keep those that did not belong" off of the Underpass, and so allowed railroad workers to stay, since it was property belonging to the railroad.

JFK Assassination: Shades From The Fence

Add to this the fact that in 1963 Police officers did not have any form of personal communications, such as personal radios. There simply would not have been any way for anyone to coordinate an effort to seal off such an area. Instead the officers used their own initiatives to head towards where the sounds of the shots told them to go. Some officers headed to the TSBD, while others went down the Elm Street extension, to the railroad yards and Grassy Knoll. (Dealey Plaza being an echo chamber in many respects, further confused the issue.) Their intent was to catch the shooter, as their primary duty was to stop the suspect from endangering the public further. Of course, running into an armed shooter without backup is always questionable, but unlike today, with modern personal communication equipment, the officers would have had to scramble to their vehicles to use the police radio (on Channel 2).

In addition to the 10 DPD officers assigned to Dealey Plaza, there were the officers in the motorcade itself, as well as the Dallas County Deputy Sheriffs standing in front of their offices on Main and Houston Streets. These deputies also did not have personal communication devices, and although most of them also spread over the Plaza to look for shooters and gather reports from witnesses, there was no way to coordinate their efforts. It therefore took almost 10-15 minutes for various officers to determine the TSBD as a likely source for the shots and then seal off the building. Accordingly, the first effort of those going to the TSBD was the search, find and apprehend the shooter. Only three officers in the Motorcade stopped in Dealey Plaza for any length of time: Officers Marrion Baker, Clyde Haygood, and Bobby Hargis.

Motorcycle Officer Marrion Baker, who was part of the motorcade, saw pigeons fly off the roof of the TSBD at the sound of the shots. He raced to the Elm Street end of Houston, parked his motorcycle, and ran into the building to try to get to the roof. Even though he was sitting in front of his radio on his motorcycle, he did not broadcast that he was going into the TSBD. His intent was to find the shooters, and not seal off the building. By putting together a number of films, we can determine that Baker was on the front steps of the TSBD within 22 seconds of the fatal head shot at Zapruder frame #313 (Z313). Again, today's law enforcement are told to call for backup before trying to find a shooter, but Baker was apparently caught up in the immediacy of the event, and the desire to get the shooter.

Once sealed off, the TSBD was searched in a number of waves. The first wave of Officers and Deputies in the building were naturally looking for shooters or other suspects. After it was decided that there was no immediate shooter threatening anyone, the subsequent waves of law enforcement were looking for evidence. During these searches some of the employees were allowed to return into the building, while some were not (apparently depending on the time of their arrival, and which officer was at the door).

Many have expressed concern about the TSBD being left open to employees, reporters, and even strangers later that afternoon and over the weekend. The press was allowed into the building later that evening, and took numbers of photos, and also rearranged the boxes in the "sniper's nest." Additionally, there are stories of complete strangers entering the building during the course of the weekend, finding it unlocked and un-attended. (I have not confirmed these reports.) After years of watching television shows like "Quincy," and "CSI," even the average person today would think that the crime scene should have been secured for a much longer time. While they are probably right, the reader should remember that many things that happened in Dallas that November actually caused major revisions in how law enforcement handles crime scenes, evidence and prisoner protection.

In this case, it appears that once they had removed evidence such as the rifle, casings, paper bag, and even a Dr. Pepper bottle, and also taken photos and finger/palm prints in the sniper's nest, the investigators decided there was no further evidentiary value in the TSBD. They knew that Lee Harvey Oswald worked there and would find his fingerprints all over the building, if they wanted to. Since there was no "concrete evidence" (I hate that phrase) pointing to an additional shooter in the building, and the existing evidence had been removed, they left the TSBD open. Of course, by today's standards that would be unacceptable, but again, many of today's standards were a result of the most analyzed investigation of the 20th century.

Much has been made by the movie "JFK" and other researchers over the years about the number of people who rushed to the Grassy Knoll soon after the shooting. Many cite this rush as evidence that a large number of people must have heard or seen a shooter from this area. While it is true that some witnesses (such as Jean Hill, and others) did say they saw or heard shots from up on the Knoll, there may also be another explanation for many of these people.

As mentioned earlier, the overpasses were supposed to be clear of people. However, Officers White and Foster allowed about 20 railroad employees to gather across the Triple Underpass, right over the motorcade route on Elm Street. (They did shoo away some Newsmen and other 'unauthorized' individuals.) Police Chief Jesse Curry noticed the small crowd of people on the Underpass[11], and as things started to happen in Dealey Plaza, this was the first discrepancy he was aware of. He knew that those people were not supposed to be up there, according to motorcade security plans.

As soon as he knew the President had been hit, he got on the radio to tell his officers that they were going to Parkland Hospital. He immediately ordered his men to go up to the railroad yard, and find out what happened up there.[12] Since this was something amiss, in his opinion, he may have naturally assumed that shots had come from there.

---

[11] Jesse Curry, "JFK Assassination File"

JFK Assassination: Shades From The Fence

Only two of the motorcade officers reacted to these orders. Bobby Hargis parked his motorcycle on the south side of Elm Street, left it running, and crossed that street, and briefly ran up onto the Grassy Knoll close to the fence. He then returned to his motorcycle, drove to the far side of the Underpass and again ran up the hill. He reportedly did this a third time, on the Stemmons Freeway overpass. Additionally, Motorcycle Officer Clyde Haygood also stopped his bike, on the north side of Elm, by the sewer. Haygood then ran along the fence to the railroad "bridge," where he climbed up onto the concrete railing/abutment. Many people followed Haygood, including Reporter Robert McNeil.

In truth, many in Dealey Plaza may have also run up the Grassy Knoll simply because they had seen two officers, and others do it previously. Some of them may have just assumed the Policemen who went up there knew something, and followed because of that reason. Again, some may have seen or heard something, but many may have been simply following others up that direction.

Arrest of Oswald, His Rights and Attorney Selection

The arrest of Lee Harvey Oswald is sometimes also questioned. I have been asked about the fight that ensued between him and the arresting officers in the Texas Theater, and whether excessive force had been used. In addition, a question of Oswald's various rights, especially his rights to an attorney, has also come up many times.

A Police Officer must show reasonable cause to arrest a person. When Johnny Brewer had box office cashier Julia Postal call Police from the Texas Theater, the only reasonable cause they had on Oswald was that he had gone into the Texas without paying. However, since they were looking for a suspect that had shot and killed a Dallas Police Officer, JD Tippit, in addition to looking for a suspect in the JFK shooting, many of the officers naturally assumed that Oswald was their man. However, Officer McDonald did follow normal procedures, in simply asking Oswald to stand up. Oswald reportedly then took a swing at Officer Nick McDonald, scratching him severely on the left side of his face. Oswald allegedly then pulled his pistol and attempted to shoot McDonald.

At this point, after having attacked a Police Officer, and allegedly attempting to shoot him, Oswald was subject to as much force as was necessary to subdue and arrest him. Of course, the emotions of the Dallas Police over having a fellow officer shot and killed by Oswald, would naturally play into their emotions during the scuffle, and may have caused some additional force to be used.

I have heard many of the policemen speak on this subject, and a number of them had already related the Tippit shooting to the shooting of the President, while some had not. For many of them, the shouts of the crowd in the front of the Texas Theater about the President were the first time they made that connection. Some officers have stated that when they first surrounded the entrance their guns were trained on the theater where the suspect was, but by the time he came out, many had their guns pointed towards the hostile crowd outside of the Texas Theater (putting the suspect in danger). Many of the crowd knew nothing of the Tippit shooting, and simply assumed the arrest was of someone involved in the JFK shooting.

Lt. Jim Leavelle was the Detective in charge of the Tippit investigation, while Captain Will Fritz was in charge of the Kennedy shooting. To this day, Leavelle complains that he got about 10-15 minutes with Oswald before the suspect was "taken away from him" by Fritz. According to Leavelle, and others, Captain Fritz had returned from the TSBD with instructions to Sgt. Gerald Hill to go out to Irving (Ruth Paine's house) to pick up an employee of the TSBD who was missing. Hill asked why Oswald was wanted, and when told he informed Capt. Fritz that he could save him a trip, cause "there

JFK Assassination: Shades From The Fence

he sits." Oswald was then taken by Fritz for the Kennedy investigation, and Leavelle hardly got a chance to question his suspect for the Tippit murder the rest of the weekend. Leavelle also relates that in casual conversations with Fritz, they emphasized that Leavelle should do a good job on the Tippit investigation, because that was the stronger case for a murder conviction.

> [12] The following excerpts are from the Police Radio log - Channel 2
> **Curry:** Get a man on top of that triple underpass and see what happened up there. ...
> **Decker:** Have my office move all available men out of my office into the railroad yard to try to determine what happened in there and hold everything secure until Homicide and other investigators should get there.

There have also been complaints that Oswald went two days in jail without legal representation. However, he did have the opportunity to call a lawyer. He tried to call New York Attorney John Abt, and later tried to get Ruth Paine to also call Mr. Abt. After he asked for legal representation over the television, the head of the Dallas Bar Association, Louis Nichols,[12] did come to talk to him, and was told that he wanted Abt, or maybe someone from the ACLU first.

Mr. Nichols left, satisfied that Oswald's civil rights were not being violated. It is not within the authority of the Police to *force* a lawyer onto Oswald (even under Miranda, which was a US Supreme Court decision in 1965).

Captain Will Fritz and the Stenographer/Recorder Question

Captain Fritz was an "old school" Officer, in that he learned on the job. He was very good at coming across as being friendly to his suspects, and getting them to give additional

---

[12] Jesse Curry, "JFK Assassination File"

information, and sometimes confessing. (He had a good record of doing that.) Procedures were not as strict in those days as they were after the Miranda ruling; however, they did follow standardized guidelines to protect the suspect's rights. Fritz was trying very hard to get Oswald to loosen up, and after the fact complained (to Jim Leavelle and others) that every time he would get Oswald talking, another person in the room (such as FBI James Hosty) would interrupt, and Oswald would clam up.

Fritz was trying to not only get on Oswald's good side (if such a thing existed), but also get other information that would allow his officers to look for accomplices, or confirm what happened. It was more of an informal "information gathering" phase, that did not interfere with the rights of the person being interviewed. Of course, after Miranda, anything Oswald said before being offered an attorney would be inadmissible, but the assumption was that if Fritz could get him to say it once *off the record*, he could probably say it again, or sign something *on the record*.

If they had a stenographer, or a tape recording, during this "informal" phase, a good Defense Attorney could actually use that record to have any information gathered be ruled inadmissible, simply because there was a record showing that the information was given before Oswald's attorney had been present. An *official* record could therefore be an actual nuisance in that case.

But, remember, this was before the Miranda ruling. Such informal questioning was standard practice in those days. Even today, they can *ask* informal questions, but if they get anything major before the suspect is read his rights, that information runs the risk of being rejected by a judge. (Providing there is PROOF of when this information is given, which a steno or recording would provide.) Captain Fritz being "old school" trained would also be a negative, in that he often simply did procedures his own way.

Many have said that this was a problem with the TSBD "snipers nest" crime scene preservation. These problems included the paper bag being moved before being photographed, the moving of the boxes, casings, and other items in the crime scene, and the control of the evidence. There have also been allegations of the shell casings being moved before the crime scene could be properly photographed. Fritz may have thought that Tom Alyea's film of the snipers nest was sufficient, not realizing that the film would end up on the cutting room floor and lost. Or it may have been that Fritz was less concerned about the exact placement of the casings in photos. Of course, by today's standards this is a very sloppy investigation.

The snipers nest photos made by Studebaker have been alleged to be staged shots, instead of the original placing of the shells. We can time stamp at least one of these shots, as the one taken from the western end of the sniper's nest shows Houston Street out of the window. On the street there is a utility truck

[14] Zero degrees is Houston Street curbs and walls of Records building, etc. Done on Nov 12, 2009 – Daylight savings removed (not in effect in 1963)
1:00 PM 10 degrees
1:15 PM 15 degrees
1:31 PM 20 degrees
1:49 PM 25 degrees
2:09 PM 30 degrees
2:31 PM 35 degrees
2:53 PM 40 degrees
3:16 PM 45 degrees
3:40 PM 50 degrees
4:09 PM 55 degrees
4:40 PM 60 degrees
5:02 PM 61 degrees
5:26 PM sunset

and other objects with the sun's shadows at a 45 degree angle from the direction of the street. I have done shadow studies in Dealey Plaza, and in November the sun will hit this 45 degree mark at approximately 3:15 PM.[14] It is likely that all three photos were taken at the same time, instead of Studebaker stepping over the shell casings while processing the nest for fingerprints and moving boxes. This seems to strongly support that these photos were staged and taken much later than the 1:30 to 1:45 that Studebaker arrived in the sniper's nest.

Fritz also caused some controversy that still confuses many researchers today. He kept one of the three shell casings in his office, instead of keeping it with the other two casings in the Dallas crime lab. This led to a receipt showing only two casings, at the time these materials were given to the FBI, on Nov 26th. However, FBI Agent James Hosty gave Fritz a separate, hand-written receipt for the remaining casing, Oswald's wallet, notebook and other materials, when he turned them over to Hosty around 1:00 AM on Nov. 27. The Evidence Receipt included in the Dallas Police files of evidence shows two shells, while the Receipt in the Warren Commission evidence has apparently been altered to show three. The Dallas Police files of evidence also include the hand-written receipt, while the Warren Commission evidence does not.

Fritz usually got a conviction, and may not have been as concerned about crime scene and chains of evidence as he should have been. It is speculation of course, but given the type of jury that Oswald would have most likely drawn in 1963, it is very likely that this misfit would have been convicted anyway. Perhaps if Fritz, and the Dallas Police, had lost more cases, they would have been more careful about procedures.[13] But his techniques generally got his suspects talking, and he generally got convictions, so any sloppiness was not as apparent as it should have been.

Dallas Police and the World Press

---

[13] Texas Innocence Project website, "The State of Texas is home to more verified wrongful convictions than any other state in the Nation. 38 individuals have been exonerated by DNA testing, and several more have had their wrongful convictions overturned on other grounds." This may because Dallas is unique among larger jurisdictions, in that they kept their old rape kits going back to the early 1980's. These have been subjected to modern DNA tests, overturning many unvalidated or improper forensic science applications.

JFK Assassination: Shades From The Fence

The Dallas press had a great working relationship with the Dallas Police Department, and other law enforcement, as there was a mutual respect, and relationship between the two entities. I have spoken to many members of the 1963 Dallas press establishment, and they all say good things about their relationship with the DPD. As long as they respected the police needs for security and safety, and to protect the rights of the people and suspects, the police were very obliging to the press. I have heard countless stories of incidents where the press and police worked together.

In fact, there was an order, "General Order 81" (WC Talbert Exhibit #1 – also in DPD files), that stated the DPD were to cooperate with members of the Press. "It is the policy that members of this Department render every assistance, except such as obviously may seriously hinder or delay the proper functioning of the Department, to the accredited members of the official news-gathering agencies and this includes newspaper, television cameramen and newsreel photographers." The order was written in June of 1958, and had been a part of Police policy for years.

In February of 1963, there was an incident where a photographer had been refused access to a crime scene by two officers, complained about it, and those officers were severely scolded (short of an official reprimand). At that time, Curry made it clear to the DPD that compliance was not at the discretion of the officers. It was clearly known by DPD that they were to cooperate with members of the press. In fact, this went two ways, in that members of the press would often help out their officer buddies by assisting the poorer typists with some of their written reports. Unlike the photographer who complained, most members of the press were very careful to stay on the good side of the officers, for fear of being shut out of future stories and events, and to possibly get exclusives from the officers who knew, and trusted them. It was a matter of mutual respect.

However, this relationship and arrangement with the *local* press became a major issue when the members of the national and international media started to flood the city that weekend. The trust and mutual respect the DPD had with the local press was certainly abused by many of the national and international press. The DPD was inundated with hundreds of strange faces and reporters that they did not know and could not respect. These national and international reporters took advantage of every opportunity, and often abused the access that they enjoyed that weekend. The halls of the Dallas Police Department, especially the 3rd floor, were jammed with hundreds of people. In fact, local CBS Television Newsroom Manager Eddie Barker at one point even "threw out" the members of CBS national press from his newsroom.[14] He also had a major disagreement with Dan Rather, after Rather went on the air with a story about Dallas children cheering for the shooting of JFK without clearing the story first.

Local Politics and Oswald Security

There is little excuse that anyone can give the Dallas Police Department for the shooting and murder of Lee Harvey Oswald while in their custody, and I have never tried to make excuses for them. Chief Jesse Curry simply made a terrible decision that ended up costing Oswald his life, and possibly forever preventing us from solving the JFK assassination. There were partial reasons for this decision, although I will certainly never say there were **good** reasons for Curry's decision. The Dallas leaders were very concerned about Dallas "image," especially after the Stevenson incident and the "City of Hate" label. They were extremely sensitive to the perception how a left-wing pro-Communist would be handled by a Police Department which was considered very right-wing, in a city considered right-wing. The city leaders therefore, put pressure on Jesse Curry to have everything as public as possible.

In fact, on Friday evening, a national television figure was reported to have shown a photo of Oswald from earlier in the

---

[14] Eddie Barker, "Eddie Barker's Notebook"

day, and then said, "This is what the man who is charged with shooting President Kennedy looks like, or at least this is what he did look like. We don't know what he looks like now after being in custody of police…"[15] implying that in the hands of the Dallas Police, Oswald may have been subjected to police abuse. This comment was what instigated the famous "Midnight Press Conference," where Curry gave into pressures to allow the press to see Oswald. The primary purpose of this press conference was to show that Oswald had not been abused in any way behind closed doors, while in custody.[16] However, it was soon ended because of the uproar the newsmen created. Oswald appeared to enjoy the publicity, but not the confirmation from local TV newsman Bill Mercer[17] that he had indeed been charged with shooting the President.

By Saturday afternoon, most of the Dallas Police officers working the Oswald case, and most of the press had been awake since early Friday morning. As they had worked throughout the night, most were getting very punchy and tired. However, they would not leave, for fear that they might miss something happening. Jesse Curry told the waiting press that they should go home and get some sleep (he, and his men were also in need of rest), and had to assure them that they would not miss anything if they did so. In addition, he was giving Oswald Saturday night to try to rest. He went as far as to tell them that if they were back at DPD by 10:00 AM on Sunday morning, they would not miss anything. This was not a scheduled time to transfer Oswald, but simply the time by which they should be back, so as to not miss anything.

This promise to the press, plus the political pressure he was getting from Dallas leaders to keep the transfer of Oswald open

[15] Jesse Curry, "JFK Assassination File"
[16] Even though the scuffle at the Texas Theater, created obvious bruises on his face.
[17] Bob Huffaker, Bill Mercer, George Phenix, Wes Wise, "When the News Went Live"

to the press, combined to make a very bad decision on Curry's part, and make the transfer in full view of print reporters, television cameras, and unknown bystanders.

Legend has it that Bill Decker was concerned about having the transfer in broad daylight, at an announced time. Decker supposedly also complained to, and suggested they move Oswald in secret, as they had received many phone calls threatening Oswald's life. The normal procedure was for a Deputy Sheriff to come and get the prisoner. Al Maddox, who still lives in the Dallas area today, did many of these transfers. However, when Curry insisted on moving the prisoner as scheduled, Decker told him to "bring him down." The legend goes that Decker did not want to be responsible, or have his men involved in this dangerous transfer, after the many threats had been received.

FBI Special Agent Gordon Shanklin also allegedly told his Dallas FBI to stay away from the transfer, after he made a phone call to Curry while most of his Agents were in Shanklin's office, listening to his side of the phone call.[18]

Jack Ruby and Police Friends

Much has understandably been made of the ease in which nightclub owner Jack Ruby was able to get in and out of the Dallas Police building all weekend. Justifiably so, as there are really no good excuses for the security surrounding Oswald, which allowed Ruby to kill him among over 60 armed policemen. Some simply say that Dallas Police were happy that Jack Ruby silenced Oswald, or that Ruby was allowed to get to Oswald intentionally. I can't say for certain that he did not have help, but there were some other factors that could have clouded the issue.

After the Oswald shooting, Chief Jesse Curry had his entire department questioned as to whether the Officers knew Jack

---

[18] James Hosty, "Assignment: Oswald"

Ruby prior to the shooting. He states that he had never heard the name Jack Ruby, and that less than 25 officers had any knowledge of Ruby before the shooting of Oswald. Mainly these were members of the Vice Squad, and those that worked the areas of the two nightclubs that Ruby operated.[19] Undoubtedly, this number was probably a little higher, as I would guess that some may not have been completely honest to this question.

I know some people that knew Jack Ruby, including having known some of his dancers. They say that Jack was a "wanna-be." in that he always wanted to be where the action was and be part of the action. He would appear at police headquarters, radio stations, or any other happening event, and try to hand outing business cards, and introducing himself. Many of the people that knew him state that because he was rather talkative, and a show-off, he was one of the last people you would trust for a conspiracy.

But, you have to remember that Dallas Police department was inundated with *hundreds* of national and international members of the press. In that crowd of unfamiliar faces, it is small wonder that a familiar face might be allowed in. I am not saying that every police officer working security knew Jack, just that they may have seen him at DPD in the past, or even earlier that weekend. There are even reports that Jack was seen pretending to hold a small notebook, trying to blend in with the newsmen.

Once he was in the building, even someone who does not know him might recognize him from the prior day, or evening, and simply allow him in at a later time. He was allegedly asked once or twice what he was doing there, by people who did know him, and he told them he was interpreting for members of the press. He also pointed out Henry Wade and other officials to various members of the press, in addition to handing out cards and trying to promote his Carousel Club to almost anyone who would listen.

---

[19] Jesse Curry, "JFK Assassination File"

JFK Assassination: Shades From The Fence

He may have been allowed in by some of his friends on the Dallas Police force. It may never be proven or disproven. However, that does not *automatically* mean that they were in on a plot to kill Kennedy, or even silence Oswald. One can surmise that, simply based on his apparent ease of access but it is a pretty broad conclusion to jump to. Granted, Dallas Police really blew the Oswald security, but that is still not enough of a basis for accusations of intentional involvement in either killing. In my opinion, there must be much more supporting evidence of involvement before such a charge is leveled, especially against the entire department.

Passions and Perceptions

In the 1970's, Dallas Mayor Wes Wise was once attending a national convention of Mayors and was asked (paraphrased) by another Mayor, "How does it feel to be the Mayor of the city that killed Kennedy?"[20] Los Angeles is not hated as the "city that killed Bobby Kennedy." nor is Memphis despised as the "city that killed Martin Luther King, Jr."; however, even to this day, Dallas is often looked at in this way. Of course, Los Angeles and Memphis did not have the "City of Hate" reputation, and did not subsequently allow their prime suspect to be shot and killed in the basement of their own police department!

Obviously, to say an entire city or even the Dallas police were responsible for the death of John Kennedy is a vast oversimplification. Yet it shows the extent of the emotions surrounding the event. But these emotions went both ways. In addition to the anger and shock felt throughout the country, those here in Dallas also had their share of emotions as well, including the Dallas police.

However, briefly put away that blame and look at the situation from the individual officers' viewpoint, even if you

---

[20] Bob Huffaker, Bill Mercer, George Phenix, Wes Wise, "When the News Went Live"

JFK Assassination: Shades From The Fence

have to force yourself to *pretend* they were not involved. They had passed laws to try to protect the President from the type of hate incident that Adlai Stevenson endured, and did everything the Secret Service (the "experts") asked of them... yet the President was gunned down in their city. One of their fellow officers was also shot and killed (they believed) by the same shooter on a Dallas street. It was surprising that it turned out to be a Communist sympathizer, instead of the right-wing extremists which Dallas was known for. The Dallas law enforcement investigation was in many cases "overridden" by Washington, and Dallas investigators were told to not pursue conspiracy issues or makes statements concerning conspiracies. Most importantly, the evidence was removed from their hands and taken to the FBI in Washington almost immediately. To top everything off, they then have the prime suspect gunned down in their own basement. You can imagine the shock, anger, resentment and finally embarrassment that the common Dallas police officer must have felt, even if he was not part of the conspiracy(s).

Almost every Dallas police officer I have ever spoken to believes that Lee Harvey Oswald was the shooter. I have met only a couple who will even consider that Oswald might have been part of a group and the others were never named. Even then, they point out that there was no evidence to point to another shooter in another location. The investigation naturally reflects this opinion, possibly intentionally. Naturally, this frustrates many researchers who point out that investigation in other directions should have been a requirement.

In addition, many pieces of the puzzle have since been found to be missing. For instance, there was allegedly a list of the people allowed out of the TSBD parking lot that day, and a list of patrons of the Texas Theater at the same time as Oswald. The Dallas police state that they made these lists, but after Oswald's death they simply disappeared. It could be that someone took them as souvenirs, or that someone simply figured they would no longer be needed. Once you have decided that Oswald was the lone gunman, and once that

89

gunman was silenced, apparently such evidence is no longer needed. For many years it was believed that there were no notes taken during Oswald's interrogations; however, decades later, hand-written notes by Captain Will Fritz and FBI Agent James Hosty were found, and given to the Assassination Records Review Board.[21]

Naturally, all of us who continue to research the case would like to have these lists and other missing "evidence" available. But without knowing exactly what is on these materials, we cannot say for certain that it is actual evidence.

Summary

I cannot just sit here and tell you that "Dallas" was not involved in a conspiracy to kill Kennedy. I certainly cannot state for a fact that Dallas Police were not involved in either the conspiracy to kill Kennedy, or in the killing of Lee Harvey Oswald. However, to simply state that they were, just because security was more lax than any of us would have wanted, is making a tremendous leap of logic (or simply an emotional reaction).

Obviously, the local law enforcement were in over their heads in the Kennedy investigation. I can't say if they realized that it would be the most scrutinized investigation in history, but even if they did, I don't know if they would have changed anything. However, they had many murders in Dallas in 1963. (Dallas County Coroner Dr. Earl Rose listed the Kennedy inquest (which didn't happen) down as Inquest #210, indicating the number of sudden deaths that year. So it was not as if Dallas officials were unfamiliar with violence.

The Dallas Police did manage to keep crime down, and usually got their man (whether he was the right one or not). Plus, here in the conservative, Bible belt, south, a jury usually convicted the people the authorities said were guilty. Very seldom would we have a person acquitted on a technicality (like not photographing a paper bag). So....the police could do things that would not be acceptable in a less conservative area.

There was undoubtedly a lot of "CYA" after the fact, so all of the reports and affidavits written after the fact should be viewed in light of that. But, they were trying to look for other conspirators and suspects, until the Feds took over and shut them down. Hard to do good work with the FBI taking your evidence, and the White House calling about every public comment you make.

Additionally, if the Warren Commission was set up with the purpose to convince the American public that Oswald was a *lone nut*, regardless of other clues and information (and discrepancies) then the reports of the Dallas Police would probably also reflect that intent. Therefore, any information presented here from that source, or other books and references should also be view with the same skepticism as the Warren Report.

Dallas law enforcement made lots of mistakes, especially in Oswald's security (THEIR responsibility). But the President's security is the sole province of the Secret Service, and it is up to them to ask for local support (or military) as they deem fit. The President's security was pretty much standard for many other Motorcades and cities he had visited. If the purpose of the trip was to let Kennedy be seen by as many of the voting public as possible, and that, in itself, poses all sorts of risk. Kennedy himself allegedly had a certain fatalism, after his many brushes with death, and he himself allegedly said that a shooter with a rifle could get to him almost any time.

The Kennedy Assassination rewrote many of the rules on security and presidential protection. It also re-wrote many of the rules in handling a high-profile murder suspect. Many of the procedures in place today are because of the Kennedy assassination, as well as the Oswald shooting.

Handling and mishandling of evidence and the crime scene was also a problem. A lot of this was because of the procedures the Dallas Police used, which may have been less than formal. But much of it was also caused by the Feds taking the evidence and the transfers of various pieces of it between Washington and Dallas (multiple times).

I have been accused, many times, of making excuses for Dallas and the Dallas Police. I do feel that if anyone in Dallas were involved, they should be prosecuted to the full extent of the law, and I do not want to make excuses for them. I have simply tried to recap the many procedures, reasons, facts and even rumors surrounding the event, and let the reader at least consider this information.

7. The Trials (that never happened)

Lee Harvey Oswald died an Innocent man. (For that matter, so did John Wilkes Booth, over 98 years earlier.) Since under our justice laws, a man is "presumed innocent" until convicted in a court of law, and Oswald never had a trial, he remains an innocent man to this day. However, he has been "tried" in the court of public opinion, multiple times. Many find him "guilty" and many think he was completely set up as an innocent "patsy" and was not involved in the killing of JFK at all.

The same cannot be said of Jack Ruby. In January, 1967, he died as a guilty man, because he had been tried and declared guilty by a Jury in a legal court of law. His attorneys did get him granted a re-trial, based on a "change of venue" argument where the appellate court said he could not receive a fair trial in Dallas, because the citizens wanted to somehow atone for JFK being killed in Dallas. He died before this retrial could be conducted. Had he been retried, and his conviction overturned, he would have died an innocent man, but it did not occur. He died while living in the Dallas County Jail, overlooking Dealey Plaza.

Of course, the lack of a legal trial of Oswald has created many problems.

Dr. Humes is alleged to have burned both his notes, and the first draft of the Autopsy report in his fireplace on Sunday, Nov. 24th. He told the ARRB that he was trying to protect "the privacy and the sensibilities of the President's family", in doing so. Of course, Dr. Finck later said that it was not a "complete autopsy". But we must wonder if there had been a trial, if we would have seen a much more complete record of the autopsy. Had they actually done a better job, than the information we have today indicates? Would a proper murder trial, with its rules of evidence, have produced the X-rays, brain sectioning, photos, and more carefully preserved records? We may never know...

JFK Assassination: Shades From The Fence

On Nov. 25th, Assistant Attorney General Nicholas Katzenbach, wrote the infamous Katzenback Memo, to Bill Moyers of the new Johnson Administration. In it he wrote in paragraph 2:

"The public must be satisfied that Oswald was the assassin; that he did not have confederates who are still at large; and that evidence was such that he would have been convicted at trial."

…and in the following paragraph:

"Speculation about Oswald's motivation ought to be cut off, and we should have some basis for rebutting thought that this was a Communist conspiracy or (as the Iron Curtain press is saying) a right-wing conspiracy to blame it on the Communists. Unfortunately the facts on Oswald seem about too pat--too obvious (Marxist, Cuba, Russian wife, etc.). The Dallas police have put out statements on the Communist conspiracy theory, and it was they who were in charge when he was shot and thus silenced."

This led to the formation of the Warren Commission, which many believe was simply formed to "whitewash" the Assassination and lay the blame firmly at the feet of the dead Lee Harvey Oswald. Many consider this a "Conspiracy of non-investigation", that may well be separate from any Conspiracy to kill Kennedy. Others join the two, in what I call a "Grand Conspiracy".

Of course, an adversarial trial, would give Oswald the chance to be represented and declare his guilt or innocence. We will never know if Oswald would come up with a better alibi than the ones he attempted to give to Captain Will Fritz during his interrogation that weekend. He might have been able to name names, if he did have any co-conspirators, although that would not make him less guilty, if he participated in the killing in any way.

JFK Assassination: Shades From The Fence

Additionally, with all of the problems with the evidence that has surfaced over the years, it is possible that a clever attorney might be able to get Oswald "off", somehow. As it was, Oswald was not represented in the WC's investigation. His mother, Marguerite Oswald, wanted attorney Mark Lane to represent Oswald's interests, but although he was interviewed by the Warren Commission, he was not allowed to participate and protect Oswald.

Ambulance driver Aubrey Rike was a family friend of mine. In the late 60's he became a police officer, and he was instrumental when a member of my extended family was the victim of a kidnapper. (Not from the "poor" side that I am from.)

When Rike passed away in 2010, Jim Leavelle, a mutual friend and I had lunch together after the burial. One of the things that Jim told me was that he and Captain Will Fritz had lunch on Saturday, Nov. 23rd, close to the downtown Dallas police station. Fritz was the Captain in charge of the JFK killing investigation, while Lt. Leavelle (lesser rank) was in charge of the Tippit shooting investigation. Fritz told Leavelle that he should do a good job on the Tippit shooting, because that was the much stronger case! (I believe Jim has said this in some of his public statements, also.)

Police Chief Jesse Curry famously stated about the JFK killing that "nobody could put Oswald in that window with a rifle in his hand". I am certain he meant somebody that could positively identify Oswald, which the witnesses that stated they saw someone in the building did not do at the line-ups. Nobody inside the building saw Oswald, except prior to or immediately after the 12:30 shooting. I cannot put Oswald in that window either; however, I also cannot put him anywhere else in the building (see my articles later).

The Tippit shooting had multiple witnesses of the event, or of Oswald's escape immediately after. He was arrested with the weapon, tried to punch and then shoot Officer McDonald in the Texas Theater according to several Officers and witnesses at

JFK Assassination: Shades From The Fence

the scene. Had nitrate on his hands (not face), when tested in the Dallas jail that weekend.

I am about 97% convinced that Oswald was the shooter of Officer JD Tippit. For that matter, with my area of expertise on the TSBD and the reported movements inside, I am 90% convinced that Oswald was a shooter in the TSBD. However, that does NOT eliminate him being part of a Conspiracy. (More on that later.)

IMO he would have been initially convicted in either trial, although the Tippit shooting would be enough. However, the U. S. citizens would insist on the shooter of their President being named and convicted. This is especially true, using 1964 justice and forensic standards. In addition, a very right-wing Dallas citizenship would likely form a Jury that would be more than happy to convict a pro-Castro/Communism individual of either crime.

Like Ruby, however, Oswald would have likely been granted a retrial for "change of venue" reasons. If Jack Ruby, who shot Oswald before millions of people on live television, was granted a retrial, Oswald certainly would have also! He possibly would have been convicted with no overturn resulting from the retrial. However, we will never know, and technically Oswald died an innocent man.

Clay Shaw tried in New Orleans

In January 1969, the only official trial concerning the JFK Assassination occurred in New Orleans. The New Orleans District Attorney Jim Garrison investigated the connection that Lee Harvey Oswald had to the City of New Orleans. Oswald had moved to New Orleans in April of 1963, after allegedly taking a shot at the Dallas resident General Edwin Walker, through Walker's window on the night of April 10th. Marina later joined him, and he spent the summer in questionable associations with pro- and anti-Cuba factions and activities. Garrison later wrote several books on the subject, and the Oliver Stone movie "JFK" is based on this actual event.

JFK Assassination: Shades From The Fence

Garrison felt that Oswald was connected to 3 main individuals in the New Orleans area: David Ferrie, Guy Bannister and an individual allegedly name "Clay Bertrand". Garrison connected this name as an alias used by the gay founder of the New Orleans Trade-Mart named

Clay Shaw. By the time of trial, the first 2 individuals were dead, and beyond Garrison's reach. So Garrison proceeded to bring Clay Shaw to trial, under charges of being involved with Oswald in a "conspiracy" to murder the President. In March of 1969, it took the Jury less than an hour to conclude Shaw was innocent of the charges.

But Garrison took the opportunity to try to prove a Conspiracy in the Assassination. He investigated many leads, and brought to light many questions that Researchers are still looking at today. He often went to the extreme on the Conspiracy side, and sometimes used questionable interrogation and leverage tactics.

In many ways, it ruined Clay Shaw's life.

The 'Mock' trial(s)

In 1986 there was "On Trial: Lee Harvey Oswald". It was also broadcast in Britain as "The Trial of Lee Harvey Oswald", as well as the U.S. and other countries. It was a TV movie/documentary featuring Prosecutor Vincent Bugliosi, and Defense Attorney Gerry Spence. (Produced by Mark Redhead and Richard Drewitt.) It was over 21 hours of filming, which was trimmed down to 5.5 hours for the telecast and the DVD.

The outcome of the trial was "Oswald acted alone", according to the Jury.

Of course, Oswald was not there to control his own defense, or offer any information whatever. But many of the witnesses and pertinent investigators did take part. These include Ruth Paine, Buell Frazier, Cyril Wecht, Bill Newman and others.

Another problem with the trial was that it was held in London. Of course, that is far away from Dallas, Texas, where most witnesses would be readily available. They offered to pay witnesses to travel to London, and therefore only had the witnesses they made the offer to, and were able to arrange to take the time for the trip. This could hardly be considered fair to a defendant, if he had actually been defending his innocence.

Bugliosi did an excellent job as a prosecutor, a role he has done for much of his career. He examined people like Frazier and Wecht, and forced them to make admissions that their statements and versions over the years may not be as cut and dried as many Researchers often feel they should be. Wecht, who has famously speculated that the "magic" bullet could not happen, admitted that he was unable to give an alternative exit path for the bullet that hit Kennedy in the back. Frazier was forced to admit that the package he saw Oswald carry into the building, could very well have extended above the armpit to the front, or shoulder, of the jacket. Gerry Spence did a lesser performance, as he kept trying to invoke sympathy for "Lee", who could not be there to represent himself. Instead of trying to point out reasonable doubt, he often seemed to be trying to blame other forces for the killing of the President. The goal of a defense attorney should not be to come up with others to blame the killing on, but to poke holes in the prosecution's case, and raise reasonable doubt.

It was an entertaining show, and I highly recommend it to the reader. Just be aware of the obvious limitations. As always: think for yourself.

There have been a number of other mock trials of Oswald, some with an actor playing Oswald himself. But most of these have been with actors portraying the participants, instead of the actual people involved. Naturally, they are working from a script, or WC statements. They are not really subject to cross-examination, as the WC did not have an adversarial Oswald representative.

Often, when I see mock trials done at conferences and by students of the assassination, too much focus is done on whether Oswald was "alone" or not. According to everything I can find about the Texas laws that Oswald would have been tried under, his participation in the event alone would be enough to convict him on. There have been many Texas cases where even the "get away" driver, who is outside of the bank being robbed, is also guilty of murder when someone in the bank is shot and killed!

If Oswald took any shots at all, pretended to take shots, supplied a rifle, or helped others access and egress the TSBD, he could have been convicted of murder. Any participation at all, even without pointing to other "conspirators", could mean a conviction.

The infamous Clyde Barrow, of the infamous Bonnie and Clyde duo, was actually waiting out in the get-away car when the grocer John Bucher was killed. Raymond Hamilton, a friend of Clyde's, probably killed Bucher, while Clyde was outside in the car. However, it was one of the 1st murders Clyde would have been charged with, had he ever been captured and tried.

Some LN Researchers ask the question all the time, "IF....why...?" A paraphrase is "If Oswald was being set up as a patsy, and others did the shooting...why didn't he step forward and name them?" They seem to think that this means Oswald acted alone, because he did not name others. However, even if he could have named others, that would NOT exonerate him from a murder conviction, according to Texas law. (I am not an attorney, remember.) Naming others would simply confirm that he was a participant in the plot, or at minimum: knew about it.

Some Prosecutors in these mock trials are trying to prove Oswald acted alone. This is not required for a murder conviction. IMO, it is a big mistake for a "prosecutor" to try to prove there was no Conspiracy to kill JFK, alone. If they attempt this, it is easier for the defense to poke holes in their case. The logic is that if Oswald was not "alone" as the prosecutor is trying to support, then other parts of their case must also be questionable.

On the opposite side, it does no good whatsoever for a defense attorney to try to defend Oswald by claiming he was set-up and others are at large. It does not matter that others got away, if Oswald cannot show he did not participate. He could (and probably would) have still been guilty of murder, regardless of alleged participation or advance knowledge of others.

Jack Ruby trial

The one trial that did happen, was the trial of nightclub owner Jack Ruby, in his shooting of assassination suspect Lee Harvey Oswald.

Jack Ruby was at the Dallas Morning News at the time of the JFK shooting, in Dealey Plaza, 3 blocks away. He was allegedly taking care of advertisements for his strip club, the Carousel. He was also there to complain about the "black bordered" ad that appeared at the

Dallas Morning News that morning. It was signed Bernard Weissman, and The American FactFinding Committee. Its title was "Welcome Mr. President", but in the text of the ad, it criticized JFK quite severely.

My 1st cousin (twice removed), Edward "Ted" Dealey, allegedly did not see the ad. However, once he read it, he told his son Joe Dealey (Sr.) that he would have approved it. He saw nothing in the ad, that he had also not been saying for many months in his editorials. Joe Dealey, the President of the newspaper was allegedly very shocked about the ad. However, he also did not see it that morning. It was the "advertising" department that allowed the 'ad' to be published. That normally would not require approval from the management, or editorial, departments. (Even though, G. B. Dealey, founder of the DMN, always required any advertisement that gave a political view to be reviewed by the management of the paper.)

According to the investigation into the case, Jack Ruby appeared at the Western Union office to 'wire' $25 to one of his dancers over in Fort Worth. The Carousel club had been shut down on Friday and Saturday of that weekend out of 'respect' for the slain President. That was true of many businesses in Dallas, Texas, that weekend. The dancers, who depended on 'tip' money were unable to make any because of the shutdown.

The phone call from the dancer, occurred around 10:15, and allegedly woke Ruby up. He threw his dog, Bathsheba (dachshund) into his car and drove downtown to a parking lot at 2035 Main St. This was across the street from the Western Union office. He left the dog in the car, with the windows cracked, and walked across the street to 'wire' the money. Some theorists assert that Ruby would not have left the dog in the car, if his intent was to kill Oswald. However, according to many of the dancers, and others, who knew Ruby, it was his common practice to take the dog, and leave it in his vehicle. (I know/knew many of these ex-dancers, although when I knew them, they were much older and probably much less attractive... But then, again, I ain't a spring chicken either.)

The time stamp on the Telegram receipt is 11:17 PM. I am still uncertain whether this is the accurate time stamped, when Ruby pushed the telegram across the counter. In those days, there was no internet, and many clocks were set "loosely" to the actual time. Often, this was based on watches and other estimates of time. People would also set their clocks based on the TV schedule. To prevent missing their 'favorite' TV show, many would set their watches a little ahead. The time of any event of the assassination will always be questionable, unlike today when we have cell phones that adjust the time based on a signal.

The time of the shooting of Oswald, is 11:20.

Oswald was escorted our of the jail elevator by police, on his way to be transferred to the Dallas County Jail. The jail at the downtown police office was usually just a "holding cell", where serious offenders could be held, while being booked, fingerprinted, and the initial interrogation could be conducted. Serious prisoners, of felony charges, would be transferred to the County jail, which was the more secure confinement.

According to multiple Deputy Sheriffs I have known over the years, the normal procedure would be to send a Deputy

JFK Assassination: Shades From The Fence

Sheriff down to Police headquarters to "pick up" the prisoner. Many phone calls threatening Oswald's life had allegedly come into both the City of Dallas, and Dallas County switchboard overnight. The calls threatened Oswald. County Sheriff

Bill Decker was concerned about the transfer of the prisoner, and suggested to Chief of Police Jesse Curry that the transfer should occur in the middle of the night. Curry, who was being pressured by Dallas leaders that he show Oswald was not being unduly 'pressured' in a backroom, by the ultra right-wind Dallas Police Department, had promised the Press that Oswald would be transferred in full view of the media. Curry therefore waited until after 10:00 AM to transfer Oswald, intending it to be within full view of the Press and their live TV cameras.

There is still debate about how Jack Ruby got access to the basement that day. Ruby did know a lot of the downtown Police, as he cultivated friendships with many of them. Naturally, many of the "vice squad" based in downtown Dallas, where his stripper bar was located, would naturally know Jack Ruby. Ruby also used to have "police night" at his club, where police were invited to attend for "free". (In reality, almost any Police officer, on any night would likely be admitted for free into his club.) Ruby also had a police record, having been arrested for actions such as pistol whipping a customer who was out-of-line in his club.

The Warren Commission determined that after sending the telegram, Ruby walked the short half-block to the Dallas police department. They contend that he walked down the northern ramp, without being seen.

That ramp was guarded by Sgt. Roy Vaughn, who insisted to his dying day, that Ruby did not ascend the ramp he was guarding. However, the ramp on Main St. was normally the entrance ramp into the 'one-way' basement driveway. Because the exit ramp had a armored vehicle in it, blocking the exit, Dallas Lt. Rio Pierce, exited the 'entrance' onto Main St. Vaughn allegedly stopped traffic briefly to allow Pierce to turn onto the road. This would mean that Vaughn would have his

102

back to the ramp, while stopping the east bound traffic. Pierce also stated that he did not see Ruby, whom both of the officers knew. Of course, Pierce would also be looking towards oncoming traffic, to look for a clear moment, and may have not noticed Ruby walking from the opposite direction. Ruby himself, would later identify Pierce as leaving in his car, and say that he walked down the ramp at that time.

When Oswald came out into the basement, Ruby took his snub nosed 38 out and fired on shot into Oswald's abdomen. There was no chance for a second shot, as he was immediately subdued by several Officers, disarmed, and taken up the jail elevator. Once on the 5th floor, he was immediately placed in the same cell that Oswald had just vacated.

According to police officers I have talked to, Ruby initially thought he would be a "hero". He said that he knew they could not 'do it', and thought he would be praised for killing Kennedy's assassin. In many telegrams he received later, he was praised for doing so.

In April of 1964, he was convicted of killing Oswald. His defense attorney, Melvin Belli, had tried to claim "psycho-motor epilepsy". The basic premise was that Ruby, in his anguish and concern, basically 'blacked out' and shot Oswald without knowing what he was doing. Ruby himself allegedly objected to this line of defense, as he thought it implied that was that he was "crazy". He was convicted, with the Jury rejecting that defense.

He was later granted a retrial, on the "change of venue" basis, where it was argued on appeal that he could not be given a fair trial in Dallas, Texas, where the public wanted to somehow make up for the President being killed on their streets.

However, he would die of Cancer in January of 1967, before the re-trial could be arranged and conducted.

8. Terms we use (or misuse)

I am not an attorney, so I cannot give the legal definition of these terms. These are simply opinions in what I usually think they mean. So, as always, the things in this book are simply opinions, and not designed to be definitions. Others will, and have, debated much of this.

In the debates on the subjects of the Assassination and the other 2 shootings, there are certain terms that are thrown around a lot: 'Facts", "Evidence", "Proof/Prove", "Testimony", "Chain of Evidence" and "Reasonable doubt". Again, not being an attorney, I cannot give the legal definition of these terms, but will simply give my opinion. "Think for yourself!"

Facts

> "Archaeology is the search for fact... not truth. If it's truth you're looking for, Dr. Tyree's philosophy class is right down the hall."
> – (Henry) Indiana Jones, (Jr).

Since COVID19 last year (now 2021), I have stopped giving tours. However, one of the things I used to tell people during my tours:

"There are only 3 undisputed 'facts' about what happened that weekend:

1.   Connally and Kennedy were shot while riding through Dealey Plaza, and Kennedy later died. (Qualifier: One of the 1st theories I heard in the late 60's was that Kennedy was a mental 'vegetable', lived in Parkland hospital, and later on one of Onassis' islands.)

2.   Someone shot and killed JD Tippit in Oak Cliff that afternoon.

3.   Jack Ruby shot and killed Oswald on Sunday morning, on live television. (Qualifier: Whether it was Lee

JFK Assassination: Shades From The Fence

JFK Assassination: Shades From The Fence

Harvey Oswald, Harvey Oswald or Lee Oswald, I still can't tell you…)"

(The qualifiers were always included in my tour, and I usually had to explain that last qualifier. It is because there is a school of Researchers out there that believe Harvey and Lee were 2 separate people, looking so similar that even Marina had trouble determining.)

Of course, there are other 'facts' that are not disputed, but they are the minor ones. For instance: Jackie wore a pink dress, the limo was dark blue, etc. These are the main points that are almost universally accepted by everyone in the Research community. And it is an extreme rarity in the Research community to have anything that we all agree on.

One person's 'fact', is another person's opinion. The Research community tends to throw around the term: fact. Many seem to feel if they can say "the facts are" that they have proven their point. Of course, many cannot support, debate or defend their facts. They seem to believe that if these 'facts' are repeated enough, by enough people, or even constantly repeated by themselves, they somehow become real and accepted.

You can present anything you want as a fact, but it will be interpreted as being your opinion, or maybe some other author/researcher's opinion. For it to become a fact, you must be able to explain and support it to others. It is all subject to the evaluation of the persons involved in the statement. If they agree, or can at least see your argument, you all can agree to treat it as a fact and move on to other debate. However, if 2 of you both stipulate it is a fact in discussions between you, fully expect others to question it.

True facts, have to be agreed upon, or they are only opinion.

In most of the groups I moderate, if you state something as a fact, you must cite the source. For instance, if you say: "Bob shouted "Hey!", you must cite where the quote came from (testimony, recordings, etc.)

But many try to state a fact, because someone else said it. The biggest mistake is pointing to some author(s), or some video they saw, where someone says something happened. It is the author's opinion, you are pointing to. Even if they allege it as a fact, such as a statement (in quotes or otherwise), it may simply be how an author interpreted it, or managed to get someone to say something. Even sworn statements are not facts. They are simply what the witness remembered or recalls.

Evidence

I have had far too many debates on what is "evidence". They often get into highly technical definitions, both legal and otherwise.

Some have debated that evidence must be the truth, and accurate, or it is not technically evidence. To me, this completely eliminates phrases such as "false evidence" or "weak evidence", as how can something that is completely true be weak or false? The truth is the truth, right?

My use of the term "evidence" is the much broader one: Information pertaining to an event. (Or, legally, to a criminal case.)

It can be physical evidence, such as a weapon, bullets or a knife. It can also be location, or something else you can physically point to.

But it can also be something much more subjective, such as testimony, documents or photos/films. For instance an "Autopsy Report" is actually someone's opinion, and his observations and findings. If the person making the report is found by the Court to be an expert in their field, then the evidence is certainly much stronger and informative. The Court (and Jury) may even consider this evidence as a fact, when it is based on "expert opinion", but it is still opinion written down. It might even be subject to the mistakes of the expert, such as the rewritten Autopsy notes in the JFK case. (Not saying there are errors, only that the report is subject to errors.)

Now, some of you are already wondering why I included photos/film, as "subjective".

After all, there is the old expression, "pictures do not lie". That expression was true, at the time it was quoted. Back in those days, we did not have the technology to easily modify films and photos. Hollywood, and some Agencies, were surely able in the 1960's, but it was not always easy. (See the chapter on Alterations, later in the book.)

However, although an unaltered photo/film does not lie, it is subjective to the person looking at the photo and film. Different people will see things differently, plain and simple. A photo is only as strong as what the viewer sees, or thinks they see. If presented carefully, you might be able to convince all members of a Jury that they see the same thing. However, others may see something different. A good opponent might be able to introduce other interpretations, or viewpoints.

Therefore, a photo/film/video can never be considered hard evidence, and fact. While it does physically exist, it must be interpreted. Some photos are much easier to interpret than others, depending on what they show and how complicated they are. But even then, there are such things as optical illusions, Rorschach tests and the ability to influence people to believing in what you want them to see. Magicians do it all the time.

Proof/Prove

When I was a kid, in about 3rd grade or so, there always seemed to be the stubborn kid in the schoolyard that would say, "Oh, yeah? PROVE it!" Unfortunately, I have run into too many Researchers who seem to have never outgrown this childishness. (Again, no names...) To every point you bring up, they will ask you to 'prove' it. At the same time, they will claim that their own information (or evidence) is 'proof', and you will never convince them otherwise. (Probably, the

TRUEST statement they will ever make, so don't bother trying for too long..)

"Beauty is in the eye of the beholder." IMO, so is 'proof'. In the case of a trial, proof is in the eye of the Jury or Judge. It is only proof, if you can convince a Jury or a Judge that it is.

There is no such thing as "absolute proof", although it is a good title of Robert Groden's book, it does not exist as a thing you can point to.

For instance, I can state that "Fred was walking down Main St., when he saw..." Bypassing the 2nd part of what he allegedly saw, I cannot prove that Fred was walking down Main St. Even if I have testimony from Fred, other witnesses putting Fred at the scene, and a street video of him walking, some may not readily agree it is Fred. They may not know and recognize Fred, or cannot see him clearly in the video, or insist that Fred and the other witnesses are mistaken or lying. However, if the phrase comes up in the course of a criminal case, where what Fred 'saw' was a crime occurring, his walking down the street may easily be disregarded. If the Jury accepts that he was walking down Main St., it become unnecessary to try to prove it.

Many in the Research community will nitpick over every single detail. We were talking about Oswald bringing his rifle into the building. Suddenly, I was assailed with "Oh, yeah? Prove it!" The Researcher wanted me to track back to Oswald's mail order of the rifle, the PO Box receipt that the rifle was delivered, track the rifle for its complete history to New Orleans, and prove that he carried that rifle in the paper bag that Frazier saw him with that morning. It was all completely immaterial to the point that Oswald was a participant in the shooting. However, these Researchers are often just trolling, or wanting to argue.

I can't say this enough: the ability to find and ask legitimate questions of the official version is not the same as proving Oswald could not have participated.

JFK Assassination: Shades From The Fence

If the Jury/Judge accepts it as proof, that is the best we will ever have. Short of a proper trial, with adversarial debate, and defendant's representation, there is NO such thing as "proof". Proof is what the Jury accepts, whether guilty or not guilty.

A Researcher insisting on proof, will almost always be disappointed. Proof is what the jurist is willing to accept as being true. It is nothing else, and is highly subjective to the arguments, presentations and corroborating evidence and information. Nothing stands alone, or is absolute proof – unless you think it is, in which case you might think of it as "proof".

Testimony

One of the most misused concepts is that of Testimony. Many seem to believe that any statement made by a witness should be considered on the same level as Testimony. Just because someone made a statement to some author, Researcher, interviewer, etc. after the fact, and sometimes many years later, does NOT have the same weight as Testimony.

The non-legal definition of Testimony is that it is a "sworn" statement made to a legal authority. The most stringent of these is statements given in a legal Court of law. Any statement made to any Court, after taking the "Oath", is considered to be Testimony.

However, there is other Testimony.

Any "Statement" made to the Court, or any Investigative authority, is also considered Testimony. Sometimes, such as a Court, there is a "swearing in" of the witness. This is obvious Testimony, and subject to the laws, and criminal penalties, of Perjury. Even if made before the "swearing in" can actually take place, any statements made to any "officer of the Court" can be considered as Testimony.

However, often the witness cannot appear in Court. In these scenarios, the Court, Prosecutor or the Defense may get a legal statement from the individual. These are known as an Affidavit, or Deposition. Even though these statements are not made in the presence of the Judge/Jury, they are as legally

JFK Assassination: Shades From The Fence

binding as any statement made in the courtroom, at trial. They are equally subject to Perjury and other laws.

Some question has come up over the years, about the presence of a Notary Public when statements have been made. I am a Notary Public, although I have never had to be present in Court to present Testimony and records about any document, or Affidavit/statement, that I have witnessed in my 'official' capacity. What many do not understand, according to current Texas Law, almost any Law enforcement may "notarize" a statement made by an individual, as long as it pertains to their duties. (They cannot "notarize" a contract, bill of sale, etc.)

This means that any statement made to Law Enforcement by anyone, during an investigation, is considered a "legal" statement, subject to Perjury laws and penalties. Any Affidavit made in the aftermath of the shooting of JFK, or any other crime, is therefore considered Testimony, in the 'eyes' of the law. Even if there was not "Notary" present during the interrogation, it is the same as any notarized statement and subject to the legal process of perjury. In addition, it is currently illegal to make a false statement to the Federal Bureau of Investigation (FBI), or other Federal investigators.. The laws go back to the 1940's, however, I am not certain of the date of "1001" of the Federal criminal code.

This would make many of the statements made to the FBI, immediately after the shooting, or over the next several months, subject to perjury charges. They are considered "sworn statements" even if there is not Notary present, and the witness was not required to raise their hand to make an oath.

Statements made to others, regardless of when they were made, should be subject to skepticism. This includes statements put under quotes. They are simply 2nd hand information, in a court of law. They may be actual quotes, but there is no guarantee as to them actually being made by the individual. They are entirely subject to the credibility of the individual allegedly quoting them.

Often, an author, or interviewer, can manipulate these people into making statements that are not accurate. This might

110

be unintentional, but many Researchers will keep asking questions until they get the results they are looking for.

Therefore, take every statement, with a "grain of salt".

Reasonable Doubt

This is probably the most misused (misunderstood?) term used in the Research Community, or even among students and others interested in the JFK case. Often, it is used just as a Grade Schooler will use the term Proof/Prove.

(Again, the 3rd grader might challenge anyone else with, "Oh yeah? Prove it!")

Too often it is mistakenly confused with the idea of "no doubt". Almost anyone can come up with some "doubt" about anything if they try hard enough! LAW.COM defines it as:

> n. not being sure of a criminal defendant's guilt to a moral certainty. Thus, a juror (or judge sitting without a jury) must be convinced of guilt of a crime (or the degree of crime, as murder instead of manslaughter) "beyond a reasonable doubt," and the jury will be told so by the judge in the jury instructions. However, it is a subjective test since each juror will have to decide if his/her doubt is reasonable. It is more difficult to convict under that test, than "preponderance of the evidence" to decide for the plaintiff (party bringing the suit) in a civil (non-criminal) trial.

In layman's terms, it means what a 'reasonable' Jurist would consider as proof, without a major reasonable objection, that their conscience would use to let a defendant off. It is NOT the lack of all doubt, as many seem to want to portray it.

If it seems that they defendant committed the crime, to a Jury of reasonable intelligence, they can be convicted under the law.

JFK Assassination: Shades From The Fence

The idea of "reasonable" is, of course, highly subjective. There are many who will raise the smallest of "what-ifs", and thus cast doubt on the statement under question. The ability to question something with minute details is easy. Many of us can do it.

However, if a Jury of someone's 'peers' are almost completely convinced of the involvement of someone in the crime, that person can be convicted. It has little to do with "absolutes", in any form.

Too many Researchers feel that their ability to raise questions, means that Oswald would have gotten off. Additionally, they will raise questions about the integrity of the Investigators, and the "chains of evidence" presented.

These are valid questions, to be sure. (See my chapter on Seeds of Doubt). However, if a reasonable Juror does not feel they rise to the level of Reasonable Doubt, these little problems can be (and should be) overlooked.

The Jury (or Judge) has final say on what is reasonable doubt, and the "proof" of any case. Having said that, it is again the burden of the Prosecution, to present a case "beyond a reasonable doubt". If the Prosecution fails, in the opinion of the Jury, to do so, our system of Justice requires a verdict of "not guilty". This protects all of us.

Of the criminal cases I have been on a Jury for, one armed robbery stands out in my mind. I did actually believe the defendant was very likely guilty; however, the Prosecution did not provide a convincing case "beyond a reasonable doubt". We found "not guilty", and after the trial explained to the Judge, Prosecutor and Defense attorney, why we thought so. (I only hope the Defendant did not go on to perform other crimes.)

Once again, anyone's ability to create doubts, is important. However, it alone does not mean the person accused did not do the crime, nor should they be released. If the Prosecutor can present a case that causes the reasonable Jurist to believe the defendant did the crime, the Jury should return guilty.

JFK Assassination: Shades From The Fence

Unfortunately, this often means that the guilty will go free, or that the innocent may be incarcerated. But it is the best system of Justice that we have. But many Researchers believe that if they can raise any doubt about anything, that Oswald was innocent. We will never know. Oswald was never tried.

Conspiracy

The United States legal definition, according to the Legal Information Institute is:

An agreement between two or more people to commit an illegal act, along with an intent to achieve the agreement's goal. Most U.S. jurisdictions also require an overt act toward furthering the agreement.

Therefore, even if Oswald was the "lone" shooter, but was being helped, encouraged by another with an actual plan or act, or even was told he would have help escaping, it is still a Conspiracy. Technically then, if we spend time thinking Oswald was a "lone" gunman, but with help, that makes us a CT.

Conspiracy to Kill a President was a Federal Crime in 1963, while the Murder of a President was not. It was still a State crime. (A few years later you could probably prove that depriving someone of like, was a violation of their Civil Rights – but the Civil Rights Act had not been passed in 1963.)

Chain of Evidence

This term is hotly debated to this day.

A "Legal Term" dictionary defines its meaning as:

"A process and record that shows who obtained the evidence; where and when the evidence was obtained; who secured the evidence; and who had

113

control or possession of the evidence. The "sequencing" of the chain of evidence follows this order: collection and identification; analysis; storage; preservation; presentation in court; return to owner."

In the Research Community many people believe that there were too many "cooks in the kitchen". Dallas Police, Secret Service, the FBI and many others were handling various pieces of evidence, so many believe there was too much opportunity for mishandling, losing, substituting, and creating evidence. Others believe that as long as the evidence was being tracked as it went through the various law enforcement / agents and other officials, the "chain" is preserved.

The rifle, the gun, the shells and bullets, were all sent to the FBI crime lab on Friday night, to the resentment of the Dallas Police Crime Lab. It was later returned, but there was much communication mistakes between the entities. The limo itself was taken back to Washington that evening, by the Secret Service.

Even Vincent Bugliosi (Prosecutor for the Manson killings) admits to serious chain of evidence problems in this case, in his book "Reclaiming History".

9. The Investigations

In 1963, the murder of the President of the United States was not a Federal crime. (Of course, this was changed in 1964.) Murder fell under the jurisdiction of the State of Texas, or any other state in which it occurred.

As mentioned in the Events of the Day chapter, there was a 'tug-of-war' over the body of the President in Parkland Hospital that day. The Dallas County Medical Examiner Earl Rose was insistent that the Autopsy had to be performed in Dallas County. The law required it, according to Rose. (Recent research seems to show that moving a body out of the County was actually a very minor misdemeanor offense, subject to a $100 fine.)

But the Secret Service knew that Jackie would not leave her husband's side, and they additionally wanted to get everyone safely out of Dallas as soon as possible. They eventually allegedly contacted a Dallas County Justice of the Peace, who authorized releasing the body to Jackie, as long as it was accompanied by Admiral Burkley, JFK's physician. Many today argue that the Secret Service 'illegally' stole the body, but it was released legally to his wife and physician, by Dallas County Justice of the Peace Theran Ward. (There is still debate about this, as some say Ward would not make a decision.)

Dallas Police were initially involved in both the Tippit and Kennedy murders. However, the Federal Bureau of Investigation immediately got involved in the matter. That Friday night they requested all of the physical evidence, such as the rifle and shells, be packed up and sent to their lab in Washington. The Dallas crime lab resented the intrusion, but complied. Lt. Carl Day, who had photographed fingerprints on the trigger guard never told the FBI about them. He felt that if they were the 'all mighty' FBI, they should be able to find the fingerprints themselves!

JFK Assassination: Shades From The Fence

They didn't... But the Kennedy shooting was mainly investigated by the FBI and the Secret Service.

After Oswald was shot on Sunday morning, the investigation turned to Jack Ruby, for the most part. Lt. Jim Leavelle did do some follow up investigating, and spoke to many witnesses in Oak Cliff. However, Leavelle and the Dallas Police had other crimes to investigate and did not do a lot of follow up on the JFK assassination.

The Secret Service and FBI did do more investigating into Oswald, his history, background, movements, etc. They continued taking statements for the next several months. However, they wrote a preliminary report within 2 weeks of that weekend, saying Oswald fired 3 shots, and got 3 hits.

After Oswald was shot and killed on Sunday morning, Deputy Attorney General Nicholas Katzenbach wrote a report to President Johnson's assistant Bill Moyers. Here is that report:

> It is important that all of the facts surrounding President Kennedy's Assassination be made public in a way which will satisfy people in the United States and abroad that all the facts have been told and that a statement to this effect be made now.
>
> 1. The public must be satisfied that Oswald was the assassin; that he did not have confederates who are still at large; and that the evidence was such that he would have been convicted at trial.
>
> 2. Speculation about Oswald's motivation ought to be cut off, and we should have some basis for rebutting thought that this was a Communist conspiracy or (as the

Iron Curtain press is saying) a right–wing conspiracy to blame it on the Communists.

Unfortunately the facts on Oswald seem about too pat — too obvious (Marxist, Cuba, Russian wife, etc.). The Dallas police have put out statements on the Communist conspiracy theory, and it was they who were in charge when he was shot and thus silenced.

3. The matter has been handled thus far with neither dignity nor conviction. Facts have been mixed with rumour and speculation. We can scarcely let the world see us totally in the image of the Dallas police when our President is murdered.

I think this objective may be satisfied by making public as soon as possible a complete and thorough FBI report on Oswald and the assassination. This may run into the difficulty of pointing to inconsistencies between this report and statements by Dallas police officials. But the reputation of the Bureau is such that it may do the whole job.

The only other step would be the appointment of a Presidential Commission of unimpeachable personnel to review and examine the evidence and announce its conclusions. This has both advantages and disadvantages. It [*sic*] think it can await publication of the FBI report and public reaction to it here and abroad.

JFK Assassination: Shades From The Fence

> I think, however, that a statement that all the facts will be made public property in an orderly and responsible way should be made now. We need something to head off public speculation or Congressional hearings of the wrong sort.
> *Nicholas deB. Katzenbach* Deputy Attorney General

LBJ was initially inclined to let the Texas Attorney General Waggoner Carr handle the investigation, using a Texas Court of Inquiry. Carr even traveled to Washington the week after the event to meet with LBJ, and others. However, both houses of Congress started talking about doing their own investigations of the event. Johnson was allegedly concerned about conflicting investigations "popping up all over the place".

Additionally, Johnson advisors insisted it might look bad to have Texas do the investigation. After all, Johnson was from Texas, and it might reflect badly on him politically to have the investigations in his home state. (It was bad enough that Kennedy was killed in Johnson's home State.)

So Johnson followed the advice of Katzenbach and used the "Johnson treatment" to convince several high ranking members of the government into serving on a Presidential Commission. Chief Justice Earl Warren was pressured into serving on the Commission although he initially resisted, and to this day we simply call it the Warren Commission. Many of the other members also did not want to participate, and were pressured into serving.

President's Commission on the Assassination of President Kennedy

The Warren Commission (WC) was given 2 official tasks. One was to 'invstigate' the Assassination, while the other was to review Secret Service procedures surrounding the event.

JFK Assassination: Shades From The Fence

Johnson allegedly told Earl Warren that this would be little more than approving the FBI report that was being compiled.

Johnson wanted the Commission to represent all parties and major interests of the country, so he cajoled individuals from the North and South, both parties, and other former members of various offices of the government.

Earl Warren – Chief Justice US Supreme Court
Allen Dulles – Former Director of the CIA
John McCloy – Advisor to Presidents FDR to Kennedy
Sen. Richard Russell – (D) Georgia (close friend to LBJ)
Sen. Sherman Cooper – (R) Kentucky
Rep. Hale Boggs – (D) Louisiana
Rep. Gerald Ford – (R) Michigan (later Vice President and President)

LBJ felt these "seven honorable men" would be diverse enough to satisfy the American people, and head off any investigations in the Senate and House of Representatives.

The WC was originally told that they simply had to review the report of the event that the FBI was putting together, and also review Secret Service procedures. However, in one of their earliest meetings it was decided that they should at least interview many of the witnesses, friends of Oswald, stage recreations and evaluate Oswald's history.

They had no "investigative" arm, so used the FBI and Secret Service quite heavily to do the recreations and other investigative work. They did however, have attorneys perform thousands of interviews. The various Federal agencies did:

FBI: 25,000 interviews, 2,300 reports, 25,400 pages

SS: 1,550 interviews, 800 reports, 4,600 pages, filmed recreations

CIA: "Investigative analyses of particular significance and sensitivity in the foreign areas" IRS, State and military intelligence handled additional investigative requests.

JFK Assassination: Shades From The Fence

The Commission also did hundreds of interviews, but without any adversarial representation for Oswald. Therefore, the ability to cross-examine witnesses these witnesses did not exist. The WC would often go "off the record", raising suspicions about what was discussed during these periods.

Researchers today are mixed on how well the event was actually investigated. The trial is usually the true test of the value of any investigation, and this case was only 'tried' in the "Court of Public Opinion". (And continues to be debated there…)

The initial FBI report had said that 3 shots were made by Oswald from the window, and that all 3 shots hit Kennedy and Connally. However, the Warren Commission were told about, and concerned about James Tague, a bystander who was injured by a bullet which he said hit the curb in front of him. Since a bullet going downward into Kennedy or Connally could not come back out, travel an additional 100+ yards and cause photographed damage to a curb, they determined there must have been a missed shot. Since one shot was obviously a skull shot, which also could not have caused damage that far away. They came up with a "single bullet theory" (SBT).

That theory said a bullet went into JFK's upper back/low neck, missed major bones, exited his low throat, and proceeded into Connally sitting in front and to the left of him. Connally's entrance wound was elongated as if the bullet had started to tumble. It hit Connally's 5th rib sideways, breaking through it, and exited below his right nipple. It then entered his wrist, broke the bone, exiting the bottom side of his wrist. It then went slightly into his left thigh. A mainly intact bullet was found on a stretcher in the emergency room of Parkland

Hospital that afternoon. It is Commission Exhibit 399 (CE399). It is slightly flattened at its base (maybe hitting bone sideways?) and lead is extruding out of the bottom of its metal jacket. WC said that this was the bullet that went through both bodies. Critics have named it the Magic Bullet, as they contend it should be more damaged.

JFK Assassination: Shades From The Fence

However, they were under great political pressure to finish a report by the election in 1964. Johnson wanted the report to be done, as he was running to be re-elected as President.

Many therefore look at the Report as a cover-up, and a rush to judgment. They often simply went "off the record" to clear things up, and did not seem to follow up on any answer that pointed beyond Oswald, or other shooters.

IMO, they were charged to come up with a viable Oswald acted alone theory, which the American people would accept. (This is precisely what the Katzenback memo #1 requirement was.)

Although Oswald's mother, Marguerite Oswald wanted attorney Mark Lane to sit in all of the meetings and represent the good name of her son, it was denied. Mark Lane was interviewed, but was not allowed to represent Oswald. He would become one of the earliest published critics of the WC.

Not surprisingly, the WC determined that Oswald did indeed kill Kennedy. While they said they could not "rule out" a conspiracy, they stated that they "could find no evidence" of a conspiracy, nor of other shooters/actors. The Secret Service also did a complete overhaul of many of their procedures, although no real penalties for the lax actions of that day were ever suggested.

They delivered a Report to LBJ in September 1964. They additionally compiled Exhibits and Interviews in another 26 bound volumes, although it took until November 1964 for this material to be compiled and released to the public. It was released with no index, and is difficult to find what is wanted. (In the computer age, some of the earliest researchers created a CD index.) You can still buy the volumes (used) on eBay for a couple of thousand. They should cure your insomnia....

(At minimum, the serious student of the event should read the Warren Commission report book – just be aware that it is considered a white-wash by many.)

JFK Assassination: Shades From The Fence

Clark Medical Panel

During the 1967/8 investigation and trial of New Orleans businessman Clay Shaw by New Orleans District Attorney Jim Garrison, there was pressure to get the autopsy x-rays and photographs of JFK. United States Attorney General Ramsey Clark prevented these materials being given to Garrison. Instead, Clark appointed 4 medical experts to examine the medical photos, x-rays and other materials related to the death and autopsy of JFK.

The Panel determined that only 2 bullets struck JFK. One was obviously the head shot from behind the skull, destroying the right side of the skull. The other shot struck the right side of the spine at the base of the neck, and traveled through the upper abdomen and exited the lowest throat. While the head shot shattered, having struck dense skull bone at high speed, the back shot struck no bone and exited the body.

The Clark Panel did not speculate about where the bullet went, since they only had the photos and materials on the President.

Ramsey Clark's final day in office as Attorney General, on January 25th, 1969, the order was given to permanently deny the x-rays and photographs from Jim Garrison, and his staff. (They have been leaked over the years, however.)

Church Committee

After the Watergate incident in the early 70's, there was a clamor to investigation the FBI, CIA, NSA and other national security institutions. Watergate uncovered many abuses from Nixon's White House that used these agencies to spy on Americans, and other alleged activities.

The "United States Senate Select Committee to Study Governmental Operations with Respect to Intelligence Activities" was formed in 1975. It was headed by Senator Frank Church, so commonly called the Church Committee.

Among its investigations was the use of the CIA to assassinate leaders of other countries. It had long been rumored that the Kennedys were using the Mafia, through the CIA to attempt to kill Fidel Castro, the President of Communist Cuba. The Committee dedicated a 112 page Volume V to the Assassination of President John F. Kennedy. In it, they researched if Oswald was an FBI informant, and put together a Chronology of Oswald's life, defection to the USSR, return, and pro- and anti- Cuba activities.

Volume V's "Findings" starts out with the sentence, "The Committee emphasizes that it has not uncovered any evidence sufficient to justify a conclusion that there was a conspiracy to assassinate President Kennedy." Once again, the investigation does not eliminate a conspiracy, just states that it is unable to find "any evidence" to support one.

Good Night America – Geraldo Rivera

Although it is not an official 'investigation', an episode of Gerald Rivera's Good Night America on March 6, 1975, has a strong influence on the Kennedy investigations. On this episode comedian Dick Gregory and Researcher Robert Groden appeared.

More importantly for our purposes is the presence of Robert Groden on the show. Robert had been a consultant during the Clay Shaw trial, which had borrowed a copy of the Zapruder film taken in Dealey Plaza that day. While Time/Life had purchased the film and rights, and had released stills of the film, the American public had never seen the film. Robert had a bootlegged copy of the film, and it was first shown to the American public that night. It was grainy from multiple copying, and had some missing frames and splices; however, it showed the gruesome shooting as seen through the lens of the only person that recorded the entire sequence that day.

Other episodes also covered the JFK killing, such as the March 27, 1975 episode. This one included Deputy Press Secretary Malcolm Kilduff, Senator Ralph Yarborough, Author Jim Bishop, Coroner Cyril Wecht, Attorney Mark Lane and Comedian Dick Gregory.

JFK Assassination: Shades From The Fence

To say the least, the shows made public a number of questions that had been bothering WC critics for years. The public furor they raised was most likely them main cause of the U. S. House of Representatives to re-open the case and start the HSCA investigation.

House Select Committee on Assassinations (HSCA)

Because of the uproar created by the bootleg Zapruder film, Watergate and other assassination critics, faith in the Warren Commission was largely waning among the American people. In 1976 the U. S. House of Representatives authorized the House Select Committee on Assassinations. The HSCA met beginning in late 1976, and eventually published their report in 1979.

The HSCA expanded studies of the Assassination into areas which they felt the earlier investigations did not adequately study. These included multiple panels of scientists and investigators to look into related areas. These included photograph and film analysis, FBI and CIA, the Mafia, and acoustic study and analysis. They also looked into the 1968 shooting of Martin Luther King.

For the most part, they agreed with the Warren Report and said that Oswald was the shooter, and could find no involvement by the Mafia, CIA, FBI or others.

However, the Acoustics panel firm of Bolt Beranek and Newman Inc. studied a Dictabelt recording of an 5+ minute "open microphone" over the Dallas Police channel #1. (The routine channel, and not the channel #2 that was used by the officers for the motorcade.)

After setting up sound tests in Dealey Plaza, with shots from both the 6th floor window of the TSBD, as well as test shots from behind the picket fence, "grassy knoll", they determine there was a match. Since the equipment had a built in noise filter, the panel said that instead of hearing actual gunshots, the sound was kind of an 'impulse' that had to be found scientifically. They said they could detect 4 shots, and therefore there was a 95% probability of a 2nd shooter from behind the picket fence. Based on the medical and autopsy analysis, they determined this shot was a miss.

They asserted that Dallas Police Officer H. B. McClain was the officer with the stuck open microphone. However, H. B. told me, and others, on many occasions that it was not him. He was on Channel 2, and clearly heard all of the communications on Channel 2. Additionally, tests done in the Plaza with microphones placed in various locations along Houston and Elm St. determined where the stuck microphone would have to be located to match the 'impulses'. The few films of the motorcade that we have consistently show McLain approximately 50 feet out of these required positions when these impulses occur.

The entire recording is readily available to researchers today. IMO the sounds seem to be a motorcycle officer racing from a position across town, to the Trade Mart. You can hear the varying speeds of the motorcycle engine, as the rider makes his way through Dallas streets. After he arrives at the Trade Mart and stops, you can hear sirens approaching his position, passing by, and then fading into the distance. If it had been a motorcycle in the Motorcade, these sirens would be more consistent for the entire trip to Parkland Hospital (where McLain went).

Additionally, the equipment was designed to record human voices and similar frequencies. Yet, you cannot hear any of the large crowds that where cheering, clapping and shouting along the entire Motorcade travel in the downtown area. If it had been part of the Motorcade, these sounds should be there.

Every Dallas Police officer I have gotten an opinion from insists that this is not a motorcycle on the Motorcade, or anyplace in Dealey Plaza or downtown Dallas.

In 1980 and 1982, respectively, the FBI lab and the National Academy of Science performed their own testing, and determined the Acoustic Panel was mistaken.

JFK Assassination: Shades From The Fence

ARRB

Prior to 1963, there was a law/tradition that records from an official government investigation, which were not specifically released to the public, were to be locked up for 75 years. This was a basic procedure to protect foreign entities from determining investigation methods, for the sake of National Security. This meant that much of the investigations into the Kennedy Assassination would be secured until the year 2038/9.

But because of the Research community, and mostly because of the Oliver Stone film "JFK", the public demand to release these records was ever increasing. The President John F, Kennedy Assassination Records Collection Act of 1992 was passed. It created the Assassination Records Review Board (ARRB).

The ARRB was not truly an investigation, formed to make a conclusion on the Assassination. Instead they were charged with gathering records from the various Departments, Bureas and Agencies that related to the investigations of the JFK Assassination. The ARRB worked as a collector and logger of the records, gathering over 6 million Assassination records. In September of 1998, they met for the final time and released their report on the records they had collected. These were transferred to the National Archives and Records Administration (NARA).

However, if any record was deemed to be a National Security risk, by showing our intelligence means and methods, many parts of those documents could be redacted (blacked out). Additionally, there is reported to be approximately 50,000 documents that were so sensitive they have still not been released by the various entities. The Research Community is still pouring over these 6 million records and documents.

It is a slow process.

Other "Investigations"

These constitute the official investigations of the JFK Assassination itself.

JFK Assassination: Shades From The Fence

Of course, both the Jack Ruby trial and the New Orleans Clay Shaw trial were also official investigations. The Jack Ruby trial investigated the shooting of Oswald, and dipped a little into Jack Ruby's background. It was determined that Jack Ruby did not know Oswald, and there is no proof that he was in any way involved in the shooting of JFK.

The New Orleans Clay Shaw trial attempted to investigate many factors of the JFK Assassination, as it was trying to prove that Clay Shaw was a party to that crime. It spent a lot of time in the details of the JFK shooting, that are still debated today.

Many private "investigations" of the case have been done by Researchers over the last 58 years. Again, it is arguably the most investigated crime in the 20th century.

If you are reading this book, it can be said you are investigating the crime, although for this particular book, you are barely being exposed to the surface of the case.

10. Hurray for Hollywood.....?

Since 1963, there have been a number of films and documentaries about John F. Kennedy, and (for our purposes) about his Assassination. It is obvious beyond the scope of this book to discuss all of them. However, some of the major documentaries and films which greatly influenced me, and most of the Researchers, will be covered very briefly here. Mainly I will discuss the general impacts these films have had on many in the Research Community. (I have missed many of them, especially with internet video, but these are the main ones that appeared over the years.)

A CBS News Inquiry: The Warren Report (1967)

This 4 hour documentary aired over 4 nights in June. Walter Cronkite and Dallas CBS' Eddie Barker interviewed several of the actual witnesses and employees of the TSBD. It wet the appetite and caused many of us to read the Warren Report fully (if we had not done so already). The preceding year would also see the release of many of the early books by critics of the WC, such as Mark Lane's "Rush to Judgement" which was also turned into a documentary. 1967 also saw the release of Josiah Thompson's "Six Seconds in Dallas" (I have both of these) which is likely why CBS decided to create the program.

Executive Action (1973)

One of the earliest Hollywood films about the Assassination. It was pure fiction, but got people interested in the case. However, at that time the only thing we could do about it would be to try to find books we could read. The movie starred Burt Lancaster, Will Greer and Robert Ryan as high financiers/conspirators who train a team to do the Assassination, and blame it on Lee Oswald.

Kennedy (1983)

JFK Assassination: Shades From The Fence

Although it does have the Assassination towards the end of the film (and over 3 minutes of annoying siren) it is basically a mini-series about John F. Kennedy (Martin Sheen), Robert Kennedy (John Shea) and the rest of the family. It aired over several nights starting on Nov. 20th, 1983 on NBC. However, that first night it was up against the ABC "The Day After", which occupied most of American television.

CBC The Fifth Estate (1976-)
Canadian Broadcasting Corporation (CBC) had a weekly news program similar to "60 Minutes" in the United States. Over the years they have had several shows about the Kennedy Assassination. Not living in Canada, I do not recall seeing any of these shows. However, Fred Litwin discusses their investigation at length in his book, "I Was A Teenage Conspiracy Freak", so it had some impact for those who saw it.

I list it here as a main documentary because Fred's book covers it so much. It represents a number of documentaries about the Assassination that have been broadcast over the years.

"JFK: Inside the Target Car" (2008 – The Discovery Channel), and "JFK:Beyond the Magic Bullet" (2004 – The Discovery Channel).
These both use more modern recreations to attempt to prove that the SBT could have happened, and that the head shot was from behind. Gary Mack was instrumental in these investigation documentaries. He put Jackie in the wrong position during discussion of the head shot, as they had her behind Kennedy at Z312, opposite him from the grassy knoll. In fact, she was leaning forward trying to look into his face at that moment. I was there during filming, but the Assistant Director would not let me talk to anyone about it. (I did mention it to the actress playing Jackie, but to no avail.)

The Men Who Killed Kennedy

JFK Assassination: Shades From The Fence

This multipart documentary was created in the United Kingdom by Nigel Turner. It was filmed beginning in 1986-7. It was a multi-part documentary released over several years. "Coup D'Etat" (1988) , "The Forces of Darkness" (1988), "The Cover-Up" (1991), "The Patsy" (1991) and "The Witnesses" (1991) , were the first 5 parts. Whenever they released and aired a new episode, they would also replay the prior episodes, which gave the impression that they were created and released at the same time (depending on when you saw them). It was an extensive look into many of the more sensational Assassination theories circulating at the time.

It was well done and featured many of the actual witnesses, employees and investigators of the Assassination. It covered many different theories, and highly questioned the results of the WC and HSCA investigations.

It was the first major documentary raised on the subject of the Assassination and raised many issues/concerns that are still discussed by Researchers today. Many of the people interviewed have since died, so it is a major record of their interviews, etc.

Affectionately abbreviated as "TMWKK" by Researchers today, it is still often referred to and the theories discussed by many in current Groups and Forums.

Additional episodes were also released years later: "The Truth Shall Set You Free" (1995), "The Smoking Guns" (2003), "The Love Affair" (2003), "The Guilty Men" (2003).

This last episode was very controversial. It basically accused Lyndon Johnson as being aware of, or actually responsible for, the Assassination. It aired on the History Channel the week of Nov. 17, 2003. The Johnson family immediately went into action protesting the episode. Eventually, even President Gerald Ford gave the History Channel his objections to the program. (Many consider Gerald Ford to be the most FBI apologist on the Warren Commission.)

The History Channel hired a team to evaluate the program, and did not again air the program while they were doing so.

JFK Assassination: Shades From The Fence

The Channel eventually publicly apologized, and deciding they should be more selective on what they allowed on their channel, promised never to air the program again.

Fortunately, my wife ordered me a DVD copy of all of the episodes that week, knowing that I was interested. To date, DVDs of those final episodes are not available for sale.

"JFK"

The biggest blockbuster surrounding the Assassination is Oliver Stone's 1991 release of "JFK". It stars Kevin Costner as New Orleans District Attorney Jim Garrison. It is loosely based on the Clay Shaw (Tommy Lee Jones) trial that is to date the only actual trial of anybody for the Assassination. It is based on the book "On The Trail of the Assassins" by Jim Garrison, as well as "Crossfire" by Jim Marrs.

It is a major Hollywood drama, and "who dunnit" (everyone likes a good "who-dunnit", right?). However, much of what happens in the film is very much fictional. Stone, and his consultants, threw in a lot of information that was not available during the actual trial in 1967/8. For instance they have Garrison meeting in Washington with a "Colonel X" (Donald Sutherland), who gives him a background of the involvement of the military intelligence in the shooting. This is loosely based on Fletcher Prouty, a ex-military man who came out with his book, "The Secret Team" in 1973.

Additionally, they have TSBD employee Carolyn Arnold testifying during the 1967/8 Clay Shaw trial, and quote almost verbatim a statement she made 15 years later to Dallas Morning News reporter Earl Golz, in 1978! (In November 1963 Arnold made a sworn affidavit to the FBI that she might have caught a "glimpse" of Oswald in the TSBD doorway, but could not be certain. In the spring of 1964, she also made a FBI statement that she did not see Oswald that day.) In her 1978 interview it is alleged that she said she saw Oswald in the 2nd floor lunchroom, at 12:25, eating his lunch alone.

It is a very entertaining movie, and I certainly commend Oliver Stone for making this blockbuster. It reopened the JFK

JFK Assassination: Shades From The Fence

Assassination in the minds of millions, and rekindled interest in the Assassination itself. I still watch it a couple of times a year, or so.

I have given tours of Dealey Plaza and other Dallas sites surrounding the Assassination to friends and family going back to 1984, when I moved back to Dallas area permanently. But the rekindling of interest in the Assassination which "JFK" rekindled allowed me to start making spare cash doing professional private-party and bus tours, so I cannot complain about "JFK".

However, too often I run into people that think the drama is like a documentary, and that things shown in the movie actually happened in the investigation and trial of Clay Shaw. Even more experienced members of the Research Community will occasionally mention a quote, or event, that is from the Hollywood movie – and did not actually happen, in 1967/8 (at least). Some of them 'could' have happened, as we can only speculate on many of the events. But many are simply Hollywood treatment, as entertainment, even though the movie is "based on an actual event": the trial of Clay Shaw.

It is entertainment, and NOT a factual documentary.

As I am writing this in 2021, there is a new Oliver Stone movie set to be released, titled

"JFK Revisited: Through the Looking Glass". It is narrated by Donald Sutherland and Whoopie Goldberg, and James DeEugenio wrote the screenplay (based on the book).

IMDB.com lists it as a Documentary this time, although they also show it is linked to "JFK" (1991), so it may contain scenes from that film. It has not been released yet, so I am unable to give any kind of accuracy review, etc. I do know Jim DeEugenio, and am not very hopeful, about the show's content. IMDB.com shows the Storyline to be:

"Declassified files related to President Kennedy's assassination in a far larger context, aiming to shine more light on what really happened in 1963."

JFK Assassination: Shades From The Fence

Stone has shown "Revisited" (short name) at the Cannes film festival. The reviews on Indiewire says that he tried to sell the documentary as 4 one-hour episodes for TV, but could not find any buyers. So Stone reworked the 4 hours into a 2 hour film. It is purported to show how the FBI and CIA lied to the Warren Commission, which overlooked evidence that has since been unveiled. Stone worked on the film during the pandemic, and Indiewire believes his intent was to bring public "up to speed on what really happened in 1963." Anne Thompson spoke to Stone at Cannes, and quotes, "To make this documentary is to prove our case. We proved it as far as possible. There is no absolute proof."

Since writing the preceding paragraphs, I have seen the film on Showtime. It is indeed a documentary, including many films from the period, and a number of Researchers that we all know.

It focuses on the many discrepancies that people have turned up in the past 58 years, and that the Warren Commission and other investigators ignored or did not catch 57 years ago. It implies that these discrepancies were intentional on the parts of the government involved.

It is a well made film, by a famous Hollywood Director, Oliver Stone. Of course, much of the speculation has been around for decades, and really presents nothing new.

It has been panned by most of the Research community as being misleading and manipulative. For example, it shows the WFAA TV (ABC in Dallas) broadcast that took place live within minutes of the Assassination. About 1 PM, Nov. 22nd, news director Jay Watson interviews witnesses Bill and Gayle Newman. In the WFAA version, Watson is sitting on Newman's right, and Newman points to his left temple area while speaking about the fatal head shot. In the film, they use a reverse image to make Newman point to his right temple instead. Manipulative? Are they trying to convince you that

JFK Assassination: Shades From The Fence

Newman 'pinpointed' an exact shot location, by using Hollywood tricks? (Let the viewer beware....)

From That Moment On

My first participation in a film or documentary was this 2005 documentary from James Lambert. James was in college at the University of North Texas, and did the documentary as his final thesis for his Journalism degree project. It was very limited in its release, although I do have a copy of it.

For the most part, James shows the impact the Assassination made on many citizens of Dallas. These include some witnesses at Parkland Hospital or Dealey Plaza. I am interviewed because of my name, and discuss the impacts it had on the city. In fact, YouTube still has over 2 hours of unedited video that was recorded for the film. (If you can't sleep some night... search FTMO Jerry Dealey.) Not sure why he uploaded it, but have no objection. Hopefully, I didn't insult anyone!

Oswald's Ghost

Director Robert Stone released this film in 2007. It is a pro "Oswald did it" film that features discussion of many of the aspects of the event. It was released as a theater film, although IMDB.com shows its theater Gross as a little under $2,000. In 2008, it was shown on TV by the program "The American Experience". I do have a DVD of it. IMDB.com has the following Storyline:

> "It accounts the events before and after one the most important events during that time, and they were told through eyewitnesses who were living at that time."

My association on this film was that Robert and his film crew took a Dallas Historical Society bus tour for this film. In the film, you can see my friend Kenneth Holmes, Jr. in his cowboy hat, speaking in Dealey Plaza. (You might get a glimpse of me, carrying the speaker connected to his wireless microphone.) I was on that tour as a Docent for the Society. So while traveling, I was sitting behind the film crew on the bus, where Robert and I were chatting throughout the 4 hour tour. The theater debut was at the Texas Theater many months later, where Gary Mack hosted an after film debate between Robert Stone, Hugh Aynesworth and Josiah 'Tink" Thompson, which I also attended.

JFK: The Lost Bullet

Robert Stone would also return to Dallas and work on the Documentary in 2011. This one features Max Holland (author of "The Kennedy Assassination Tapes"). It promotes the theory that the first bullet in Dealey Plaza that day was the one that missed (and possibly injured James Tague). Initially they believe it hit a light pole that went across Elm St. at the Houston St. intersection. However, unable to find any damage on the cross pole, they review the Secret Service film, and seem to see a hole in the flat panel that surround the actual traffic light (no longer the original).

I was in Dealey Plaza and talked to Stone briefly the day of filming, but do not have any appearance or other connection to the film. It was made as a TV movie, but IMDB.com does not show any airing, until it was aired in an episode of National Geographic Explorer in 2011.

Killing Kennedy

This National Geographic dramatization was released in 2013, and based on the book of the same name by Bill O'Reilly and Martin Dugard. It starred Rob Lowe as Kennedy, and Will Rothhaar as Lee Oswald. It features Oswald with am actual personality, more than many films and documentaries. I told Will that I could see a lot of the book "Marina and Lee" by Priscilla Johnson McMillan, in his acting and characterization of Oswald. He did an excellent job in presenting Oswald as a family man and human being, unlike how Oswald is portrayed in many films. Will said it was high praise that I thought his portrayal as a person was so good, and admitted that he used the book for research.

It is purely an Oswald-did-it film. It focuses on Kennedy in the White House, while at the same time a dual following of Oswald and his family life. Of course much of both Oswald's and Kennedy's relationships with their wives and at home is dramatic license and loosely based speculation.

Kennedy is shown living in the White House as he plans for the Dallas trip. Jackie is played by Ginnifer Goodwin, and the film covers their relationship. It even covers speculation of Jackie's knowledge of Kennedy's 'womanizing' (including a White House pool party, with skinny-dipping).

Oswald is also shown with much of his family life, again based on McMillan's book which was initially written with Marina's stories and approval. (Marina is reported to have since been quite upset with McMillan.)

Freda Dillard, a fellow tour guide and also a friend of the late Kenneth Holmes, was contacted several weeks before the pre-release of the film by National Geographic. They wanted a 5 hour tour, for the Press, to precede the pre-view release of the film at the Texas Theater. Freda felt I would be the better tour guide for that particular group, and put us into contact with each other.

I was given a non-reviewable link to view the film before the tour, so that I would be familiar with it ahead of time. I met the group at the Hotel Texas in Fort Worth, and proceeded to give the bus a tour. On the bus was the director Nelson McCormick and screenplay writer Kelly Masterson. Additionally, the actor Will Rothhaar who played Oswald, was also on the bus tour, pre-view screening, and went to the Sixth Floor museum with us afterwards. Will is still a Facebook friend of mine, as is his father, although we are not real close friends.

The film does have a number of errors, such as Oswald standing while shooting (which the Director/Writer noted that night when I showed them the sniper's nest). However, many of the errors are very minor, and are only obvious to some of us who have been to the sites hundreds of times. Overall, it is an excellent film if you want to see possible portrayals of Kennedy and Oswald as people.

A Coup in Camelot

I also appear, and am credited, in this 2015 documentary, by Directory Stephen Goetsch and Writer Art Van Kampen. It is narrated by Peter Coyote, and features a number of Researchers. In order of appearance: me, Barry Ernest, Sherry Fiester (Guiterrez), Doug Horne, David Mantik, Vince Palamara and Dick Russell.

Steve and Art contacted me several months before wanting a Tour. I met them and found out that they were working on this film. So we did a 2 hour tour (I usually do longer ones) and they took me to a filming location, to do an interview. For my part, I simply talk about the history and politics of Dallas, and a few factual details about what happened that weekend. But I do not really get into any of the controversies and theories of the Assassination.

Several of the other Researchers get into more controversial topics, such as Sherry's belief that the fatal head shot came from the knoll on the south side of Dealey Plaza (unlike the famous "grassy knoll" which is on the north side). Doug Horne (ARRB) and Dr. David Mantik focuses on the head shot, from a medical and x-ray point of view. Vince Palamara has written several books, and specializes on Secret Service procedures and 'misconduct'. Barry Ernest wrote the book, "The Girl On The Stairs" about his search and interview of TSBD workers Sandra Style and Vickie Adams, who came down the stairs about the time that Oswald would have used them. Dick Russell wrote the book "The Man Who Knew Too Much", about Richard Case Nagell who was allegedly hired to kill Oswald and prevent the Assassination.

The film also spends a lot of time on the "casket game", where 3 different caskets were at Bathesda Naval Hospital that night. Some say there were also 2 different bodies, but that story has never been supportable. One of the caskets was the Britannica casket that JFK flew from Dallas in. A second was a plain shipping casket, and the 3rd was a casket ordered by Jackie that night. She wanted a better casket, and sent some aides out that night to pick one out. This 3rd casket was the one that Kennedy was buried in, and lay in the Capitol rotunda. They make a mystery of why the extra casket was there (and if there was another body). To me, it is simply that it may have been ordered by Kennedy brother-in-law Sargent Shriver while the airplane was returning, just in case it would be needed to ship the body to Massachusetts, Florida or elsewhere.

The show never really had much of a Theater run, and pretty much went straight to DVD instead. (I do have a "one sheet" movie poster hanging in my dining room.)

Once again, I appeared at the Texas Theater for the premier of the film, followed by several drinks and party. Additionally, I appeared on a podcast of "Night Fright Show", with host Brent Holland along with Vince Palamara, where we discuss the film and various aspects of the Assassination. Doug Horne, Dick Russell and David Mantik also spoke on episodes of the podcast in December of 2016. (Search for A Coup in Camelot, if interested.)

Obviously, there are dozens of films, TV shows and documentaries about JFK and the Kennedys themselves and dozens about the Assassination(s). This is simply a list of the ones that influenced me the most, or that I have appeared in or had some association with.

11. Television (The Tube)

Now that we have covered Hollywood, the next topic is about Television. Many of the documentaries I have listed in the prior chapter only appeared on Television, but this chapter is another article about the impact of the Kennedy Presidency and his Assassination on television in general. (Even "Gilligan's Island" was impacted. During the introduction and theme song you can see many flags at half mast, because that scene was filmed on the week following the Assassination.)

As I have given tours over the years, I have naturally run into students just learning about the Kennedy years and the Assassination. I have also done lectures and bus tours to history classes and other student groups.

It is not uncommon to hear about assignments given by a social studies or history teachers to research Kennedy and the legacy of his Presidency and his death. The exact legacy is often brought up in the Research Community as well. Often, the question of how would the world be different had he lived, but I will not try to conjecture on that.

The most common answers to JFK legacy seem to be either the Space race and landing on the moon, Vietnam or Civil rights.

While it is true that his challenge to land on the moon by the end of the decade did push NASA to achieve that goal, it was LBJ who was actually the biggest promoter of NASA and the space projects.

Additionally, the Civil Rights Act was probably almost dead in the Congress while Kennedy was alive. It was his tragic death that allowed the bill to be pushed through against strong opposition from many sides, by LBJ.

Vietnam is also often mentioned. He had an order to withdraw 1,000 'advisors' by Christmas of '63, and many believe that was the start of a total withdrawal from the war. However, it must be remembered that we started with advisors during the Eisenhower administration, and Kennedy had us more involved for over 3 years.

IMO (as everything in this book is), Television was the biggest impact of the Kennedy years. And TV news was the single biggest impact of his Assassination.

Kennedy was the first to use Television on a regular basis. He and Nixon had the first televised debates, Jackie gave a televised tour of the White House, and Kennedy had regularly televised press conferences. (I recommend the video "Thank You, Mr. President", which shows Kennedy's wit and intelligence in these press conferences.)

On the weekend of the Assassination, TV news went live the entire weekend. This was a first for national television news which was not much of a player in the weekly TV schedule.

After that weekend, it became a nightly show on all 3 of the major networks. The book, "When The News Went Live" by Dallas newsmen Wes Wise, Bob Huffaker, George Phoenix and Bill Mercer covers this event from a TV news viewpoint.

Rather than re-invent the wheel on this chapter, I am cutting and pasting a "white paper" that I wrote and never published. I used to give a copy to history teachers that I knew had such assignments, as I felt I should have to write one also. It was never published anywhere, but I do think I had it on my web page for a while, and wanted the teacher to be able to detect if some student had simply copied it.

The 1960's were arguably the biggest decade of cultural change this country, and the world, has ever had. The 1910's had World War I; the 1920's prohibition; the 1930's the Great Depression; the 40's World War II; and the technological changes of the 1980's and 1990's with computers and cell phones. However, the 1960's had the largest social changes, in addition to the space-race, and other technical changes.

JFK Assassination: Shades From The Fence

The Kennedy Legacy

I am a Dallas historian, and also a member of the Dealey family, after whom Dealey Plaza was named. Of course, in November of 1963, President John F. Kennedy was shot and killed in Dealey Plaza. I am a member of the JFK Assassination Research community, and attend many of the functions and conferences about the Assassination. In addition, I frequently give tours of the related sites around Dallas. I am often asked what Kennedy's biggest legacy was.

Many would say the Space Race and the landing on the Moon by the Unites States in 1969. Kennedy was a strong supporter of NASA, as was his Vice President, Lyndon B. Johnson. Kennedy also made the famous speech which set the goal of landing an American on the moon by the end of the 1960's, a feat which was accomplished in the summer of 1969.

Civil Rights was also a major issue which came to the forefront during Kennedy's presidency. However, many feel that the Kennedys were dragged into Civil Rights, and did little on their own in this area. The 1961 Freedom Rides, the 1962 incidents at the University of Mississippi, when James Meredith tried to enroll, and the 1963 attempt of black students trying to attend the University of Alabama, virtually thrust this issue into the lap of John Kennedy. He did come forward and make some major speeches on Civil Rights, and started legislation to pass the 1964 Civil Rights Act.

Television was the main legacy of the Kennedy presidency, and, unfortunately, his Assassination.

John Kennedy was the first President (and candidate) that seemed to fully understand the power and capabilities of television. Although Eisenhower appeared on television a few

JFK Assassination: Shades From The Fence

times, he never utilized it as well as Jack Kennedy. Kennedy handily won the Kennedy / Richard Nixon debates to the television audience, as he came across as healthy and confident, compared to a weak Nixon image. In addition, Kennedy was the first President to hold weekly television news conferences. Jackie also did tours of the White House and other television interviews. They both seemingly had an inherent understanding of the power of television, and showed their youth and cultural elegance to a wide audience. It also helped that they had young children in the White House, although Jackie strove to keep their privacy.

Unfortunately, Kennedy's Assassination was also a major television event. That 3 day weekend was the first time that television went live for such a long period of time. Television news "came of age" during that weekend, with millions of Americans following every change as it occurred. Even the live shooting of Lee Harvey Oswald on CBS, showed what television news was capable of.

It should be remembered that even Walter Cronkite, America's most trusted newsman, was only on about 15 minutes a night, prior to September of 1963. They expanded to 30 minutes that month, with NBC soon following suit. ABC did not expand until after the Kennedy assassination, once the power of television news was better understood.

The Assassination of President Kennedy has at least 3 cultural changes tied to it. In addition to television news coming of age, there was a major emptiness felt by the American people at the death of a young, healthy, vibrant President. This sadness was partially filled by the British Invasion in music, which quickly helped the younger people of our country recover. Yet, it did not fully satisfy the loss of the idealism that the Kennedy years seemed to inspire. Even those who did not particularly like John Kennedy and his policies felt this loss and emptiness after his tragic assassination.

142

JFK Assassination: Shades From The Fence

For many, the 3rd cultural change that the Assassination caused was one of distrust of the federal government. For many, it was a distrust of LBJ, but for most of us it was the idea that the Warren Commission had not told us everything. This was compounded by the announcement of the sealing of the records for 75 years. This naturally led many to simply assume that there was some secret the government was hiding.

William Manchester, in his book "Death of a President" came forward with a weak minded idea that people need a great villain to commit a great crime. This theory says that people don't believe Lee Harvey Oswald did it, because it makes them feel better to believe there had to be a larger villain behind it. Although I have heard other offer this feeble theory since then, I feel that it is hogwash, and even those who make this statement do not believe it. We had just gotten past the Cuban Missile Crisis, and other confrontation with the Soviet Union over Berlin, it was the height of the Cold War, and Lee Harvey Oswald was a pro-Castro, pro-Russian, MarxistLeninist who had defected to the Soviet Union once already. Quite simply, to any logical person, that spells conspiracy. Whether actual or not, the idea of conspiracy in this situation is natural, and not because a "great villain" would "make us feel better".

Who was Feeding Whom?

After the Assassination, the television industry started working very hard to improve its own capabilities. The weekend of November 22, 1963, had shown the networks how an expanded, more mobile news force and technical capabilities were needed. Along with expanded time each evening, and expanded technical capabilities, such as sound film and mobile cameras, they started searching for news stories. They needed more news to fill this time, and the added nighttime, lunch and morning news shows they were putting on the air.

JFK Assassination: Shades From The Fence

Prior to 1960, the Press was much more selective in what they would put in a newspaper, magazine, radio, or on television, and the Presidency was a respected institution. Kennedy's 'dalliances' with other women were off limits, as were the little problems with previous Presidents and their administrations. Care was taken to represent the Presidency carefully, and newsmen often overlooked any little discrepancies (such as FDR's alleged affair).

But with the competition that grew after 1963, almost every story was fair game. From LBJ's dog being lifted by its ears, to LBJ's surgical scars, almost everything came pouring out into our living rooms, to fill the additional time. In addition, the distrust that many Americans had of the government also was shared by some of the news media, so many started searching for problems and lies. Because of competition, the day of "looking the other way", and selfcensorship, was long gone. The Press went into major competitive mode, and anything was likely to be aired to fill the time, and to get a leg up on the competition.

This pouring out of news stories into our homes grew as the decade progressed. The race riots and other violent stories came across the airwaves, and a rather prodigious flow. The worst of this were the stories and film out of the jungles of Viet Nam. Americans, who had suffered disillusionment at the Assassination of John Kennedy, were flooded with images of war, death and other violence across our nation. This lead to further fear, disillusionment, and a general feeling that our government had lost whatever control it may have once had.

The "counter culture" (or anti-Establishment) movement grew from this. The baby boom generation was basically weaned on television. They are considered the generation from 1946 to 1955, and with the creation of television in 1948-9, most do not even recall the "radio days". They got their news, and entertainment from television. As these people saw the problems presented by television news spill into their living rooms, the distrust of the government and emptiness from the Assassination grew. They saw problems with America, that the "establishment" just seemed to be unable to answer, or solve. The main problems were Civil Rights, and the Viet Nam war.

It is not television news fault that these events occurred, but the television and the events happening in the country seemed to feed each other. As events happened, the television news would simply put them into our living rooms, as we had a right to know. When America saw these events, they would get disillusioned and often angry, when they would express this anger, television news would be right there to record it, and feed it to others. It was a vicious cycle, that was not anyone's particular fault.

It ballooned into such events as: Viet Nam, the race riots, Kent State, the death of Martin Luther King Jr. and Bobby Kennedy, the 1968 Democratic convention protests in the streets of Chicago, and on and on. It caused many to simply 'drop out' and try to find a better answer, and caused others to embrace violence. The Hippie movement was also a by product of the television coverage these 'drop outs' attracted. It promoted music, drugs and dropping out of the American establishment. It highlighted in Woodstock, and at the same moment, the murders done by the Manson clan.

Actually, the protests were a good thing, in that they showed that people still believed they could change something. It was only after the disillusionment of the 1970's, and Watergate, that the public seemed to feel that they could not change anything. In many ways this apathy of the 70's was much more depressing, than the idealistic protests and statements of the 60's.

JFK Assassination: Shades From The Fence

Government erodes its own credibility

As mentioned, the Kennedy Assassination and the report by the Warren Commission started many in America to start to distrust their government. This was compounded by the television news stories that spilled into our homes. After the Warren Report, New Orleans District Attorney Jim Garrison brought an ill advised trial of businessman Clay Shaw. Although Shaw was acquitted, the Garrison investigation questioned many of the facts of the Warren Commission, and gave the public the suppressed Zapruder film of the Assassination. These doubts generated caused the Clark Panel to review the medical evidence of the assassination, which revealed that much of the evidence had been "lost".

Television news fed upon this distrust, and along with the Washington Post and other members of the press, uncovered the Watergate break in, and other abuses by the Nixon White House. This in turn, fed into the Church Committee to investigate abuses by the FBI and the
CIA. This, in turn, fed into the House Select Committee on Assassinations, to again look at the JFK and Martin Luther King assassinations. These investigations were continually covered by the news media, and help feed distrust into those watching.

Eventually, Watergate became the ultimate turning point in our culture. Those that had protested, in the belief that they might actually change things, were quickly disillusioned, and gave up. The public lost respect for our higher offices, and the protests slowed as being useless. The Press soon felt their job was to report on the abuses of those in power, instead of reporting only facts and events. The more the Press took on the role of "watch dog", instead of simply reporting the facts and hard stories, the more the public were dissatisfied. This dissatisfaction was also aired, which further fed the distrust. Of course, this would be later compounded by 24hour cable news, where even opinions are aired, and every little story is likely to be blown way out of proportion.

Loss of innocence? Or lack of communication?

In the days prior to television news "coming of age", we lived in a simpler time. People lived their lives more locally. They got their news from the local newspaper, and the national news was more remote. They learned their values from their parents, their church, and their community. Their entertainment was radio, and movies.

Television was a simpler, more innocent entertainment medium at first, with selfimposed values and censorship. The most popular shows, such as the "Honeymooners" (195556) or "I Love Lucy" (1951-57) would not even show the bedrooms on their early shows. Even when the bedroom was finally shown on television, the husband and wife had twin beds: "The Dick Van Dyke Show" (1961-66). Controversial shows, such as "The Smothers Brothers Comedy Hour" (1965-67) were actually cancelled and taken off of the air, when they became too controversial in their criticism of the government and the Viet Nam war.

With Viet Nam, the Race Riots and the campus protest violence, such as the Kent State tragedy, spilling into our living rooms on the national news every night, such innocence was quickly lost. Some shows, such as "Rowan & Martin's Laugh-In" (1968-71) started out as
"silly", but soon developed an edge that protested the problems with the establishment. "All in the Family" (1971-79) and other shows of the 1970's, soon reflected this more edgy sophistication, and deteriorating family values. We "grew up" and our "teacher" was the violence, hate and war spilling from our television sets each night. Sex and violence became a

mainstay of prime time programming, with the public being used to the violence from the news.

Cable TV, and 24-hour news channels have compounded this education. They now compete with anything that might be considered news, or even news related. Opinions are now broadcast, to fill the time, by an industry that used to validate facts, and report events. The recent problems of Dan Rather show how information can now get on the air, that is not properly validated and confirmed before hand. It is the result of the competition, and television news' current role of being America's "watch dog". With so many channels that satellite and cable provides, the competition becomes much more fierce. Consequently, the more sensational shows and news is sought.

This is now compounded with the Internet. Now, we can get our news any time of day, even with a cell phone or other device that we carry around with us. Since anyone can put their opinions on the Internet, like on a Blog, we have no way of knowing how accurate anything is anymore. Television is trying to compete with the Internet, and only has the edge in the quality of its productions. But the Internet is catching up, and has the advantage that anyone may now decide what others should see and hear. Its content is no longer controlled by network and news executives. Of course, in competition's name that control had largely been lost a long time ago.

Once opened, Pandora's Box can never be closed. The same is true for the cultural change that television and advanced communications has brought. Once available, nobody would want to go back to that slower, more sheltered time.

In this election year, we have 2 candidates that are now pronouncing "change" as their slogan. One is an African-

American, while the other has a woman as a Vice-President running mate. Regardless of which side wins, there will be "change". (Paper written in 2008.)

I cannot help but look back on the "change" brought by the Kennedy Presidency, and wonder what the near future will hold.

12. The Witnesses

So, we will start to go into details about the JFK Assassination. The Tippit shooting will not be covered in detail, but mentioned. We will discuss the major witnesses in Dealey Plaza and that worked in the Texas School Book Depository.

First of all, witnesses are never as reliable as we would like. They are not computers or video cameras recording every detail of an event. They are human beings trying to recall what they saw and when they saw it. Time and memory will influence them a great deal. They are also subject to the influence of others, and the emotions of the event.

Even then, whatever statement a single witness makes must be evaluated and compared (or corroborated) with other witness statements. Memory and what people notice are certainly different.

The Tippit shooting has a prime example of this: Virginia Davis and Barbara Davis were sister-in-laws who lived in the corner house at 10th and Patton. They were relaxing in their living room, when they heard the sounds of the shots. They hopped up and both looked out the front screen door, and saw the shooter walking across the front of their house on the sidewalk, and cut across the corner of their yard.

Even though they both saw only 1 man, Virginia's testimony says he was wearing a light tan jacket, while Barbara's says it was black. They did NOT see 2 individuals. In fact, the jacket found behind the gas station that afternoon is kind of a off-white gray (WC exhibit 162). Of course, some Researchers believe this means it was NOT Oswald, since the color is incorrect. However, it is much more likely that the 2 different ladies were simply focused on other things, or had forgotten this minor detail.

The colors of the jacket are different among the many Oak Cliff witnesses that saw it. This does NOT mean there were a bunch of different men shooting Tippit, like some like to believe. Nor does it mean that the witnesses' statements should simply be thrown out because Oswald was wearing a different color than what a particular witness says. In fact, all of the witnesses corroborate that the shooter was wearing a jacket, and thus strengthen the case that Oswald was the shooter since he left his rooming house with a jacket, was not wearing one in the theater, and a jacket was abandoned.

Many Researchers will simply focus on these errors, and try to tell you that it means they were "lying" or saw different men. Often the Researcher will be very selective on which witness they choose to use, and believe that if they can discredit any part of his testimony, he is therefore unreliable. ONE witness is unreliable, and nobody should ever be convicted because of one witness' statement. However, if several witnesses see the same thing, even if a few discrepancies exist, it is highly likely they saw the same person.

The Texas School Book Depository (TSBD) Employees

Dallas Police Chief Jess Curry said, "Nobody's yet been able to put him (Oswald) in that building with a gun in his hand." He was not seen by anyone who could positively identify him, such as a co-worker, with a rifle or long package in the building. A shooter was seen in the window by several people in the Plaza, but they did not know Oswald and would not positively identify him in a line up.

So, much of what we have as far as TSBD employees is what they did NOT see.

Buell Wesley Frazier and Linnie Mae Randle

The exceptions to this are Buell Wesley Frazier and Linnie Mae Randle, who knew Oswald and saw him with a long package that morning, before he went into the building.

Oswald had gone 'home' to the Ruth Paine house with Frazier on Thursday, Nov. 21. He normally went on Fridays, and returned on Mondays. When Frazier asked him about this, he said he had to pick up some curtain rods for his rooming house. Frazier gave him the ride and did not suspect anything.

That Friday morning, Frazier's sister was at the kitchen window when she saw Oswald carrying a long package towards Frazier's car. She mentioned to Frazier that Lee was outside, so Frazier quickly grabbed his stuff and went out to drive to work. Frazier glanced at the package in the back seat, and asked Oswald about it. Oswald said they were the curtain rods he had mentioned the day before, so Frazier thought no more about it. Both Randle and Frazier would later recall that they thought the package was a little over 2 feet.

When they parked the car by the north warehouse, Frazier stayed to rev up the engine and charge up his battery a little. Oswald went ahead, and after several seconds Frazier followed him.

He later said he could not see much of the package cupped in Oswald's right hand. He believed it was tucked into Oswald's armpit, but later said in the London Trial that it could have been in front of Oswald's shoulder, or under his jacket in front. Oswald always stayed more than 50 feet in front of Frazier, and went in first.

It was simply not something that Frazier was really paying attention to. Frazier might have seen Oswald at times that morning, while both were working, but could not say for certain in his testimony. He never saw the long package again.

Frazier would tell Researcher Gary Mack, during a interview, that he did see Oswald after the shooting turning the NorthEast corner of Houston and Elm Streets. Oswald was walking south and turning east, as if he had come from the dock area of the TSBD. However, Frazier is unclear about how much of Houston St. he saw Oswald walk, so Oswald could simply be avoiding the crowds instead of coming all the way from the dock.

Frazier eventually wrote a book in 2019-2020, along with his son Rob Frazier. Buell came to my office in 2019, and I spent a couple of hours going through all of the photos I had of the interior of the TSBD, which I specialize in. The book is mainly about his entire life, and only some about the JFK Assassination. However, he does tell a story that he had never disclosed before, about how after the Assassination he went down Elm St. towards the parking lot, and encountered a man with a rifle coming towards him.

Jack Dougherty

On April 8, 1964, Jack Dougherty gave his testimony to Warren Commission's Joseph Ball. He stated that he was at the wrapping table, and saw Oswald come in the back door "out of the corner of his eye". He did not recall seeing Oswald carrying anything as he came in. (Just as I doubt the reader can say exactly what your own co-worker had in the hands last Friday.)

He states the last time he saw Oswald was around 11:00 AM, while Dougherty was getting stock off of the 6th floor. Dougherty also ate his lunch in the 1st floor domino room, between 12:00 and 12:30.

He returned to work around 12:30, and was on the 5th and 6th floor retrieving stock for an order. He says he was on the 5th floor when he heard a 'shot' sound. He was about 10 feet from the elevator. He did not see anyone, and would get on the west elevator and go down to the 1st floor with the books. There he would encounter Janitor Eddie Piper who would inform him that the President had been shot.

Some Researchers insist that if Dougherty did not see Oswald with a package, then Oswald did not bring one into the building. It may simply be that Dougherty did not notice the package, or Oswald could have stashed it in the shipping building between the back door and the dock, to retrieve it later that morning when the "coast was clear".

Researchers also question why Dougherty did not see Oswald cross the 5th floor, if he were only 10 feet from the elevator. Dougherty was working, and not simply standing by the stairs/elevator observing others. Photos of the 5th floor show a large set of shelves just south of the stairs and elevator areas, that blocks the view of the stairs area.

JFK Assassination: Shades From The Fence

There are many reasons why someone does not see something. Again, they are not video cameras focused on an area of access/transit. They are humans engaged in their own activities, thoughts and area of attention.

Charles Givens

Charles Givens was one of the warehouse workers who was working to overlay the floor boards with plywood that morning on the 6th floor. Unlike what is shown in the movie "JFK", the group of workers overlaying the floors were all employees. There was not any outside work crew working inside the building.

They stopped working a little before noon, and raced the 2 elevators down. Also in the crew were Supervisor William Shelley, Bonnie Ray Williams, Bill Lovelady, and Danny Arce. Many of them stated that they saw (or heard) Oswald on the 6th floor asking them to close the gate on the west (automated) elevator, so that he could call it back up.

Once Givens got down to the 1st floor, he realized that he had left his jacket on the 6th floor, with his cigarettes in it. He took the east elevator back up to retrieve them. As he was leaving the 6th floor, he saw Oswald walking north along the east aisle, with a clipboard in his hand. Givens asked Oswald if he was going to break for lunch, and Oswald said he might in a bit. Oswald asked Givens to make sure the west elevator gate was down, so that he could call it. When Givens got down to the 1st floor, the elevator was gone.

Givens states that he talked briefly to James Jarman Jr. and Harold Norman, once on the 1st floor. He left the building, and walked a few block away to visit a friend of his. He would later initially have trouble re-entering the TSBD once it was sealed. He also was a person of interest for the Dallas police when they realized he was missing. Law enforcement knew him because of some trouble he had gotten into, in the past.

JFK Assassination: Shades From The Fence

Bonnie Ray Williams

Bonnie Ray Williams was actually based as a warehouse worker at the Texas warehouse a few blocks north of the TSBD. However, he had been reassigned to the TSBD location to assist while they were overlaying the floors with plywood. He was one of the people who raced the elevators down that day, and did not really know Oswald that well. He was friends with Harold ("Hank') Norman and James ("Jr.") Jarman. These 3 individuals would be right below the 'sniper's nest' during the shooting, on the 5th floor.

Williams and the others had discussed the Motorcade coming by that day, and that the 6th floor would be a great place to watch the event from. After Williams cleaned up and grabbed his lunch, he returned to the 6th floor thinking that the others would join him there. He arrived on the 6th floor around 12:10 or so, and ate his chicken lunch in the 3rd and 4th set of windows from the east. (Sniper's nest was the 1st and 2nd set.) He was there about "5, 10 or 12" minutes, and left around 12:20 to find the others. He took the elevator down to the 5th floor, and found Jarman and Norman there. He saw or heard nobody, while on the 6th floor.

Harold Norman and James Jarman

These 2 workers were friends with Williams, and usually played dominoes in the 1st floor "Domino Room" in the mornings and during lunch. On this day, they went to the domino room after cleaning up, got their lunches and were standing on the 1st floor close to the front door eating. They heard on a police radio that the Motorcade was on Main St. (starting about 12:20-3), so had enough time to go back upstairs and get a bird's eye view of the motorcade. They went around the building to the dock, and took an elevator up to the 5th floor. Here, they met Bonnie Ray Williams and the 3 of them knelt down in the 3 eastern windows to watch the Motorcade.

"Jr." was the name given by Oswald during Fritz's interrogation as one of the people who "walked through" the Domino Room during Oswald's eating his lunch there, according to Oswald's alibi. Some have stated that he could not know this unless he was actually there to see it. However, he had been working there for almost 5 weeks, and would know the patterns of most of the warehouse workers, who also kept their lunches in the window of the domino room. It is obviously not a very strong alibi, in my opinion.

After the shooting, the 3 5th floor witnesses went quickly to the west facing windows to see if they could see the Motorcade, or shooters, etc. They lingered there for several minutes, and Williams did see Manager Roy Truly and Officer Marion Baker cross part of the 5th floor, from the stairs coming up from the 4th to the eastern elevator. None of the 3 saw Oswald, or any other shooters.

Billy Lovelady

Billy Lovelady was also one of the workers who was overlaying the floorboards on the 6th floor. He saw/heard Oswald as they were racing the elevators down, a little before noon.

Lovelady was standing out front of the TSBD, in the porch at the top of the front steps. He was there with about 10 other TSBD employees. Over the years, these 10 have listed who they recall were out there with them, and none have said Oswald was out there.

Lovelady and the others can be seen in the background of the Altgens 6th photo, and since Lovelady resembled Oswald, many Researchers believe that Oswald the one in the photo. (See chapter on Alterations and Logistics.)

Mrs. Robert Reid (Geraldine)

Geraldine Reid worked on the 2nd floor of the TSBD. Her desk was towards the back of the 2nd floor. She was the Clerical Supervisor, and would often make change for the warehouse workers so that they could use the Coke machine in the 2nd floor lunchroom, or the Dr. Pepper machine on the 1st floor by the stairs. She did not know Oswald well, but sometimes gave him change. She stated she did not give Oswald change, nor see him that day.

She ate her lunch in the 2nd floor lunchroom, with the "usual girls". The ladies would usually eat lunch in there, while the warehouse workers would usually use the domino room on th 1st floor. She says that the several ladies left the lunchroom earlier, so they could go out front to watch the Motorcade. She was running a little late, and left almost 12:30. She did manage to get out front, just before the Motorcade came into Dealey Plaza. None of these ladies reported seeing Oswald in the 2nd floor lunchroom.

After the shooting, she went back up to the 2nd floor, so that she could call her husband and tell him about it. As she was crossing the office area of the 2nd floor, she saw Oswald coming out from the lunchroom area, and coming towards the front of the building. She stated she said that President might have been shot, and that Oswald mumbled something back that she did not catch. Oswald had a Coke in his hand.

Caroline Arnold

One of the most intriguing TSBD witnesses is Caroline Arnold. She is mentioned most often as the witness who had seen Oswald in the 2nd floor lunchroom around 12:25; indicating he was not upstairs in the sniper's nest. However, this statement is highly controversial and unreliable, IMO.

Ms. Arnold was never interviewed by the Warren Commission, nor by the House Select Committee on Assassinations. She is shown in the movie "JFK" as being a witness and testifying in the New Orleans trail of Clay Shaw. However, this is Hollywood liberties, as she did not testify in that trial. (Hollywood embellishment?)

She made her 1st statement to the FBI, on Tuesday, November 26th, 1963. This in itself is a little unusual, as it is the only statement taken after the weekend by a TSBD employee. In this allegedly "sworn" statement to the FBI, she says she might have "caught a fleeting glimpse" of Oswald when looking back at the front door from her spot on Elm St. She said she could not be certain it was him. She puts the time at 12:15.

Like all of the rest of the 73 employees of the TSBD, she made an additional "sworn" statement in April of 1964 (Commission Document 1381). In this document, she states she did not see Lee Oswald that day. Additionally, none of the other employees state they saw Oswald any time in either lunchroom, or out front by the steps.

But in 1978, Researcher John Armstrong and Dallas Morning News reporter Earl Golz allegedly interview Ms. Arnold, and she states she saw Oswald in the 2nd floor lunchroom around 12:25! This is 15 years after the event, in an unsworn statement. It is used most often by Researchers who are dying to prove that Oswald was not on the 6th floor.

To be fair, she says that she is surprised by the contents of her FBI statements. However, knowing that Oswald was taking the blame for the event, and had children and a wife, I find it very hard to believe that she waited 15 years to make the statement that would have spared his family's guilt.

Roy Truly

Roy Truly was the Warehouse Manager, and was also the man who hired Oswald back in the 2nd week of October. He was standing out in front of the building on Elm St. when the shooting occurred.

Right after the shooting, Motorcycle Officer Marion Baker parked his bike on Elm St. and sped into the building. Truly, knowing that the officer did not know the interior of the building, followed him in to assist him. He led Baker into and through the building, within a couple of minutes of the shots,

Baker and Truly encountered Oswald in the 2nd floor lunchroom, buying a Coke. Truly reassured Baker that Oswald was an employee who belonged in the building, so Baker and

Truly left him and continued up through the building to the roof.

Truly would later realize that Oswald (and Givens) was missing, and felt the police should know. He gave Captain Will Fritz the name and address for Oswald from the employee files, before Fritz left the building around 2 PM. Having just seen a gun aimed at Oswald's stomach, he naturally had Oswald on his mind.

Sandra Styles and Vickie Adams

Two other TSBD employees should be mentioned, because they did not see Oswald. Sandra Styles and Victoria Adams were on the 4th floor at the time of the Motorcade, as were several other ladies. After seeing the shooting, they decided to go down the stairs to exit the building. Their Supervisor, Dorothy Garner, walked with them to the mid-building wall that separated the offices in the front of the 4th floor from the warehouse that ran across the back of the building. She saw them go down the stairs, and several seconds later saw Roy Truly and Officer Baker come up and go across to go up to the 5th floor. She saw nobody else on the stairs. Vickie and Sandra also saw nobody else on the stairs, including Baker and Truly!

Now, in the movie "JFK" they imply that they should have seen Oswald coming down from the 6th floor. In the movie they show a "stairwell", instead of single flight stairs that the TSBD had. Many believe that they should have seen Oswald, if he was coming down the stairs. (By the same logic, they should have also seen any "other" shooters.)

Knowing the configuration of the stairs and elevators in the building, it is my opinion, that Oswald crossed the 4th floor by the stairs before the girls cleared the mid-building wall and were able to see the corner. (Not sure how high the stacks of boxes were on 4.) The only place they could descend these narrow, single flight stairs and the narrow path crossing each floor, without seeing any of the 3 men, was if they passed the 2nd floor lunchroom when Baker, Truly and Oswald were all in there.

JFK Assassination: Shades From The Fence

Once again, a prime example of what a witness did NOT see....

Dealey Plaza Witnesses Seeing A 6th Floor Person

The events in Dealey Plaza were highly emotional in many different ways. For most in the crowd that had gathered to see the President and Jackie there was much excitement. During the shooting, there was confusion and trying to understand what exactly the noises were. Afterwards, there was much shock, disbelief and horror, according to what they thought had just happened, reacting to the screams of the crowd and the spoken words of those claiming there were shots and people were hit.

It is difficult for human beings to be precise as to what they see and hear in these types of critical events. Discrepancies are always going to be present, as humans are not recording devices and react and notice different things.

For this book, we are not going into detail about all of the statements about what the crowd saw, source of shots, number of shots, etc. If you want to dig into that, it will take a lot more research in the books I list in the back, and other sources.

However, there were a number of individuals that saw something in the TSBD window(s), or believed they saw Oswald. Unlike the TSBD employees, none of these individuals knew Lee H. Oswald, and would not be able to positively identify him. An individual looking similar to Oswald, such as Bill Lovelady, might be mistaken for Oswald when they see him on television or in the papers at a later time.

Howard Brennan

Howard Brennan was a pipe fitter that had been working on the new Courthouse being constructed at Commerce and Houston. During his lunch, he went to Dealey Plaza and sat on the wall surrounding the north end of the north fountain. He approached Dallas Police Officers at the front of the TSBD soon after the shooting, and said that he saw a man firing a rifle from the corner of one of the upper floors. He gave a description of about 5' 10", age 30, white male, which was broadcast over police radio about 12:45.

He did later attend one of the many lineups, and did not identify Oswald. He later told the story that he did believe Oswald was the man, but was afraid to identify him. He said the Officers told him that they had positive identifications on the Tippit shooting, so Brennan did not feel a very strong pressure to come forward with a positive identification.

Amos Euins

15-year old Amos Euins attended a school that allowed their students to leave, if they wanted to go and see the Motorcade that day. He was standing behind a concrete block on the rail wall by the north reflecting pool.

Before the limo had turned onto Elm St., Euins noticed a "pipe" sticking out of an upper floor window. At the sound of the 1st shot, he looked around to find the source of the sound. He saw the "pipe" as the 2nd shot was fired. Euins ducked behind the concrete, and saw the 3rd shot also. He states that he only saw the shooter's hands: one on the trigger and the other on the "barrel thing".

Amos ran to the grassy knoll railroad yards because a number of policemen were going that way. There, he told Sgt. D. V. Harkness what he had seen. Harkness gave him a lift sitting on the back of his Patrol 3-wheeler to Houston, where he placed him in Captain Sawyer's car to be taken in for a statement.

Arnold and Gena Rowland

Mr. Rowland had come to Dealey Plaza with his fiancé to watch the motorcade. They were located on the east side of Houston St. close to the Elm St. corner. They were discussing the security present, and about 12:15 he noticed a man in an upper floor corner window of the TSBD. The man was holding a rifle, with a scope on it. He pointed it out to her, and they decided it was a security person, possibly the Secret Service. He felt the man was a thin, light skinned latino or Caucasian, with black hair, wearing an open light shirt and a t-shirt on underneath. He was 'standing' 3-5 feet back from the window, and Rowland could only see the upper 2/3rds of him. (Low windows, so a sitting person would look to be standing.)

When he tried to point the man out to his fiancé, he had disappeared back into the shadows, and she never saw them. He stated the time to be about 12:22 or so. He also states that he saw a colored man in the west corner of the same floor briefly at about that time. (Bonnie Ray Williams?) He also saw multiple people looking out various windows and floors in the building.

Tom Dilliard and Bob Jackson

Tom Dillard was in an open car several cars back in the motorcade (position #6). They were approaching the TSBD on Houston when the shots sounded. Bob Jackson mentioned that a rifle was being drawn back into the building, and Dillard quickly raised his camera and got a shot of the front. However, by that time the rifle had drawn back in and nothing discernible can be seen in Dillards photo on the 6th floor. The 3 workmen on the 5th floor are clearly discernible, since they were leaning out of the windows into the sunlight.

Pierce Allman and Robert MacNeil

Dallas Radio Newsman Pierce Allman was covering the Motorcade in Dealey Plaza when the shots rang out. After his initial shock, he started looking for a telephone so that he could call the news into his radio station. Within minutes he went to the door of the TSBD, where he believes he ran into Lee Oswald leaving the building. Oswald pointed into the building, to a telephone, and then leaves. We do have an audio recording of Allman's report, with him inside the building and out of breath.

JFK Assassination: Shades From The Fence

Robert MacNeil, of PBS' MacNeil / Lehrer Report also tells of getting directions to a phone from Oswald at the front door, within minutes of the shooting.

James Worrell

A bystander at Elm And Houston St., James Richard Worrell Jr., also gave Dallas Police an affidavit that day. In it he says he was standing against the building when he heard a sound he thought might be a fire cracker. He looked above his head and saw a pipe sticking out a window several floors above him. As he was looking, he saw the barrel discharge another shot. As he ran away in fear, he heard "two more shots". He ran north to Pacific street past the TSBD dock area. After he turned around he saw a white male (5'10", dark hair, open shirt or jacket to his waist) run out of the building and go "the opposite way" (towards Elm?). The man had nothing in his hands.

Roger Craig

Dallas County Deputy Sheriff Roger Craig told that several minutes after the shooting, he was standing across Elm St. from the grassy knoll, and heard a whistle. A man who looked like Lee Oswald runs down the hill on the north side of Elm St. and jumps in a green Rambler station wagon that had stopped on the street briefly to pick him up. Such a station wagon can be seen in several of the photos taken in Dealey Plaza after the shooting. Later that afternoon Craig went to DPD headquarters, where he glimpses Oswald, and tells Captain Fritz about the sighting. Oswald is asked about it, and allegedly says to leave Ruth Paine "out of this", as Ruth also drove a green Rambler. About the time he saw this event, Oswald would have already been on a bus where is former landlady Mary Bledsoe had seen him. Mary definitely knew Oswald, while Roger Craig did not.

Roger Craig would also be part of the law enforcement on the 6th floor when the rifle is found. He hears another officer say it looks like a Mauser, and would later insist that he saw the word Mauser on the top of the weapon. However, the Carcano rifle found had "Made in Italy" stamped on its barrel. Perhaps Craig, who only got a glimpse, mistook the "Ma…" as Mauser, after the verbal suggestion had been heard.

A third controversial thing that Roger Craig also said is that at one point he walked to look into the Sniper's Nest, and saw all 3 bullet casings lined up side-by-side on the window sill/ledge. I can believe this one, as while Studebaker (crime lab) is fingerprinting and processing the sniper's nest, he would naturally lay the casings down, and not try to tip-toe around them on the floor.

Obviously there are hundreds of witnesses in the JFK shooting, as well as dozens of witnesses during Oswald's trek to Oak Cliff, the Tippit shooting, and the Texas Theater. However, for the purpose of this book, we are focusing on the JFK shooting itself, and not the other events of that day. Nor are we going into Oswald's history and life. For those topics, I would refer the reader to the various books listed throughout this one.

JFK Assassination: Shades From The Fence

(For those new to the case, this photo of Dealey Plaza is provided to help you with your bearings. The street going down the center of the grass is Main St. and is a West/East running street. Houston St., by the buildings, runs North/South.)

13. "The Sewer Troll Gets a Lift"

The Kennedy Assassination is very likely the most studied crime in the 20th century. Since it never went to trial, and Oswald never spoke his side of the story (if any) there are many unanswered questions. With the advent of the internet, almost anyone with a computer and any curiosity can do any amount of study they wish. Most, just have a casual interest and expose themselves to movies, documentaries, YouTube videos, books, blogs and groups on Facebook.

Others try to research deeper, and soon find there is a quagmire under those churning waters.

There are simply too many facets of the case that have been raised over the last 58 years for anyone to try to focus on all of it. As I mentioned in the Research Community, if anyone ever claims to be an Expert in the entire Assassination, take a firm grip of your wallet and do not let go. They are either kidding themselves, or trying to Con you.

Because of the last name, I have always tried to specialize on Dallas, Dallas' history and politics, and Dealey Plaza itself. My first book, "D in the Heart of Texas" (2002) was simply focused on these topics, with only a mention of the Assassination, and Dallas organized crime figures.

However, over the 25 years of Moderating forums, some of the theories I have heard led me into a different area of specialization: the Texas School Book Depository itself. I have given dozens of presentations on the interior, walking through the building floor by floor, discussing the movements the various investigations have determined, and what witnesses have testified their own movements were.

In 2008, in preparing for such a November in Dallas conference, I got Gary Mack and Steven Fagin, Curators of the Sixth Floor Museum to take full photos of all of the freight elevators as they stand today in the Museum. Gary said I am the only person to ever make such a request. They do have the photos in their archives, if you know what to ask for. (I also still have them, but cannot release without the Museum's explicit permission.)

I also went down the Dallas Public Works Department and got full sewer diagrams and photos of the sewers in Dealey Plaza, both as designed in 1934, and as they are today.

In addition to many of my Conference presentations, the result is the series of "Dealey Plaza Echo" articles that I am reprinting in the next several chapters. This being a book instead of a "Journal" for education purposes, Copyright rules are much different here than "Dealey

Plaza UK" would have faced to do its Journal. Therefore, the following will not have the photos and documents that the Journal might have used, that are not from a government agency.

This first chapter is my first pass at the interior of the building, as well as the storm drains under Dealey Plaza. It was probably launched because of the theories of a storm drain shooter escaping through the drains after the event. Additionally, it just seemed to me that too many were talking about strangers accessing the TSBD, without much understanding of the interior of the building, and the configuration of the stairs and elevators throughout. The actual 1963 TSBD configuration raise multiple concerns about access and planning logistics. As in any endeavor, these logistics must be worked out.

Here is the text of the article, cut-and-pasted here.

First of all, I want to thank my many friends of the Dealey Plaza UK, who recently gave me a *Dealey Plaza UK Honorary Life-Member Award*. I am even more honored that I am probably one of the few, or only, recipients that has not yet made his way over to England to speak. It is either because my charm is so good that it can spread

thousand of miles, or you are still looking for permission to use the name! (If it is the later, you have MY permission, although I cannot speak for all of the Texas Dealeys.) Either way, it is an honor (or should that be honour?).

A number of months ago, my Echo article, "The Ups and Downs of the TSBD" was published. (Book note: the next chapter is that article) In that article, I stated that I hoped to write a follow-up article, which would include new testimony from the HSCA, or other sources.

Unfortunately, there is a dearth of any 'new' evidence, as the HSCA mostly used the Warren Commission testimony. Hence, a follow-up article was not readily forthcoming.

However, at the November in Dallas 2008 conference, I was asked by Deb Conway, Stu Wexler and Larry Hancock, to do a TSBD "Walkthrough" presentation. This was largely due to Larry seeing my ECHO article, and realizing that no NID conference had ever had a walkthrough of the building. (Hard to imagine that something so basic had never been presented.)

In addition to simply walking through the building, using the FBI investigation photos, I did a bit of research to bolster the information I was presenting. Not only did I walk through the TSBD floor by floor, but I presented the history of the Plaza and its buildings, the parking lots, an analysis of the storm drain system, the Dealey Plaza extension, and a focus on the operation of the freight elevators ("LIFTS" for my British friends) within the building and the placement of the people in the building at the time of the Assassination.

Much of the history of Dealey Plaza, and the buildings, is in my book, "D in the Heart of

Texas", and much of the floor by floor / witness location information was in my earlier Echo article. However, a lot of additional information was gathered, which naturally prompts me to put together another Echo article. In this article, I will present a brief overview of information gathered which is not in those previous sources.

JFK Assassination: Shades From The Fence

History

The presentation had a great deal of the history of Dealey Plaza, and the various buildings. Much of this information was from my book, but there were a few items of interest that are not in the book.

Larry Hancock had a brief presentation on the occupants of the Dal-Tex (Dallas Textile) building in 1963, including a couple of unusual, non-textile companies. I therefore focused on the "TSBD", which was built in 1898, as a 5-story building, by the Rock Island Plow Co. Prior to this building, the Rock Island Plow Co. occupied a 4-story building that was across Houston and Elm from this building, where the Records Annex stands today. But in 1901, it was struck by a lightning strike, and burned to the ground. It was rebuilt as a 7-story building, but the passenger elevator in the front of the building continued to only service floors 1-4, with its lift mechanism on the 5th floor.

The building continued to be occupied by the Southern Rock Island Plow Co. until it was purchased in 1939 by Dallas Oilman David Harold Byrd ("DH" or "Dry-Hole" Byrd, as he was known.) In 1940, the Sexton Grocery Supply Co. moved into the building, and occupied it until 1961. Byrd was also an owner of a company called Temco (which my maternal grandfather worked for), which would later merge with Ling and Vought companies, to form LTV Corporation, a military equipment manufacturer.

In late 1961, early 62, the Texas School Book Co. leased the building, and moved in. Up until that time, the TSBC had occupied the "North Houston" warehouse, which was located on Houston and Munger, which is a few blocks north of Elm. (CE361) They had also had their offices on the first floor of the Dal-Tex building. They moved out of the TSBD about 2 years after the assassination. The building then sat empty for many years, when it was acquired by Dallas County in 1977. In 1978, the "Annex" building (railroad shipping building) was torn down, when it was discovered it was on railroad property. The

169

JFK Assassination: Shades From The Fence

Hertz sign was also removed in 1978, and put into storage. The County saved the building by purchasing it, as Byrd intended to raze it.

I additionally covered history of the Plaza, and the Dealey Plaza Annex (the park west of the Triple Underpass). It was the Annex land which George Bannerman Dealey once owned. No area of Dealey Plaza was ever owned by any member of the Dealey family (to my knowledge), but it was named after GB Dealey because of his work in civic improvements. It was named in 1936, and GB had the honor of being in the first car to drive through the Triple Underpass.

The Plaza and the Annex were dug out of the ground in 1934-1936, to create a grand western entrance into downtown Dallas. The 'Grassy Knoll' area constitutes the natural slope of the ground, and the railroad tracks have been there since 1872. They tunneled under the tracks, and the term "Triple Underpass" is the official name. (As shown in the 1934 plans.)

The Annex has curbs which run from the triple underpass between the streets. This median is about 3 feet wide at its narrowest, and about 6 inches tall at the curb. It has been suggested that it was little more than a 'speed bump', or some minor verge, which would be not problem for a motorcade to cross. However, consider how a low-riding limo, motorcycle escorts, press busses, running board ridden convertibles and the other vehicles would have to slow to clear such an obstacle.

Storm Drains

The storm drains, and the pipes running under the streets, have long been of interest to Researchers. There has been much speculation and myths about the size of these, and the ability for a shooter to possible escape through them. (There have been actual claims of doing this, by various people, but no photos of films of these people actually trying to get into these pipes.) I therefore went down and worked with the Dallas Engineers in the Dallas Public Works department, to clarify what is down there.

I was allowed to have a copy of the original design drawings of Dealey Plaza, as they were done in planning the Plaza in 1934. This photo is a snapshot of my copy of the plans. In addition, I was allowed to look at the survey/storm drawings they have redone of Dallas in the 1990's. (Under controlled conditions, as these are now kept secure since the Oklahoma City bombing, and other terrorist considerations.)

These show the sewers from the Elm St extension (in front of the TSBD) to be a 15 inch pipe, leading into the manhole area down on Elm St. in Dealey Plaza. This also has a 12" pipe coming into it from the storm drain on the north end of the triple underpass/railroad bridge. The drain pipes then continue along a 15" pipe, to join a 24" (east of the junction) / 30" (west) pipe, in the center of Main St. This 30" pipe continues under the triple underpass, where it is joined by other storm drain pipes on the west side, in the Dealey Plaza Annex. There it expands to 33" and continues to another drain pipe down own the center of Industrial.

JFK Assassination: Shades From The Fence

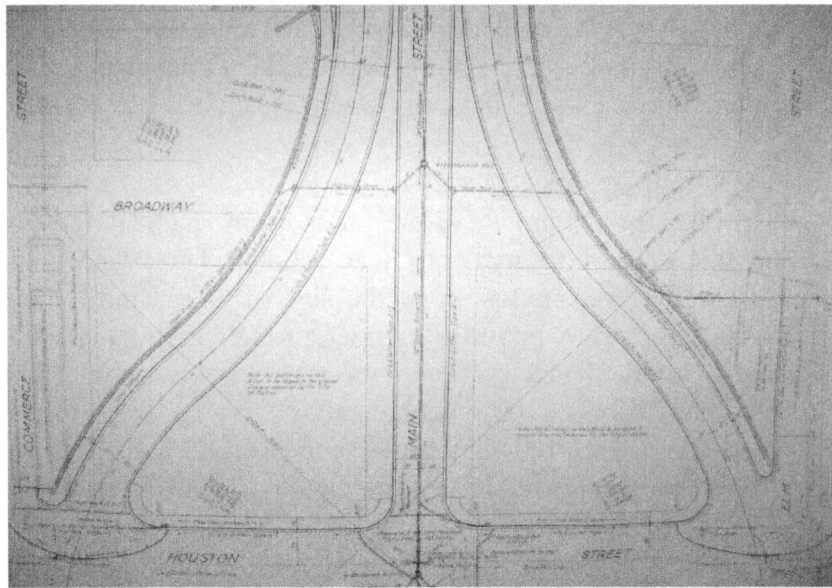

For a number of years there has been a lighter, plastic lid to the man-hole cover in Dealey Plaza, and I have opened it and shown the interior in many of my tours of Assassination sites (even to some of my British friends). However, this last summer, a man injured his leg opening and getting into the storm drain, prompting the City of Dallas to again put in a heavy iron, locked man-hole cover. But as of last spring, I can confirm that the pipes documented in the 1934 plans, as well as the 1990 survey, fit the size of the pipes that I have seen there multiple times. However, here are some photos of /from the interior, as done by Michael Parks for an earlier NID

JFK Assassination: Shades From The Fence

Conference.

North wall of drain showing the 10" feeder from the Knoll.

Inside of drain. Note the 13" feed on the east wall coming from up Elm and Houston plus a 10" feed from the Knoll on the north wall.

Additionally, the angle to make a shot leaves a lot to be desired. It would require the rifle to be actually pushed out of the storm drain to align the barrel with the head shot location, and a shooter to either have some form of 90 degree scope, or to shoot blind. In addition the clearance of the asphalt (today) leaves very little gap for a shot, although the depth of asphalt has undoubtedly grown in the last 45 years. Again, some photos from Michael Parks, showing the view from inside the drain, while getting the camera as far right as possible. Greg Jaynes can be seen from inside the storm drain (in the 1990's), but is actually standing several feet west of the location of the head shot.

Taken from where Zapruder stood showing Greg in the same location as last picture. This would put Kennedy around Z361 as the earliest point seen from the drain. This is a point west of Altgens.

JFK Assassination: Shades From The Fence

Greg Jaynes

From inside the drain looking as far east as possible.
Note Greg Jaynes and the street lamp.

There has often also been speculation about a storm drain on the southern end of the triple underpass. It is assumed that Dealey Plaza was symmetrical in design, and if there is an opening on the north end, there should have been one on the south end as well. Some have speculated that this storm drain has been paved over, and that it existed in 63.

However, there have never been any photos showing such a storm drain, nor is there any record of such a drain in the Dallas Public Works department. None of the available overhead photos of 1964, and later, show such an opening, and no evidence or photo of such a storm drain has ever been produced. Not only does the Dallas Public Works have no record of such a storm drain, but they have 1962 overhead photos of the area, which also does not show such a storm drain. These photos are part of that overhead. The north drain is clearly shown in the left photo (just after the shadow starts), while no south photos shows any such drain.

The above photo is the south end, and the following is the north end of the overpass.

JFK Assassination: Shades From The Fence

I cannot emphatically deny that such a drain ever existed, or that the storm drain pipe sizes were as they are shown in the 1934 plans, the 1990 survey, and as I have seen them myself. However, without any other substantive evidence that they existed, the idea of a storm drain shooter on Elm St., and their ability to escape through the drains, has to be strongly rejected. The "Troll" who lives in those storm drains, can now rest easy that his domain will not be disturbed by tourists. (But I will have my petroleum jelly ready for anyone who wants to try.)

Parking

In preparation of my presentation, I also researched the parking lots. FBI Agent Robert Gemberling did the reports on the Parking lots. Both he, and Deputy Sheriff Roger Craig mentioned a parking lot where the Deputy Sheriffs could pay and park. What threw everyone is a discussion about a locked gate, when no such gate (or chain) can be readily seen in any of the Grassy Knoll parking lot films and photos. But overlooked is this photo taken immediately after the Assassination. There is a fenced gate behind the Dallas Public Works vehicle. This small area is immediately west of the TSBD Annex, and overhead shots show vehicles parked within. This could easily be the area that Gemberling and Craig were speaking of.

I also covered the parking lot where Frazier parked, over by the north warehouse. The photos showing this area, are photos 38 and 39 of Commission Document 496, which is on the Mary Ferrell website. In fact, almost all of the photos on the interior of the TSBD is contained within this document. Some additional photos can be found with the Dallas Police files, and in the book "First Day Evidence".

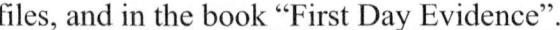

JFK Assassination: Shades From The Fence

TSBD Walkthrough

As part of the presentation, I stepped through all of the photos of CD496 (above). Again, there is little documentation aside from what the FBI provided in this Commission Document. If they were not interested in a floor (such as #3, #4, #5 and most of #7), they simply did not include any photos of that floor. The fifth floor does have some photos made when reviewing Williams, Norman and Jarman's locations in the building. (Which we also looked at.)

Most notable in the photos for this presentation, was the location of the warehouse phone that the 15 warehouse workers were allowed to use. This location is confirmed by Buell Frazier's testimony, where he labeled the location of the phone on a floor plan. The quality of the image is rather poor, but the phone can clearly be seen on the little table in front of the pillar, in the back center of the 1st floor. (CD496 includes floor plans where the direction the camera was shooting is labeled.)

There has never been any photo of a payphone in the 2nd floor lunchroom, and the warehouse people were not supposed to use the phones on the desks of the office workers. If Oswald was in the 2nd floor lunchroom, waiting for a call, he was violating the rules about phone usage

9. MR. TRULY'S OFFICE (MANAGER).

TEXAS SCHOOL BOOK DEPOSITORY
FLOOR PLAN OF FIRST FLOOR

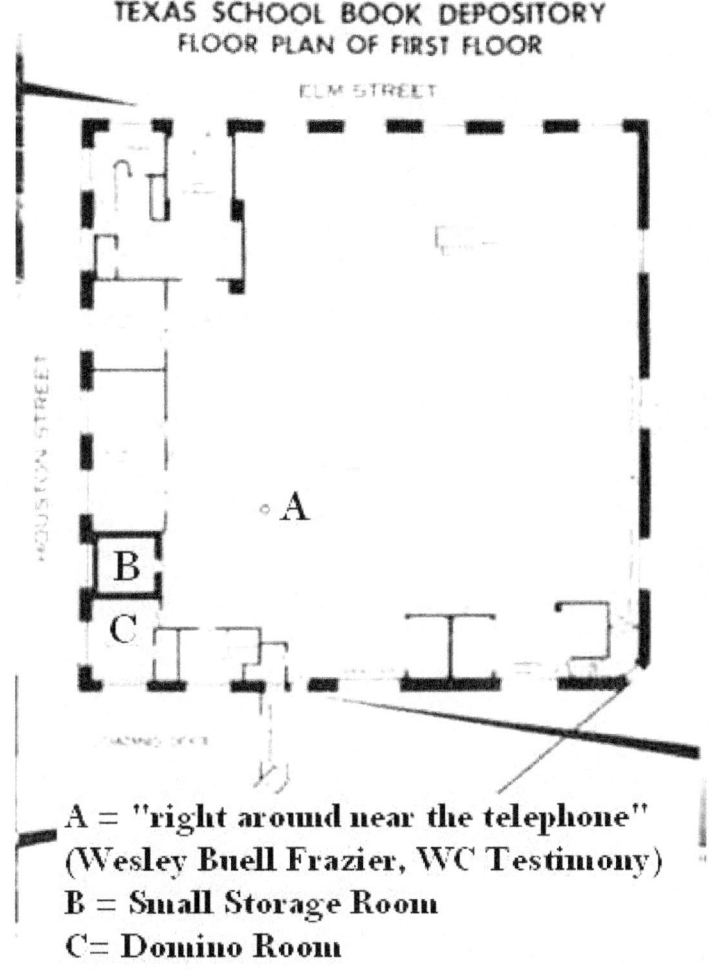

A = "right around near the telephone"
(Wesley Buell Frazier, WC Testimony)
B = Small Storage Room
C = Domino Room

Another interesting note was brought out during the Conference, by Ian Grigg's guest, Paul Wilkins. The 7th floor layout in CD496 states that in the middle back of the floor, there is a "ladder to the roof". This had always puzzled me, as there was what appears to be an extension of the stairway in the NW corner of the roof, like the stairs continued up there. In addition, no overhead shot shows any hatch or opening for this ladder. Former Officer Wilkins confirmed that this was a ladder into an "attic", and not the roof.

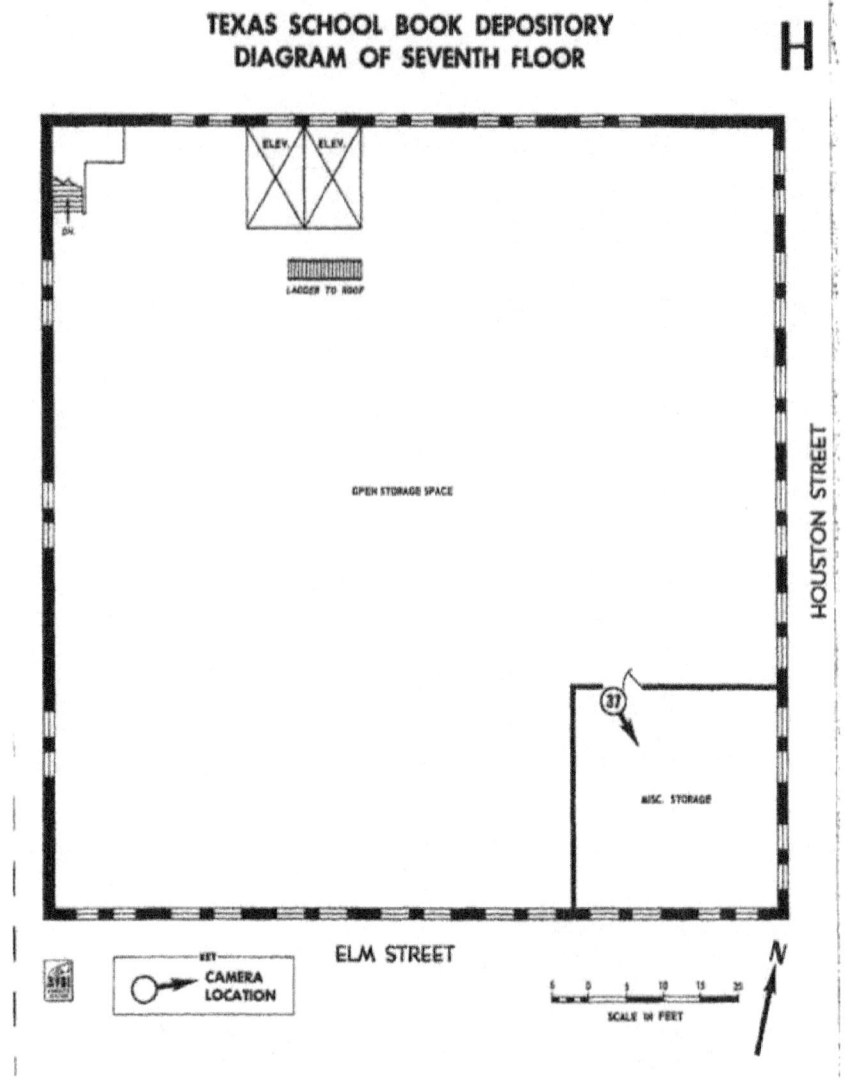

TEXAS SCHOOL BOOK DEPOSITORY
DIAGRAM OF SEVENTH FLOOR

H

A third interesting points is in photo #15 of CD496, which shows the bench in the "Domino Room", laid down so that the dimensions of the hollow bottom is shown. This is never explained why this was of any interest, but it is like the FBI was conjecturing that under this bench could have been a hiding place for the paper wrapped rifle. Also of interest is the FBI photo of the sniper's nest (#32), which is the one that clearly has an airbrushed cartridge. This is one of the 2 taken by the Dallas Police, supposedly before the shell casing were disturbed; however, the FBI version has the apparent alteration.

"Lifts" (hence called Elevators)

None of the FBI, or Dallas Police photos really show much of the freight elevators. Photo 6 of the CD496 shows just the inside south wall of the elevator, and the roll-up gate. ("First Day Evidence" also shows a little glimpse of the elevators, but too small to see much detail.) These photos have prompted a fellow researcher to contact me the last few months on the structure of these elevators. Based on "First Day Evidence", he believed that the elevators were similar to some he used in the US military, with a solid metal slatted outer gate, and a hydraulic "push" system underneath, instead of a lifting system from above. This prompted me to work with Gary Mack to get detailed photos of the interior of the freight elevators, which are now forever stuck on the Sixth Floor. (I showed some of these during my presentation, with permission, but do not have the Copyright to include them here.)

The freight elevators were a dual gate system. The gates were slats of wood, with gaps between them held together by linkage. The outer gate was a full one, which rolled into the holder that is seen above the elevator in photos 6 & 7 of CD496. The inner gate was a ¾ gate, standing about 4 feet from the floor. It lifted into the shaft to open, and the elevators would not move unless both gates were closed (for safety reasons). Additionally, the gates on any other floor would not open if the elevator was not on that floor. (I suppose they could be "jimmied" in some way.)

JFK Assassination: Shades From The Fence

6. FIRST FLOOR LOOKING SOUTHWEST FROM REAR ENTRANCE.

The north wall of the elevator was a complete wall, and the lifting mechanism was attached within that wall. As can be seen in the photos, the south wall was a ¾ wall, and the interior of the elevator shaft could be seen from within it. Additionally, the 2 freight elevators shared a single elevator shaft, and the elevator walls between them was also a ¾ wall, with a wire mesh on the remaining ¼ to the roof. This means that the shaft and other elevator could be seen from within each elevator. (Probably helped when the warehouse guys were "racing" to be able to see where the other elevator was.) With the wooden slatted gates, and the ¼ mesh between both elevators, it was very easy to see through the shaft and gates, to determine if the near, or far, elevator was present. There was no solid gate to obstruct the view, nor was there any problem seeing through either elevator to the other side. (Truly seeing the elevators on the "5th floor" from the 1st, and his knowing at each level if the elevator was present is easier to understand from this description. Hence when he and Baker came out on the 5th floor, he could easily see the elevator on the far (east) side.

184

JFK Assassination: Shades From The Fence

The ceilings of both elevators are a metal roof, with a close pattern of ¼ inch holes. (Perforated metal roof.) In addition, each elevator has a hole of about 10" in the center, with a single light bulb within it. This means that anyone in the elevator can clearly see the elevator shaft above him, and would detect if the other elevator were on a higher floor. (Truly said the western elevator was NOT on 5, 6, or 7, and that it did not pass them while going up to 7.)

These elevators did have a lifting mechanism, housed in the small structure on the roof, as seen in outside photos. They did go all the way down into the basement, as well as all the way up to the 7th floor. The west elevator was the "automatic" elevator that could be called from any floor, providing the gates were closed. It had a panel of pushbuttons for each floor from 7 down to the basement. The east elevator was a manual elevator, where you had to hold the up, or down, button until you got to the floor you wanted. It could not be called, but could only be operated by being in the elevator.

Today, the east elevator also has a full push-button panel in it. It is not documented whether this elevator was updated some time in the last 45 years, or if the panel were moved from the west elevator (which today just has the wiring), to the east elevator for "looks" when considering a JFK Museum. I tried to get Gary Mack to grab a screw driver and take a look behind the panel, to see if the wires were there, but he declined. Fair enough, as I really can't see any purpose in a "Elevator Control Alteration Conspiracy".

As part of the presentation, I also walked through both elevators movements, per the FBI, WC and HSCA. Briefly, here is a review:

11:55-12:00 Both West (auto) and East (manual) are raced to the 1st floor by six of the floor crew employees. Danny Arce says they pass Oswald on 5th floor who asks that they close the gate so he can call the West elevator. They don't do it.

12:05 After Charles Givens has washed up a little, he goes back to the 6th floor in the East (manual) elevator to get his

185

jacket, and cigarettes. He encounters Oswald on the east wall of 6th, who asks him to lower the gate on the West (auto) elevator when he gets back down to the 1st floor. Givens states that he does check the gate when he returns to the 1st floor, but the elevator is gone by the time he gets there. (Does not mention passing the elevator, which he should have been able to see, if he were paying attention.)

12:05 After washing up, getting a Dr Pepper and grabbing his lunch, Bonnie Ray Williams takes the West (auto) elevator to the 6th floor. He possibly passed Givens going down in the East (manual) elevator, although neither man recalls seeing the other elevator.

12:20 James Jarman and Harold Norman had eaten their lunch in the Domino room (as did others), and went in front of the building to watch the motorcade. They state that they heard on a nearby police radio that the motorcade was on Main St., and decided they had time to go back upstairs for a better view. (If they knew about the motorcade route, and knew Dallas, they could have known the location of the motorcade from the radio before Main St. was mentioned, and also known they had time to go upstairs. The first mention of Main St. on the radio transcripts appears to be about 12:23.) They avoided the crowd on the front steps, by going in through the dock, and then up in the East (manual) elevator to the 5th floor.

12:15 to 12:20 (estimated) Bonnie Ray Williams has finished his lunch, and realized that his friends were not going to be joining him on the 6th floor, although it had been discussed that morning as a good vantage point. He then takes the West (auto) elevator down to the 5th floor, where he finds his friends.

12:30 We are unaware of the location of the 2 elevators from the meeting of the 3 guys at 12:20 (or so). That meeting had the elevators on the 5th floor, which is where Roy Truly says the elevators were when he and Baker got to the shaft on the 1st floor, after the Assassination. (I also re-covered Baker and Truly's movements, which are in the earlier article.)

JFK Assassination: Shades From The Fence

12:30 Jack Dougherty has returned to work to fill orders, after having finished his lunch. He says he is working on the 5th floor, filling orders, about 10-20 feet from the West (auto) elevator, when he hears "one shot". After a few seconds, he takes this West elevator down to the 1st floor, where he comes to the front of the building, and is informed about the Assassination by Eddie Piper. He says he never heard Roy Truly calling for the West elevator up the shaft, although Truly and Baker said they lingered long enough to holler up the shaft 2 times.

12:32-34 Baker and Truly emerge onto the 5th floor, and see the East (manual) elevator. Again, this is done quite easily by looking through the wood slat gate, and past the space where the West elevator travels. (Presumably, the West elevator was ridden by Jack Dougherty to the 1st floor, while Truly and Baker are on the steps, or near the 2nd floor lunchroom.) Baker and Truly then take the East (manual) elevator to the 7th floor, and use the steps to go up on the roof. They linger there, and then take the East elevator back down. Tom Alyea films Baker reporting to his superiors on the 4th floor (per Baker). Truly insisted that he did not pass the West elevator while going to the roof, and he should have been easily able to see it, if he had.

It is possible that Oswald, or some other strangers used the elevator within the many gaps of their 'known' locations (per testimony). However, this testimony is very consistent between the various people giving it (Arce, Givens, Williams, Dougherty, and Truly). Any use of the elevators during these periods, would require the elevators being returned to the originating floor, so that the consistency can be preserved. However, the back stairs and the passenger elevator are completely unaccounted for during this entire period (with the exception of Jack Dougherty using the stairs to return to work on the 5th floor).

But consideration has to be made as to the logistics of accessing the building. The only accesses to the building were the front door, and the back door at the dock. The dock and the

JFK Assassination: Shades From The Fence

TSBD Annex building were both enclosed, with a number of overhead doors into the main building. The Annex had a small door on the west side, but this was usually locked, and was in the fenced area that the Deputy Sheriffs used to park. There was also the overhead doors on the dock and Annex (we assume) which were used for shipping, but these were generally closed unless a truck was loading of unloading. (I could find not photos of these doors around the time of the Assassination.)

In addition, the only way to access all of the floors was by using the back stairs or freight elevators. The passenger elevator only accessed up to the 4th floor, and was generally used by the office people. The front stairs only accessed the 2nd and 1st floor.

These back stairs were narrow, single flight stairs. In other words, they had no landing, so once you access a floor, you would have to cross about 20-25 feet of that floor to get to the stairs up to the next level, and so on. This meant that anyone traveling within the building using the stairs, could easily be seen by the normal employees of the building. The 2nd, 3rd and 4th floors were office floors, so they had a wall blocking the view of the back stairs, but the 1st, 5th, 6th and 7th were open warehouse spaces. Of course, stacks of books would also block views of the back stairs.

Other than Danny Arce giving restroom directions to an elderly man, who left before the motorcade arrived, there were no strangers in the building reported by the 75 or so employees. The men laying the 6th floor were all normal warehouse workers, although some of them more frequently worked the north warehouse. Contrary to what Garrison says in "JFK", there were not work crews of outsiders doing the floors.

In addition to these access considerations, the use of the stairs and elevators for the 75 employees during their lunch hour is another difficulty. Any conspiracy group would not have any way of knowing when they would encounter an employee using the elevators or stairs, on their way to lunch. Granted most probably used the front elevator, but there is really no way of telling. Such possibilities would have to be considered by any group of outsiders who were planning on shooting from the building.

Also to be considered, if a group of Conspirators are using the building, and setting up Oswald, as a completely innocent patsy, is Oswald's location itself. If he wanders out into the front of the building to watch the Motorcade, and is photographed, it makes it much more difficult to set him up as a lone patsy. Additionally, if Oswald himself actually spots a "team" of shooters, he himself may quickly move to expose them. Of course, is Oswald was "part of the team", then he might assist them in access the building, and might have even built the sniper's nest wall ahead of time.

I cannot say that these things didn't happen, just ask the reader to consider the complexities and problems involved in planning such a caper. There is certainly plenty of unaccounted for time to get outsiders into and out of the building. It is possible, but does have logistical problems that should be considered.

Other Oswald sightings

As part of the presentation, I also briefly went over the other Oswald sightings in the building that have been mentioned over the years. Many of these were reported years later, and some on that day. Many are contradicted by the testimony gathered by the FBI in 63 and 64, but the reader should consider the FBI evidence carefully, as they have been caught altering evidence on more than one occasion in the case.

Carolyn Arnold's FBI statement of March 19-1964, says that she left the 2nd floor lunchroom with other ladies. For "Conspiracy", and Dallas Morning News , in 1977, she says she saw Oswald alone in the lunchroom around 12:15, and was shocked with what the FBI said she said in 1964.

Mary Hollies' FBI statement of March 19, 1964 says she was not acquainted with Lee Harvey Oswald, but recalls seeing him in the lunchroom in the past. For a magazine (American

JFK Assassination: Shades From The Fence

History Illustrated, November 1988), she states says she saw Oswald that morning and he responded that he had "fishing rods" in the package. She says that right before the Motorcade she was on the 4th floor and Oswald went by them in the freight elevator going up. After the Motorcade he again passed them on the freight elevator, and she thought he went to the first floor. He did not stop either time.

Vickie Adams told the WC that she and Sandra Styles went down the back stairs about 1½ minutes after the shooting. They did not see Oswald, but encountered Billy Lovelady and Billy Shelley as the first people they see on the 1st floor. Lovelady and Shelley said they went into the railroad yards after the shooting, and then went into the back of the TSBD. Sean Murphy has recently had an exchange with Sandra Styles in which she said Vickie gave them a time that was way too short.

Ochus V Campbell, Vice President of the Texas School Book Company (Truly's boss) said that he did not know Oswald, and would not recognize him by sight. However, later that day, he was quoted by a New York newspaper, that Oswald was encountered by a policeman in a small storage room on the 1st floor. Could this be a misunderstanding of information he heard from Roy Truly?

Danny Arce, Harold Norman, Bill Shelley and Bill Lovelady all eat their lunch in the Domino Room on the 1st floor, and then go out front with James Jarman. Jarman had eaten his lunch in the 1st floor entry area, and after getting his cigarettes, Charles Givens eats his lunch in front of the building, before leaving to meet up with a friend a couple of blocks away. None of these people recall seeing Oswald, since passing him on the 5th floor (Danny Arce – the other passengers only heard his voice).

Mrs. Reid and Pauline Sanders eat their lunch in the 2nd floor lunchroom. Mrs Reid says they ate with the "general one that usually eat there with me every day:, but does not specify who these ladies are. They say they leave the lunchroom around 12:15-12:20. Mrs. Reid also sees Oswald as he walks out on the 2nd floor (during the presentation I pointed out her desk, close to the dumbwaiter).

Mrs Donald Walker, Betty Dragoo, Carolyn Arnold, Judy Johnson, Bonnie Richey, Virginia Baker, Georgia Ruth Hendrix, Gloria Holt, Delores Andrews and Joyce Stansbury – all say that they "left" around 12:15 – 12:20, but do not specify if this is leaving the building, or simply leaving the 2nd floor lunchroom. The warehouse workers were certainly allowed to use the 2nd floor lunchroom, and the coke machine was in there (I pointed out the Coke and Dr Pepper machines in the presentation). However, the warehouse workers usually used the Domino Room, where they could be a little more rowdy, while the office workers typically used the 2nd floor lunchroom.

Summary

The information provided in this article, the prior article, and the historical information presented in my book, should all be considered background material in the Research of the Assassination. There is certainly no earth breaking truths being revealed, or anything new that will help us solve the case. However, this is basic structural, historical and logistical information that needs to be considered for everyone who is trying to determine what happened.

I still post on the JFKLancer.com forum frequently, so please let me know if you have any further discussion or questions you want to make. One day, I hope to make it over to the DPUK conference, but so far finances have restricted me from doing so.

14. "The Ups and Downs of the TSBD"

This next chapter is again a reprint of one of my "Dealey Plaza Echo" articles. This first one is about the building, and the movements inside the building based on their affidavits and Warren Commission testimony. MaryFerrell.org definitely has full archival copies of this article in the Echo, for those interested.

Again, this 1st article (of three) focuses on the Warren Commission testimony and version of what happened.

(This article is repetitive of some of the things in the previous article, and I apologize. However, each was to be 'stand alone' so the reader did not have to refer back to previous articles for information.)

The following Walkthrough of the Texas School Book Depository was written for the March, 2008 volume of The Dealey Plaza Echo, the journal of the British Assassination Research group: Dealey Plaza UK. It ran exclusively in that journal, and many months later put, this version was put on-line by Jerry Dealey. Back issues of The Dealey Plaza Echo are available at the Mary Ferrelll Foundation web site: MaryFerrell.org. (To find this article, do a search on the term "Elevator".

The Ups and Downs of the TSBD

The entrances and exits of the Texas School Book Depository in November 22, 1963, along with the stairs and elevators, have always been an interesting sub-topic to me. IF, as many contend, there were other shooters in the TSBD, they would have had to enter and exit the building. Presumably, these would be strangers to the normal workers in the building, and they ran the risk of being seen.

Commission Exhibit 1381 was put together by the FBI, at the request of General Counsel J. Lee Rankin. It contains statements from the 73 TSBD employees that were in the building that day. (And even the statement of Franklin Emmett Wester, who said he was in the north Houston warehouse, and did NOT step foot into the 411 Elm St. building that day.) It excluded 3 employees that were absent that day.

Mrs. Robert Reid, and Pauline Sanders both state they were in the 2nd floor lunchroom that day, and left around 12:15 – 12:20. They do not say who else was in that lunchroom, but Mrs, Donald Walker, Betty Dragoo, Carolyn Arnold, Judy Johnson, Bonnie Richey, Virginia Baker, Georgia Ruth Hendrix, Gloria Holt, Delores Andrews, and Joyce Stansbury all state that they left around 12:15 to 12:20 to watch the Motorcade. Some left the building, while others stayed in the building, so "left" could refer to the lunchroom. How many of these were the

"general ones that usually eat there with me every day" that Mrs. Reid refers to in her Warren Commission testimony is anyone's guess.

There were a number of people who reported staying in the building:

1st floor: Eddie Piper, Roy Edward Lewis (front window) and Troy Eugene West (the shipping wrapper) by back doors.

2nd floor: Geneva L Hines (desk), Carol Hughes (desk)

3rd floor: Stephen Wilson (desk), Doris Ray Burns (walking), Edna Case (desk), Sandra Sue Elerson (window watching Motorcade)

4th floor: Vickie Adams, Sandra Styles, Elsie Dorman (together at windows watching Motorcade), Dorothy

Garner (at her desk by window, with Adams, Styles and Dorman), Mary Hollies and Bettie Foster (together at window watching Motorcade), Yola D. Hopson and Ruth Nelson (together at window watching Motorcade), Ruth Willis (?)

5th floor: Bonnie Ray Williams, Harold Norman and James Jarman Jr.

6th floor: Jack Dougherty (also on 5th floor)

Most of the other employees report that they were outside, in front of the building, or in other locations throughout Dallas.

All of these statements, with the single exception of Danny Arce, say that they did not see any strangers in the building that day. They also discuss if they knew Oswald, and whether they had seen him during that day at any time.

In the movie, "JFK", Director Oliver Stone contends that strangers were in the building, laying the floors of the sixth

JFK Assassination: Shades From The Fence

floor. However, the workers that were doing the floor work were actual employees of the Texas School Book company. These included Bonnie Ray Williams, Danny Arce, Bill Lovelady, and Charles Givens. The contention that there were 'strangers' in the building doing the floor work, is not supported anywhere. (There was one elderly gentleman that went into the front of the building a little while before the Motorcade, to use a restroom. However, he left soon after, according to Danny Arce. –WC Vol6, p366)

First, a quick discussion about "time" and memory. This document is being written in 2007, where we are in the computer age. In addition to computers, we have digital watches and clocks, cell phones that automatically set the time, and watches and clocks that are set by radio wave from the National Institute. Back in 1963, it was a much different world. These capabilities were not available to the average person, and they generally estimated time, based on when TV shows started, or other criteria. Additionally, when they looked at a clock, they tended to estimate the time on the face. It is not uncommon for someone to say that they did something at 12:30, when in reality they probably did it around 12:15 and 12:20. Additionally, they did not know at the time of these events (such as leaving the lunchroom) that the time would later become a critical factor. Of course, memory of these events will naturally be "fuzzy", and it is unreasonable to assume that if someone says a time that conflicts with other motions, that person is automatically lying or trying to hide something. These were real world events, and the average person in 1963, was not operating by a stopwatch.

This document will attempt to follow the movements on the freight elevators and stairs according to the testimony given the Warren Commission by the employees. Of course, the FBI, Secret Service and Dallas Police also interviewed these employees, and I hope to supplement these movements from those reports at a later date. It should be remembered that the Warren Commission talked to these employees in the spring of

1964, and by that time they could easily have modified or been influenced in their recall of the events.

First, let us start with a floorplan of the 1st floor of the Texas Schoolbook Depository, and discuss all of the features.

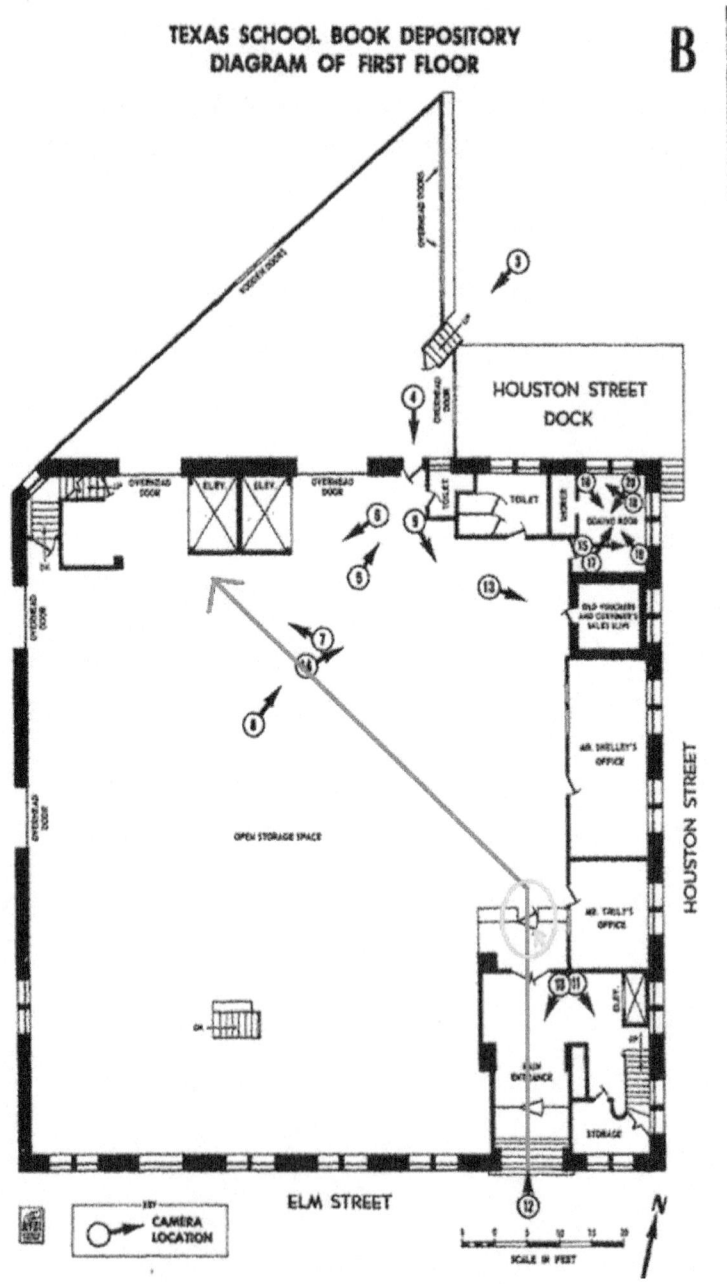

The primary outside entrance into the Depository, were the 2 sets of double glass doors on the south side of the building. Immediately east (right) of this entrance was a set of stairs that only went from the first to the second floor. In this lobby area by the entrance, there was also a small passenger elevator, which only went as high as the 4th floor. (The TSBD was originally built in 1895 as a 5 story building. This elevator was installed with the lift equipment on the 5th floor. After the building burned in 1901, they rebuilt it and added the 6th and 7th floor.) The passenger elevator serviced the office personnel who worked on the first through fourth floors. Although they would use the other elevators on occasion, these were generally left for the order fillers' use. All employees used the stairs.

In the second glass doors from this lobby area, there is a "Will Call" counter (circle), with a half door and a latch which swings towards the entrance. To the left of this lobby area, were a set of stairs that went into the basement. There was no outside access to the basement.

There was also a door on the north side of the building, which opened out onto the dock area. In addition, there were a series of 4 'overhead' doors on the north and west walls. These would be locked from inside, but would be opened as needed to reach the dock, and the "TSBD Annex" building on the west side. This annex building was originally used to offload/load from the railroad tracks which curved around the north and west side of the building.

The only access to the 6th and 7th floors of the building were by the pair of freight elevators on the north side of the building, and the steps in the northwest corner. The stairway was very narrow. It was a 'one-way' type of stairway, in that it only went between 2 floors, and then you had to exit the stairway, and walk across the floor to re-access the stairway again for the next level. The north wall entrance would be going up, you would turn mid-way, and then reach the next highest floor on the west wall.

21. STAIRS BETWEEN SECOND AND THIRD FLOORS.

The photo shows the door on the north wall of the second floor. You would take these steps up, turn midway, and then go up to the 3rd floor. Then you would have to cross about 20 feet of the 3rd floor, to go up to the 4th floor, etc. Any strangers in the building using these stairs would have to cross the floors at each level, risking being seen by the workers in the building. Some floors had hallways and walls that would hide this area of the building (2nd and 3rd floors did, and the 4th floor had walls between this area and the offices in the front of the building).

Stacks of books could also block the view of these areas.

There were also 2 freight elevators on the north side of the building.

The EAST elevator was hand controlled and you had to be in the elevator to hold the up or down direction switch. The WEST elevator could be called, provided the gate at each floor, and the gate on the elevator itself was closed (double gated). You would then push the button for the floor you wish to move to.

It is the movements of these freight elevators, and known movements on the stairs that this document will attempt to track, as these are the only access points to the 6th floor, which is the floor of Lee Harvey Oswald's "snipers nest". We will not address the movements up the front stairs and passenger elevators, as these were not readily important to the Warren Commission and other investigators. We can assume that the office personnel used these front elevators and steps as needed.

TEXAS SCHOOL BOOK DEPOSITORY
DIAGRAM OF THIRD FLOOR

D

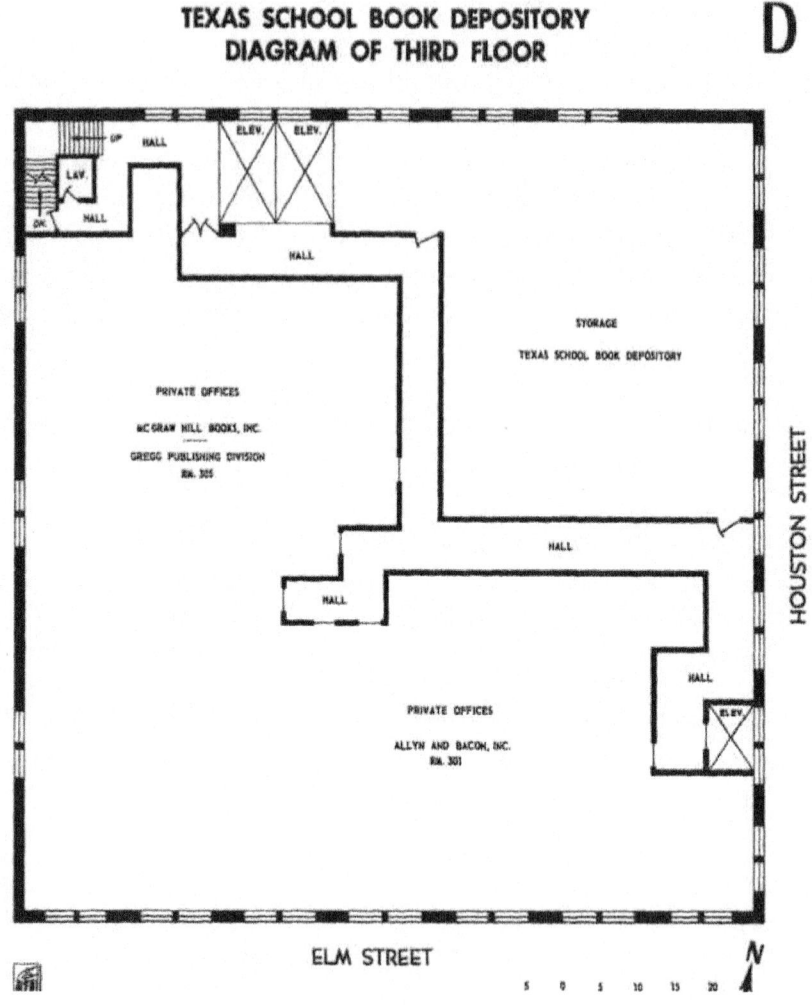

We will start our timeline with the movement of the "floor installation" crew down the freight elevators, when they broke for lunch at around 11:45-11:50 AM. Bonne Ray Williams, Harold Norman, Danny Arce, Bill Lovelady, Charles Givens and Supervisor Bill Shelley all stated that they raced the elevators down from the 6th floor. (Williams v3 p167,

Lovelady v6 p336, Arce v6 p364) (Nobody ever says which elevator won in the race.)

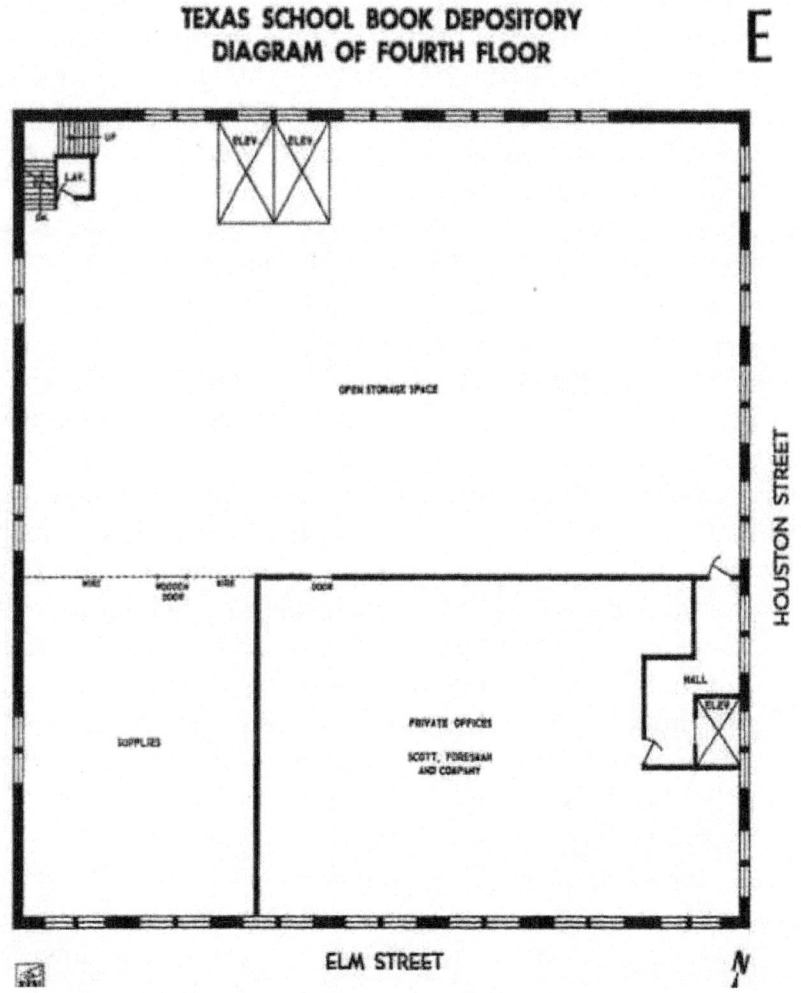

As they passed Oswald on the 5th floor (Givens v6 p349), he asked them to put the gates back down, so that he could call the west elevator when he was ready to come down. (Arce v6 p364)

Charles Givens gets to the first floor, and soon realizes that he had left his cigarettes in his jacket, in the northwest corner of the 6th floor, where they were laying floor all morning. He

JFK Assassination: Shades From The Fence

takes the east elevator back up to the 6th floor, and gets his jacket and cigarettes. (Givens v6 p349)

He says that as he returns to the east elevator, he sees Oswald walking up the east side of the floor carrying his clipboard. He is about 10 ft from the east wall, walking away from the south (front) side of the building, the general area of the 'sniper's nest'. Givens states that he had not paid any particular attention to that corner. Givens asked if Oswald is going downstairs, as it is near lunchtime. Oswald says no, but again asks that Givens lowers the gates on the west elevator, so that Oswald can call it back up when he needs it.

Givens then goes back down the east elevator (hand operated) to the 1st floor, and walks around to the west elevator to close the gate. He states that the elevator was not there when he checks it. The time is about 11:55. (v6 p351) Givens then joins James Jarman and Harold Norman on the first floor by the window, and they discuss going out front to watch the motorcade. Charles Givens eats his lunch while standing in front of the building, and decides to go see a friend of his that works at a parking lot at Main and Record streets. This is where he will be when the motorcade comes by. (He, and Oswald, will later be the 2 warehouse employees that are missing from the building, after the shooting.)

While Givens had gone back upstairs, Harold Norman (v3 p188) had washed up and eaten his lunch in the "Domino room", in the northeast corner of the first floor.

James Jarman (v3 p201) says they quit for lunch about 11:55, and after going down he washed up and got a pop from the second floor lounge/lunchroom, then went down to the front window on the first floor. He ate his lunch standing there, while he was watching the crowd gather out front. Presumably, this is where he was joined by Charles Givens and Harold Norman.

Danny Arce states that he had his lunch with Jack Dougherty, in the Domino room. (v6 p365) He then went out with Bill Shelley and Bill Lovelady, and joined James "Junior" Jarman, and was standing outside in front of the building

202

awaiting the motorcade. It was at this time that he saw the older gentleman with the "kidney problem", gave him directions to the restroom inside, watched him come into the building and saw him leaving a couple of minutes later.

Oswald himself claimed that he was eating lunch in the lunchroom. This was supposedly later confirmed in 1978 by Carolyn Arnold, who was not interviewed by the Warren Commission. Ms Arnold's FBI statement of April 18, 1964 makes no such claim. No other person states that Oswald was in the lunchroom.

Bonnie Ray Williams says they quit about 5 or 10 minutes before 12:00, and he went down in the west elevator (v3 p167). He also recalls hearing Oswald yell for the elevator, but being on the west elevator; he could not see Oswald and was uncertain which floor Oswald was on. On the 1st floor, he washed up, then got his lunch from the Domino room. He then returned to the 6th floor, presumably on the west elevator, which would explain why it was no longer on the 1st floor when Charles Givens looked to lower the gate on it. Williams had earlier heard Bill Lovelady and Danny Arce discuss eating lunch on the 6th floor, where they would have a good view of the motorcade. So he assumed that is where everyone was going to meet.

Bonnie Ray Williams finishes his lunch on the 6th floor, in the area just west of the 'sniper's nest'. The lunch consists of a bag of Fritos, a chicken sandwich, and a Dr Pepper from the vending machine on the 1st floor (v3 p169). He leaves his lunch bag, bottle and trash on the 6th floor, which is later found and photographed by investigators.

About 12:20 (v3 p173) Williams finishes his lunch, and takes the west elevator down to look for his friends. He stops on the 5th floor, where he finds them.

Harold Norman and James Jarman hear that the motorcade has reached Main St., so they decide that the 5th floor would be a better vantage point to watch the motorcade. (Jarman v3 p202, Norman v3 p190). (Presumably, they hear this on the

JFK Assassination: Shades From The Fence

Police radio of a nearby officer. The first mention of Main St. is at 12:21 on the police channel 2. Based on this Williams estimate of 12:20 is probably a little early, if they had to go around the building, and up to the 5th floor first.) They go around the building, because there are too many people blocking the front door. They take the east elevator back up to the 5th floor. They raise the windows on the northeast corner of the 5th floor. Here they are joined by Bonnie Ray Williams, and they will remain here until after the shooting.

Officer Baker and Roy Truly would later say that both elevators were on the 5th floor, and we are at that position at this point in time. However, there is also some limited use of the elevators by Jack Dougherty.

Jack Dougherty was a stock worker, who supposedly saw and spoke to Oswald when he came in that morning (v6 p377). He seems extremely positive that Oswald had nothing in his hands when he spoke to him, but only after Mr. Ball questions him multiple times. However, in his WC testimony (v6 p381) he later claims that "some of the fellows" saw Oswald with a large package. He cites Bill Shelley saying this "the day after it happened". (Shelley does not say this in his testimony.)

Dougherty's testimony is rather confused, and Mr Ball has to constantly remind him of his earlier FBI testimony. He eventually states (v6 p377-379) that he quit working for lunch about 12:00 noon, ate his lunch in the Domino room (Arce v6 p364), and returned to work about 12:30. He was doing his normal order filling duties that day, and not assisting with the laying of the new floor. At around 12:30, he went briefly to the 6th floor, using the west elevator, to get some stock, and then returned to the 5th floor on that elevator (v6 p379).

He was standing about 10 feet away from the elevator, when he heard one shot. He insists he only heard one, and it sounded like a car backfiring; however, he does say it sounded like it was from overhead. (Mr Ball then points out that in the FBI testimony, Dougherty said it sounded like a "loud explosion".) (v6 p380)

JFK Assassination: Shades From The Fence

Dougherty says that he heard no call for the elevator, nor heard anyone going up the stairs. He also never saw Officer Baker and Roy Truly. (below)

He says that he continues to pick up his stock on the 5th floor, and then takes the west elevator down to the first floor. It is here that he speaks to janitor Eddie Piper, and is told that the President had been shot.

Eddie Piper had spoken to Oswald about going to lunch about 12, but Oswald just said "Yeah." and then mumbled something Piper did not catch (v6 p383). Piper sat inside the second window on the 1st floor, but could not really see the motorcade because of the crowd blocking his view. Piper moved his position after the 2nd shot, to a better vantage point, and then heard the 3rd shot. He still could not readily see anything, because of the crowd. He could not tell where the sound of the shots came from. He estimates it was about 12:27 (v6 p385). Eddie does not recall Baker's uniform and helmet, as he states he was not sure if it was an FBI man or policeman, but he hears him ask where the elevators were, and says he says, "I don't know, sir, Mr. Truly."

Officer Marion Baker's timeline of getting off his motorcycle, and coming into the building with building Supervisor Roy Truly, is being covered by Richard Van Noord, Sean Murphy, Jeff Rollins and Chris Davidson (with me assisting by staying out of their way) for a presentation for JFK Lancer. I will cover Baker and Truly's path through the building.

Baker runs into the front door of the building, on his way to the roof, where Baker has seen pigeons take wing at the sound of the shots. Building supervisor Roy Truly sees him and follows him. They make connections somewhere in the front, or in the entryway (Arce v6 p385).

Truly then leads the way, to show Baker the way to the roof.

Truly runs into the half-door at the Will Call counter, which is latched (v3 p322). Baker then runs into the back of Roy Truly. Baker and Truly then back up, so that they can swing the door open, and enter. They then proceed from the southeast entrance to the north wall, for the freight elevators (the only access to the 6th and 7th floors, and the roof). (see red line on first floor diagram above).

Truly sees that both elevators are apparently on the 5th floor (v3 p223). Presumably the west one (callable) is in use by Jack Dougherty, or left there when Jarman and Norman took it back to the 5th floor. The east elevator (manual) was taken to the 5th by Bonnie Ray Williams, when he took it down from the 6th floor.

Truly pushes the button, and call bell, and shouts for someone to "release the elevator" by lowering the gate. According to both Baker and Truly, he does this at least twice (Baker v2, p249, Truly v3 p223). Jack Dougherty states that he never heard them (v6 p381).

Baker and Truly then proceed up the stairs, in the northwest corner of the building. They proceed into the stairs on the north wall of the 1st floor, and come out on the west wall of the second.

As Baker is following Roy Truly across the 20 feet (or so) of the 2nd floor, Baker notices a man through the glass window in the vestibule door in front of the 2nd floor lunchroom, walking away from him. He opens the door and yells for the man (about 20 feet away – v3 p250) to stop.

Baker asks Truly, who has turned back to find out where Baker was delayed, "Do you know this man? Does he work here?" Truly yells, "Yes!", and the two simply continue up the stairs.

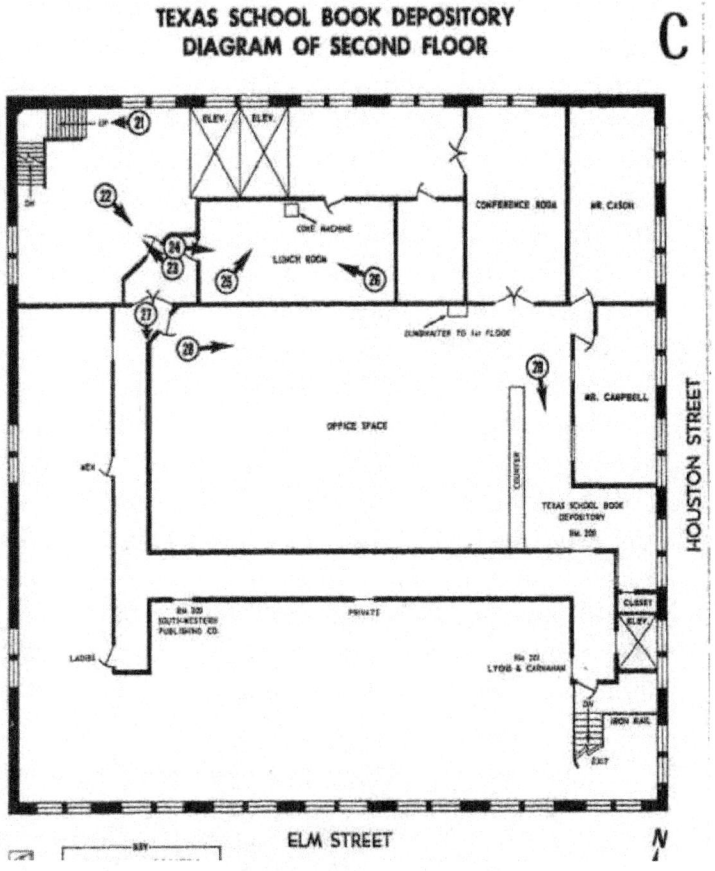

**TEXAS SCHOOL BOOK DEPOSITORY
DIAGRAM OF SECOND FLOOR**

C

Two re-enactments done for the investigators take 1 minute 30 seconds, and 1 minute 15 seconds to reach the 2nd floor lunchroom (v3 p252-253). Baker says that there was no time taken during the re-enactments for his scan of the crowds down Elm St, nor for his having to work his way through the crowds on the front steps/entryway/lobby. (We do not know about time for the half-door collision, or any other delay of Baker looking for suspicious people as he travels through the building.) He states that the actual time was probably longer, and that these times were most likely the minimum times it would take to reach the 2nd floor lunchroom.

Of course, the man Baker encountered is Lee Harvey Oswald, who has (according to the Warren Commission) taken

3 shots at the motorcade, taken his rifle from the southeast corner, dodging rows of books, to a location just south of the down stairway on the west wall, towards the northwest corner, and stashed it under a number of cartons. He has then proceeded down the stairs on the west wall, emerging on the north wall of the 5th floor. He has crossed the 20 feet of the 5th, 4th, and 3rd floors, and has ended up on the 2nd floor. He has entered the lunch room, just prior to Baker and Truly emerging from the 1st floor, and is seen walking away through the glass window in the vestibule door.

Oswald is not seen crossing any of the floors, including the 5th floor, where Jack Dougherty is getting stock and putting it on the west elevator. The 3rd floor has the stairway area readily blocked from view (see layouts above), and the 4th floor is similarly blocked, if you are standing in the office area at the front of the building. (Book note: some state that Dougherty should have seen Oswald crossing the 5th floor; however, he was filling an order and not staring at the area of the stairs. Photo shows that the stairs area view was blocked by shelves and boxes.)

Baker and Truly continue up all flights of stairs, until they reach the 5th floor, and Truly spots the east elevator. By this

JFK Assassination: Shades From The Fence

time the west elevator is no longer on the 5th floor, or Truly would have been unable to see the east one on the other side of the west elevator shaft from the stairway. (Truly v3 p229, Baker v3 p255) Presumably, Jack Dougherty has taken the west elevator back down to the 1st floor, during their race up the steps or encounter with Oswald. They then proceed to take the east elevator and continue up to the 7th floor.

Baker states that he had his pistol drawn the entire time, and was alert to any movement by any individual. He recalls having seen people on the 1st floor, and Eddie Piper is one of the employees who recall seeing Truly and Baker come through. (v6 p384)

Baker and Truly then take the ladder to the roof. On the roof, both men lift themselves up onto the wall that surrounds the roof, which requires them to stick their toes in a crack and lift themselves up to peer over. Baker decides that it is unlikely that a rifleman could hold himself up in that position, while shooting a rifle.

He also climbs about 10 feet of the ladder that goes up onto the Hertz sign, as well as checks out the elevator control shed on the roof (v3 p260).

Baker and Truly then come back down the ladder, and take the east elevator back down. (Baker is a little vague in his testimony here, insisting that the elevators did not go to the 7th floor, and that they had to go down a level of stairs. However, he later says they got on the elevator on the top floor. (–v3 p260-261.) On their way down in the east elevator, they pause at the 4th floor, where Baker reports to Inspector Sawyer that he had checked out the roof. However, they do not actually get off the elevator, and after talking to Sawyer, they proceed down to the 1st floor. Baker leaves the building, and later estimates that he had spent approximately 15 minutes in the building (v3 P262).

Baker then follows the motorcade to the Trade Mart, then Parkland where he helps with crowd control, and later Love Field.

209

JFK Assassination: Shades From The Fence

At this time, we lose all reference to the freight elevators. We had lost the placement of the west elevator when Jack Dougherty got off, and now lose track of the east elevator when Baker and Truly are through with it. However, at this time the building is also filling up with Policemen and other investigators, as they begin their searches for suspects and evidence. Stairway: At the time of the shooting, Bonnie Ray Williams, James Jarman and Harold Norman on the 5th floor hear the sounds of the shots right above them. They run to the west side of the building, because they see a number of people in Dealey Plaza going up the steps to the railroad yard. They linger on the west side of the 5th floor for a few minutes, and do not see anyone in the stairway area of the building. This area is actually blocked from view from the west wall by a number of boxes and a short wall. They never hear any running from the floors above them, nor running on the stairway; although, while at the open west window, they were probably subjected to the noise from outside.

They move to the area next to the stairway on the north wall, to see if they can see anything out that direction. Only Bonnie Ray Williams recalls seeing Baker come across the floor, to go to the east elevator (v3 p180). The other 2 do not recall seeing either (Jarman v3 p206, Norman v3 p193). They then proceed down the stairs.

In the movie "JFK", Oliver Stone discusses the travels of Victoria Adams and Sandra Styles down the stairs immediately after the shooting. He places their movements in the time that Oswald would have had to come down the stairs, stating that they do not see him or hear him.

Vickie Adams and Sandra Styles watched the motorcade from a front window on the 4th floor. They were there with Dorothy Garner and Elsie Dorman (who attempted to film the motorcade from the front windows, but filmed too high as she didn't want to look through the small viewfinder and miss seeing the President and First Lady in person). (Adams v6 p386) From that point at the front of the building, they could not see the stairs area, as there is a wall (see 4th floor diagram).

JFK Assassination: Shades From The Fence

Adams is initially unwilling to state a length of time between the last shot and when she went down the stairs. (v6 p392) However, Mr. Belin gets her to estimate that it was about 30 seconds after the last shot until she "start(ed) toward the stairway". He then gets her to say it was less than a minute after leaving the window that she was down on the 1st floor. (In 3" heels, no less –v6 p389.) She also states that the elevators were not moving.

However, she then states that immediately after arriving on the 1st floor, she sees Bill Shelley and Bill Lovelady by the "Houston Street dock" (v6 p389-390). She does say the dock, so this is possibly outside.

Bill Shelley and Bill Lovelady say that they "didn't do anything for a minute" (Shelley v6 p329). They state that they saw Truly and Baker go in, but state it was "3 or 4 minutes" (p329). They then went to the railroad yards (Lovelady v6 p339, Shelley v6 p330), and worked their way to the back of the building, where they entered into one of the overhead doors on the west side. Lovelady does say that is when they saw Vickie Adams. (I have not been able to pick out Shelley and Lovelady in the photos and films of the crowds in the railroad yards.) It appears that someone is confused somewhere, as that is a lot of ground for Shelley and Lovelady to cover in the 1 ½ minutes that Adams says she made it down to the 1st floor. It is questionable whether Adams and Styles came down the stairs that quickly. **In 2008, researcher Sean Murphy had a telephone interview with Sandra, in which she says it was more time. She was surprised at Vickie's estimate.** The last witness to movement inside the building is Mrs. Robert Reid.

Mrs. Reid ate her lunch in the 2nd floor lunchroom, starting around noon. (v6 p271) She ate it "rather hurriedly" so that she could go find a good position for the motorcade. She estimates that she left the lunchroom around 12:15-12:20. She remembers that the "usual girls" were there, and they left before she did. She could not recall if anyone was left in the lunchroom when she left. Mrs. Reid says she was standing almost directly in front of the entrance to the TSBD during the motorcade (vol 3 p272).

After the shots, Mrs. Reid went into the building, up the stairs by the entrance, and to her desk. (v3 p274). Her desk was located close to the dumbwaiter on the north wall of the office area on the second floor. (see diagram) Oswald came into the office area from the door on the northwest corner (diagram by circle 27 & 28). Mrs. Reid told him the President had been shot, and he was calm and mumbled something she did not catch. Oswald had a coke in his right hand, and proceeded out of the building. Mrs. Reid did not notice his path out of the building, as she was not watching him. In a re-enactment, they estimated Mrs. Reid was at her desk approximately 2 minutes after the final shot (Reid v3 p275).

Oswald apparently went down the front steps, or front passenger elevator. He supposedly gave a couple of people directions to a phone, and left the building. (Newsmen Pierce Allman, and Robert McNeil both later state they got directions from Oswald, but Oswald thought it was a Secret Service agent he gave directions to.)

Ochus V. Campbell, VP of the Texas Schoold Book Company, was quoted in the NY Herald Tribune Times on Nov 23 that he saw Oswald in the ground floor storage room immediately after the shooting, but this statement was not made in the CE 1381 FBI signed statement, and Mr. Campbell was not interviewed by the Warren Commission. He also told the Dallas Morning News on Nov 23, that it was at the 1st floor storage room that an officer with a drawn gun encountered Oswald. (It is uncertain if he was talking about Truly, or someone else Oswald encountered.)

The study of the stairways, elevators and movements inside the building are highly interesting to me. If there were more than just Lee Harvey Oswald shooting from inside the Texas School Book Depository, they would have to use these stairs and elevators to get access to, and escape from the building. This naturally puts them at risk of being seen by the regular employees of the building, or even being trapped without a means of escape. If they are setting Oswald up as a patsy without his knowledge, they also run the risk of being seen by Oswald himself.

Of course, the witnesses that made statements about movements within the building could be mistaken or lying about when these movements occurred. Additionally, there are natural gaps in time where the stairways and elevators could not be seen by employees, and others. The stairs have a gap from when most employees left the building at 12:15-12:20, to when Baker and Truly ascended at about 12:32. The elevators appear to have a gap between 12:15-20, when the 3 men convened on the 5th floor, and when Jack Dougherty used them around 12:28 or so. A large team of conspirators accessing and escaping the building would naturally take time and planning. The stairs and elevators are not easily seen from most floors, but there is always the risk. Only one stranger was reported in the building that day, by Danny Arce. These are all factors that must be considered.

Naturally, all testimony can be influenced by both the person asking the questions, as well as conversations the witness has heard and had between the time of the event and the time of making the statements. None of this evidence is cast in stone, and should be taken with proper skepticism.

This is a first swing at this topic, and I feel it is very important to include HSCA statements, press statements, and other statements that could fill the gaps and further clarify the access, egress and movement within the TSBD.

15. "The Ups and Downs of the TSBD - Revisited"

This next chapter is again a reprint of one of my "Dealey Plaza Echo" articles. This second one is again about the building, and the movements inside the building, but is more based on the HSCA version and other information that has come out later. The "ECHO" Journal had different Copyright restrictions than my book does, so photos are not included here.

MaryFerrell.org definitely has full archival copies of this article in the Echo, for those interested.

This article also included the HSCA Summary of the known movements in the building, which can be seen in their materials. It also included the hand-written notes taken by Capt Will Fritz during his interrogations of Oswald.

Again, this 2st article (of three) focuses on the HSCA testimony and version of what happened. Like the others, it also talks about some of the many theories. It was written in 2015.

(I apologize if many things are repetitive, but each article was intended to 'stand alone' with the information and not required to reference other articles.)

The Ups and Downs of the TSBD - Revisited

The Dealey Plaza Echo , March 2008 volume, contained my original writing on the inside of the old Texas School Book Depository, on November 22, 1963. It discussed the layout of the building, the location of many of the 73 employees in the building on that fateful day, and the movements within the building of those employees, and the single stranger reported within the building. The article was based on the Warren Commission and the FBI reports gathered within the following year, leading up to the Report written by the Commission, and

JFK Assassination: Shades From The Fence

the supporting volumes. At that time, I said that a future article should be written that encompasses the information gathered by the House Select Committee on Assassinations, as well as other documentation, interviews, theories and comments issued after that date. This is that follow-up article. (Perhaps the DPUK Echo Editor will also re-print the mentioned article, as it contains the layouts of the floors and other discussions that would be useful.)

As mentioned in the first article, the use, history and study of the interior of the building (as well as the Dal-Tex, and the other buildings in Dealey Plaza) has long been an interest of mine. As the reader may know, I have given professional tours of the events surrounding the assassination, and always try to include a discussion of the interior of the buildings, and the known movements.

I have had researchers who have looked at my previous article (it is online), call it an "exposé" on the subject. However, my intention was to simply explain that any theory that includes strangers within the building to do the shooting, or simply to plant the shells and weapons that might implicate Oswald, must consider the difficulty and *logistical* restrictions that such an endeavor would require. You can't simply have such conspirators appear on the 6th floor, and then simply disappear again. ("Mr. Scott" could not have even 'beamed' them in, since even Star Trek was a creation of later years.)

Accessing and Sealing the TSBD

I am not saying that the stairs and elevators did not have an amount of time where they could be used, before 12:30. They did. As long as about 15-20 minutes, from the time Bonnie Ray Williams went back to the 6th floor (12:05), until he went down to the 5th floor and met James 'Junior" Jarman and Harold Norman (12:25), the area of the stairs and the elevators themselves were available for movement. But it is more of a logistical and planning problem, than an actual execution problem. How would a team (or single) of conspirators know that such a window of opportunity would present itself? How long does it take to build a 'snipers nest"? Would not these conspirators run the risk of being seen at any of the 6 floors they had to pass to accomplish such a feat? The same problems Oswald would have in *leaving* the building, would similarly be faced by any conspirator that has to not only leave the building, but also access the building, without being seen by any of the 73 employees, 20 or so having stayed in the building.

Similarly, after the assassination, we have a gap in time that the stairs were not used. After Styles and Adams, descended the stairs, and after Baker and Truly went up the stairs to the 5th floor where they found the elevator, we know of little use of the stairs. Film photographer, Tom Alyea, was the only member of the Press who accessed the upper floors, and filmed the search being conducted by the police on the upper warehouse floors. Presumably, this took a while to get started, as the building entrance in the back was not sealed off until D V Harkness arrived, around 12:38 to 12:40 (WC Vol XI p 310). Harkness did state that he saw 2 "secret service" agents as he arrived at the back of the building, but did not get them identified. (Naturally, David Belin simply ignored the statement.)

Inspector Sawyer arrived at the TSBD around 12:34, because he had heard the 12:34 broadcast about the building on his car radio. He immediately went inside and took the passenger elevator to the "top floor" (the elevator only went to the 4th). He walked through the floor very briefly, looking for a shooter. He says he only spent a maximum of 3 minutes in the building (Vol VI p315). He then says he returned outside, and assured that the 2 patrol officers at the front door had sealed the front entrance. He sent the Sargeant (presumably D V Harkness) around the back to seal off that entrance. At 12:40, Sawyer called on the police radio for more officers, to hold and search the building. He insists that after that point, no one except employees and law enforcement were allowed into the building, or out. In fact, even film cameraman Tom Alyea was not allowed to leave the building and had to throw his exposed film to a co-worker to take to WFAA and develop without him. (A future article about Alyea and his statements will be in the future, as I have spent a great deal of time working with Tom the last several years.)

Baker and Truly bypassed the 6th floor on their elevator ride from the 5th to the 7th, in their effort to get to the roof. However, the 3 employees on the 5th floor, also lingered by the stairs area, but this was only after seeing Baker and Truly going by. Shooters may have lingered on the 6th floor for a few minutes, before slipping down the stairs. Many of the employees came in and out of the 1st floor dock entrance, before the building was sealed off, and searched. After it was sealed, some employees were kept out even after identifying themselves as employees. This included Charles Givens (Vol VI, p355), even though there was a description of him put out over the police radio about 12:48(Vol VI p322).

If the estimates by the Dallas Police are accurate, the building was sealed off by about 12:40, and no one entered or exited the building without being checked by the officers at the doors first. This gives the "conspirators", a very short window after the movement on the stairs previously discussed, and the sealing off of the building. In addition to that, multiple officers were making their way up and down the building, searching the various floors, as Tom Alyea's film shows. We are uncertain how much was done on the 6th floor, versus the back of the 4th, and the 5th floor. Any conspirators waiting on any of these floors to leave, would be subject to being seen.

However, the planning and logistics considerations still remain, as the conspirators would not know these windows of time existed, and ran the risk of being seen by the various employees in the building.

Of course, if Oswald was party to such a conspiracy, he would have had time to build a "sniper's nest", and could possibly assist other shooters in accessing and escaping the building.

However, the question comes up as to why he would not simply leave with his co-conspirators? Although he did stay long enough to be seen by his manager, Roy Truly, and thus establish his presence in the 2nd floor lunchroom, it was not as if he "ran interference" with Baker, so his friends could escape. It seems circumstantial that Baker and he had the encounter they did have.

Oswald himself would have very little trouble accessing the building, since he worked there. He also had basically unsupervised access to the south east corner of the 6th floor, and would have had plenty of time that morning to move the boxes away from the window in that area, and move the Rolling Readers cartons from the middle of the 6th floor, to the "sniper's nest". There was a crew of 6 employees overlaying the floor on the southwest corner of the building, but they were busy and not paying attention to Oswald, and he could easily have accomplished the preparation work, as it was not that uncommon to be moving boxes in his normal line of work.

Some have suggested that the rifle and shells could have easily been planted. Many have said that this could even be done hours, or day, ahead of time. The drawback of that, is that such advance planting, assumes that Oswald, or one of the other workers, would not stumble onto such items in the normal course of their work. Even someone coming in and planting the weapon/shells at the time of the motorcade, has to have access to the 6th floor, without being recognized as a stranger in the building by any of the 73 workers there that day.

I know of a few Researchers that believe that other employees of the Texas School Book Company were involved. Naturally, they had the same access to the areas of the floor that Oswald would have. They also could just as easily access the building, as Oswald could. In fact, I have run into a few individuals that feel that many of the other employees are lying (maybe induced by the 'investigators' after the fact), or heavily involved in either the shooting, or the setting up of Oswald as a patsy. I cannot argue against that, if such is the case; however, I can't simply state they were all lying.

Oswald as a Patsy

There are 3 inherent problems that you have to address, if you are setting up Oswald as a Patsy, when he is not assisting, or involved in every way:

1.   **You must *control* Oswald's location.** You cannot have Oswald as a free agent during the time of the shooting, allowing him to be anywhere he wants to be. You not only run the risk of him being on the 6th floor, where your real shooters / weapon planters are, but of him being with someone else, where he has an alibi. He could easily be out front, where he can be photographed (see the Altgen's 6 photo article, where many believe this is where he was). Most of the theories has him in the 1st or 2nd floor lunchrooms, "waiting for a phone call". However, there are no phones in either lunchroom. The phone that Oswald and the warehouse workers used (and knew the number to) was in the center of the back of the 1st floor, where anyone waiting in the area can easily see the entrances to the building, as well as the elevator and stairs areas. If you tell Oswald to wait by some other phone, such as the 2nd floor office area, he may get suspicious.

2.   **You must be able to sneak in and out without being seen as "strangers" by the 73 employees.** These employees used the stairs and even the freight elevators at any time they wished. Additionally, during their lunch hour, they may be at any point in the building. You cannot guarantee that they would all be out front, watching the Motorcade (most were), when you plan to access the building. If they see strangers in the building, they are very likely to report it, and thus move suspicion off of the "patsy". (In fact, only Danny Arce reported any stranger in the building, and he stated this gentleman left and got into a black car, long before the Motorcade came down Main St.)

3.   **Most importantly, Oswald himself must not see any stranger, or known 'associate' in the building.** It is

unlikely that Oswald will intentionally set himself up as a patsy, and if he sees someone in the building, he is going to realize that he is being set up. (Again, he could have 'assisted' someone, but his staying in the building afterwards simply does not make sense.) If he realizes he is being set up, he may start whistle blowing quite quickly. His natural arrogance would not likely allow him to let someone set him up, if he knows about it.

Oswald as a patsy, also exposes a number of other questions, such as: Why would you let your Patsy run around town as a 'loose cannon' after the event? Would you not want to control him afterwards as well? (These will be discussed in a future article about Oswald's "escape plan" and actions, and a theory that might explain those actions, and this question.)

Elevator and Stair Access Limitations

91-001 / 077

The previous article covers the Elevators and Stairs needed to access the 5th, 6th and 7th floors of the building quite extensively. However, I did not necessarily *stress* the limitations and problems with these access points.

The stairs were single flight stairs, without a "stairwell" as we normally think of them. This means they were not shielded from each and every floor, where you can simply access the stairwell, and then go up and down the building at will. In a modern stairwell, you have landings at each floor, so that you can continue down the next flight, all within the confines of the walls surrounding the stairway, shielded from each floor you need to pass.

A single flight of stairs was about 3-4 feet wide, and only went between 2 floors. When going up, you entered on the north wall, went up about 5 feet, turned 90 degrees, and continue up the additional 5 feet to the next floor, where you emerged on the west wall. **You then had to cross 20 to 25 feet of the floor, to access the flight of stairs going up to the next floor.** Of course, coming down the stairs, you simply reversed this process, using the same set of narrow stairs.

This means you have to cross each and every floor, on your way up to the 6th floor. The 2nd and 3rd floors, did have walls close to the stairs and elevator areas, so that most of the floor was shielded from a direct view. Also the office space in the 4th floor was shielded from the warehouse spaces by a wall which ran east and west through the center of the floor. But the 5th, 6th and 7th floors were completely open warehouse spaces, and anyone in these floors could possibly see that corner of the building, depending on how high the various stacks of boxes were.

Again, there are periods of time where we know of no use of these stairs, and no employees in the stair area (except the western side of the open 1st floor, where Shipper Troy Eugene West was making coffee and having lunch), but it is still a planning and logistical problem. How do you plan to get your shooters in and out of the building, without being seen, with these access limitations?

The Elevators had similar visibility problems. They were located in the same corner of the building, and could be spotted on any of the open floors, or by anyone in the general area on the other floors. In addition, they made at least some noise. (Not sure how much, however, since there is some movement of the elevators that Truly and Baker missed.)

The freight elevators were the only elevators that accessed the 5th, 6th, 7th floors, or the basement. The small passenger elevator in the northeast (front) lobby of the building only went up to the 4th floor, as it was originally installed between 1895 and 1901, when the building was only a 5 story building. The lift mechanism was housed on the 5th floor. Afire in 1901 'gutted' the back of the building, and the 6th and 7th floor was added when they rebuilt/repaired it. The passenger elevator was largely undamaged, so it remained as it was.

These were 2 elevators in the same shaft. They were basic 7-foot steel cages, with back walls that went up about 5 feet. The corners and sides then continued up to a perforated steel ceiling, with no access hatches. The back meant that you could see through the chain-link fence like material on the upper 2 feet of the cage, into the other elevator (if it was there), or into the elevator shaft, and floor beyond. The only part of the ceiling that was not perforated metal, was a single bulb light fixture.

The lift gates into both elevators were slatted wood gates. This includes slats of wood of about 1" to 2", separate by openings between the slats of the same size. These gates, when fully lowered, were also about 5 feet, so you could easily see every floor you passed, as well as being fully visible from each floor. The "automatic" elevator on the western side of the shaft, had 2 gates. One on the elevator itself, and one on each floor. The manual elevator on the east side used a single gate system, with no gate on the actual elevator. The additional gate on the west side was also wood slats, that apparently ran up and down, instead of vertically.

JFK Assassination: Shades From The Fence

Again, both elevators shared the same elevator shaft. This means that while it was possible to "repel down the shaft" as some Researchers have suggested, you would be blocked by the elevator itself. (Bruce Willis movies usually feature a bank of elevator shafts, so you can move between the elevators themselves. *Can't say from personal experience, however.*) In this case, the elevator itself used up the entire single shaft, from wall to wall. If the elevators were on the 5th floor at the time of the shooting, where Roy Truly and the known movements put them, you *could* probably climb over the 2 foot gap of the 6th floor gate, and stand on the elevator cage and roof. Remember though, that the roof of the elevator is perforated steel, and you would be visible to anyone in the elevator. There was also a row of windows in the elevator shaft itself, so you would be well lit. But you would be unable to bypass the elevator in the shaft. You might go down the stairs below the elevator, on the 4th floor and access the lower elevator shaft from there. (We have all seen the Mission Impossible series of movies and television shows, and know that this is *possible*; however, this would be highly visible and would tend to draw attention to anyone working any of the floors, so highly doubtful.)

The elevators did have a solid back wall, but the top 2 feet of this wall was an open fencelike screen. This means you could see from one elevator into the other, for the top 2 feet at least. Additionally, this also meant that parts of the elevators themselves were basically see-through from every floor they passed. When the elevators were not on the floor, these slatted wood gates were all you had to look through to see across the elevators into the floor on the other side. This meant the stairs area, elevator area, and the 20 -25 feet of open space you had to cross to get to the next floor was exposed from the opposite side. Unless the elevators had stacks of boxes in them (extremely rare), anyone riding the elevators would be visible from every floor they passed.

For safety reasons both elevators were designed to not function when the gate was not properly put in the down (closed) position. Similarly, the gates were not able to open unless the elevator was at the matching level of the floor, where a release mechanism was in place. This might address Luke Mooney's (Vol III pp283-284) using the west double gated elevator to come up partway up the building, and dropping a couple of ladies off at the 2nd floor. He said that he could not get the elevator to function after this, and thought it was turned off. It could be simply that he only lowered the elevator gate, and not both gates, and did not understand why it would not operate. He said he ended up taking the stairs on up to the 6th, and also that he crossed paths with a couple of plainclothes officers coming down which he assumed "were Deputy Sheriffs". (HE was a Deputy Sheriff Detective, so he should have known them.) Maybe he did recognize them, but by the time he made the statement he forgot who they were?

Again, the consistent positions of the elevators that we know of, and the placement of the employees still within the building during the motorcade, do not preclude the use of the stairs or elevators to sneak shooters/conspirators into and out of the building. But it does present some logistics and planning problems to anyone trying to discretely access the building.

Even if you did access the stairs or elevators without being seen, you still had the problems of being on a floor that had Oswald, or other employees working on them. Even if you are just accessing the 6th floor to *plant* the rifle, and shells, you had to plant them in a location where they would not be spotted by Oswald and the other workers in the building. Any employee could access any floor of the building at any time, for any number of reasons. It certainly could have happened, but such operations need to be *planned*, and these factors do interfere and are difficult to plan around.

I am attaching many pages of the House Select Committee on Assassinations reported movements by the employees in the building, leading up to the assassination time of 12:30. *(Edit: Reader will have to find these.)* However, the remainder of this article will discuss alternative theories and reports that I have encountered throughout the years.

Narrative   364

(6) Charles D. Givens, Negro - lists no names (24:210)
This man has been convicted under a narcotics charge. 37, 6' 3", 165 #, Dallas
Sheriff Department # 37954 (17:419)
(7) James (Junior) Jarman, Negro: *Summary of all lists:*   (not listed by:)

1. Bill Shelley, white
2. Billy Lovelady, white
4. Danny Arce, Mexican
6. Bonnie Ray Williams, Negro
5. Charles D. Givens, Negro

(on list) 1. Shelley — 8 lists
(2 lists) 2. Lovelady — 8 "
(2 lists) 3. Dougherty — 4 "
(1 list) 4. Arce — 8 "
(no list) 5. Givens — 8 "
(2 lists) 6. Williams — 7 "
7. Norman — 1 "
(1 list) — Jarman

8 lists

Lovelady - list B
Dougherty
Williams list A
Jarman

Lovelady - List A
only on Williams list B

November 22, 1963 - Friday   10:00 A.M.

At 10:00 a.m. Eddie Piper comes to work at his usual starting time at the TSBD. (26:544)
Piper sees Oswald on the first floor. Oswald describes Piper as a ' little short negro'.
(6:383) *only time Piper sees LHO 11/22. (CD 206:13)*

At 10:00 a.m. Oswald is filling orders for books to be shipped. (Life 2/21/64)

TSBD employee Billy Lovelady, white, says that Oswald asks him the location of certain
books on the 6th floor. (22:662) *Lovelady sees LHO on 6' floor. (CD5:332)*

At 10:15 a.m. Harold (Hank) Norman, a Negro, sees Oswald looking out of the Elm Street
windows on the first floor. (3:188) *10:20/10:30 Norman sees LHO. (CD 329:14)*
These windows have a decorative screen of pierced concrete panels and the view is restricted.

During the morning, Bonnie Ray Williams says that many employees are planning on watching the Presidential Motorcade from the 6th floor. (3:169)
10:30 - R. E. Lewis sees LHO on 1' floor. (CD205:23) (TAG1:462 says sees LHO @ 10am)
(TAG 5:64)

November 22, 1963 - Friday   11:00 A.M.

At 11:00 a.m. Wesley Frazier sees Oswald on the first floor. (24:209) *For last time. (CD5:318)*
11:00 am Benny Rice sees 0 7 pieces of paper on 6' floor. (CD 205: 2)
At 11:00 a.m. Jack E. Dougherty sees Oswald on the 6th floor getting books. (6:377) *(CD 206:14) (CD 51346)*
Dougherty says he does not see LHO afterwards. (CD206:___ 'FBI teaches: 34)
At 11:30 a.m. Oswald eats lunch with Negro TSBD employees Eddie Piper and James (Junior)
Jarman on the first floor. (24:267,482) *Cheese, bread, and 2 apples.*
Could it be Harold Norman instead of Eddie Piper ? (Meagher: 125)
On 11/22 Oswald tells Captain Fritz that he eats lunch with 'Junior' and some other employee
on the second floor at the time of the assassination (12:30 p.m.). (4:224,231) *(24:264/)*

Oswald tells Captain Fritz that he eats his lunch in the lunchroom on the second floor
and possibly 'Junior' and a short Negro TSBD employee walk through the lunchroom while
Oswald is there. Oswald has a cheese sandwich and an apple z lunch which he brought

JFK Assassination: Shades From The Fence

from Mrs. Michael Paine's Irving residence. (24:19)

Oswald tells Captain Fritz, according to FBI agent Hosty, that he eats lunch on the first floor and is still there at 12:30 p.m. (17:786)

Recall that the TSBD lunch period is from 12:00 noon until 12:45 p.m. (3:214; 22:162; 24:872; 25:601; DFP 12/7/63:A-2)

At 11:45 a.m. James (Junior) Jarman, a Negro, says that all the workers on the 6th floor, including himself, leave and are out on the street by noon. (24:213)

Between 11:30 a.m. and 12:00 noon James (Junior) Jarman, a Negro, sees Oswald get on an elevator on the first floor to go and get some boxes. (24:213) *7 order followed. (CD5:334)*

At 11:45 a.m. Bill Shelley, a white supervisor, does not see Oswald on the 6th floor. (24:206) *Shelley last saw LHO between 11:45 & 12 noon. (CD5:371)(11/22)*

Between 11:30 a.m. and 11:50 a.m. Billy Lovelady (white) says that he, Bill Shelley(white), Jack Dougherty (white), Danny Arce (Mexican), Charles Givens (Negro) leave the 6th floor to see the President. (6:337; 24:214)

Between 11:40 a.m. and 11:45 a.m. Bonnie Ray Williams (Negro) sees Oswald on the east side of the 6th floor. (22:681) *(1/8/64. Williams says he sees O on 5th floor & O asks elevator be sent back. (CD329:13)*
At 11:50 a.m. Bill Shelley, a white supervisor, sees Oswald on the first floor near a telephone. (7:390; 22:673)

At 11:50 a.m. Billy Lovelady (white) says that he and Bonnie Ray Williams go down on the west automatic elevator from the 6th floor and Oswald is standing by the east non-automatic elevator on the 6th floor. (6:337) *(6/22/63 - Lovelady @ 11:50 7 Givens; Arce; another Negro male start down from 6th floor on 2 elevators. O calls for them to stop on 5th but they don't. (CD5:332))*
At 11: a.m. Bonnie Ray Williams (Negro) says that he and Charles D. Givens, a Negro TSBD employee who is a narcotics ex-convict, go down from the 6th floor on the east non-automatic elevator. (3:168) *@ 11:50 (CD5:335) 1/8/64. Williams sees LHO on 5th floor.*
At 11:30 a.m. Charles Givens says he went downstairs to the bathroom. (11/22 -24:210) *(CD1064th:10)*
At 11:45 a.m. Charles D. Givens, a Negro TSBD employee who is a narcotics ex-convict, says that he, Bonnie Ray Williams (Negro), Danny Arce (Mexican) and Billy Lovelady (white) are on an elevator going down from the 6th floor when they pass Oswald on the 5th floor. (6:349)

Between 11:40 a.m. and 11:50 a.m. Danny Arce (Mexican) sees Oswald on the 5th floor. (24:199) *near elevators. (CD205:8)*

At 11:55 a.m. Danny Arce (Mexican) says that he, Bonnie Ray Williams (Negro) and Billy Lovelady (white) ' race down ' on the east non-automatic elevator. Arce thinks that Oswald is on the 5th floor. (6:364)

Shortly before noon Jack E. Dougherty (white) sees Oswald on the 6th floor. (24:206)

At 11:55 a.m. Charles D. Givens (Negro ex-convict) takes the east non-automatic elevator to the 6th floor to get his cigarettes. *(CD1064(1) @ 10 say @ 11:45 a.m. & LHO is standing in SE corner of bldg.)* Givens sees Oswald on the 6th floor, walking northward (toward the wall that the elevators adjoin), 30' - 40' north of the building's south wall (along Elm Street) and 10' west of the building's east wall (along Houston Street) with a clipboard in his hand.

227

JFK Assassination: Shades From The Fence

CD296:3 (Insp. Holmes' report of 11/24/63 Oswald interview) - At lunchtime colored fellow invited Oswald to go with him. Oswald said, "You go on down and just send the elevator back up and I'll join you in a few minutes."

CD5:329 - Givens on 11/22 says the exchange re: elevators is at 11:30)

Givens asks Oswald if he is going to lunch. Oswald says, "No. Close the gate on the west (automatic) elevator," or "Not now. Just send the elevator back up." When Givens returns to the first floor on the east non-automatic elevator, the west automatic elevator is not there. (6:349,351; 24:491; WP 12/1/63:E-4; FBI Report, CD1:6)

Bill Shelley says Rolling Reader boxes used to conceal Oswald's position were 1/2 building width away from their correct position. (7:391)

At 11:50 a.m. Bonnie Ray Williams (negro) says that he gets a Dr. Pepper and takes the east non-automatic elevator to the 6th floor where he sits down by the 3rd set of two windows on the south building wall (Elm) counting from the east building wall (Houston). Williams ate some chicken and drinks the Dr. Pepper. 1/8/64 Williams says he eats on the 6th; goes to 5th at 12:05. (CD 329:13) As no one else comes up and it is so quiet, Williams puts the empty bottle down by a cart and goes down to the fifth floor where he finds Harold (Hank) Norman (Negro) and James (Junior) Jarman. (3:171,172,173) Check CE 2003 (Meagher:40) Williams goes to 6th floor; stays 3 minutes; goes down stairs to 5th; hear 2 shots overhead. (CD5:330)

Check on the location of chicken bone fragments and 'lunch sack(s)' on the boxes surrounding Oswald's hiding place as it might indicate how close Williams comes to Oswald. (Meagher:39,40)

November 22, 1963 - Friday   12:00 Noon

At 12:00 noon, Eddie Piper sees Oswald on the first floor. (6:383) DPD Statement 2/18/64=Piper tells LHO he is going to eat sandwich and Oswald mumbles something that he is going up to eat. (TAG 1:467)

At 12:00 noon Charles D. Givens, a Negro ex-convict, goes to visit a friend at a parking lot at Elm and Record. (24:210; CD 1069(c):11) This is the 100 block of North Record. ("Friend" Edward Shields says 601 Main. James Lacy = friend. (See N.385)

On 11/21 Jack Ruby had visited the AAA Bonding Service, 106 N. Record, around noon. Re: Phil Hodges, bonds, 607 Main; Best Cafe, 601 Commerce (1962 City Directory) (25:190,215,321,322)

A list of Dallas gamblers on April 2, 196 , includes:
         "17. Smith and Stovall, 106 S. Record, bail bondsman"(23:166)

On 1/8/64 Jarman says he, Norman and Williams eat lunch on 1st floor around noon; 12:25 take west elevator to 5th floor. Hear shots and go downtown. (CD 329:12) On 1/8/64 Norman says Jarman and he eat lunch on 1st floor; go outside. Go to 5th on west elevator and Williams joins them. (CD 329:14)

Between 12:10 p.m. and 12:25 p.m. James (Junior) Jarman and Harold (Hank) Norman take the west automatic elevator to the 5th floor.(3:210; 24:229)

228

They see the east non-automatic elevator at the 6th floor. (3:190)
(12:10/12:25 would indicate Williams came down at 12:15 p.m.??)

)   Bonnie Ray Williams (Negro) says that James (Junior) Jarman and Harold (Hank Norman have already reached the 5th floor on the west automatic elevator when he comes down from the 6th floor on the east non-automatic elevator. (3:172) At 12:05 (CD329:13)

12:10 p.m. (CST) = 10:10 a.m. (PST)   (CD 1107:82,83)
Two experiences (6 years) telephone operators on a toll call line servicing 12,000 phones in Oxnard, California, report:
    (1) Voice of middle-aged woman.
    (2) At 10:07/10:08 a.m.: "The President is going to die at 10:10" (12:10 CST)
    (3) This said so rapidly that it might have been read: "The Justice, the Supreme Court, there is going to be a fire in all the windows; the Government is going up in flames."
    (4) Named 12 courts in order of importance starting with the Supreme Court to Probate Court and Juvenile Court.
    (5) "The President is going to die at 10:30." (12:30 CST)
    (6) Courts again mentioned.
    (7) "The Government takes over everything; lock, stock and barrel."
    (8) One of the operators heard: "thermostat, rheostat, heostat."
    (9) Lasted 10-15 minutes. Operators switched to other calls. This caller was never connected to anyone else. At one time when operator offered help, the voice said, "Please get off the line; I'm using the phone." (This was a party line.)
      (Legacy of Doubt:234 says Bobby Kennedy very curious about call and investigated Oxnard 5/28/68) Call from Oxnard-Camarillo area 50 miles north of Los Angeles.

At 12:10 p.m. TSBD president Cason leaves the building to go home.(22:640)

12:15 p.m.(-) - Mrs. R. E. (Carolyn) Arnold tells FBI on 11/26/63 that Oswald was in hallway between front door and double doors a few minutes before 12:15. (CD5:41 - Archives - Meagher:225)

On 11/22 Jack E. Dougherty says that he works on the 6th floor until noon and then goes to the first floor to eat his lunch. At 12:45 p.m. Dougherty goes back to work and is on the 5th floor getting some stock when he hears a shot. (CD5:366; CD206:11)

12:15? - LHO is seen on 5th floor (CD 1210:4 - Sgt. Gerald Hill)

At 12:   p.m. Jack E. Dougherty (white) goes back to work on the 6th floor (This indicates ! that Dougherty calls the west automatic elevator down from the 5th floor and returns on it to the 6th floor.)

12:15/12:20 ? - Danny Arce assists old man with kidney trouble to men's room on west side of 2nd floor of TSBD. (6:366,367) Sees him leave in black car. Arce describes (on 11/22/63) as real old man in old brown suit and western type hat. Arce sees him leave TSBD and drive off in old black Buick. Old man is in TSBD after lunch but not carrying anything in hands. (TAG 1:5)

TSBD superintendent Truly says that the normal lunch period is from 12:00 noon until 12:45 p.m.; however, as Dougherty comes an hour earlier than the other employees in the morning, perhaps his lunch period is different.

Jack E. Dougherty (white) takes the west automatic elevator on the 6th floor and goes to the 5th floor where he is about 10' from the elevator when he hears something that he thinks
(a) is a backfire
(b) is a shot overhead (CD206:11; 3:228,229; 6:379,380; 22:645; 24:206)

White male, 28, sallow complexion, foreign appearance, very prominent nose, goes to Anderson Studios, Cedar Springs and Harwood, and asks to make Long Distance collect call to Indiana. Leaves without completing the call. Nervous. Just as reports of shooting come in. (CD5:439(Rel? W. D. Sanders

Geneva Hine, only employee in TSBD second floor office, says power went off and phones went "dead" in TSBD as pilot car of motorcade approached TSBD. (6:395; CD5:3_ _)

Carolyn Arnold, and Oswald in the 2nd Floor Lunchroom

In the movie, "JFK", Oliver Stone shows a number of rather misleading scenes and statements that continually raise questions. One of these is the "team of shooters" he shows accessing the 6th floor, pulling weapons out of cases, building a sniper's nest, and then leaving. The actor speaking (Kevin

Costner?) talks about the "workmen" that were replacing (overlaying) the 6th floor that day. The problem with this, of course, is that the actual workmen laying plywood over the old flooring, were all employees of the building. They were not "outsiders", although at least one of them, Bonnie Ray Williams, did normally work the northern warehouse a couple of blocks north of the TSBD. (But it gave the movie more drama, and allowed Gerry Patrick Heming an role in the movie – he is the big guy pulling the rifle out of a box.)

Another misleading scene is the one where they showed Carolyn Arnold testifying in the Clay Shaw trial. They show Oswald eating his lunch in the 2nd floor lunchroom, and her voiceover says:

> "He was sitting in one of the booths on the right hand side of the room. He was alone as usual and appeared to be having lunch. I did not speak to him but I recognized him clearly. I remember it was 12:15 or later. It coulda been 12:25, five minutes before the assassination, I don't exactly remember, I was pregnant and I had a craving for a glass of water."

This has been brought up numerous times, and it gives Oswald an alibi. However, Carolyn Arnold never testified in the Clay Shaw trial.

CD-5

FEDERAL BUREAU OF INVESTIGATION

Date ___11/26/63___

        Mrs. R. E. ARNOLD, Secretary, Texas School Book Depository, advised she was in her office on the second floor of the building on November 22, 1963, and left that office between 12:00 and 12:15 PM, to go downstairs and stand in front of the building to view the Presidential Motorcade. As she was standing in front of the building, she stated she thought she caught a fleeting glimpse of LEE HARVEY OSWALD standing in the hallway between the front door and the double doors leading to the warehouse, located on the first floor. She could not be sure that this was OSWALD, but said she felt it was and believed the time to be a few minutes before 12:15 PM.

        She stated thereafter she viewed the Presidential Motorcade and heard the shots that were fired at the President; however, she could furnish no information of value as to the individual firing the shots or any other information concerning OSWALD, whom she stated she did not know and had merely seen him working in the building.

on 11/26/63	at Dallas, Texas	File # DL 89-43
by Special Agent RICHARD E. HARRISON /rmb		Date dictated 11/26/63

This document contains neither recommendations nor conclusions of the FBI. It is the property of the FBI and is loaned to your agency; it and its contents are not to be distributed outside your agency.

In the attached HSCA document, you should see a reference to her FBI statement, made on Tuesday, November 26th, 1963. In that statement, taken 4 days after the assassination (attached below) Carolyn was standing outside, in front of the building, so she could see the Motorcade. She looked behind her, and thought *"she caught a fleeting glimpse of LEE HARVEY OSWALD standing in the hallway between the front door and the double doors leading to the warehouse, on the 1st floor."* She said the time would have been before 12:15 or so. This was the report taken within days of the assassination where the memory would have been fresh.

Additionally, Commission Document 1381 (CD 1381) contains the statements of all 73 employees of the TSBD who were there that day. It was taken in the spring of 1964, by the FBI. Naturally, being much later than the above statement, it was more subject to what the employees had discussed and heard about. In that statement, Carolyn Arnold says she did not see Oswald that day.

Carolyn Arnold's statement about seeing Oswald in the 2nd floor lunchroom was made as late as November 26, **1978**, in an interview with Earl Golz, Dallas Morning News. (Summers, *Conspiracy*, p. 108) In all fairness, Summers says that Arnold was surprised by her FBI "testimony", and allegedly misquoted. However, even the HSCA did not include the 2nd floor story in its discussion of movements within the building in their 1978 Report. I have not found where they talked directly to Ms. Arnold – only the reference to her Nov. 26, **1963** FBI statement.

Victoria Adams and Sandra Styles

"JFK" also discusses Sandra Styles and Victoria Adams. This pair of TSBD employees (Scotts-Foreman Publishing employees) were sitting in the front of their office spaces, with fellow employees Dorothy Garner and Elsie Dorman (who filmed the event, but aimed too high). Also watching from another end of the 4th floor were Mary Hollies, Bettie Foster, Yola Hopson, and Ruth Nelson (Willis?). In the movie, it shows them running down the stairs right after the assassination, but stresses that they never see or hear Oswald.

JFK Assassination: Shades From The Fence

They imply that Oswald would have had to pass them on the stairs on his way from the 6th floor, down to the 2nd.

In the previous article, based on the Warren Commission, I stressed that they said they immediately saw Bill Shelley and Bill Lovelady, once they came down the stairs onto the 1st floor. There was some discrepancy in how soon they came down the stairs, because Shelley and Lovelady went to the railroad yards for a period of time before returning to the building.

Lovelady does say he saw at least one of the "girls" when they returned. (He volunteered without anyone asking that he was not sure it was "Vicki". So it could have been anyone.)

In Barry Ernest's excellent book, "The Girl On the Stairs", he discusses his many years of investigation with mentor Harold Weisberg. He finally tracks down Vickie Adams, and gets clarification. Vickie confirms that she and Sandra started towards the back wall of the 4th floor office areas, about 30 seconds after the shooting. They are accompanied by their "no nonsense" Supervisor Dorothy Garner. (Vickie says she was an intimidating woman.) Vickie insists that it took about 1 minute to descend all of the stairs, crossing the 20-25 feet at each floor, to reach the 1st floor. These were times that Vickie estimated, after being pressed on this point by the WC questioner. They put Sandra and Vickie on the 1st floor about 12:32, on their way out to the railroad yards.

They never see, nor hear, Oswald while on the floors or on the stairs. Vickie insists that she would be able to at least hear Oswald, as they were wooden stairs and anyone on those stairs make a great deal of noise. Additionally, she never sees Baker or Truly coming up the stairs on their way to the 5th floor, where they take the manual elevator up to the 7th floor and proceed up to the roof. She also does not see them when she reaches the 1st floor. Sandra Styles supports all of these statements in an interview Barry had with her.

Now, both Sandra and Vickie were there that day, and I was not. They were also familiar with those rickety, creaky wooden stairs, and when they both say they should have been able to hear Oswald, or anyone else on the stairs, either behind (above) them, or ahead (below) them, I have to believe they are sincere in that belief. (I am NOT one of the researches who seem to believe that **everyone** except LHO that worked there is lying, or in on it.) Barry was very specific about the point of them being able to hear anyone on the stairs, even if they were ahead of them. Both ladies believed that they should have.

However, the fact that they did not see, *or hear*, Baker and Truly on the stairs is problematic. We know that Baker's foot hit the front steps of the TSBD about 22 seconds after the head shot (we put together films and photos and can reconstruct that). Assuming an interaction between Baker, janitor Eddie Piper and eventually Roy Truly, somewhere in the front lobby area of the 1st floor, that would put Baker and Truly at the west elevator about 1 to 1.5 minutes after the first shot. This is about the time when Adams and Styles calculate they emerged from the stairs onto the 1st floor. Very hard to believe they would not notice a Police Officer with his gun out, waiting for an elevator right there by them. Very hard to believe that they could have emerged from the stairs and left the building before Baker and Truly were across the open shipping floor.

As earnest as Vickie and Sandra believe that they would have heard Oswald, I have my doubts. Both girls had just seen the President of the United State shot, and were in a very stressful state of mind. They proceeded down these loud, creaky wooden stairs, in an attempt to get outside and find out what happened. In addition, they were both wearing 3" high-heeled shoes, as ladies in downtown Dallas office positions were almost always wearing in 1963. They would not be thinking about listening for others on the stairs, and would have been making a lot of noise on those same stairs themselves. Because the stairs were dark, and also because of the heels, Barry says that they went rather slowly and carefully, and insist they should be able to hear Oswald. He stressed this point very carefully in his interviews with both women, and they sincerely believe they should be able to hear him.

JFK Assassination: Shades From The Fence

From what I can tell from the Police inventory, Oswald was wearing some form of loafers (no shoe laces is mentioned). He could have been ahead of them, having passed the 4th floor before they cleared the mid-floor wall, where they could see the elevator area. He only weighed about 140 lbs, and may have been trying to be stealthy as he descended. I think it is very possible they did not hear him.

Dorothy Garner remains by the back wall of the 4th floor office space, which is halfway between the front windows and the stairs. In his appendix Barry Ernest produces a letter he found in the national archives, which he calls the Stroud Letter. Martha Joe Stroud was an Assistant United States Attorney. In this letter, there are corrections to Vickie Adams testimony that she asked to be made, and were never there.

In addition, Stroud says that Dorothy Garner stated that she continued to stand at the middle wall after Sandra and Vickie went down the stairs, and later saw Truly and Baker come up, on their way to the 5th floor. She also does not report seeing Oswald, or anyone else on the stairs. Dorothy's statements in this letter are very important, as it confirms how soon after the shots that the three ladies went toward the back warehouse space of the 4th floor. It also confirms that nobody used those stairs from the moment she could clearly see the area and the 2 ladies went down, until Baker and Truly came up.

Baker and Truly being seen by Dorothy Garner very soon after Styles and Adams leave the 4th floor, and the fact that neither of the girls saw Truly and Baker also becomes problematic. It tends to support that Oswald was ahead and below them, as the obvious place that Baker and Truly could be, where Styles and Adams missed them, **is with Oswald in the 2nd floor lunchroom!** It could be during these brief seconds when all 3 of the men are out of the path of the stairs and crossing areas, that the 2 girls bypass them. The exchange when Baker asks Truly if Oswald belonged in the building, appears to be the exact moment that Styles and Adams rush past, on their way to the 1st floor.

JFK Assassination: Shades From The Fence

An additional consideration to all of this is Jack Dougherty use of the western (automatic) elevator. It somehow went from the 5th floor, where he was filling orders and Roy Truly saw it, to the 1st floor. Jack said he was working on the 5th and briefly on the 6th, and heard a noise that sounded like a backfire, so took the elevator to the 1st floor where he encountered Eddie Piper. (Vol VI p380) Nobody noticed it passing them, so it probably did not make a lot of noise. Certainly it made less noise than that made by footsteps of the people on the different flights of wooden stairs

Now.... many Researchers argue that this simply proves that Oswald was on the 2nd floor lunchroom all along. That is certainly one way that he could be there without Styles, Adams and Garner seeing him.

But..... *"what is good for the Goose is good for the Gander"*. If the fact that Adams, Styles and Garner do not see or hear Oswald, 'exonerates' him, **then it also exonerates any other shooter or conspirator** on the 6th floor! You can't have it both ways. At least during the number of minutes right after the assassination; when Adams, Styles, Garner, Baker, Truly (as well as Jarman, Williams, Norman and shipper Troy West) are in the back stairs area. There is possibly a very few minutes beyond the time that the three workers on the 5th floor (Williams, Norman and Jarman) came down to the 1st, before the police sealed off the building and used the stairs and elevators to begin the search.

If there was a shooter, or fake shooter (*sticking a gun out the window to be seen)*, they also have to make their way out of the building. The building will later be searched by Dallas Police, including the roof (Baker) and the crawl spaces above the 7th floor, the closets, storerooms, lunchrooms, etc.

If Styles, Adams, Garner, Baker and Truly (shipper Eugene West and others on the 1st floor, or spread throughout the building) did not see Oswald, they also did not see anyone else! If there were other shooters, such as Malcolm Wallace, Loy Factor, and so on, they are subject to the same rules as Oswald, and anyone except the Invisible Man. They have to access the escape the building, and there are very limited ways of doing that. There are very limited times that the area was not seen by someone, and the planning and logistics problems are still present.

The "Psychic" Oswald and the Domino Room

According to the 5 pages of handwritten notes that were allegedly written by Captain Will Fritz (FBI Agent James Hosty also wrote some notes that have materialized), Oswald claimed he was eating a cheese sandwich in the 1st floor lunchroom, or domino room. Nobody else confirms his presence there, although one of the 19 warehouse workers thought he might have seen Oswald briefly. (NOTE: The notes are attached, and right before these statements the date 11-**21**63 appears. We have presumed these claims from Oswald do apply to Friday, 11-**22**-63 – and it was just a slight error by Fritz. Not sure why he would be asking about Oswald's lunch on Thursday. But elsewhere Oswald says he ate his lunch by Bill Shelley out front (Friday?). Could the different statements by Oswald really mean different dates, asked by Fritz?)

Additionally, there were about 10-12 ladies that usually frequented the 2nd floor lunchroom, and none of them recall Oswald that day either. Generally, the warehouse workers would frequent the 1st floor "Domino Room" to eat lunch, where they could laugh and joke and have a little more coarse language, while the office ladies tended to frequent the 2nd floor lunchroom. Oswald also allegedly told Will Fritz that a couple of the negroes came through the room briefly, while he was there. He thought one of them was called "Junior" (Jarman), and the other was a shorter man (Harold Norman?).

During 2013, I had an on-stage 'debate' (had to take the Lone Nut side, although that is not my firm belief) with Robert Groden, after the traveling Broadway stage play "Oswald" The Interrogation" at Fort Worth'sCasa Manana theater. Sitting in the audience was Researcher Jim Marrs, who raised his hand to ask us a question, but was not noticed by the Moderator with the microphone. During the NID conference, I asked Jim what his question would have been, and he said for the audience benefit he was going to ask:

"How would Oswald know that Junior had come through the Domino Room, if he was not present to see it?"

I have had a number of Researchers bring this up. Some have gone as far as to state that Oswald either must have been in there to know this, or Oswald was a very accurate "psychic".

Instead, I will offer a less "black and white" alternative, at some shade of "gray" in between.

The Domino Room was called that for a reason. It was used to play dominoes by many of the warehouse workers. Not sure how many of my readers have been involved in a work environment where workers play games during the lunch hour. I have worked at a couple of places that played the card game "Spades", or the domino game "42". Plus I have been around many people who play Cribbage, Gin, Bridge, Poker, and other games during their lunch breaks, and many other breaks. (We used to play Spades every chance we got.)

In addition, the Domino Room had the men's room attached to it, as well as it's window being the place where most of the warehouse workers stored their jackets (Oswald's blue jacket was left in the window that day), as well as their sack lunches. They might even buy a lunch off the catering truck that usually arrive mid-morning, and store that lunch there until their 11:45 – 12:30 lunch time.

Having worked in the building for 5 weeks, Oswald would know that most warehouse workers would go to the restroom and clean-up, then grab their lunches, if not eat their lunches, in the Domino Room. He could have even noticed that morning, which had a lunch sack (name on them) or a lunch box in that window. Just common sense would allow Oswald to name somebody that almost always did this, and say they 'walked though'. It is almost a given, and does not require any psychic ability to say this, and hopefully have a valid 'alibi'.

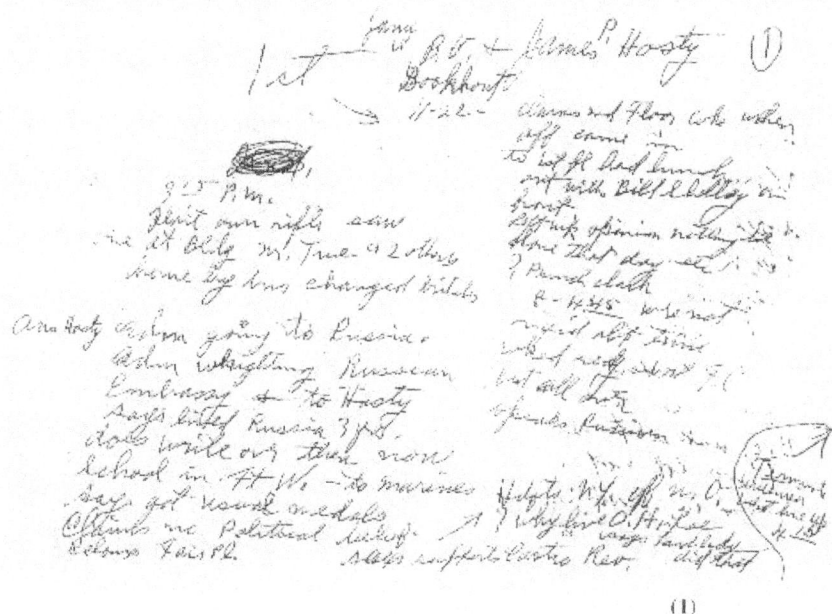

(1)

1st 11-22
B.O. + James P. Hosty
Jame W Bookout

3:15 p.m.
Didn't own rifle saw
one at Bldg M. True + 2 others
home by bus changed britches

Ans Hosty adm going to Russia
adm wrighting Russian
Embassy + to Hosty
says lived Russia 3 yrs.
Does write over then now
school in Ft W. - to Marines
says got usual medals
claims no political belief
belongs Fair Pl
Hdqts NY off N.O.
says supports Castro Rev.

claims 2nd floor Coke when
off came in
to 1st floor had lunch
out with Bill Shelley in
front
lft wk opinion nothing be
done that day etc.
? punch clock
8-4:45 wre not
rigid abt time
wked reg 1st Fl
but all over
speaks Russian

?Why live O.H. Lee
says landlady did that

Terminate interview
with line up
4:15

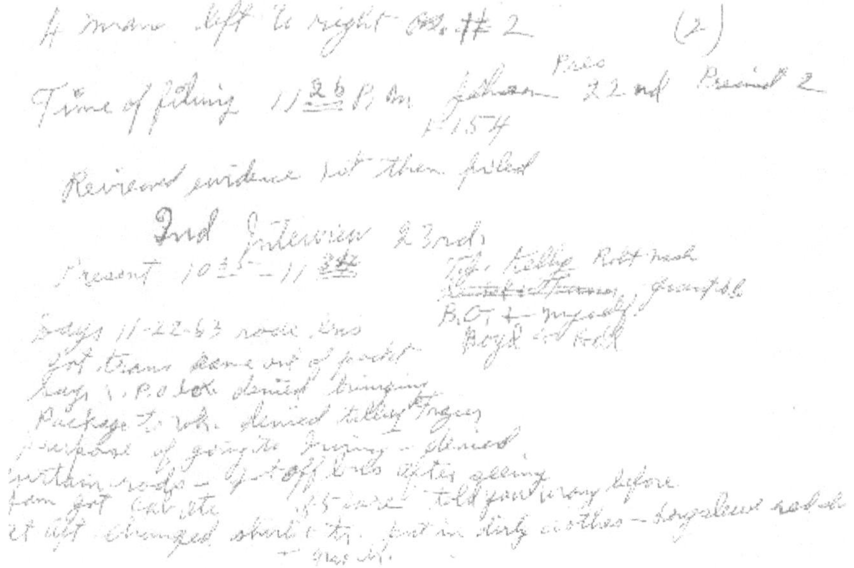

JFK Assassination: Shades From The Fence

[handwritten notes]

4 man left to right as #2   (2)

Time of filing 11:26 pm Johnson Pres 22nd   Precinct 2
                        F154
Received evidence 1st then filed

2nd Interview 23rd
Present 10:35-11:34
T.J. Kelly Robt Nash
Grant ??
B.O + myself
Boyd + Hall

Says 11-22-63 rode bus
got trans same out of pocket
says 1 p.o. box denied bringing
 package to wk. Denied telling Frazier
purpose of going to Irving - denied
curtain rods - got off bus after seeing
jam got cab etc .85 fare told you wrong before
at apt. Changed shirts + tr. Put in dirty clothes - long sleeve red sh
                + gray tr.

242

morning 23rd. (3)
says 11-21-63 say two negr came in
one Jr. + short negro - ask ? for lunch says cheese
sandwiches + apple

says doesn't pay cash for wife staying with Mrs. Payne
denies owning rifle in garage or elsewhere admits other
things these
Came there 63 - N.O.
Says no visitors at apt. Claims never order
owns ???? for gun
denies belonging to Com party
says bgt gun 7 mo Ft W. didn't know what Place.
ams to grest ant questioning
Arv. July 62 from U.S.S.R. Int by F.B.I. Ft W
says Hard + Soft meth etc   Buddy
says on interview of Payne by F.B.I. He thought she was intimidated

(4)

Desires to talk to Mr. Abt. I ask who
says Smith act att.
Says did live N.O. 4706 Magazine St. From Apt.
Wked Wm B. Riley Co 640
says nothing against Pres does not want to
 talk further -   No Pahy at time in past had
refused
Oswald A.C.L.U. member he says says
Mrs. Payne was too. I ask abt organization
he says to pay lawyer fees when needed
B.O. asks about Heidel selective s. Card - adm having
would not admit signature - wouldn't say
why he had it. Says add. Book has names of Russian
Emigrants he visits - denies shooting Pres   says didn't know
Gov. shot

3rd 11-23 - 6:35

(5)

Shows photo of gun. Would not discuss photo
denies buying gun from Kleins.
Comp of wanting jacket for line up.
Says I made picture super imposed

arr 10-11:15
4th.   11-24   Insp Holmes - Sorrels - Kelley et al

        Chief

Summary

My good friend, the late Ken Holmes, used to scold me on
a regular basis. He used to just look at me and ask, "So **YOU**
can put Oswald on the 6th floor with a rifle?" The phrase is a
quote from Chief of Police Jesse Curry, who insisted that
"nobody could put Oswald in the window with a gun." **I can't
either.** However, I also can't prove he was *anywhere else*
either.

Unlike the Warren Commission, who had a magical ability
to ignore anything that did not point to the "Lone Nut",

JFK Assassination: Shades From The Fence

Oswald, I simply cannot ignore all of the other statements, preknowledge, evidence, activities, witness statements and Oswald's background. I am enough of a "fence sitter" (my reputation, unless you ask a CT'er or LN'er), to be unable to just accept the Lone Shooter theory. However, I cannot prove the Conspiracy theories either. (At minimum, there was a "conspiracy" to not investigate or present any evidence that pointed beyond Oswald, but that does not make it the same conspiracy that killed Kennedy. A future article, perhaps.)

However, any pet theory that the reader wants to believe, must be supported with logic and common sense. There were very small windows for both accessing and escaping, and it certainly could have happened. However, it is not enough to simply state that other shooters were in the building, unless you can at least think through and figure out how they got there, built the "sniper's nest", and how they exited.

This article was simply a further discussion on the difficulties involved in accessing the building. Nothing is impossible, but not considering the planning and logistics involved is simply not thinking the problem through.

16. "The Ups and Downs of the TSBD - Aftermath"

This next chapter is again a reprint (without photos) of one of my "Dealey Plaza Echo" articles. This third one is again about the building, and the movements inside the building, but is more focused on the period of time after the shooting. It is based on the Testimony from Dallas Police and various members of the Press that managed to access the building before it was sealed off. MaryFerrell.org definitely has full archival copies of the Echo, for those interested; however, I am uncertain that this latest article is there.

This article does include speculation of the movements and use of the stairs and elevators in the critical 2-3 minutes after the shooting. This has been called "horrendous speculation" by at least one Researcher on the internet. I immediately agreed with him that it was "speculation", as I have never said otherwise. However, I challenged him to show why it was "horrendous" by showing me any other "timeline". He never came back to me. While I am certain that somebody else has done a timeline of movements, comparing the statements of the various participants, but I have not seen one. This graphic lays these movements side-by-side so that the reader can readily see how these statements 'could have' been related.

Again, this 3rd article (of three) focuses on the movements after the shooting, including discussion of the law enforcement sealing and search of the building. Like the others, it also talks about some of the many theories. It was written in 2017.

The Ups and Downs of the TSBD – Aftermath

This is my 3rd article on the interior of the Texas School Book Depository, on November 22, 1963. The 1st article (Echo

JFK Assassination: Shades From The Fence

March, 2008) focused mainly on the Warren Commission version of the employees of the building, and their movements. The 2nd article (Echo Winter 2015) expanded into both the HSCA investigations and interviews, major books and other theories I have run into over the years. For the most part, they focused on the time and movements in the building up to 12:30, and the stairs after the shooting. This article will focus on the TSBD after the shots. Since each article should 'stand alone', there will be limited repetition in this article.

Of course, all of this information is pure speculation. 1963 was before we had video cameras in the workplace. Although CCTV was available, it was extremely expensive and seldom used for anything less important than a bank vault or government building. Even then, it was seldom recorded. Therefore, we have no real proof of the movements in the TSBD in the eight to ten minutes after the shooting, until the building was "sealed off" by Dallas Police.

The article will focus mainly on those first 10 minutes, but will also cover a little of the investigation within the building for the next couple of hours.

The Texas School Book Depository Employees

All of the TSBD Employees had access to the entire structure. On that day, there were 73 employees in the building. About 22 of these stayed within the building during the Motorcade, but most left the building to watch the motorcade in the Plaza out front.

Obviously, Lee Harvey Oswald, as well the other employees, would have plenty of time to build a "sniper's nest", move Rolling Readers from their spot in the middle of the 6th floor to the NE corner, and fire a rifle (or plant one). The Secretaries, and other women, would not have the same opportunity since their moving boxes around in the warehouse spaces would be unusual.

The FBI was asked to interview every employee by the Warren Commission, and did so in March and April of 1964.

JFK Assassination: Shades From The Fence

The document containing those interviews is Commission Document 1381 (CD1381). In those interviews each employee was asked the same 5 questions. These included where they were at the time of the shooting, if they had seen Oswald on that day, and if they saw any strangers in the building around the time of the motorcade.

Only Danny Arce said he saw any stranger in the building, and he stated it was around 12:05 or so that an older man needed a restroom. Danny showed him where the restroom was (presumably by the Domino room on the 1st floor), waited, and saw the man leave the building and climb into a black car, well before the time the Motorcade arrived. None of the other 72 employees reported any stranger in the building.

Attached is a summary from CD1381 of the employees inside the building at the time of the shooting.

Some researchers believe that Malcolm Wallace or other strangers were in the building, and that Oswald was either in the 2nd floor lunchroom, or the Domino room (1st floor lunchroom). While it is certainly possible that strangers were in the building, there is the *logistical* problems of accessing the building, moving the Rolling Readers, creating a sniper's nest, and exiting the building, *without being seen by Oswald or any of the other 72 employees.* Some believe that Oswald could have assisted others, by building the sniper's nest, moving Rolling Readers, and helping them access the building without being seen by anyone. It requires the idea that Oswald would let someone else shoot from his place of employment, and then **not leave with them!** It does not make sense that Oswald would help incriminate himself, and then not escape with them. It was not like he ran interference to Officer Marion Baker, to protect his escaping comrades.

Other researchers simply believe that other TSBD employees were "in on it", and conspired to set Oswald up as a patsy. A few have mentioned Roy Truly, Bill Shelley, Jack Dougherty, Bill Lovelady and others. Some have blamed Jack Cason (the President), because his politics were such that he hated Kennedy. A very few have actually postulated that the entire Texas School Book Company was a sham, set up to kill JFK (ignoring the number of years the company was in existence).

Still others insist that they see Oswald on the front porch in the Altgens 6 photograph, the Couch or Darnell films, or other photographic evidence. This is partially based on Oswald *stating* he was there (Suspects NEVER lie about their location....right?). This is despite the statements of every other TSBD employee on that porch or just inside, who insist Oswald was not there. There were 12 employees that also stated they were on the front porch area: Bill Lovelady, Bill Shelley, Buell Frazier, Sarah Stanton, J R Molina, Mrs. Charles Davis, Ruth Dean, Carl Jones, Judith McCully, Madie Reese, Pauline Sanders and Otis Williams.

Regardless, they simply insist that "Doorman" or "Prayer Man" is really Oswald, and any employee that does not agree is simply "lying". These Researchers see what they want to see, and simply remain stubbornly emphatic. If they see it, then it either must have happened, or the films / photos were "modified" (although they cannot explain how there was time to do so).

The Lunchrooms

There were 2 lunchrooms in the Texas School Book Depository, that all of the employees were allowed to use.

The 1st floor lunch room was called the "Domino Room". This is because many of the warehouse workers would play Dominoes in this room at every break, lunch or before work. It was located in the back of the 1st floor, close to the dock. It also had small restrooms attached to it, which was more convenient for the warehouse workers than the larger restrooms on the 2nd floor. In addition, the warehouse workers would store their jackets, lunches and other personal items in this room. Since the women seldom used this lunchroom, it allowed for more coarse language by the warehouse workers.

JFK Assassination: Shades From The Fence

The 2nd floor lunchroom was located close to the back stairs and freight elevators, in the back center of the 2nd floor. It was also just off the office area where most of the women's desks were located. This is where most of the women would take their lunches every day, although it was accessible to all employees. There was a Coke machine located in this lunchroom, and a Dr Pepper vending machine by the stairs on the 1st floor.

Many Researchers insist that Oswald was in the 1st floor lunchroom at the time of the shooting. This is based on his statement to Capt. Will Fritz that he was in there (would he lie?). Additionally, he said that 2 of the warehouse workers walked through, one of them named "Junior" (James Jarman Jr.) and the other a shorter one (Harold Norman?). Many believe the only way Oswald could know this, is if he were really in there. However, having worked there several weeks, he was completely familiar with the pattern at lunch where workers used the adjoining restroom, picked up their lunch from the window, played dominoes, etc. It does not take psychic abilities to determine that they likely "walked through", as they did every other day, especially if he saw their lunches there, or heard them talk about getting them.

The 2nd floor lunchroom is a location that many Researchers place Oswald during the shooting, based on his being there within 2 minutes of the shooting. The main reason for this contention is a statement made in the mid 70's by employee Carolyn Arnold that she saw Oswald around 12:15 – 12:25. This was Arnold's 3rd statement, 12+ years later. Her earliest statement said she was standing out front, and looked back and thought she *might have* seen Oswald in the entry area (November 27th, 1963 affidavit). Her CD 1381 statement said she did not see Oswald that day (March/April 1964). Additionally, several of the women employees ate lunch there that day, and left the lunchroom about 12:15-12:20. None of them reported seeing Oswald in there, until Arnold's statement over 12 years later. Yet some Researchers site this as **proof** Oswald was there. (I was not there, so I can't dispute it.)

JFK Assassination: Shades From The Fence

I have asked many of these Researchers to present a scenario where the Conspirators could give a good reason for Oswald to wait in these lunchrooms, without him getting suspicious. I have also asked for a scenario where the 'shooters' can plan, access, build the sniper's nest, shoot, and exit the building. They remain silent, except for those that insist many of the employees were "in on it" or simply lying. Practical logic seems to give way to extremism, when a Researcher wants to believe Oswald as an unwitting patsy.

The Freight Elevators and the Stairs

Again, since every article ought to stand on its own 'legs', I am repeating much of the material I cover in detail in my earlier articles. In this article, I will move much more quickly over it.

There was no way to access the 5th, 6th and 7th floor from the front of the building. There was a small lobby in the entrance area, which had a set of stairs that only went up to the 2nd floor. Additionally, there was a small passenger elevator that only went up to the 4th floor.

The stairs that could access the entire building (except the basement) were located in the northwest corner of the building. These were single flight stairs, with a 90 degree turn in the middle. You had to go up the north wall halfway up, then turn 90 degrees to the left and west wall to go up to the next floor. Once on the next floor, you had to cross about 25 feet of that next floor, to access the next flight of stairs. There was no stairwell, so you could not just enter an enclosed stairwell and access all of the floors. While using these single flight stairs you would be visible to anyone close by at each floor, as you traversed. The stairs were about 3 feet in width, and constructed of wood on a wooden inner wall and brick outer wall.

The 2nd floor had walls a few feet away from the stairs/freight elevator area, but a small open area surrounding them. The lunchroom vestibule door had a window that looked out into the area. The 3rd floor was the only floor with walls

252

close to the stairs, where you would be hidden from anyone on that floor as you crossed it in a small hall. The 4th floor had a wall about the middle of the building that separated the office space from the warehouse. Anyone using these stairs could be seen by any of the employees with no obstructed view (depending on the height of the box stacks).

The Freight Elevators were located in the northwest area of the building, close to the stairs. They were 2 elevators in the same shaft, with no space between the elevators and the shaft walls (Bruce Willis fans shudder). Additionally, there was a row of windows in the shaft that kept it pretty well lit. The doors to the elevators were slatted wood gates, with gaps between the boards. This meant when the elevator was not there you could easily see through the shaft to the stairs (except 3rd – with its hall). The elevators were only ¾ solid, with a chain link material separating them. Therefore, even if the elevator(s) were there, you could see through.

All movements beyond the 4th floor would require using one of these 2 methods.

The Critical First 2 Minutes

The bulk of this article will cover the movements in the building during the 3 minutes after the shooting. This is approximately the time it took Oswald to leave the building. We will focus on the 4 groups that were doing most of the movement in the building, according to testimony, statements, and analysis.

Of course, if your theory *insists* on other shooters in the building, I cannot dispute you! There were certainly gaps in time leading up to 12:30 that could have been used by others to access the building, regardless of the possible exposure to the employees they faced. If your theory puts others into the building, you should work on analyzing their movements and fitting them into the movements and statements of the other individuals involved, who did NOT see them (unless lying, of course).

Again, this is all speculation, as there were no video cameras inside the building.

Knowing the layout of the building, the times involved are speculation. For instance, a person 'in a hurry' going from 3rd floor down to the 2nd is projected as taking about 10 seconds: 4 seconds down the stairs, and 6 seconds to cross the 2nd floor to the top of the next flight of stairs. The reader may have a better time.

Four groups of reported movement will be discussed, and a time chart estimate presented below. I will then talk about other employees, press and police, for the 10 minutes it took to seal the building.

Shooter/Oswald – If you don't believe Oswald was the shooter on the 6th floor, then you can certainly substitute your shooters. At least until the 2nd floor lunch room encounter, which we know was Oswald (or identical twin). However, if you do substitute your own shooter (or team) you will have to determine their movements inside the building. Like Oswald, they would have to exit the building, without unusual movements and speed. But, unlike Oswald and the other employees, they had additional problems or entry, as well as the time and knowledge it would take to build a sniper's nest.

You would also have to decide how they intended to "control" Oswald to make sure he was not photographed, or with someone who would give him a complete alibi. Simply asking him to wait in some room would raise his suspicions. You have to give him instructions he would think as normal, so that you don't raise his suspicions and have him figure out he is being set up.

The most common version has him waiting in a lunchroom for a phone call; however, neither lunchroom had a phone in it. Additionally, the phone the warehouse workers normally used, and knew the number to, was in the back center of the 1st floor, in full view of the dock, front, elevators and stairs. To ask Oswald to use any other phone could easily arouse suspicion.

Oswald had an encounter with Roy Truly and Office Baker in the 2nd floor lunchroom, where he was identified as an employee by Truly and let go. He supposedly finished buying a Coke from the machine, as he is seen walking across the 2nd floor office spaces by Mrs. Robert Reid (Geraldine) from the lunchroom area, carrying said Coke. He probably went down the stairs in the front lobby, and leaves the building through the front door. Two newsmen have come forward saying they got directions to the closest phone from someone who they later think was Oswald, at the front door. Pierce Allman, a radio newsman, did make an out-of-breath report from inside the building that we have the audio of today.

Baker and Truly – Dallas Police Officer M. Baker and warehouse Manager Roy Truly are the 2nd group we will chart. Baker is seen running into the building in the Couch and Darnell films, and we can see his foot hitting the bottom step at 22 seconds after the fatal shot. Truly follows him into the building. After a brief exchange between janitor Eddie Piper, Baker and Truly just inside the 2nd glass entry door, Truly leads Baker across the open 1st floor to the freight elevators. Truly says that he saw both elevators were on the 5th floor, and jammed the call button a number of times. The elevator (Automatic – unless the door was open) did not move, so Truly yelled up at least 2 times to "release the elevator". After several seconds, Truly and Baker took the stairs with Truly leading. As they crossed the 2nd floor, Baker saw movement in the 2nd floor lunchroom, and diverted into the lunchroom. There he encountered Lee Oswald. Truly, who had started up to the 3rd floor, came back looking for Baker and found him and Oswald in the lunchroom. Truly identified Oswald as an employee, so they moved on.

Baker and Truly continued up the path of the stairs and crossing of each floor, until they reached the 5th floor. Once there, they saw that the automatic elevator was no longer there, but the eastern manual elevator was. They crossed over and took the manual elevator up to the 7th floor. They then went up the stairs to the roof, and spent several minutes up there. Baker even climbed the Hertz sign, in addition to lifting himself onto the parapet walls of the roof. He determined that a shooter could not easily fire from the walls, as they were too high.

After several minutes on the roof, Baker and Truly came back down. Baker reported to

Inspector Sawyer on the 4th floor, saying he had checked the roof. (The encounter was filmed by Tom Alyea.) Baker then left the building and went to Parkland hospital. Baker estimated he spent 10 – 15 minutes in the building.

The Fifth Floor Warehouse Workers – Bonnie Ray Williams, James Jarman Jr., and Harold Norman were on the 5th floor during the shooting. They were at the front 3 windows in the southeast corner of the building, and were photographed kneeling in those windows for several seconds after the shots rang out. One of them later said he recalled hearing the bullet casings hit the floor above their heads after each shot.

After the initial few seconds, and their natural "what happened?" reaction, they moved quickly away from the east side of the building, to the west – the direction the limo went. They said they spent a few minutes on the west side, looking out the windows to see if they could see anything. Then they moved north of the building, to some more western facing windows close to the stairs. They again spent a few minutes there, looking out to the grassy knoll/parking area west of the building. Bonnie Ray Williams said that while the other two were looking out the window, that he saw Truly and Baker cross the 5th floor to the manual elevator. (However, he could not remember seeing Baker's motorcycle helmet.) After a few minutes, they took the stairs down.

Jack Dougherty – Not a "group" in himself, so he is being mentioned here. Jack had returned to his work of filling orders at 12:30, apparently not having any interest in the motorcade. He reported he took the automatic elevator to the 6th floor briefly, then went to the 5th floor to get some books. He was a few feet from the elevator when he heard a sound that sounded like a "backfire or firecracker" (inside the building?). He continued to fill the order, and then took it down to the 1st shipping floor. There, he was told by janitor Eddie Piper that there had been a shooting. He said he never heard Truly hollering to "release the elevator", and saw nobody during this time.

The women of Scotts Foreman Publishing – The next critical group were the ladies on the 4th floor. These were Victoria Adams, Sandra Styles, Dorothy May Gardner, Elsie Dorman, Mary Hollies and Bettie Foster. These 6 were at the front windows towards the southeast corner, in the office of Scotts Foreman. Additionally, outside of the office area and in the warehouse area on the southwest corner were Yola Hopson and Ruth Nelson. Elsie Dorman filmed the motorcade going through Dealey Plaza, but did not look through the viewfinder to do so, and filmed too high.

After the shots, the ladies were stunned. Within 30 seconds, Vickie Adams and Sandra Styles headed through the office area in the front of the floor, through the door in the wall midway across the building, and towards the back stairs. In 3" heels, they rushed down the stairs, and out the dock door of the building. They went to the parking lots on the west side (grassy knoll), and were within a yard or two of the railroad tracks, when a Dallas Police Officer sent them back to the building.

They came back in to the front of the building, and started to use the passenger elevator.

The elevator was "off" (police will shut off an elevator when looking for suspects, so that nobody would use it). They then went back to the freight elevator and joined Deputy Sheriff Luke Mooney in the automatic elevator. Mooney and the girls went to the second floor, and dropped them off.

Their Supervisor, Dorothy Garner, had also followed the girls back out of the office space. However, Dorothy stopped at the doorway in the wall across the floor that separated the office space from the warehouse space. She stood there, and said that she later saw Baker and Truly emerge from the stairs coming from the 3rd floor, on their way to the stairs to the 5th. She was joined by some of the other ladies that stayed on the floor, and they went to the west windows to see if they could see anything. When the 3 guys from the 5th floor did come down the stairs, they did say that they saw several ladies at this west window. She never left the building, until the building was closed around 2:00 to 2:30 PM.

Sandra and Vickie have since told interviewers that they believed they *should* have been able to hear anyone else ahead or behind them, as they were noisy wooden stairs. However, they were in a hurry, and wearing 3" heels, so were probably making a great deal of noise themselves. If Oswald was trying to be quiet, I doubt they would have heard him ahead of them, with the noise they were likely making themselves.

Dorman did see Baker and Truly coming by the 4th floor. Additionally, Bonnie Ray Williams saw Baker and Truly crossing the 5th floor, to the manual elevator. But Sandra Styles and Vickie Adams did not see anyone at all, while crossing the floors and descending the stairs!

Baker and Truly, who were looking for an elevator, also did not see the girls, nor the automatic elevator pass them on its way down (presumably with Jack Dougherty). The 3 foot stairs and 25 foot crossover on each floor would be shared by bother people coming up, as well as people coming down. None of these people saw any other movement on the stairs or the elevators.

So....based on all of the above....I have created a speculated time chart of the critical 2 minutes or so after the shooting. Again, I was not in the building, and there were no video cameras inside, so this is all speculation. I am just unable to come up with a better time frame for all of the movements of these 4 groups.

There were a number of re-creations done by the Warren Commission, and these times are noted on the right of the chart. Marion Baker was asked to see how long it would take him from 100' or so south of Elm on Houston (where the 1st shot scared birds off the roof), park his motorcycle and go to the 2nd floor lunchroom. His 1st re-creation was 1 ½ minutes, and his 2nd was 1 ¼ minutes. But, in both of them he did not linger at the elevators or the lobby, as happened on Nov. 22. In his testimony, he said this 1 ½ was a "minimum" time.

JFK Assassination: Shades From The Fence

A 24 year old Secret Service Agent recreated the shooter/Oswald path from the sniper's nest, stashing the rifle, and coming down 4 flights of stairs. His recreation was 1 minute 17 seconds (1:17). Coming down the stairs, he was not winded. Baker and Truly said Oswald was acting quite normal, and not out of breath. To be fair, however, Baker did not know Oswald and would not know what 'normal' was. Truly only looked at Oswald long enough to identify him, and then he and Baker moved on. It was not as if they stopped to take his pulse or blood pressure, as they were in a hurry to get to the roof.

As best as I can tell, the purple circles are the only place/time that Baker/Truly, Styles/Adams and Jack Dougherty could possibly pass each other without seeing each other in that limited pathway. With all of them traveling the same path, only while Baker and Truly were in the lunchroom, with Oswald, could Adams and Styles pass by them without seeing them, or being seen by them. Dougherty could actually pass by with the western elevator while people were on any flight of stairs, as the elevator was likely not as loud as their own feet on the stairs, and blocked from view by the stair wall.

The only other possibility is that somehow Adams and Style came down so quickly that they **beat** Oswald down, and also cross the back of the 1st floor to the dock **before** Baker could see them. Remember, that Baker had his weapon out, and was looking for anyone coming down the stairs. I simply find it doubtful, that they were that quick on 3" heels! Of course, this is reinforced by Dorothy Garner seeing them go down, and remaining before Baker/Truly came up.

Oswald would have to cross that area.

Again, if your theory has other shooters in the building, you are welcome to plug them in where you think their exit could have happened. Be sure to let me know.

Sealing the Building and Other Movements

JFK Assassination: Shades From The Fence

Sgt. D. V. Harkness – Dallas Police Sgt. Harkness was the highest ranking officer in Dealey Plaza at the moment of the shooting. He was one of several police officers located at Elm and Houston, with his 3 wheeler. It was probably on this 3-wheeler radio that Junior Jarman and Harold Norman heard that the Motorcade was on Main St. around 12:22/5, prompting them to go back upstairs to the 5th floor.

Like many of the police officers, Harkness initially went to the railroad yards, on his 3wheeler. He says he initially went to the Dealey Plaza Annex, on the other side of the railroad yards, but returned to the grassy knoll area when he did not see any shooter in the Annex.

In the railroad yard, he is approached by 15-year old Amos Euins. Euins had been by the fountains on Houston St. and saw a shooter in the "5th floor". Harkness, puts Euins on the back of his 3-wheeler, and returns to the front of the TSBD. While on the 3-wheeler he radio reports a witness says the 'bookstore' (TSBD). He puts Euins into Inspector Sawyer's car and lets Sawyer know Euins is in there. Sawyer and Harkness discuss the building being sealed, and Officer's White and others had the front door blocked. Harkness and Sawyer orders them to keep it sealed. He gets on the radio at 12:36, and asks for more Dallas Officers to come help seal the building.

Harkness therefore goes to the back of the building, with a couple of other officers. Once back there he encounters "some Secret Service agents. They told me they were Secret Service.", whom he allows to leave. Secret Service are not in Dealey Plaza until closer to 1:00 PM. He estimates that the back dock door was sealed by 12:38 to 12:40.

Inspector Sawyer – Sawyer was stationed during the Motorcade at Main and Akard or Harwood. After the motorcade passes, he gets back into his car and cruises west on Main. He hears the commotion on radio channel 2, including Sheriff Bill Decker instructing Station 5 to send his men into the railroad yards at 12:31. At 12:34 he hears Harkness report that a witness (Euins) reports seeing a shooter in the building, so that is where he heads.

JFK Assassination: Shades From The Fence

He arrives at the building about 12:34/5, and enters. He goes up the elevator to the "top floor" (passenger elevator only goes to 4), and walks briefly to the back. Not seeing anything, he comes down the back stairs to "see about building security". He says he walked right through, and was probably only in the building "one minute" or so. He talks to Harkness, and sends him to the back to seal off the building. He then sets up a command post in front of the building.

Luke Mooney, Eugene Boone, Paul Wilkins and other Police – Deputy Sheriff Luke Mooney, Eugene Boone, Buddy Walthers and 6-8 others were standing in front of the Sheriff's Office/Courthouse when the motorcade passed. Upon hearing the shots, most of them raced to the grassy knoll. However, it did not take long for this flat, open area to be searched for shooters. Amos Euins' reported that the shots came from the Texas School Book Depository, which quickly changed the search for shooters to that building.

Mooney and Deputy Sheriff Vickery and Webster entered the building through the parking cage on the west side of the building, and the 'Cyclone' fence gates there. Mooney told the other officers that he would take the west (automatic) elevator, while they took the stairs. Two ladies walked up (Styles and Adams?) and asked to be taken up to the 2nd floor. He let the ladies off, but could not get the elevator to function after that (possibly left the outer gate up – as both have to be closed to operate it), so he takes the stairs to the 6th floor. He reports that he passes "plain clothes men – possibly Deputy Sheriffs" coming down the stairs. (He is a plain clothed Deputy Sheriff, so should *know* them – but doesn't say he did!)

He does not see anything on 6th, and makes his way up to the 7th floor. There he finds the entrance to the attic/crawlspace, but it is too dark to see anything. Eugene Boone had taken Hugh Betzner (photographer) to the Sheriff's Office, and is tasked to bring back flashlights. (Fire department eventually supplies them.) Dallas Police Officer Paul Wilkins will be the poor guy who eventually has to crawl through this dirty space, but does not see anything.

JFK Assassination: Shades From The Fence

Mooney then goes down to the 6th floor, where the floor-by-floor evidence search is taking place. He squeezes between some boxes, and finds the sniper's nest. He gives the time as approximately 1:00 PM, although he does not really look at his watch to note the exact time. Fritz will then assign a couple of officers to watch and secure the area. (It is reported that 1 officer picks up the brown paper bag, and examines it.)

Once Eugene Boone returns, and joins in the search, he allegedly finds the rifle about 1:25. Paul Wilkins also states that he was the Officer who first saw the rifle, but about the same time as Boone.

Captain Will Fritz was at the Trade Mart during the actual shooting, awaiting the arrival of the President. Chief Stevenson came to him about 12:35 and told him of the shooting. He went to Parkland Hospital initially, arriving about 12:45. He then headed to the Texas School Book Depository, arriving about 12:58. They were in the midst of the floor by floor search, having done an earlier search for suspects. Soon after he arrives, he is told about the finding of the sniper's nest in the southeast corner of the building. He assigns 2 officers to watch the sniper's nest until photographs can be taken by Lt. Carl Day and Studebaker, of the crime lab. He leaves around 2:00 PM, with Oswald's name and address (Paine house) in his pocket, as Roy Truly lets him know the boy that had the lunchroom encounter with Baker was missing.

Various other Law Enforcement officer are part of the searches and evidence gathering of the building, but the above are the critical players.

Tom Alyea – Tom was a film journalist that worked for WFAA (ABC channel 8) on November 22, 1963. Alyea, Pierce Allman (radio newsman) and Robert McNeil were about the only press that accessed the building before it was sealed off. The films we have of the search inside the TSBD, the finding and fingerprinting of the rifle, etc. was filmed by Tom Alyea.

I worked extensively with Tom several years ago, when he was thinking of writing a book, and needed a proof reader. He only got up to about 6 chapters, and due to family health, I think he dropped the project. I am not at liberty to discuss everything he said due to the trust we have, but I will discuss a few things which he has said in a newsletter he published for a while and some public speaking he was involved in.

Tom and a co-worker were actually in Dealey Plaza when the motorcade came through, but they were heading east on Commerce St. approaching Houston, stuck in traffic. Once the shots ran out, Tom grabbed the camera he was using and ran across Dealey Plaza. He filmed the entrance to the TSBD and a number of people and officers in the area. He then got inside, before they sealed it off, and spent most of the next hour and a half inside. Arrived about 12:34/5. (After Oswald would have left.)

Tom says the search of the building was in 2 major phases. The initial search was naturally for the shooter, and the police worked their way through all floors, crawl space and roof. After several minutes, without success in finding a shooter, the 2nd phase was the search for the weapon and other evidence. Much of Tom's film that we have all seen is this 2nd search. You see them moving boxes and looking behind with flashlights, etc.

The sniper's nest was found around 1:05 or so, and the rifle found about 1:22/5. Tom's film shows Lt. Carl Day (who arrived right before the rifle was found) handling the rifle, and dusting for fingerprints.

Summary

Again, an awful lot of the above is highly speculative! I wished we could put a better time stamp on the movement inside the building, but are unable to. Unlike the outside, where we can often time stamp things that happened based on photographs, the Hertz clock on the sign, and even shadows (sun dials have been around a long time).

I will not state that there were not other shooters in the TSBD, as I cannot make such an assertion as a FACT. In fact, there are many things in the above (such as Mooney's "Plain clothes Deputy Sheriffs", or Harkness' "some Secret Service" agents) that could very well point to other shooters in the building.

Book Addendum: **Deputies in the Depository**

In the last week (Aug 2023), I received a letter from a Researcher who is not on Facebook (from what I can see). He had purchased my book, but raises an issue that has been discussed for years about the case. I will address it here, and may update parts of my book (the advantage of eBooks). My apologies for anyone who has already purchased a book.

He complains about "page 261, but also elsewhere". On that page I mention that Luke Mooney said in his Warren Commission testimony that after entering the TSBD, and going up the stairs, he encountered 2 officers in plain clothes, coming down the stairs. He says that I had a "short shrift" treatment of the event. (Minimized.) He says this is not "negative", as many others in the Research community have also made this event into a minor event.

I do agree that this could be a valuable problem with the WC version of events. If these 2 officers were 'strangers' in the building, then letting them walk away could be a major issue. This Researcher goes on to say that it is possible these 2 accessed the building well before the shooting, hid among boxes during the initial search, and exited the building. Indeed, this could be nefarious, as many in the Research community insist.

This Researcher says in his letter, that Boone "could not" identify these individuals. This is despite the fact that Boone was also a Deputy Sheriff, and should have known the other individuals in his own Department.

JFK Assassination: Shades From The Fence

I will say that Boone DID NOT identify these individuals in his WC Testimony, which (according to Vol 3 preface) was on March 19th, or April 1st, 1964. This is a far cry from "could not" as this Researcher, and others contend. The interviewer for the WC, Joseph Ball, certainly did not ask for clarification of their identity, and it was never pursued by the WC or other investigators.

Nobody knows the exact movements in the building in the minutes after the shooting. In my book, I try to explain estimates based on testimony. However, I will be the first to admit these are only estimates, and a general idea of what is Logistically possible. Of course, if the people giving Testimony are mistaken, poor memory of times, etc, this is all questionable. (As a Fence Sitter, I am uncertain.) Naturally, if you want to believe that Law Enforcement of Dallas, or some of employees of the TSBD, were "in on it", then all testimony is questionable.

So, let us explore some of the testimony that was given in 1963/4, by the Dallas County Sheriff Deputies, and the reader can decide what they feel is the most likely scenario.

Let us start with Luke Mooney's actual Warren Commission testimony, as given at 2:15 PM that spring day of 1964. This can be found on Page 284 of Volume 3.

"...I went up the staircase myself. And I met some other officers coming down, plainclothes, and I believe they were Deputy Sheriffs. They were coming down the staircase. But I kept on going up."

Joseph Ball, the interviewer, did not push for an identity of these individuals, nor did Luke Mooney offer one. This is NOT the same as him being unable to identify them, but just that he did not do so. He may have simply been saying that the identities were not important. They may be important to us today, but can be easily overlooked as Mooney did know them at the time. Several months later, he may have simply not seen the need to identify these Officers, although as a fellow Deputy Sheriff he knew the identity of his fellow officers.

So, what are the possibilities of who these "Officers" were? We can explore that question. (Again, I do not know who they were, and we will never know; however, the reader should consider what is logical and practical.)

Unfortunately, few of the Dallas County Deputy Sheriffs actually testified to the Warren Commission in the spring of 1964. Decker, Boone and Mooney were the exception to this, but the focus of their respective interviews were NOT "who were the other Officers you encountered in the TSBD."

But Eugene Boone's testimony in Vol 3, pgs 291-292 might give us an indication of who these Deputy Sheriffs may have been.

On page 291, Boone lists several Officers he recalls being in the building with him. These are "...Ralph Walters, Buddy Walthers, Allan Sweatt, L, C. Smith. Officer Gramstaff."

On page 292, Boone says "Ralph Walters and Officer Gramstaff (sp) and I don't know whether – Officer Mooney was with them or not at that time – they headed back to get some heavy duty flashlights." This indicates that 2 Deputy Sheriffs did indeed go down the stair to retrieve flashlights to handle the darkness on the 6th, 7th, and attic area above the 7th floor. Could these be the Officers encountered by Mooney?

The rest of the WC testimony is very sparse with Sheriff Deputies' testimony. Neither of these individuals were interviewed by the Warren Commission.

However, "Decker EX(hibit) 5323" contains the Report given to the Warren Commission by Sheriff Bill Decker. It contains statements by Decker, his various staff, as well as the Affidavits the department took from various witnesses.

Ralph Walters' statement is included within this document. He does say that he returned to the Sheriff's office to retrieve flash lights. He does not mention Grandstaff returning with him, and Grandstaff does not make a report. Walters says he returned with Webster and brought lights. He also met Boone at the department, who also returned with a flash light (per Boone;s report).

Deputy Sheriff John Wiseman also reports that he went to the top floor (6th) on the stairs, and returned to the 2nd floor to organize about 50 officers to do a coordinate search "floor by floor" (for the rifle).

This makes at least 3 Officers of the Sheriff's Department that were descending during the minutes after the assassination. Of course, there being no video of the interior, nor time stamps of events, it is all conjecture. However, the Alyea film of the interior search of the building appears to have flash lights early on in the search. Certainly before the 1:22 PM discovery of the rifle, but it also seems to show the sniper's nest area after flash lights are seen in the film.

Walters says in his report that "7" officers went into the building. We certainly know of Boone and Mooney, as they helped discover the Rifle and Sniper's Nest (respectively). Looking through the "Decker EX 5323" reports, other Deputy Sheriff officers were: Ralph Walters, Buddy Walthers, Allen Sweatt, L. C. Smith, Harry Weatherford, Sam Webster and Roger Craig. Additional officers were A. D. McCauley, Jack Faulkner, Wiseman and Joe Loraine (according to the report). Grandstaff did not do a report, that I can find.

Of course, if you want to believe that Dallas LE was "in on it", then this testimony could easily be lies, or faked after the fact.

I leave it to the Reader as to what is nefarious or innocent.

JFK Assassination: Shades From The Fence

Seconds after last shot	Shooter/Oswald	Styles/Adams (Garner)	Truly and Baker	Others	Recreations
+10	Withdraws weapon, views drive away of limo underpass	"What Happened?"	Baker turns corner, parks motorcycle	Dougherty working Williams, Norman, Jarman watch motorcade away	
+20	Traveling to north TSBD along east wall			Scramble away from east	
+30	Across to west – stash rifle	Decision to go down	Baker's foot on bottom porch step **(per films)**		
+40	Crosses 5th floor (4 seconds stairs – 6 to cross floor)	Walk quickly through office front of 4th	Encounter Eddie Piper in lobby – Truly enters	Head to west window – looking some time after	
+50	Crosses 4th floor – not seen by ladies on 4	Approaches wall in front of warehouse area	Crosses 1st floor to Elevators	Dougherty on 5th floor with west elevator door open	
+60	Crosses 3rd floor – (hears Truly?)	Girls to stairs, while Garner waits at office wall/door	At elevators – hollering up shaft to release	Dougherty getting books does not hear Truly	
+1:10	Emerges 2nd floor into lunchroom vestibule	Crosses 4th floor	Takes stair up to 2nd.		Baker 2 1:15 Oswald 1:17
+1:20	Oswald in lunchroom	Crosses 3rd floor	Baker diverts to lunchroom where he has seen movement – Truly starts up	Dougherty takes west elevator down to take order and investigate sound	Baker 1 1:30
+1:30	Oswald/Baker/Truly in lunchroom	Girls cross 2nd floor – not seeing Truly/Baker/Oswald	Oswald/Baker/Truly in lunchroom	Dougherty and elevator descending	
+1:40	Oswald buys coke	Girls emerge 1st floor – leave building	Baker/Truly continue up to 3rd floor. Crosses		
+1:50	Oswald leaves lunchroom across 2nd floor office space	Dorothy Garner sees Baker and Truly cross 4th floor.	Baker/Truly crosses 4th floor	Mrs. Reid comes across 2nd office area to call husband	
+2	Oswald down stairs front of building		Baker/Truly emerge 5th floor – head to east (manual) elev	Williams sees Baker/Truly cross 5th to manual elevator	
+2:10	Oswald exits building & gives newsmen phone directions			Williams/Jarman/Norman head back to stairs	

Jerry Dealey

Commission Exhibit 1381 was put together by the FBI, at the request of General Counsel J. Lee Rankin. It contains statements from the 73 TSBD employees that were in the building that day. (And even the statement of Franklin Emmett Wester, who said he was in the north Houston warehouse, and did NOT step foot into the 411 Elm St. building that day.) It excluded 3 employees that were absent that day.

Mrs. Robert Reid, and Pauline Sanders both state they were in the 2nd floor lunchroom that day, and left around 12:15 – 12:20. They do not say who else was in that lunchroom, but Mrs. Donald Walker, Betty Dragoo, Carolyn Arnold, Judy Johnson, Bonnie Richey, Virginia Baker, Georgia Ruth Hendrix, Gloria Holt, Delores Andrews, and Joyce Stansbury all state that they left around 12:15 to 12:20 to watch the Motorcade. Some left the building, while others stayed in the building, so "left" could refer to the lunchroom. How many of these were the "general ones that usually eat there with me every day" that Mrs. Reid refers to in her Warren Commission testimony is anyone's guess. There were a number of people who reported staying in the building:

1st floor: Eddie Piper, Roy Edward Lewis (front window) and Troy Eugene West (the shipping wrapper) by back doors.

2nd floor: Geneva L Hines (desk), Carol Hughes (desk)

3rd floor: Stephen Wilson (desk), Doris Ray Burns (walking), Edna Case (desk), Sandra Sue Elerson (window watching Motorcade)

4th floor: Vickie Adams, Sandra Styles, Elsie Dorman (together at windows watching Motorcade), Dorothy Garner (at her desk by window, with Adams, Styles and Dorman), Mary Hollies and Bettie Foster (together at window watching Motorcade), Yola D. Hopson and Ruth Nelson (together at window watching Motorcade), Ruth Willis (?) **5th floor:** Bonnie Ray Williams, Harold Norman and James Jarman Jr.

6th floor: Jack Dougherty (also on 5th floor)

Most of the other employees report that they were outside, in front of the building, or in other locations throughout Dallas.

All of these statements, with the single exception of Danny Arce, say that they did not see any strangers in the building that day. They also discuss if they knew Oswald, and whether they had seen him during that day at any time.

But such access requires *planning* and *logistics* to accomplish. It is tricky to get your strangers into a building without the employees, and/or the "Patsy" (Oswald) stumbling into them. You have to be able to place your other shooters/participants in the building, and explain the exit. You also have to explain how they manipulated Oswald, into waiting somewhere. It is not enough to simply state, "He was in the lunchroom."

I am still "on the fence" about whether there was a shooting conspiracy that resulted in JFK being killed. Yes, there were multiple conspiracies in the works by nefarious characters. But their existence does not prove that Oswald was part of it. Additionally, even if Oswald WAS the only shooter in the TSBD, that does not eliminate him being part of a Conspiracy.

The times mentioned above is about the best I can put together. But I welcome any input, or debate.....

17. Alteration Theories

Many theories have surfaced over the years about the "Conspirators" controlling and Altering evidence. This certainly could happen if the killing 'Conspirators' were in charge of the investigation, and had the Federal government's access to the evidence.

The FBI clearly did have this access, and in the case of some of the evidence they did destroy or alter evidence. The Hosty note that Oswald allegedly left at the Dallas FBI office, was destroyed according to Hosty, after it was apparent that there would not be any trial.

Additionally, Oswald's address book was transcribed for the record, and the references to Hosty were not copied over. Once the 'investigators' have shown they are capable of destroying and altering ANY evidence, can we really trust any of the evidence they are in possession of? This is exactly what many Researchers believe.

The government was in charge of all of the evidence, once it came into their possession. This naturally creates a "slippery slope", once you believe the government cannot be trusted.

This is especially true for evidence hidden from the public initially. Even the Zapruder film, which was purchase from Abraham Zapruder the next day, by Time/Life, could easily be modified before a bootleg copy was shown to the American people. The autopsy photos and xrays also could have been faked or modified before they were ever seen by the public.

The Lone Nut advocates can more easily point to the "evidence" as we know it today, and see that it points to Oswald, and Oswald alone. Many run the risk of coming across fully sanguine, or even smug, in their belief in the government and the evidence they have released.

However, the Conspiracy Theorists can argue that we only have the "evidence" that the government has released well after the fact, so we can't fully trust it!

JFK Assassination: Shades From The Fence

This chapter is again a reprint (without photos) of one of my "Dealey Plaza Echo" articles.

At the time there was a very vociferous group of Researchers that believed the Altgens #6 photo had been altered, and did actually show Lee H. Oswald on the front steps and porch of the Texas School Book Depository. This is where Oswald allegedly claimed to be while being interrogated by Dallas Police Captain Will Fritz that weekend. He said he was out there, and identified Supervisor Bill Shelley as one of the people he was out there with. However, none of the people on the porch ever stated that Oswald was with them, including Shelley.

Although this article mainly discusses the particular photo, the Logistical problem is that any "alterations" done to evidence has to match other evidence. This limitation applies to body alteration, film alteration, as well as photo alteration. More so, if you want to contend that the "alteration" happened immediately!

If the film, photo, body were altered that day, and that night, you have to put plans in place to do so. This creates an enormous problem of "logistics", just as accessing and exiting the building with a team of shooters is also a major logistic problem.

If a film or photo surfaces that show something different, you have to also "alter" that piece of evidence. This would require a huge number of conspirators to station themselves all over Dealey Plaza, so they could watch the people with cameras and immediately decide whether that person has a photo or film that shows something different than what your co-conspirators are planning to modify things to show.

So, as you read this following, apply the same logistical problem to any modification of evidence allegedly done that day, or that weekend.

(By the way, I posted most of the following article to the Facebook group promoting the Altgens6 alteration theories, but kept copies just in case. Sure enough, their response was to simply delete it, kick me out, and delete any comment I had ever made in their group. But the posting turned into this article, which was published in the Dealey Plaza Echo.)

Once again, any photos are deleted. However, the altgens6 photo is readily available on the internet, along with discussions of 'badgeman', 'prayerman' and other quick nicknames for some of the people who you can see on the front porch from Altgens, and other films and photographs of that afternoon.

The article was written in 2014. It is not available as the Echo article in the MaryFerrel.org database, as these only go up to 2012. The only photo that was included in it was Altgens6, so that photo can easily be found on the internet.

JFK Conspiracy: Capability, Logistics and Common Sense?

I have spent the last several years acting as one of the main Moderators of the JFKLancer.com JFK (mainly) Forum. That Forum is now history, as Debra Conway has semiretired as far as Forum and the annual November in Dallas (NID) conferences. However, JFKLancer.com remains as a publishing organization, and as of this date still sells DVD's of most of the presentations given at those 18 years of conferences. These DVD's remain an excellent resource for Researchers.

I have spent years listening to some of the Researchers that promote various Alteration theories. Many of these are highly respected Researchers, while some are not. (My personal view is that I try to accord respect to everyone, but respect is earned by how a person ACTS, and not just whether I agree with there theories, opinions and views. I respect many people that I disagree with.) Most of the time they are talking about

274

alteration of highly subjective subjects, such as photos and films. Not scientific evidence, by any means.

They explain "Motive", which of course is the Federal "Investigators" (a loose term that) trying to control the investigation and direct it to point to a pre-arranged result. There is no question in my mind that the Warren Commission did just that, along with the FBI and any other supporting investigative bodies.

However, just because you "see" something (or think you see something) does not mean it "must have been altered". Images are still subject to interpretation. Different people can look at the same image and see totally different things, and there is no science to prove what one person sees. It is circular, childlike logic, to think that what you "see" proves anything. Just because you see a cloud that looks like an elephant, does NOT mean that elephants can fly!

Many of these Researchers rightly point out that the "Means" to modify photos and films did exist in 1963. It was possible to "touch up" photos and films at many of the hundreds of labs throughout the country. (Hollywood had been doing it for years.) Additionally, there were a small handful of highly classified labs used by the CIA, and others, that could do fairly involved 'doctoring'.

Many Researchers' explanation do include the "Opportunity" to make the modification, at very short notice, and at a very short time frame. They build an elaborate scheme of how and when a particular photo, or film, was intercepted by the "government" (or other nefarious group), modified, and then returned to the owner or public. In the case of the autopsy photos/films, this was easy, as they were in the possession of the Secret Service right after the autopsy itself. The Zapruder film was another relatively easy object, as it was escorted by the Secret Service to the lab for processing, and kept in private possession until it was sold to Time/Life the next day. As long as Zapruder himself could be controlled, it was not a problem. The film was not seen for several years, further opening the door to alteration.

JFK Assassination: Shades From The Fence

Of course, all of the above: Motive, Means and Opportunity, is what everyone usually points to. They say that all someone needs is these 3, and a circumstantial case can be brought against them.

However, what most Researchers do NOT consider is basic "Logistics and Planning". Not "all" Alteration plots require this, as some are 'after the fact' and do not have to be pre-planned. An example of this is the Autopsy photos and x-rays. Because these items were in government hands, and the public would never see them, they could be modified and changed at leisure. Similarly, the Warren Commission could be selective in what Witnesses they interviewed, and how they questioned these witnesses, to steer them away from any problem areas that arose. They did this multiple times, and often went "off the record" (which they also controlled) whenever the response seemed to be leading into these directions.

However, most Alteration plots need to be planned, and the *logistics* in place, and reasonable before execution of the event can take place. This is especially true, if there is a short window before such altered items are made public. The monitoring, interception, interpretation, modification and release of any altered objects must be highly considered and coordinated, and the owners of the object must be either "in on it", willing to comply, or unaware that such action had taken place.

(All of the above is just the Alteration itself. This writing will not even consider the Logistics and Planning of the Kennedy shooting itself.)

Over the last few years, there has been a group of Researchers that have insisted that the Altgens 6 photo was altered. They posit that "Doorman" was, in fact, Lee Harvey Oswald, and not Billy Lovelady. This is based on his shirt, which they say matches the one he was wearing when arrested (even though some think he changed shirts in his rooming house). It is also based on his statement to interrogators that he was on the front porch during the motorcade. Even though Lovelady himself said it was him in the photo, and most of his co-workers standing out front with him, say it is Lovelady, many of these Researchers insist the photo was altered to make 'Oswald' look like Lovelady. Some go beyond the single photo, and assert that many of the films, and other photos taken that day were also altered. The photos, films, documents and testimony was all altered, or controlled, to make it Lovelady and not Oswald.

However, for a moment, let us ignore ALL of photos, films, documents and testimony and just focus on the Altgens 6 photo alone for a while. However, every point that I bring up in the following discussion is expanded to every other piece of evidence. The logistics and problems are simply expanded exponentially, based on the volume of information that must be "Altered". These must all be "Altered" if there is a possibility that they may conflict with any "Altered" evidence, or confirm any other un-Altered evidence. We will, for now, ignore, getting shooters in and out of position, controlling Oswald, being seen by other employees, ballistics, body alteration, number of shots, and the myriad of other photos, films and witnesses, and the people they may have talked to, seen by, etc.

Altgens 6:

The many Researchers that discuss Alterations and other theories, do not seem to know how to support the Logistics and Planning that would be necessary to pull such a theory off.

Knowing what to Alter? One of the Logistic and Planning problems of a **public** execution of JFK is one of knowing ahead of time what you want the public to see and hear, as well as how many cameras the public will have.

You would have to have entire teams of conspirators standing around Dealey Plaza to monitor the public and see who had cameras and when they were to use them. They would have to be prepared to intercept these cameras, wherever they were. They would have to know in advance how to modify, and exactly what they want the altered material to show.

Altgens 6 was just one of dozens and dozens of film and photos that were taken that day in Dealey Plaza. How could anyone, other than "Ike" Altgens himself, know exactly what it showed, and when he was going to take a photo? How would they know that his photo showed Oswald, so that they could quickly intercept it and change it, without Altgens knowing (certainly not saying so)? There was certainly not anyone standing by Altgen's elbow in the Zapruder film.

(Or was this also modified to show Altgens by himself?)

And what about all of the other cameras in Dealey Plaza? Towner was standing directly across from the porch of the TSBD? How would they know if Towner did / did not capture the porch in a still photograph, or Tina in the film? These would have also been intercepted and modified? How did they know that Croft did not take such a photo? Dillard? Willis? Or any one of 35+ known photographers in Dealey Plaza?

There were around 400-500 people in Dealey Plaza. Are these 'Alteration proponents' saying that 300-350 of these were the "public", while another 50-100 were Conspirators standing around to watch the crowd, so that they could intercept and "sync up" any photos/films to Altgens 6? Quite a large secret to keep for 50+ years. But that is the Logistics required to intercept and modify even 1 photo in Dealey Plaza. You would have to intercept and at least look at all of the other films and photos, to make sure they showed what you wanted them to show.

Owners of the photos/film? To intercept, modify and release the Altgen's 6 photo, you would need the cooperation of Altgen's himself, unless you could find a way to separate a professional photographer from his camera and film, for the necessary time to develop, analyze it, alter it, copy it, and give an undeveloped duplicate roll back to him. This is a Media professional who has "the photograph of the century" – at least in his own mind. Of course, this is compounded by all of the other films/photos that your 'team' thinks must be looked at, in case they have to be altered to match Altgens 6.

Public release timing of an AP photograph. After taking his series of photos, Altgens had an idea of what he thought he had captured in his camera. He did cross Elm St., and is seen lingering on the grass on the northern side, in case there was a shooter or something else he should photograph.

However, once the full motorcade passed, he returned with his camera and undeveloped film, to WFAA/Dallas Morning News, about 3 blocks south on Houston St. He was joined by WFAA personality, Jerry Haynes. By 12:45, Jay Watson interrupted programming on WFAA, and began a live broadcast on TV about the shooting. He was soon joined by Jerry Haynes, and he also mentioned that photographer Altgens had witnessed the shooting and they were developing photographs.

At **1:03 PM**, Altgens 6 and 2 other Altgens photos were sent out on the AP news wire. They were quickly published and shown by newspapers and TV broadcasts throughout the country. One of the first reports that "Doorman" looked like Oswald was made by a lady in Pennsylvania, so the quality of those AP photos must have been pretty good. We still have many of these newspapers on microfilm today, so this photo is available to us. (Grainy, but available.)

So where is the Opportunity to modify the photo? Motive and Means (technical) are there, but there is simply no time.

In all fairness, Altgens did not actually develop the photograph. He gave it to a co-worker once he had returned to the office. It could be argued that there was a 'plant' at the Dallas Morning News who intercepted the photo, so that it could be modified. However, there still was not time, even assuming that the Conspirators somehow knew that Altgens needed to be modified. Was there a similar plant at every news agency, or photo processing lab?

Sure, it is TOO easy to look at the photograph 50 years later, and say it has been modified. But you have to consider the Logistics and Opportunity, in addition to Motive and Means. This is especially compounded when these Researchers start saying that all of the other films/photos of Lovelady are altered or faked. You would have to consider the time to Alter all of these other objects, but also consider that there must be PLANS to do so. The coordination of altering even 1 photo, without the cooperation and knowledge of the photographer is possible, yet impractical. To expand this to every other photo or film that actually show the same scene becomes a monumental task. In addition, you have to know about every camera in Dealey Plaza, within seconds, so that such a similar film/photo does not escape your evaluation (and alteration, if necessary).

Of course, I cannot state for a fact that any given photo or film was modified, or was not. But the Logistics of any such alteration theory must be considered.

Conspiracy?

Although considered a "fence sitter", I do think there was a "conspiracy" not to investigate past Oswald. (I do not use the word "cover-up" as that implies the same people who did not follow leads, were protecting themselves from their part in a shooting "conspiracy", and they could very well be separate). In fact, a probable reason for Conspirators to plan on shooting Kennedy in a public place, is to set up Oswald as a patsy. Why Oswald? Most likely to lay the blame on Castro/Communists. If that is the case, then the shooters WANTED Oswald to be blamed, but as a part of a larger "conspiracy" that blamed Castro/Communists.

The only ones who would profit from a "Lone gunman", is the so-called investigators. If the shooters wanted Oswald to be blamed, as part of a Castro/Communist based plot, they did not want to have Oswald as a LONE shooter. The government's "lone shooter" was actually counter to what the shooting conspirators probably wanted, as the Alvarez and other stories and efforts to blame Castro/Communists suggest. I certainly cannot prove one "Grand Conspiracy" that resulted in both the killing and the non-investigation (or "Cover up"). They could well have been 2 separate conspiracies.

As a "fence sitter" on the subject of a Shooting Conspiracy, I am uncertain that such a conspiracy caused the shooting of JFK. There were certainly a number of people who wanted JFK dead, and some of these may have built a conspiracy to get it done. But the existence of various conspiracies do not necessarily show that Oswald (or Ruby) were a part of the one that succeeded.

Unlike the Warren Commission, and some others on the "lone nut" side of the fence, I cannot simply ignore Oswald and Ruby's backgrounds, past action, etc. They are suspicious, at the very least.

I also cannot simply ignore the number of people who seemed to know the event was going to take place. Cheramie, Hemming, Hargraves, Vidal, Milteer, Nagel, Trafficante, etc. seemed to know what was happening, and some of them knew Oswald. Therefore, I cannot be a "lone nut'er", even though I have heard that is what many consider me. At the same time, the LN'ers seem to consider me a CT'er! Many just simply label me the other way, when I disagree with their 'pet' theories.

Could the 'investigators' modify and alter evidence? Yes!

Were they capable of it? Yes – as the FBI change of the phonebook, and destroyed note shows.

Did they lead witnesses and avoid other witnesses, etc. to avoid pointing away from Oswald? Yes

Did they have the Motive and technical Means to modify Altgens 6? Yes

Did they have the ahead-of-time Logistics and Planning in place to do Photo/Body alteration? NO (most likely)

Did they have the time and cooperation of Altgens to modify his photo? NO

Witness statements

A lot is generally made about which witnesses the Warren Commission interviewed, and who they did not. It is true that they could certainly avoid interviewing witnesses that they thought could be 'hostile' to the "Oswald did it alone" premise that they were trying to prove. (Something that would never be allowed in a US Court, or if Mark Lane had been allowed to "represent" Oswald's interests.) But you cannot base everything simply on WC interviews alone. All the interviews in the Volumes, by the FBI, Police, Sheriff, or even to the press, has to be considered. If the "investigation conspirators" altered/withheld evidence or testimony, they would have to silence these witness to keep other sources of statements withheld. Of course, many believe this is what happened in the years after, leading up to the HSCA investigation.

CD 1381 is one of many statements made by the Employees, and other witnesses, after the assassination. Additionally, statements made in the press, as well as honest witnesses memories, would also have to be considered down the road. You cannot simply state that because the Warren Commission did not interview them, that their statements do not exist.

Granted, the Warren Commission had to build a 'possible' scenario that showed Oswald as a Lone Nut gunman. That is what LBJ wanted, especially during an election year. Therefore, they steered away from questions, statements and witnesses that they felt would not support that. They may have even pressured witnesses to help them, but I find it difficult to believe they got hundreds of people to lie, and maintain that lie.

Logistics

Most importantly, there are Logistics and Planning considerations for every theory.

Alteration Theories are just one of the major issues that has to be expanded into Logistics and Planning. Looking at a photo or film, and saying "I see what I see, so it must have happened!" is simply not sufficient, nor is it responsible Research.

18. Seeds of Doubt

As you have read through my articles, you are likely thinking that I am a "LN". Most of my articles point out and discuss the difficulties of planning and executing the Assassination by a 'conspiracy'. It is therefore, natural that you are thinking that I believe Oswald did it "alone".

Over the years, I have attempted to logically and reasonably try to analyze every theory I have been presented. This includes the lone gunman "theory" (because it has never been proven). Some of the more extreme theories are fairly easy to dispute, if they do not include the planning and logistics that support that version of events.

However, I am definitely on the Fence about the killing of the President being part of a conspiracy or not. Even if Oswald only participated, there could still be a conspiracy to kill JFK that he was a part of, or was 'set up' by.

Unlike the Warren Commission, I am simply unable to forget Oswald's life and history surrounding his travels and acts involving Russia, Cuba and his Marxism. It seems to me that every time the WC were told about things that just did not fit the narrative and conclusions they want to project, they either changed the subject, ignored the statement, or often had an "off the record" discussion at a critical time. What was said or discussed in these "off the record" discussions may never be known.

Of course, if Oswald had lived to go to trial, maybe some of these issues would have been settled. At the least, an adversarial proceeding, such as a trial, would allow us to more closely determine Oswald's participation and guilt. However, unless Oswald let something slip, we might still never know if he acted along with others or not.

This following chapter is including about a dozen postings I made a while back on "seeds of doubt" about Oswald acting completely on his own in shooting the President of the United

States. They are not sourced. They are not "facts" that I have fully drilled down and investigated. They are certainly not absolutely "true" assertions that I am trying to make. I cannot even tell you if they are all accurate or true, or if the person mentioned actually did these things. They are certainly things that I have heard over the years, and make up the smallest "seed" of things that may make many Researchers pause over.

If you do become "hooked" on the Assassination, on any side of the fence, these are many of the issues you will encounter. I can certainly "shoot down" many of them, but it is the sheer volume (over 150) that makes me hesitate in believing the LN theory of the case. They are presented for what they are: seeds that make me wonder.

Again, this chapter is a series of lists, so may be kind of confusing for the reader new to the case.

Seeds of Doubt (recap/summary):

I recently posted on Fair Play for JFK 12 lists of categories that could cause many to not believe that Oswald shot JFK completely on his own. While doing so, Jim Hess posted a list of all of the "facts" that pointed to Oswald as the Lone shooter. (You can do a search here for both. Mine are all labeled "Seeds of Doubt", so you can search for that exact phrase here to see all 12.) This #1 through #12 categories were:

1. Pre-Knowledge primary
2. Pre-Knowledge secondary / rumored
3. Shadow warriors
4. Oswald Russian considerations
5. Oswald in Dallas 1st time
6. Oswald sightings/impersonations
7. Dealey Plaza
8. Depository deviations
9. Medical Mess
10. Oswald's odyssey (movements that day)

(Maybe Jim will "bump" his list link?)

Again, I am "on the fence" about whether Oswald was a LONE shooter or not. It was not my intent to prove a Conspiracy, but only to list many of the things that keep me from simply thinking Oswald was alone. Over 170 items.

Seeds of Doubt #1:

Ok. Let's play the other side of the Fence I sit on for a while....

True: All of the Hard Evidence points to Oswald as the Line Nut (although it can be argued that the Government suppressed anything that did NOT)...

So...how do the LN side explain the many individuals that seemingly had prior knowledge of the Assassination? (The VOLUME remains the Issue, although each individual can be explained.)

1. Rose Cheremie (crazed drug addict)
2. Joseph Milteer recorded conversation to William Somerset (FBI wiretap)
3. John Martino ("Somebody Would Have Talked" Larry Hancock)
4. Richard Case Nagel ("The Man Who Knew Too Much" Dick Russell)
5. San Giancana
6. Santos Trafficante
7. Carlos Marcello
8. Johnny Roselli
9. Jimmy Hoffa and others?

What element of doubt does this add to those witnesses that said they saw/heard other shooters?

Seeds of Doubt? #2

My first post asked about "primary" pre-knowledge of the JFK assassination, and whether the VOLUME of such reports created legitimate doubt in anyone's mind.

285

JFK Assassination: Shades From The Fence

This 2nd one expands on that with much more tenuous pre-knowledge reported from various sources over the years.

1. Johnny Roselli (in my "primary", but contended...but he ended up in a 55 gallon drum for some reason)
2. Lt. Francis Fruge - interrogated Rose Cheremi allegedly on Nov 20th

    3.Dr. Wayne Owen allegedly treated 3 men on a car accident on Nov. 19 in a Louisiana hospital. Supposedly 1 man told Dr. and multiple interns about a plot.

    4. Eugene Sunk (Dinkins) in US Army cryptographer in France 1963. Claims to have mailed a letter to Robert Kennedy in Oct. 63 warning of a plot.

    5.CIA Agent Gary Underhill supposedly knew of a plot.

    5.Roscoe White and his "deathbed confession".

7. Abraham Bolden's "Chicago" involvement, with guns, arrests, etc.
8. Madeleine Duncan Brown's alleged party on Thursday, Nov 21, at a Murchinson home.

    9.FBI Agent William Walter's alleged FBI Telex on Oct. 17.

10. David Frerrie
11. Julia Ann Mercer's alleged sighting of a man with a rifle that morning.

    Again, most of these references are tenuous(at best), and highly questionable. Major source is "JFK: Thee Book of the Film", which is questionable.!

Seeds of Doubt #3:

Again, not hard evidence, but does it tend to overall doubt about a conspiracy?

"Shadow Warriors" that appear to have links or knowledge of the shooting, Oswald or other Kennedy hating individuals.

1. David Ferrie
2. Guy Bannister
3. Clay Bertrand (Shaw?)
4. General Charles Cabell (brother Dallas mayor)
5. David Morales (We took care of that SOB!")"
6. Maurice Bishop

7. David Atlee Phillips
8. Vincent Marchetti
9. Gerry Hemming
10. Felipe Vidal

....and others.

Seeds of Doubt #4:

Oswald's entire history with things Russian is my 4th category. Could be coincidence, but many believe that Oswald was involved with the Office of Naval Intelligence (ONI), or other institutions in 'intelligence'.

1. "Self teaching" himself Russian (a hard language)
2. Marines testing him on Russian (normal?)
3. Self learning Marxism
4. Being a radar operator on a U2 base
5. Allegedly a regular at the "Queen Bee" bar in Japan
6. Financing his trip to Russia
7. Denouncing citizenship, where Snyder believes he may have been coached 8. Not "officially" denouncing citizenship
9. Marrying a niece of a GRD Colonel.
10. Loan from State Department to come home.
11. Robert Webster with similar story (fake defector program?)
12. Allegedly not of interest of CIA on return.
13. Mexico City visit, with Kosticoff and Embassy visit.
14. George DeMohrenschildt and Dallas Russian community
15. Almost 3 years in Minsk.

Again, possible reasons for doubt that he was a LONE but?

(Over a third of the way through! I think...?) Seeds of Doubt #5:

Oswald in Dallas (1st time) and New Orleans.

1. Subscribes to magazines that are being watched by the FBI.
2. Mail orders weapons, while lots of stores sell them in Texas
3. Uses aliases at PO Box
4. Walker shooting ("Fascist", Kennedy hater)
5. Creates a Fair Play for Cuba chapter (FBI tracking)
6. Offers Marine training to anti-Castro groups.
7. Handbills for Pro-Cuba ideas.

8. Address on handbills on 544 Camp St.
9. Alleged involvement with Guy Bannister, David Frerrie, others.
10. Street scuffle over the Cuba issue.
11. ASKS for specific FBI agents. (gets another)
12. Radio And TV debates. (then "drops" FPCC completely)
13. Allegedly brags to FPCC chairman about events before they happen...

Again...nothing is PROVEN by any of these events. But....they make some of us simply unable to assume the LONE part (of LONE Nut). You may certainly disregard ALL of it....

Ah hell...got some time...

Seeds of Doubt #6:

Oswald sightings/impersonations.

Again, I cannot prove any of these events. They simply add to the doubt that Oswald was a LONE actor.

1. Silvia Odio (even the WC has problems with this one)
2. Leon Yates dropping a hitchhiker with a rifle case at Elm and Houston, couple of days before, who discussed possibility.
3. Shooting at someone else's target ata shooting range.
4. Test driving a car. "Coming into money." discuss Russia and Cuba.
5. The Alvorado story in the embassy in Mexico City.
6. Clinton LA sighting with Shaw, And others.
7. Application in Clinton at East Louisiana State Hospital.
8. Registering to vote in Clinton.
9. Lake Ponchitrain wall sighting by Vernon Bundy (addict)
10. Bus trip through Texas.
11. Phone calls to Embassy (recorded, then routinely erased?) 12. Various dancers meeting "Lee" at the Carousel.
13. Oswald and Ruby having breakfast early Friday morning.

Did any of these really happen? Does it add to "involvement" , or being set up?

Let's get away from people for a while.

Seeds of Doubt #7:

JFK Assassination: Shades From The Fence

Dealey Plaza

1. HSCA given up to 7 points of impact on curbs, street, sidewalk and grass.
2. Many believe they hear more than 3 shots.
3. Curry and Decker send their men to the railroad yard.
4. Many rush up the Grassy Knoll instead of the TSBD.
5. Jim Braden/Eugene Brading in the Dal-Tex
6. "Commotion" Lee Bowers saw behind fence.
7. Deaf mute Ed Hoffman seeing gunmen in knoll.
8. Smell of gun powder.
9. Bill Newman and others vague about direction/source of shots.
10. People on fire escape of Dal Tex.
11. Shell casing found on roof of Records building (mid 70's).
12. Multiple people in actual motorcade who felt shots came from in front.
13. "Back and to the left".
14. Splatter on Bobby Hargis.

Again, many are probably just False impressions from people in the "heat of the moment", and recall of a horrible event. But they still contribute to doubt.

Seeds of Doubt #8:

Depository deviations

Based on my research and multiple articles on the movements and interior of the TSBD, I think I am about 95% certain that Oswald was the only shooter in that building. However, that does not rule out a Conspiracy to kill JFK, nor shooters in other locations.

But, even though these issues can all be rationalized as well, I would be remiss if I didn't create the list of the problems.

1. The length of the bag that Frasier/Randall saw that morning.
2. No strong testimony from coworkers seeing Oswald with the bag (Jack Dougherty possibly)
3. The bag/rifle was not seen by anyone hidden all morning.
4. The bag being picked up by Dallas Policeman instead of left alone.
5. Oswald not the best shot, although the head shot (WC's farthest) was only 88 yards.
6. Bonnie Ray William's affidavit only mentions 2 SHOTS overhead.

JFK Assassination: Shades From The Fence

7. Junior Harman affidavit stops when he was in the front porch. No Hank Norman affidavit.
8. BRW having lunch a few fett from sniper's nest until about 12:25.
9. Carolyn Arnold: Nov 27 "might have seen" in front doorway; 1972 saw Oswald in the lunchroom.
10. Rowlands and other witnesses swing multiple men on the 6th floor.
11. Sandra Styles and Vickie Adams insisted they should be able to hear Oswald on the stairs.
12. The movement of the West elevator from 5th to 1st floor, while Truly and Baker were coming up. 13. Oswald saying Junior came through Domino Room during lunch (educated guess/alibi?) 14. Building not sealed off until 12:40.
15. Sgt. DV Harkness encountering SS agents coming from the back of the building.
16. Gaps in known movements of the elevator, where access is possible.
17. Nobody saw the building of the sniper's nest, and moving of Rolling Readers.
18. Tom Alyea film not under his control.
19. Alye said Fritz handled and pocket the shell casings.
20. Studebaker photo of sniper's nest likely mid afternoon.
21. Positioning of shells in photos, versus Alyea, and others.

More later....

Seeds of Doubt #9:

Medical mess

Again these are simply categorized lists of the many concerns that have been raised over the years (and discussed/debates exhaustively). I am not trying to PROVE anything! I am simply showing why I (and others) are Undecided.

1. The epileptic seizure in DP about 12:05.
2. Aubrey Rike's saying there were many false alarms to downtown Dallas leading up to that Friday.
3. The disappearance of the seizure victim (planted CE399?)
4. The tracheostomy through the throat wound (although they had no choice).
5. The Parkland description of all wounds, from memory.
6. The removal of body from Texas.
7. Parkland not knowing of back wound.

8. The Navy controlled autopsy (no court forensic expertise).
9. Presence of 3 caskets (logical, it may be...it compounds the issue)
10. Paul O'Conner body bag, and which casket contained the body.
11. Not knowing about throat wound.
12. Divert and O'Neil quoting "looks like surgery".
13. Poor back wound measurements.
14. Family/Burkely pressuring the autopsy to hurry up, skipping procedures.
15. Kennedys and SS taking control of evidence, photos, xrays and organs.
16. Burning and rewriting of Autopsy notes.
17. Conflicting descriptions/weight of brain. (Paul O'Conner)
18. Was Ruby at/inside Parkland hospital?

I do not have the medical expertise to list the contentions that many ascribe to what the photos, fraud and drawings show.

(3 or 4 more categories still to come...)

Seeds of Doubt #10:

Oswald's odyssey

Again, no proof of anything.

1. Leaving work (a little obvious, right?)
2. Coke instead of Dr. Pepper (settle down Jim Hess) 3. Banging on the door of a bus (look at me!)
4. Bus transfer ticket.
5. Bus station, but not leaving town.
6. Front seat of a cab (unusual).
7. Whaley saying he offered can to lady.
8. 500 block of Beckley.
9. Timing of rooming house (housekeeper estimating?)
10. Why so far East of Beckley (where?) 11. Which direction on 10th? Conflicting stories.
12. Color of jacket.
13. Unable to tie jacket/laundry tag to Oswald.
14. Alleged movement person to person within the Theater.
15. Proximity of Ruby's apartment East of 100th and Patton.
16. Contention he was in theater much earlier.

Seeds of Doubt #11:

JFK Assassination: Shades From The Fence

Chains of evidence

This topic is more about the failures of the Investigators to maintain good evidence, mostly because of the Fed's interference. To me, is does not have anything to do with a Conspiracy to Kill JFK. It might interfere with a conviction in the Kennedy shooting, if not the Tippit shooting.

1. Rifle fingerprints missed by FBI.
2. Parkland stretcher bullet transport to Washington.
3. Tomlinson and Wright seeing 399 and believing the bullet they handled to be more pointed.
4. The paper bag.
5. Poe thinking he marked the shell casings at Tippit scene.
6. Automatic shell casings for a revolver.
7. Mixture of manufacturers for revolver shells.
8. Tipping scene "wallet" discussions.
9. Palm printing of Oswald at mortuary.
10. Body transport to Washington.
11. Shell cases receipts with a "2" changed to a " 3" .
12. Developing of Zapruder film.
13. Rifle clip (staying in rifle).
14. FBI destruction of Hosty note.
15. FBI change of address book, dropping Hoary mention.
16. Alleged film and photo "alterations".
17. Time/Life breaking Zapruder film.
18. Bucket at Parkland at limo.
19. Limo going to Ford factory.
20. Dry cleaning and repair of Connally's jacket.
21. Loss of lists: theater patrons, parking lot car owners, etc.
22. Mac Wallace print (debunked many times)

Seeds of Doubt #12: (last one I think)

Rush to judgement

Again, unless you believe in a Grand Conspiracy to Kill and CoverUp, this topic does not point to the Killing Conspiracy. That is the one I am undecided on. This topic is more about a "conspiracy" to not investigate beyond the dead Oswald.

1. Katzenback memo.
2. Warren Commission formation, without investigators.
3. Navy controlled autopsy.

4. Lack of Oswald representation.
5. Lack of adversarial debate (trial would have had such).
6. Known FBI destruction and alteration of evidence. (note and diary) 7. Family control of autopsy evidence.
8. Suppression of records and files for "National Security".
9. Johnson's Texas Court of Inquiry, initially.
10. Johnson, "...every shooting scrape..."
11. Warren told "...saving 40 million Americans..."
13. Movement of back wound, and other alleged inconsistencies.
14. WC going "off the record" without an adversary to object.
15. Alleged witness leading, changes to statements.
16. Redactions
17. Secret Service destruction of documents after ARR(B) Act.

(Seems like there was another category.... But I am sure many of you have some...)

I intentionally avoided most of the Tippit case, LBJ 's "cronies", and Ruby background.

19. Motives and the "LONE" factor

One thing that is weak in both the Warren Commission and House Select Committee on Assassinations, is that of Motive. Many of the Conspiracies are also deficient in Motive, as well.

Oswald Motive?

The most common motive attributed to Oswald is that he wanted to be famous, or make some grand political statement. But with analysis, there are reasons that have to make you wonder. If Oswald's motive was to be "famous", all he had to do is walk out of the TSBD and surrender. He could have simply told Baker in the 2nd floor lunchroom, "OK. You got me." He did not have to escape, travel to his rooming house, get his pistol, kill Tippit, and attempt to kill McDonald in the Texas Theater.

Of course, maybe he was waiting for the grand theater of a trial to espouse his political or social statements. But it seems he would at least leave a note somewhere, just in case he did not live to stand trial.

It often seems to me that he had given up on his life, was despondent, and had simply decided to perform "suicide-by-cop". After all, once he got his pistol at his rooming house, he shot or attempted to shoot, any police officer he encountered. Some will argue that there were plenty law enforcement officers available in Dealey Plaza, so all he had to do was carry his rifle out of the building, and point it at every police officer he saw. However, a long bulky rifle is good for distance shooting, but lousy for close combat. Additionally, he only had 1 live round left. He also may have been concerned about the innocent crowds in Dealey Plaza and the TSBD. If he wanted suicide, and did not have the nerve to simply kill himself, getting a pistol would seem the best way to have a shootout with police.

294

JFK Assassination: Shades From The Fence

Worse case scenario is you get arrested, and spend life in prison or get the death penalty. You would have the trial and the remainder of your life to make grandiose statements.

Although many consider Oswald as a social loser, or "patsy", he was actually quite accomplished for his age. Not many of us by the age of 24 have:

Trained ourselves in Marxist/Leninist ideology

Taught ourselves the complex Russian language (while serving as a US Marine at the height of the Cold War, no less)

Got ourselves into the Military and learned Radar techniques at a CIA base

Got ourselves a hardship discharge

Traveled to Russia during the Cold War

Knew how to threaten to renounce our US citizenship (without actually doing so)

Convince the Russians to allow us to stay, when they originally refused

Married a Russian national, and eventually manage to bring her back to the US

Get a loan from the State Department to get wife and child out of the USSR

Return to the US after threatening to give secrets and not be arrested

Form a Fair Play for Cuba chapter, and intelligently debate on radio and TV

Go to Mexico City, and visit both the Soviet and Cuban Embassies to try to travel to these Communist countries

Sure. Some of us have done some of these things, such as getting married and having children, serving in the military, or learning a difficult language. But few of us have accomplished ALL of these things before the age of 22 (when he returned in June '62).

(By the way, much of the above list is exactly why many cannot accept the "LN" view of the event. They say that much of Oswald's accomplishments were because he had help from someone in Military Intelligence, or another agency.)

But based on these accomplishments, it certainly appears that Oswald was not a stupid or unintelligent young man. (He allegedly did have a mild form of dyslexia.) He certainly knew that if he shot a rifle from his own place of employment, and left, it would eventually be tied to him! He certainly could not expect to simply get away with it, could he?

As I have given the tours over the years, we almost always follow Oswald's "escape". It is very hap-hazard, and seems it is not well planned at all. While doing this, I am always asking myself what I think Oswald is thinking. Where is he going?

If he is planning on suicide-by-cop, he may have left the rooming house and wandered. He knew that each afternoon landlady Johnson's grandchildren came over every school day to await their mother getting off work, and picking them up. If there was to be a shootout, he may have not wanted to have it occur around these kids that he liked.

He will allegedly tell Will Fritz that he just wanted to see a movie, since it was Friday afternoon and no more work would likely be done at the TSBD after the shooting. But he lived at the intersection of Beckley and Zang. The Texas Theater was half a block west of Zang, although about 10 blocks south. He could simply have walked south on Zang, and come out on Jefferson about half a block from the front door of the Texas. Or, he could have taken Beckley.

However, those were both very busy streets, and he may have been concerned being seen on them. An alternative would be to walk 2 blocks past Zang, onto Madison and he would be in a fairly low activity side street lined with houses. It would encounter Jefferson just a few businesses away from the Texas Theater.

His ending up several blocks east from the Texas Theater, and Beckley St. indicates that he had another destination in mind (If he wasn't just aimlessly wandering.)

About a full block east of Patton St., on Jefferson, was the library when Oswald got most of his reading material. (On my tours, I joke that he did have the book "The Shark and the Sardines" checked out, and it was overdue: explaining why he needed a pistol! Oak Cliff Librarians can be tough...) If you think about it, a library is an excellent place to "lay low" for a few hours. You can get a book and sit and read it, and nobody will bother you until the library closes. It is also a good place to 'meet' someone....

Also about 4 blocks east of 10th and Patton, was Jack Ruby's apartment. Many Researchers believe that Oswald was going to see Jack Ruby. (Not at home at the time.)

There is currently a bus service on Jefferson, just east of Patton, which serves people traveling to Mexico. However, it was not there in 1963. Many believe that Oswald was going for a city bus, either the Marsalis or Jefferson bus. He could access the Beckley bus right in front of his rooming house, or walk straight east to catch the Marsalis bus. The Jefferson bus he could have been aiming for, but that does not explain why he was going east of Patton on 10th St. He could simply have caught the bus at the stop that Helen Marham was going to, when she witnessed the shooting of Tippit.

Conspiracy Motives?

So while we are on the subject of Motives, lets explore possible motives of factions that might want John Kennedy killed.

Once again, I briefly want to discuss what I sometimes refer to as the "split" Conspiracies. I differentiate between a "killing conspiracy" and the "non-investigation conspiracy". As I said in the Foreword, I certainly feel there were people that wanted to kill JFK, as most Presidents have conspiracies against them. But unless you want to believe that LBJ and the Federal Government was part of the killing conspiracy, and wanted to "cover" their involvement up, then there might be separation.

JFK Assassination: Shades From The Fence

The Katzenbach Memo was written after Oswald's death. It was written by Assistant Attorney General Nicholas Katzenbach, and sent to LBJ aid Bill Moyers. It reads:

It is important that all of the facts surrounding President Kennedy's Assassination be made public in a way which will satisfy people in the United States and abroad that all the facts have been told and that a statement to this effect be made now.

1. The public must be satisfied that Oswald was the assassin; that he did not have confederates who are still at large; and that the evidence was such that he would have been convicted at trial.

2. Speculation about Oswald's motivation ought to be cut off, and we should have some basis for rebutting thought that this was a Communist conspiracy or (as the
   Iron Curtain press is saying) a right–wing conspiracy to blame it on the Communists.
   Unfortunately the facts on Oswald seem about too pat — too obvious (Marxist,
   Cuba, Russian wife, etc.). The Dallas police have put out statements on the Communist conspiracy theory, and it was they who were in charge when he was shot and thus silenced.

3. The matter has been handled thus far with neither dignity nor conviction. Facts have been mixed with rumour and speculation. We can scarcely let the world see us totally in the image of the Dallas police when our President is murdered.

JFK Assassination: Shades From The Fence

I think this objective may be satisfied by making public as soon as possible a complete and thorough FBI report on Oswald and the assassination. This may run into the difficulty of pointing to inconsistencies between this report such that it may do the whole job. The only other step would be the appointment of a Presidential Commission of unimpeachable personnel to review and examine the evidence and announce its conclusions. This has both advantages and disadvantages. It [*sic*] think it can await publication of the FBI report and public reaction to it here and abroad.

I think, however, that a statement that all the facts will be made public property in an orderly and responsible way should be made now. We need something to head off public speculation or Congressional hearings of the wrong sort.

Nicholas deB. Katzenbach Deputy Attorney General

This could have resulted in an Investigation that was careful to NOT look at anything beyond Lee H. Oswald. Maybe the "limited" investigation done by the Warren Commission was an intentional, "benign" conspiracy to protect the American public from a war with Cuba or Russia. This is supported by LBJ allegedly telling Earl Warren that if he serves on the Commission he might be saving "40 million Americans" from a nuclear war. Of course, still others believe that Johnson was told about the event the night before, and simply went another direction than what the killing conspirators wanted. (A shade of gray theory.)

"Split" conspiracies mean that the non-investigation may not have been a "white-wash" of involvement in the killing conspiracy. It may have been very benign in intent. After all, the Assassin Oswald was dead, and could not point to others, so let's just blame him and move on.

The LONE factor

The question that comes up in my mind all of the time, is why kill JFK in public? If you simply want him to die, there are certainly less public ways of doing it. This is especially true if you think Government Agencies such as the Administration, Secret Service, CIA or FBI were "in on it". They would likely have access, while others may not. Therefore, I really doubt the LBJ or Government scenarios.

Some also believe that the Dallas establishment was in on it. This often includes the Dallas Police, or members of that group. The Dallas Oil-Men are often mentioned, as are other members of the extreme right wing. I know Researchers that believe the owner of the TSBD, D. H. Byrd (an oilman), and many employees in the TSBD were actively part of the killing plot. Obviously, these would NOT have easy access to the President except when he was in Dallas.

(My own step-brother told me once that it was the Southern Baptists, because of a Catholic President.)

Most often the Mafia and the anti-Castro Cubans are mentioned. Members of these groups were very full of hate of Bobby and John Kennedy, for various reasons. They were certainly capable of building a killing conspiracy and setting it in motion. Revenge for past slights is certainly possible.

The most common motive given this group, as well as some members of the CIA and

Military Intelligence, is to kill Kennedy and lay the blame at the feet of Russia, or (more likely)

Castro/Cuba. That would be the reason for using a former defector, pro-Castro, Marxist like Lee H. Oswald. If they could shock the public enough, and blame Cuba, they might finally get the invasion of Cuba that they felt should occur.

JFK Assassination: Shades From The Fence

Reader, follow this logic closely:

If the above motive is true, and they wanted the shocking killing of JFK to cause an outcry and invasion of Cuba: they would NOT want the event to be blamed on a LONE gunman! (Let me say that again:) A LONE GUNMAN TAKING THE BLAME WOULD NOT CAUSE AN INVASION OF CUBA.

For the killing to cause an invasion of Cuba, or other action, the public would have to believe that Castro was behind the Assassination. If any individual just decided to kill the President, on his own, you would not blame the groups or people he knows or supports. You would simply say he was "crazy", acted alone, and move on. (Just about what happened.) You would need a Conspiracy, or the perception of a conspiracy, that pointed to Cuba/Castro or Russia, etc. Blaming one man is not enough to get the United States to invade a smaller country, even if it is one that the man likes and supports.

There is some indication that this motive to invade is exactly what happened. In the days following the Assassination there was discussion of what is known as the Alvarado incident. Gilberto Alvarado Ugarte was a Nicaraguan agent in the Cuban Embassy in Mexico City. He contacted the US Embassy in Mexico City with a story that he saw Oswald receive an envelope containing $6,000 in the Cuban Embassy. He stated that Oswald received it from a red-haired Negro, and he went on to describe Oswald (with glasses). He later recanted the story, after failing a polygraph. But it shows early attempts to tie Oswald's trip to the Embassies in Mexico City to the motive for shooting Kennedy.

There is also the story that at the Soviet Embassy in Septermber of '63, Oswald spoke with Valeriv Kostikov. Kostikov was allegedly the lead of the KGB's assassination programs in the Americas.

Of course, these stories fell apart quickly. Nobody knew exactly who Oswald spoke to, if he ever was in the Soviet

Embassy. And how can Alvarado know exactly how much is in an envelope given to Oswald in the basement of the Cuban Embassy.

Both stories seem to show a weak attempt to tie Oswald to a Conspiracy to kill Kennedy backed by the Soviets or Castro. But for that to work: their MUST be a perceived Conspiracy that Oswald is only a part of. He might be only the "tip" of an iceberg, and the only person that can be tied to the Conspiracy.

Only if the American public think there WAS a Conspiracy, backed by Castro, would there be an invasion.

Many Researchers ask why they would use Oswald. He is an inexperienced shooter, owns a relatively poor rifle, and can become a "wild card" if he is arrested and talks. However, if he is killed, or spirited out of the country, it might still point to a Conspiracy backed by Castro's Cuba. Additionally, if Oswald does not know real names, places, etc. (remember, he did not drive), he could not hurt the co-conspirators even if he is arrested, and talks. Again, he would be just as guilty under Texas Law for Murder, even if he only participated and did not actually pull the trigger on the killing shot. (Just like a get away driver for a bank robbery, who never even goes into the bank where someone else kills someone.) So he is likely not going to even attempt to indicate that he knows who really killed Kennedy, because that would still implicate him in Murder.

The "Iceberg" theory is Oswald is the only KNOWN (tip of the Iceberg) member of the killing Conspiracy, blame can still be spread to Castro, whether Oswald is arrested or not. But this motive actually requires a Conspiracy, instead of a "Lone Nut" who does the entire action on his own initiative.

Many Researchers simply do not think about this. They think a "professional" assassin, such as the Mafia and CIA use, would never use an amateur and poor slob as Oswald. But if the purpose of the method is to invoke an invasion or war with another country, you must have someone tied to that other country, and must have people believe in a Conspiracy, instead of a lone actor.

JFK Assassination: Shades From The Fence

ONLY the investigating body, would NEED a "LoneNut" acting by himself, so that they could reassure the American people that Conspirators were not at large, and could simply look at a single dead shooter.

Before we leave the subject, there is still another Motive sometime attributed to using
Oswald. The motive goes that if anti-Castro Cubans, or Mafia, could somehow be pointed to, the Attorney General Robert Kennedy would simply not investigate. This was because the Kennedy brothers were backing CIA/Mafia actors to assassinate Fidel Castro secretly. One was called Operation Mongoose, according to some. It was multiple clandestine attempts on Castro's life. Bobby would not want this information to become public, and would therefore not pursue the killers very hard.

In some ways, this might still explain why the Attorney General of the United States did not seem to have his Department of Justice investigate. Of course, the FBI was part of the DOJ, and did do some investigations. But Bobby and J. Edgar Hoover did not get along very well, and Bobby was emotionally shattered by the event.

There are many who believe that Bobby used his office and finances to investigate in private. The theory is that 'they' feared he would re-open the investigation if he became President, and he was thus Assassinated in June of 1968.

Motive is a nice thing to have, but is not essential. We do know the killing happened, regardless of the motive of the shooter, shooters, or Conspirators (if any). However, IMO the motives of many of the groups that hated Kennedy, and their ability to tie to Oswald, or blame him, should not be overlooked. The Warren Commission simply seemed to avoid many of these connections, and Oswald's history, by saying these links were simply "coincidences".

Oswald could very well have been the only shooter, and still not have acted completely alone! At the same time, the existence of connections and hateful groups, do not disprove that a LONE Oswald could have acted completely on his own.

20. Extremes – Whitest and Blackest Theories

So, let's start discussing the variety of theories that have been presented over the years. We will start with the extreme ends of the shades, and in subsequent chapters cover the many varieties of gray.

It always amuses me that when you do not necessarily agree with someone about what happened, they immediately label you as either a believer of the Lone Nut (LN) scenario, or a believer in the darkest Conspiracy (CT). Many of us are simply in the middle ground somewhere in between.

Extreme White

The 'white' end of the spectrum of theories, is obviously that Lee Harvey Oswald acted completely on his own, without anyone at all helping him plan the shooting, or telling him they would help him escape, etc.

This is exactly what the Warren Commission determined happened. However, they did not absolutely eliminate conspiracy, but said they had not found any evidence to believe that there was one. Except for the acoustics panel, this is also how the House Select Committee on Assassinations believed the event happened.

According to this theory, Oswald had acquired a rifle and pistol in the spring of 1963, after paying off the U. S. State Department for the $500+ loan they had given him. He dressed in black, and had Marina take his photo 3 times in the back yard of the Neely St. apartment with these weapons. These photos were later found in his possessions, and Marina stated that she took them.

In April of 1963, Oswald took his rifle on a bus after leaving Marina a note to help her with household/living details in case he did not return (or live). He took a rifle shot at retired General Edwin Walker, as Walker was sitting at home by a back window. The shot hit the crossbar frame, missed Walker

JFK Assassination: Shades From The Fence

by inches, and was found in a book/bookcase on the opposite side of the room. Oswald quickly went a couple of blocks away, and stashed the rifle under a railroad underpass, and then took a series of buses home. He came in late at night, and thought he had hit Walker. He returned a couple of days later by bus, retrieved the rifle, and again returned home while hiding the rifle under his raincoat.

The event scared Marina so much, that she kept the note in case she might ever need it to control Oswald. He having lost his latest job at Jagger Chiles-Stovall, she convinced him to go to New Orleans to find work there. He went ahead, while she and the 1 year-old June Lee moved in with friend Ruth Paine. Once Oswald found a job at the Riley Coffee Company, he sent for his family, and Marina joined him in New Orleans.

The Oswalds spent several months in New Orleans. During that time Lee set up the "New Orleans Chapter" of the Fair Play for Cuba Committee. While he did write the president of the national organization, he 'set up' his own chapter without waiting for permission to do so. He allegedly got Marina to sign his "membership card" with the name of the chapter president: Alex Hidell (an alias). No members ever joined the chapter, although Oswald did send honorary memberships to some.

Oswald also printed up "Hands Off Cuba!" fliers, and printed the address of 544 Camp St. on many of the fliers. He spent a lot of free time handing these fliers out, and in August got into a dispute with anti-Castro Cubans. This resulted in Oswald and the others being arrested for disturbing the peace. While in jail, Oswald was visited by the FBI, who was keeping track of dissidents in the area. He was found guilty, fined $10 and released. The event resulted in a Radio debate, and also a brief television appearance. Oswald explained his Marxist beliefs, and supposedly handled himself quite well in the debate according to the host.

Marina was quite pregnant, and during her time in New Orleans, had continued to correspond with Ruth Paine in Irving, Texas. Paine convinced the Oswalds that Marina and

JFK Assassination: Shades From The Fence

June should move back into the Paine home, when the baby was due. Ruth drove to New Orleans and pick up the 2, as well as their few possessions.

Oswald went to Mexico City in late September of 63, instead of coming to Texas with Marina. According to the investigators, Oswald visited the Cuban Embassy, and the Soviet Embassy, in an attempt to go to Cuba (which was not allowed by the United States at the time). The CIA allegedly recorded Oswald, and took his photo as he left the Embassy. However, the photo they provided the FBI later is obviously not Oswald. There is also debate about the phone tap recording(s), which Hoover talked about, but the CIA said it had been routinely recorded over. Oswald having been rejected by the embassies, returned to Dallas.

Being that the Paine house was only 2 bedrooms, for 5 people already living there (Ruth and her 2 children, and Marina and June), Oswald stayed at the YMCA for a time. He also stayed for 5-6 days at an apartment on Marsalis St. with Mary Bledsoe. Ms. Bledsoe did not like Oswald speaking in a foreign language on her phone (he spoke Russian to Marina, who knew almost no English), and asked him to find some other place to live. He found a room at 1026 N. Beckley. (Later when leaving the TSBD, Oswald will get on the Marsalis bus instead of his normal Beckley bus. Mary Bledsoe was on that bus that Nov. 22nd afternoon, and positively identified Oswald.)

Ruth Paine spoke to some of the neighborhood ladies, including Linnie Mae Randle, who lived 5 doors away from her. She told them about the situation that Marina and Lee were living in, and said that Oswald was looking for employment. Randle told Ruth that the Texas School Book Company was hiring temporary workers to fill book orders, as Linnie's brother Buell Wesley Frazier was working there. Ruth called and spoke to warehouse manager Roy Truly, who said he was still looking for temporary help and to send Oswald down. Oswald got the job on Monday, October 18th, filling small book orders for $1.25 and hour.

JFK Assassination: Shades From The Fence

Oswald would ride with Frazier to the building on Monday mornings, and return to the Paine house on Friday afternoon. The only exception to this was the weekend before the Assassination, because Ruth Paine's child was having a birthday party that weekend, and she and Marina asked Oswald not to visit. Marina tried to call Lee at the Beckley house that weekend, and was told there was no "Lee Oswald" living there! (Oswald had registered under the name "O. H. Lee". During interrogation he allegedly claimed it was a mistake by landlady Gladys Johnson and housekeeper Earlene Roberts.) Marina was quite mad at Lee, for again playing his "alias game", as she would later tell "Marina and Lee" author Priscilla McMillan.

On Thursday, Lee approached Buell Frazier and asked if he could ride with him that night to Irving. When asked why, he told Frazier that he had some curtain rods he would pick up for his room at the rooming house. Ruth later stated that this was the only time that Lee came out on any weeknight and also the first time he did not ask permission. Lee also allegedly tried to make up to Marina multiple times that night, but Marina was giving him the cold shoulder treatment. When he left the next morning, before Marina got up, he left $170 and left his wedding ring, which he never took off, on the dresser.

Frazier was having his breakfast that Friday morning, when his sister who was standing at the window in the kitchen said that Oswald was there, waiting for his ride. Randle had seen Oswald carrying a long package as he passed the window to Frazier's car on the far side of the garage. When Frazier got into the car, he noticed the package and asked Lee about it. Lee told him it contained the curtain rods he had told Frazier about on Thursday. Frazier accepted that, and did not examine the package, or think much more about it.

It had been raining that Friday morning, so when they got to the parking lot of the north warehouse, Frazier stayed in the car to run the engine and charge up his battery. Oswald preceded Frazier on the walk to the TSBD, and Frazier never got any closer than 50 feet to Oswald. At the time Frazier only got a glimpse of the package between Oswald's right arm and his body. He later stated that it was cupped in Oswald's hand, with its other end possibly under his armpit. However, he never really paid close attention to the package, and would later just estimate it being a little over 2 feet long (rifle is 34", broken down). Oswald went into the building first, and Frazier does not recall seeing him the rest of the morning. The investigators could not find any other TSBD employee that could say they saw Oswald come in with a package.

According to this theory, Oswald built a "sniper's nest" on the SE corner of the sixth floor. He did this by moving a couple of light "Rolling Reader" boxes from the center of the floor, to use as a rifle rest. He also turned several stacks of boxes from a line parallel to the southern windows, until they formed an "L" shape that could shield the 'nest' from the workers overlaying the floor in the SW corner of the building. At some time he moved his rifle to this area, and took it out of the paper bag, and possibly assembled it.

Another employee, Bonnie Ray Williams, allegedly came up to the sixth floor and ate his lunch right by the sniper's nest. This was around 12:10-15. He had heard the other workers say the 6th floor windows would be a good place from which to watch the motorcade, so he believed that is where they would meet him. However, they had gone out front instead, so around 12:25 Williams left to find them. He later said he had heard and saw nothing in the sniper's nest, and was unaware that the nest was even there. Allegedly, Oswald was sitting on a box in the sniper's nest the entire time.

After the limo turned the corner from Houston St. onto Elm St. Oswald shot the rifle. This 1st shot was possibly a miss, or struck something, causing a miss. The 2nd shot entered Kennedy in the upper back, and according to investigators, went on to exit Kennedy's throat, entering Connally's back, breaking a rib, exiting his chest, entering his right wrist which was holding his Stetson hat, breaking the hard radius bone, exiting the wrist and finally lodging itself in his left thigh. The 3rd shot hit Kennedy in the back of his head, causing the bullet to shatter and causing extensive fracture of the right side of JFK's head.

This theory then has Oswald stashing the rifle in the NW corner of the building, and proceeding down the stairs, and crossing every floor, until he got to the 2nd floor. Here he goes into the lunchroom, where he is encountered by Dallas policeman Marion Baker and warehouse manager Roy Truly. According to Baker (who did not know him) he is calm and collected. Truly says he is an employee, and thus belongs in the building, so Baker leaves him and continues to follow Truly up the various floors of stairs. Oswald allegedly buys himself a Coke, and exits the lunchroom to walk past Geraldine Reid, and down the front stairs.

TSBD warehouse employees see or hear Oswald on the 6th floor around noon, as they are starting to break for lunch and race the elevators down. Charles Givens will also say he sees Oswald walking north along the east side of the building, when Givens comes back up to the 6th floor to get his jacket and cigarettes about 12:05. No other TSBD employee claims to have seen Oswald after this, until Mrs. Reid and Roy Truly see him after the shooting. At least, until 15 years later, when Caroline Arnold allegedly tells a couple of Researchers that she saw Oswald in the lunchroom around 12:25. Her Nov. 26th, 1963, statement says she might have caught a glimpse of him by the front door around 12:15, but she could not be certain. Her April 1964 statement says she did not see him that day. These 2 early statements were official sworn statements.

He allegedly walks a few blocks down Elm St. where he bangs on the door of the Marsalis bus while it is stopped in traffic between stops. He is on this bus a couple of minutes, and gets off, receiving a bus transfer which will be later found in his pocket after his arrest. Bus driver Cecil McWatters will later identify him in a line-up.

He walks 2 blocks south to the Greyhound Bus station, where he gets into the front seat of William Whaley's taxi. According to Whaley, a lady comes up and asks if another cab would be coming soon, and Oswald allegedly opens his door to offer the lady his (escape) cab. She declines, and nobody has ever come forward to identify themselves as this person to date. (Of course, they may never have heard the Whaley account in the 1960s.) Oswald will take the cab a few blocks past his rooming house. Whaley will also identify Oswald in a lineup.

There he will get his pistol (holster was later found there), put on a jacket, and leave the rooming house. He will eventually end up at 10th and Patton, which is several blocks east of Beckley St. He will later say he just thought no more work would be done that day (he was right), and he decided to leave early and go see a movie. The Texas Theater is only 1 ½ blocks WEST of Beckley, so there is no real explanation of why Oswald angled 6 blocks east of the Texas Theater.

According to this 'white' theory, Oswald acts completely alone in his plans to retrieve his rifle, build a sniper's nest, and shoot out the 6th floor window.

What is missing in both the WC and HSCA versions is a strong "motive". Oswald allegedly likes the young President and First Lady. This lack of motive is where the term "nut" of Lone Nut comes from. According to many, if Oswald is somehow insane, a real motive is not needed since insane people are likely to do almost anything without a motive.

The most often motive mentioned by people who believe this official version, is that Oswald simply wanted to be famous. However, he could easily have done that. He could either simply stay, walk out of the building with the rifle, or simply surrender to Baker in the 2nd floor lunchroom. It seems to some that Oswald might also have had some kind of note, or "political statement" he could leave in the sniper's nest, just in case he did not live to make a statement in a trial? But then again, in a highly serious situation, plans do not always come to fruition.

Of course, his shooting of Officer JD Tippit at 10th and Patton, does seem to indicate his guilt. Additionally, his attempt to shoot Officer Nick McDonald when confronted in the Texas Theater also shows guilt. It took some time to tie

Oswald to the Walker shooting, so that was not much of an immediate factor.

Darkest Black

The film "JFK" does not really show the absolute extreme Conspiracy, but we will discuss it here in a moment as it is the theory that is most often used, and comes closest. In my opinion (IMO), the most extreme 'black' theory is that Vice President Lyndon Johnson was behind the Assassination itself, in addition to the ensuing "cover up".

Some believe that a thumbprint that could be tied to Malcom Wallace was found in the sniper's nest on the 6th floor of the building. This theory is first presented in one of the later episodes of The Men Who Kill Kennedy. In that episode they send a thumbprint to a fingerprint expert, who claims there is enough to convince him that it is Mac Wallace' thumbprint. However, there is not clear chain of evidence on where the print actually came from.

However, Mac Wallace was kind of a 'torpedo' for LBJ. Wallace was accused of killing a golf pro John "Doug" Kinser, in 1951. Wallace was convicted, but his defense was that Kinser was sleeping with his wife. His sentence was suspended. Another longtime Johnson associate was Billie Sol Estes, who believed that Wallace had participated in the Kennedy shooting. Estes allegedly gave this information, and other murders Wallace had committed, to a grand jury investigation into Estes own criminal activities; however, since grand jury proceedings are closed records, I do not think that testimony has ever been released. The 1997 book "The Men on the Sixth Floor" – Glen Sample, named Wallace as assisting in the shooting along with Oswald and Loy Factor, a Native American who claimed that he intentionally missed. Barr McClellan's 2011 book, "Blood, Money and Power (How L.B.J. Killed J.F.K.)" also implicated Johnson in several murders and other criminal acts. This darkest extreme purports that Johnson ordered the Warren Commission so that he could "cover-up" his part in the Assassination.

312

JFK Assassination: Shades From The Fence

The film "JFK" is also a very dark Conspiracy close to the very 'black' end of the spectrum that believes Government actors were part of the "killing Conspiracy". It never quite gets to the naming of Johnson as a part of the killing, but does show Johnson conspiring to get us into the Vietnam war, if nefarious characters in the scene will help him get re-elected in 1964. Kennedy had written Executive Order #273, which pulled 1,000 of the over 16,000 troops out of Vietnam. According to the film this was cancelled by LBJ, while telling these individuals to get him re-elected and he would give them their war.

But "JFK" does point the finger to anti-Castro forces. They are allegedly working with the CIA to assassinate Castro for years, by using the Mafia and other killers. According to the movie, Oswald was quite involved in these forces and was part of a plot to kill Kennedy. The plot started in New Orleans and involved Clay Shaw and many other figures in the anti-Castro movement. The intent was to get even with JFK for not supplying air attacks at the 1961 "Bay of Pigs" invasion, which failed. The thought would be that LBJ would therefore finally invade Cuba and get rid of Castro. However, Johnson went another way entirely, having a Commission point to a "lone nut" in the person of Lee Oswald, who was dead.

In the movie, they discuss how a shot while the Limo was still on Houston St. driving towards the TSBD as being the "easy shot". They claim the only reason to not shoot Kennedy as he is approaching the TSBD on Houston St., is to get him in a "triangulate crossfire" between the TSBD, possibly the Dal-Tex or Records building (east along Houston St.), and shooters on the grassy knoll. They have a team of shooters access the building, while saying that because they were over-laying the 6th floor, there were a number of strangers in the building. They also say that Oswald was part of the planning, but was not an actual shooter, instead he is waiting by a phone.

Instead, they focus a great deal of time in blaming the Industrial/Military Complex, CIA and other anti-Castro forces in the killing of JFK. The film also claims that Jack Ruby was heavily involved in the plot, including planting the 'pristine' bullet (CE399) on a stretcher in Parkland hospital.

They go into a lot of Oswald look-alikes, and their pre-Assassination appearances that might have been intended to lay the blame at the "patsy's" feet. They get into shooters in multiple places, and the control of the investigation by the government whenever it appeared to look beyond Oswald. They also focus on the allegedly "pre-knowledge" of the event by Rose Cherami and others.

As mentioned, it is an entertaining movie, and I have few complaints. While it is not the actually blackest of theories, since it does not involve LBJ directly with the Assassination plot, it comes awfully close. It is about the darkest 'shade of gray', almost to the extreme black end of the spectrum.

These 2 extremes are the ones that opponents like to 'label' whomever they are arguing with into. If someone calls you a "LN" they seem to imply that you believe in the 'official' WC version lock-stock-and-barrel.

When they call you a "CT", it is a little more open about what that means, but the most extreme version is usually used by the "LN" making the claim. It is certainly the easiest version to ridicule and shoot down, because the 'hard' evidence does not point to any Conspiracy. I call this easy ridicule, "low hanging fruit" because it is so easy to do.

Of course, the CT side will naturally point out that since the evidence was controlled by the government, we only get to see what they decided was not harmful to their case and version of the events.

And so the debate continues.....

However, there are many shades of gray between these extreme which is often overlooked by the Researchers claiming what their opponents believe. Some of these will be discussed starting in the follow chapter.

21. Shades of Gray

"Please keep hands and feet inside the vehicle at all times, we are about to start…." - Disney warning

Many Researcher tend to point at the extremes when looking at the other side. This the is because it is much easier to ridicule. A LN'er might point to the extremely black "LBJ was behind it, Oswald is innocent" when teasing a CT'er. At the same time, a CT'er will often ridicule a LN'er that he believes completely in the Warren Commission, and the whitest "Oswald completely alone" theory. This 'low hanging fruit' is much simpler to laugh at, and make fun of. However, I find that most Researchers are simply somewhere in between.

Some believe that Oswald was the "Lone Gunman" (LG), but suspect that he may be involved in a Conspiracy. (Some simply object to the "N(ut)", as they feel it is a derogatory label for the believer, instead of Oswald.) Others may feel that he was the lone gunman in the TSBD, but there were other gunmen that he may have/may not have known about elsewhere.

This chapter will list many of the shades of gray theories that exist between the extremes. We will start at the Black end of the scale, and then start to lighten and list theories until we end up at the White extreme.

To be sure, there are likely combinations that I will miss, even with 25 years of Moderating the debate. However, I hope to catch most of them. But, your particular pet theory may not be covered, so I will apologize in advance if I miss it….

There are other theories that seem to fall outside of this range, which I will cover in the end of the chapter.

Almost Black – LBJ last minute knowledge

In Madeline Duncan's book, "Texas in the Morning", she alleges that late Thursday night/Friday morning, LBJ attended a party. The party was at one of the houses of one of the Dallas oilmen's family. LBJ came into the party quite late, since he had been traveling into town from the Kennedy tour of Texas cities. She also said at times that J. Edgar Hoover showed up at the meeting, although nobody has ever been able to confirm his presence. Richard Nixon, who was in the Dallas area for a soft drink bottler's convention, is also mentioned.

LBJ greeted Madeline, and went into a back room, where he met with a number of his rich oilmen buddies. When he came out of the meeting, he again hugged Madeline and whispered something like "After tomorrow those @$@ Kennedy boys will never bother me again."

Madeline also says that in an argument with Lyndon months later, she says that many people believed he was behind it. He allegedly responded, "If you want to know who did it, talk to your Oil buddies!"

(I knew Madeline, and had many meals with her. Her story never changed that I can recall; however, I never really pushed her on the matter. She always said she had stories about MY relatives that would blow my mind, but she was too much of a "lady" to share them with me. She confirmed that most were about Ted Dealey, the family stinker.)

Now some contend that LBJ simply meant the political triumph of a successful Texas City tour, which would end on Friday night in Austin. However, others believe that in the back room he could have been told general information about the Assassination. Of course, he would not be told absolute details, as that would implicate him.

The back room conversation might go something like this, "Lyndon, the grapevine tells us that something will occur tomorrow that will make you President of the United States. We don't know any details, and it might just be a rumor. The rumor says that Castro will be blamed, and they expect it will cause an invasion of Cuba. However, we suggest you do not do that. You will become President, and that will be that."

So this version of the theory does not involve LBJ, as a killing Conspirator. It does contain advance knowledge of a rumor, without details. It does not specify the people behind the plot, and might or might not include Lee Oswald.

Many Researchers specify that at the time of the shooting, LBJ is already leaning over in his vehicle. Allegedly, he was listening to the radio to hear how successful the Dallas motorcade was. However, there are naturally some who think he was already ducking down to avoid being shot, which would indicate he knew precisely where the shooting would take place.

In a way, his Warren Commission's "blame only Oswald" might be considered a betrayal of what the killing Conspirators wanted to happen: blame and invade Cuba. It is only a betrayal if he knew in advance what the killing Conspirators' motives were. Again, it might simply be a benign 'conspiracy' to not investigate fully and just move on.

The reason this is almost completely black, is because it indicates LBJ knowing about the possible plot, even if he did not know enough to even try to prevent it. The story is very dark on Johnson's part --- if true.

Coal Black – the "JFK" film version

This is the version that is presented in Oliver Stone's film "JFK".

It is just a little further from the extreme black, because it does not actually show participation or advance knowledge on LBJ's part. It does show LBJ's willingness to get into Vietnam full time, possibly overturning JFK's rumored desire to get out. Like many of the theories, it tries very hard to show the Warren Commission as a body to simply blame Oswald, and sweep the matter under the rug.

The villains in this theory are members of the anti-Castro Cubans, mercenaries and random elements of the Military Industrial complex and other government agencies. These elements are part of Project Mongoose, and people who hate Kennedy because he would not provide air cover during the Bay of Pigs invasion of Cuba (1961). They are based in New

JFK Assassination: Shades From The Fence

Orleans area, but have links to others throughout the country and government. Naturally, gay businessman Clay Shaw is involved along with a shady cast of characters.

Oswald is part of this New Orleans group, but does not appear to be a participant in the actual shooting event. He is subsequently silenced in the basement of Dallas Police headquarters, while the film shows Dallas Police officers being involved in his killing.

(What's the old joke? "Dallas Police are not as bad as everyone thinks! Look how quickly they caught Oswald's killer…." Jim Leavelle always hated it when I used that line. I learned to avoid it when I was with him.)

But they tie the killing to the US Military, using a Colonel "X" and General "Y", in a Washington park meeting between the "X" character and Jim Garrison. Again, this is probably based on information that came up well after the 1967 Clay Shaw trial. It provided Stone to introduce much more Assassination information than what was really available at the time his film's event actually took place. (Hollywood dramatic license.)

But again, the film did raise lots of issues that need to be considered by current Researchers. I just wish some did/do not take it as truth. (I do list the book, "JFK: The Book of the Film" in my reading list. It gives the reader a chance to see the script, with footnotes for the source of much of the information in the movie.)

This theory also implicates the FBI in not being readily providing information on Oswald, and not trying very hard to investigate him. It even shows them adding a palmprint on the barrel of the rifle from his corpse at the funeral home. (TMWKK also talks about this, so it is not new.)

It does also show Hosty being ordered to destroy evidence. This was a note allegedly left at the FBI office in Dallas weeks before the shooting, where Oswald tells Hosty to leave his wife alone. This destruction did happen, as did a modification of evidence, when the FBI transcribed Oswald's pocket phone book and intentionally took Hosty's entry out of it. Once the

318

JFK Assassination: Shades From The Fence

FBI has shown it is willing to destroy and modify evidence, can they ever be fully trusted? Could they also introduce evidence after the fact, during the investigation?

This theory also includes Jack Ruby as a co-conspirator of the killings. They show him planting CE399 bullet on a gurney in Parkland Hospital. CE399, the "Magic Bullet", can be tied to Oswald's rifle by ballistics, but the people who found it on the stretcher could not identify

CE399 as that bullet. Some believe that it could have been substituted during the "investigation". Still others believe it is the bullet that went through both men, and ended up with Connally's clothes on the gurney. Others think it could have been planted by the "epileptic seizure" victim who simply walked away from Parkland.

Charcoal gray – Mafia did it

Another version is that the Mafia did the killing of Kennedy, using professional Mafia hit men. In The Men Who Killed Kennedy (TMWKK) one episode is about the "French connection" where hit men from the Corsican underworld were brought in to do the hit of JFK. One of them dressed up as a Dallas Police officer, and is the "badge man" that many see in the Mary Moorman Polaroid of the head shot.

This is supported in many ways by statements allegedly made before and after the Assassination by Teamsters President Jimmy Hoffa, and leading Mafia bosses Carlos Marcello, Sam Giancana, Santo Trafficante, Johnny Roselli and others. "He's gonna be hit!", "Cut off the tail of the dog (Bobby), and the head (Johnny) still bites you.", etc.

Many individuals seemed to have advance knowledge of the Assassination. Of course, if it was Oswald acting alone, they would not know about it. However, there was (IMO) many plots to kill Kennedy, that may not be what lead to the actual event in Dallas. But Carlos Marcello would later tell an informant that Oswald was their man. He felt that the hit on Kennedy in Dallas was on his instructions.

JFK Assassination: Shades From The Fence

Many of these individuals met untimely deaths, during the various investigations.

Roselli's body was found dismembered in a 55-gallon oil drum in a Bay, in 1976. It is believed it is because he was scheduled to appear a 2nd time before the HSCA, and he revealed too much in his 1st appearance. Giancana was murdered in 1975, shortly before he was to appear before the Church Committee. But this shady Mafia world intersects with the anti-Castro Cubans, Labor unions and even some elements of the CIA.

The Chief Counsel of the HSCA, G. Robert Blakely, who wrote the RICO law at one time in his career, was also a proponent of the Mafia backed Assassination.

As mentioned above, this theory sometimes includes Oswald as a participant. Oswald did have an Uncle in New Orleans name Charles Murret, who is alleged to be a part of the Marcello organization. Jack Ruby also is alleged to have multiple Mafia ties, being a runner in his teenage years in Chicago, and owning a bar in Dallas that is tied to darker dealings.

The Mafia certainly had a history of contract killings, and hated the Kennedy brothers.

They would not be able to control the investigation as well as a LBJ theory would, but did have some rumored control over J. Edgar Hoover, and other high ranking politicians. They were also involved in Mongoose, the allegedly Kennedy sponsored program to kill Castro. As mentioned in the Motive chapter, there are some researchers that insist that this relationship would have prevented Robert Kennedy from fully investigating, to prevent these links going public.

Dark Gray – Castro or Russia backed killing

This theory had very early traction by most of the country. It basically says that the Marxist-Leninist leaning Oswald as a pro-Russian or pro-Cuba supporter, acted on behalf of a foreign Communist enemy. This was the initial reaction of many when they first heard Oswald's background. Even Researchers that today are avid "Lone Nut" supporters, had this idea initially. LBJ himself allegedly asked if he was a target.

Castro had allegedly said in interviews, after many assassination attempts on his life, that the leaders of the United States should be aware that others can "play that game". He later said that it would have been suicide for Cuba to sponsor or support the assassination of an American President. Kennedy had agreed not to invade as part of the Cuban Missile Crisis in October 1962, so Castro had a vested interest in keeping him alive and the secret agreement active.

Russia was also considered by many. Oswald had tried to "defect" to Russian in 1959, and spent almost 3 years in the Soviet Union. Unknown to others at the time, he had also allegedly visited the Russian Embassy in Mexico City, and spoken to Vasily Kostikov who was the head of the KGB assassinations group in the Americas. It is only natural that during the Cold War, many would initially think these thoughts.

This theory had lost traction almost immediately, although there may still be some holdouts in the Research Community.

Mid Gray – TSBD employees
Many believed it was the right-wing extremists in Dallas that were behind the killing. It was the reaction of many across the country in the early interviews, with many pointing to "those people in Dallas".

This possibly included the people and groups in Dallas who objected to Kennedy's soft stance on Communism and Socialism. (DMN Editor Ted Dealey was one of these.) Some objected to Kennedy's stand on Civil Rights, and that he was a Catholic. Also in these groups many placed the Texas/Dallas Oilmen, because Kennedy was threatening to do away with the Oil Depletion Allowance (where they could deduct Oil taken out of their wells on their taxes). Other groups include the secret, hidden, shadow government that many felt (still feel) are secretly running the country.

JFK Assassination: Shades From The Fence

A member of the Dallas Petroleum Club name David H. Byrd owned the Texas School Book Depository Building. The President of the Texas School Book Company, Jack Cason, was also allegedly an extreme hater of President Kennedy and his policies.

The theory, which is still held by some Researchers today, is that many of the Employees of the TSBD were in on it. Oswald was set up by these employees, in some cases. Other versions say that Oswald was not even on the 6th floor, and the shooting was done by many of the employees instead. Bonnie Ray Williams and Jack Dougherty are most often mentioned by some, but many of the other employees are also mentioned.

Even when a Researcher does not name an actual shooter, they are quick to call almost all of the employees of the building liars. For instance, many believe that Oswald was on the front porch at the time of the shooting, either as "doorman" or "prayerman" (different figures pointed at in various photos and films of the event). Even though the several people (10-12?) on the porch say they did not see Oswald, these people are often lying according to these Researchers. Once you start bring "lying" into the equation, there is simply no way to work around it. Just like once you bring "evidence tampering" into the equation, you can explain almost anything away. The evidence was held by Federal investigators, so if they decided to destroy, alter, replace or plant evidence, reason and common sense seem to be useless in discussions with these Researchers.

While we are on the subject of right-wing, many also involve individuals of the Dallas Police. The killing of Oswald by Ruby is the most common, with DPD individuals in on the 'silencing' of Oswald. But some believe that the 'badgeman' behind the fence was Dallas Officer Roscoe White, or other Dallas Policemen. Some even contend that JD Tippit was in on the plot, and was supposed to kill Oswald – who killed Tippit instead.

JFK Assassination: Shades From The Fence

Night Gray – Oswald assisting

Any strangers accessing the TSBD without Oswald's knowledge have 3 logistical challenges (I always cover this in my tours, before walking through the interior of the building in 1963):

•   They need to control Oswald. If he is being set up as a participant, or even a patsy, it just will not do to have him standing in front of the building with the Manager Roy Truly, or anyone else who can give him an alibi (none did). In the movie "JFK", they have him standing in the 2nd floor lunchroom, and the sound says he is waiting for a phone call. However, there was no telephone in the lunchroom. The only telephone the warehouse workers were allowed to use was in the center of the back of the 1st floor, where he could see all accessing the stairs or elevators. Someone telling Oswald to wait by an Office Worker's phone close to the lunchroom, would very likely make Oswald highly suspicious.

•   You need to be able to access the building without the 70+ employees of the building seeing you, and reporting strangers in the building. Only 1 would, Danny Arce, who said a older gentleman needed the restroom around 12:05. He pointed it out, waited, and saw the man leave, long before the Motorcade was even close. (Of course, they could all be lying, right?)

•   Oswald himself must not see any stranger, or someone carrying weapons into or through the building. If he does, he might immediately realize he is being set up and run right away to be outside and establish an alibi, or even run to the law enforcement outside.

In addition to all of the above Logistical requirements, these strangers must know the building, access it, build a sniper's nest, shoot, stash the rifle, and be able to exit the building without being seen. (Star Trek's transporter beam, was not yet available…)

One way to bypass all of the above is to have Oswald himself assist the TSBD shooter(s). He can certainly build a sniper's nest that morning, or even the day before, without much difficulty. He knows the building, and the access points, and knows the approximate lunchtime patterns of most of the employees, having worked there for 5 weeks.

This theory says that Oswald either brought his rifle to others in the building, or that he assisted others in doing the shooting from the 6th floor. The book, "Men on the Sixth Floor" contends exactly the latter. The book contends that a Native American named Loy Factor, Mac Wallace (LBJ protégé), and an unnamed female joined Oswald on the 6th floor. Loy Factor claims he intentionally missed, but all males allegedly took shots. The woman worked a radio to communicate to other teams at other locations.

But the question I always raise is why would Oswald linger behind? He certainly did not seem to be "running interference" for other individuals, while they escaped. He was not even on the 1st floor, where such an escape would have to happen. He was seen by Baker walking away from the door in the 2nd floor lunchroom.

Another version of this theory is that Oswald is the only shooter in the TSBD, but is aware of other shooters in the Plaza. He is told to exit on his own, and make his best way to a meeting place.

Dark Fog – Oswald not aware of others

Another of the "light side" (Oswald involved) theory is similar to the last paragraph in the above section. Again, Oswald is the only shooter in the TSBD, but in this case he is NOT aware of any other shooters.

In the movie "JFK", they kind of allude to this when they say the "shooter teams are not aware of other teams". However, in the film they show a "team" of shooters in the sniper's nest, instead of Oswald. They show this team as being the outsiders that are working on overlaying the 6th floor that day; however, all of the people working on the floor were TSBD employees – not strangers.

JFK Assassination: Shades From The Fence

Again, if Oswald is unaware of other shooters, he is completely designing his own escape "plan' (not much of one, in almost everyone's opinion). He is told to get out of downtown the best way he can, and meet later at some pre-designated location (library?). He is, in fact, being set up as the fall guy for the Assassination by leaving his rifle at his place of work, but this may be part of the plan that he is aware of. If he is spirited out of the country to Cuba, he will still be safe. The other shooters would likely be using 'silenced' weapons, so they can more quickly escape.

They could also be shooting from the grassy knolls (north or south), the DalTex or any other location in Dealey Plaza. Putting Kennedy in the "triangulated cross-fire" that the film claims is the only reason not to shoot Kennedy while approaching the TSBD on Houston St.

I can name 3 other reasons: 1, Oswald is not a professional killer and it take a certain nerve to shoot the President and Jackie while they are looking at you. 2, Maybe he intended the 'easier' shot, but got Cold Feet, until the limo was headed away from him. 3, To take the shot on Houston, you have to square up to an open window, where you can be seen by hundreds of people, including Secret Service and law enforcement. You can no longer hide behind the corner.

Fog Gray – Oswald message shots – "Contrived theory"

When the HSCA was investigating the case, they published about 6 locations where witnesses reported a ground impact of a bullet during the shooting. Another has been rumored over the years from a couple on Elm St. that still have not come forward (last I heard).

- James Tague – hit and injured by a fragment by the Underpass
- Curb about 20 feet in front of Tague
- Sewer cover or grass on the south side of Elm St.
- Impact mark in center of sidewalk by the Stemmons sign

JFK Assassination: Shades From The Fence

• Royce Skelton (RR worked on Underpass) reported an impact on the left side of the limo, about the time of the sound of the 2nd shot.

• Virgie Baker (nee Rackley) said she saw an impact behind the limo on the left, about the time she heard the 1st shot sound (same one possibly?)

• Charles Rogers had a story from a Mike Nally that his Uncle (not named) was one of the Motorcycle cops, and heard a bullet rattling around in his front wheel spokes/fender during the shooting.

• Randolph Carr reported seeing a furrow in the grass on the south side of Elm that pointed towards the Criminal Courts building

• The couple that never came forward told Researcher they saw an impact between them and the limo. They were standing on the north side.

Now, this is more than 6 locations, but some are highly questionable, and some may be duplicate reports of the same shot.

Since Tague was injured by a shot. A shot shattering Kennedy's head would likely not have enough momentum to clear the windshield and injure Tague. It certainly would not have enough to damage a cub in front of Tague. Any bullet going into human bodies at an initial downward angle would obviously not have enough momentum to raise out of the car and travel another 100 yards to injure Tague or the curb. I can buy that 1 impact somewhere by a missed shot would still have enough direct momentum to still injure Tague. However, if more than 2 of these reports actually happened, there have to be multiple shooters!

So, with this in mind, I got to thinking. (Jim Hess, founder of Fair Play For JFK group, calls this my "contrived theory".) I created a theory that both explains the number of impacts, as well as Oswald's rather "nonchalant" actions on the bus and taxi during his escape.

JFK Assassination: Shades From The Fence

Maybe Oswald was approached by a plotter and told to fire at, but NOT hit, JFK? If successful, he would be taken out of the country, and given safe haven in Cuba. There he would be a hero of the Revolution.

This would scare Kennedy, and send a message that he could be assassinated. The fact that Oswald is gone, and his rifle is in the building, would certainly show that the message was from Castro. Especially if he could be taken to Cuba in a way that definitely shows Cuba was involved.

Oswald, is not overly concerned about any laws about shooting close to the President. It is minor. So he agrees, and does so. He intentionally gets off 2 or 3 shots, but misses the limo by shooting above it. (Another reason to wait until after the turn, where it is much more open – and nobody might get hurt.)

Anyone who has fired a high powered rifle knows that with the kickback you seldom see the results of your shot (unlike Hollywood enactments). That is why many snipers are paired with spotters, depending on the characteristics of the rifle.

So, Oswald leaves his place of work, leaving behind a rifle that he knows will be tied to him. He walks a few blocks and gets on the Marsalis bus, instead of the Beckley bus he normally takes, because the meeting place is up Marsalis. While on the bus, when it is stopped in traffic, a kid tells the bus that Kennedy has been shot. Oswald, is probably thinking, "No. He has been shot AT." and is still not overly concerned.

They let Oswald go completely on his own, because he really does not know anything that could possibly hurt them. All he knows are fake names, etc. If they HAD shown up in Dealey Plaza, to pick him up, they run the risk of being caught themselves when they show up unexpectedly, and he realizes too quickly that he is being set up.

When the bus gets stuck in traffic, he gets off and receives a bus transfer he probably will never need in his life. He shoves it into his pocket (later there when arrested) and walks the 2 blocks to Whaley's cab by the Greyhound bus station at Lamar and Commerce St.

He gets into the front seat of the cab (not afraid of being identified by the cab driver) and tells the cab the 500 block of N. Beckley. While there, a lady comes up and asks Whaley if another cab would be there shortly. Oswald, unlatches the door and offers his (escape) cab to the lady. Why not? He has time....

The cab passes his rooming house, so Oswald can see if anyone is there ahead of him, and drops Oswald off 3-4 blocks south. Oswald walks to his rooming house, a few minutes before 1:00 PM. He goes into his room to grab a jacket, and gets his revolver while there.

When Oswald enters, Housekeeper Earlene Roberts is attempting to tune in local TV news, as a friend has called her to give her a 'heads up'. Around 1:00 PM, WFAA Jay Watson has been live on the air for several minutes. His guests around this time are Bill and Gail Newman, and their 2 young children. Bill Newman is relating how he has seen the President's "head explode and his right ear fall off".

Oswald, in the next room of the rooming house, overhears this confirmation that the President has actually been hit! He now panics.

He either starts to realize he has been set up, and there were other shooters in the Plaza that he knew nothing about, or maybe he thinks he has "accidentally" hit the President in the head himself! He knows he is not the best of shots, after all. (Maybe the latter, if he continues onto a planned meeting place as a patsy. However, he still needs to get out of town to Cuba...) From this moment on, he tries to kill every cop he encounters.

Again, some call it a contrived theory. It is built backwards from Oswald's actions, seeming casual attitude up to a certain point. But it explains the impacts and many of the movements and actions of Oswald after he leaves the building.

JFK Assassination: Shades From The Fence

At least many of the people I gave tours to over the last several years were entertained? Some liked it, and I have even heard from some of them by email much later that they were convinced something like it was a valid possibility.

As you will see towards the end of the chapter, it is as good as many theories out there in the Ethernet.

Light gray – Oswald acting on behalf of others

One of the lightest grays is the point where Oswald really IS the only shooter, but is doing it at the direction of others. He is told to do the best he can, without much guidance and planning assistance. But he is told that if he DOES succeed, they will rendezvous' at some designated location, and he will be taken out of the country, to Cuba, where he will again be a "Hero of the Revolution".

He acts and plans completely on his own. They again do not pick him up, because they don't want to risk being associated with him in any way.

Oswald will either be silenced, while somehow pointing to Cuba, or really taken out of the country. Even if he is captured, he knows nothing and cannot be associated with anyone who could get arrested as an accomplice. If he succeeds, the plotters get what they want. If he fails, he does not know enough to hurt them.

Off-white – Oswald trying to impress

The final theory within the range of the extremes is very similar to the WC's version of Oswald acting completely alone. The only limitation is one of motive. Maybe he is trying to impress Marina, the Russians, the Cubans, or anyone else. In this case he has not even been told he will be assisted in leaving the country. He is simply trying to do it to "Show" someone.

Bizarre or Other Theories

The theories that fall within the above range, are the ones that involve Oswald in some way, either as a shooter, as a participant or as a patsy.

However, there are some theories that involve some of the people there that day, and some that are complete fantasy. Some are bizarre enough that I cannot dignify them with serious thought to even contest them in a legitimate debate.

Some Researchers have listed a number of "mysterious deaths" by various witnesses over the years. These are deaths that have been accumulated for just those involved in the JFK assassination. They are sometimes compared to taking a page of names out of a phone book, and those being the people who die. They claim the odds are astronomical. However, it would have to be EVERY name on the page to hit those astronomical odds. It was not EVERY involved person in the JFK assassination, although some deaths might well be mysterious, or related.

SS Agent Greer shoots JFK. In the Zapruder film, some believe that when Limo driver

Greer looks back at Kennedy, he is holding a pistol in his left hand. He uses the pistol to shoot Kennedy in the head. (And nobody else in the Limo notices, except for SS Agent Kellerman, who may be "in on it".)

"Mortal Error" theory. Based on the book by Bonar Menninger (NOT in my suggested reading list). This theory says that Secret Service Agent Hickey, who is sitting on the back of the follow-up convertible, Queen Mary II, shoots the fatal head shot. Hickey, who is clearly seen turned and looking completely behind him and the Altgens #6 photo (taken at Zapruder frame 255), turns back forward, scoops up the automatic rifle sitting on the floor boards, removes the safety, and raises the rifle high enough to miss the windshield. Then, when the driver applies the brakes to avoid running over Clint

JFK Assassination: Shades From The Fence

Hill, who has jumped off and is attempting to reach the Limo, the lurch causes Hickey to fire the weapon and hit JFK in the head (Zapruder frame 312). All of this happens in 3.11 seconds. None of the 9 Secret Service Agents report Hickey, because they don't want to get him into trouble.

Hickey does raise the weapon before they go under the triple underpass; however, the Nix film does not show the weapon at the time of the headshot. There are die-hard Researchers that insist this is what happened.

<u>Jackie Kennedy shoots JFK</u> Offensive, and not worth a comment. Whenever this theory shows its ugly head, and group/forum I moderate will have it deleted and we will consider banning the person posting.

<u>Dal-Tex roof.</u> Not an entire theory in itself. There are many theories that believe there were shooters in other locations around Dealey Plaza. Most include the "grassy knoll" on the northwest side of the Plaza, and some even believe the southern knoll is a better spot. Many believe the roof of the Dal-Tex, a lower floor of the Dal-Tex or even the roof of the Records Building Annex (a secure Dallas County building in 1963). There are some reasonable reasons to believe in the possibility, and even a shell casing found on the roof of the Annex in the early 70's. The angles involved are really not much different than that of the 6th floor of the TSBD.

<u>Dal-Tex through the TSBD windows.</u> This theory has gotten its main supporter banned from many FB groups. It says that a "professional" sniper was on the raised air handler tower on the roof of the DalTex, thus giving an additional 12 feet (or more) height. The proponent says the sniper picked this location because of the excellent escape possibilities.

But he goes on to say that the sniper shoots into an eastern window of the Depository, past any Oswald or boxes in there, and again out of the partially opened south window of the sniper's nest. When you point out that the eastern window was never photographed as open, and could not even BE opened (upper part is fixed, and sashed lower part disabled), he says that one of the TSBD employees opened the window, or even removed a pane of glass for the shot. Same with the stacks of boxes that photos taken that weekend show blocks access to the window, as well as the stacks that made up the sniper's nest.

He shows how it can be possible, by showing the view of the entire window from 5 feet away from it. He does not realize that a shooter 80 additional feet across Houston does NOT have the same view, as you would only have a 'tunnel' view of about 20x30 feet of Elm St. Within 5 feet of the window, you can pivot and see a wider range.

(He will remain nameless, as do many of the Researchers that believe any theory I discuss.)

BBS comedy "Red Dwarf" – episode "Tikka to Ride" The BBS had an old comedy show about 3 people stationed in space. They use a time machine to come back to 1963, to Dealey Plaza. They go into the Depository and somehow manage to knock Lee Oswald out the window before he can shoot. He tries to climb back in, but does not make it and Kennedy is not shot.

They again use the time machine to go to the 1960's future, where they encounter Kennedy being arrested. He has made a bad shambles of things, and is now paying the price. They manage to talk JFK into coming back to 1963 with them, and he ends up shooting himself from the fence on the grassy knoll.

The "Hat" Industry There was a joke with many of the Researchers at the JFK Conferences that it was the "Hat People". Kennedy famously did not like to wear hats, and since he and Jackie were so instrumental in leading fashion trends, it was costing the Hat People a lot of money! That morning in

Fort Worth, they gave him a hat as a test, had it put it on (he didn't) they would have "called off" the Assassination. "Just follow the Money…"

Again, as I specified in the beginning of this chapter, I tried to include almost every theory I could think of. I am not rating them in any way, as to how likely I think they are. (Even my "Contrived" theory is not high on my belief system, just something that should be considered.) Accept, adopt or reject any and all of these theories. I cannot tell you any of them actually happened, nor would I want to try. They are presented as food for thought, and to explain that there is very little "black and white" in the Research Community.

THINK FOR YOURSELF! (As always…..)

22. Fence Sitting 101

I am one of the "fence sitters" (FS) in the Research Community. These are the people that are uncertain that *JFK was killed as a result of a Conspiracy.*

I said in the Foreword that there WAS a Conspiracy to kill Kennedy. In fact, there were likely many of them. This includes the suicide bomb that Richard Pavlick would try to kill Kennedy, while he and Jackie were attending church services in December, 1960. Pavlick was a "postal worker" (aren't they ALL?...sigh) with a history of mental illness. He allegedly wanted to show Kennedy that the Presidency was not "for sale". He had 10 sticks of dynamite and some blasting caps in his vehicle when arrested in Florida. He had made previous statements about his intent, and the Secret Service got wind of it, and managed to arrest him before he could act on his plans. He had a history of writing angry letters, and it back fired.

There were others. Undoubtedly, as much as the Kennedys were hated by various groups and figures, there was very likely many "conspiracies" to kill him. It is rumored that early in November, 1963, another plot was foiled in Chicago.

So, while there is little doubt in my mind that there was one or more "conspiracies" to kill Kennedy: I AM UNCERTAIN THAT ANY RESULTED IN HIS DEATH. Kennedy could have been killed by a 'lone wolf' that day. At the same time, he could have also been killed by a 'lone gunman', that was still part of a Conspiracy! (The other statement I made in my Foreword.)

Oswald could have been the only gunman, but might have been encouraged or even involved with others, still creating a Conspiracy. The others might simply have told him something like, "If you succeed, meet us afterwards and we will take you to Cuba, like you want, where you will be a Hero of the

JFK Assassination: Shades From The Fence

Revolution!" This would still constitute a conspiracy that just happened to involve Oswald as the shooter. I usually refer to this type of Conspiracy as an "Iceberg", in that it is obvious that there are others involved and Oswald is only the part of the Iceberg that can be seen. Since he does not know real names, or how to implicate others, he can't hurt them. Even if he could "name names" that would only show he was a knowing participant, and still guilty according to Texas law. It would not do him any good.

At the same, time Oswald may have simply been the only shooter in the TSBD, with other shooters at other locations. This could be with, or without, Oswald's knowledge. He was set up as a "patsy" to take the blame, but not an innocent one. This would also explain why he did not "spill the beans" about others, because that would simply confirm he was in on the plot, and therefore still guilty per Texas law.

At the same time, Oswald could just as easily been the only actor that day, and any planned Conspiracies to kill Kennedy were not active in Dallas that day. That does not mean they did not exist, which would make any of us who believe some did exist a "CT", while we might also be a "LN" at the same time!

The following is an online article I wrote in 2011, about being "On the Fence" about the Kennedy Assassination.

Straddling the Fence on the JFK Assassination

OK. On a thread out on JFK Lancer's forum I finally wrote that I continue to some degree to "straddle the fence" between the "Lone Nut" Theories, and the "Conspiracy Theories". This naturally resulted in a response from various people, of both support, as well as requests for explanations.

335

JFK Assassination: Shades From The Fence

I suspect that there are more than a few of us, that prefer one of the "shades of gray", somewhere between the "BLACK and WHITE" views:

1.   Oswald did it, and the Tippit shooting, completely alone, with no accomplice, just as the Warren Commission concluded.

2.   It was planned, executed, and covered-up, by some party/parties in our Government, and Oswald was always a Patsy, with no knowledge or participation of any type, including the Tippit shooting, and Ruby's elimination of Oswald for the conspirators.

There are all sorts of in-between shades, that I will not go into in detail. (In fact, I seem to recall a recent thread that discussed the many types of "Researchers", and the levels of their belief in the theories.)

The following it some of my opinions, and why I still vacillate between the extremes.

Could Oswald have done it alone?

It is POSSIBLE that a Lone Shooter (Oswald or another) could have done the JFK shooting. Heck, it is possible that a straw can split a telephone pole during a Tornado, although nobody can re-create it! Just the fact that the shots were difficult and Oswald was a "poor shot", does not mean he could not "get lucky".

Of course, the problem with this is the Single Bullet. (I claim no forensic or ballistic expertise, this is a layman's view.) A metal jacketed bullet is designed to go through multiple people, and Connally and Kennedy do appear to be properly aligned at some point (if not more) in Zapruder.

336

JFK Assassination: Shades From The Fence

However unlikely, it is POSSIBLE that a bullet could go through soft tissue, slow down, fracture bone, and remain relatively intact. If it could stay as intact as the "pristine bullet CE399", is an extreme, and I do not have the expertise to say.

The other half of this problem, is the "bullet that missed". If there were any other bullet hits in Dealey Plaza, this missed bullet had to account for all of them. The James Tague curb hit is the most obvious of these, and the only one that the Warren Commission actually admitted to have existed. Some conjecture that the bullet hit something, such as a tree limb and splattered, and then hit the curb, and possible other locations within the Plaza. FBI analysis of the curb, supposedly showed no metals other than what would have been in the core (the whole "Testing the Patch controversy understood). If there were other strikes throughout the Plaza, they would have had to come from this shattered missed shot, or from fragments from the head shot. (The head shot fragments would not explain any hits witnesses claim behind the car.)

I do not understand ballistics enough to know if you can "have it both ways". Can a type of bullet that can go through 2 men, breaking and shattering bones, going through clothes, muscle and skin, and remain relatively intact – yet be shattered by a tree branch enough to splatter all over the Plaza with remaining high velocity as they strike the ground in multiple places?

If Oswald did "get lucky", he could have come down 4 flights of stairs in a matter of seconds, and be calm and cool when Baker encountered him. Indeed, Baker's time frame was just an estimate after all.

Naturally, Oswald could have done everything attributed to him during his escape, including shooting and killing J D

Tippit, as reported. There is nothing in this chain of events that is not POSSIBLE.

But he did own a rifle. He did own a pistol. He did go home the night before, which was unusual. According to Frasier and his sister, he carried a package back to work the next day (even if Frasier was unsteady on size). He also left Marina some money, along with his wedding band, which also would be considered unusual.

I do tend to give Oswald credit for intelligence, beyond what the term Lone "NUT" implies. I feel that if he was going to do this all by himself, he was not thinking it all the way through. He is shooting with a rifle from his own place of employment! Is there anyone who would be foolish enough to think they are not going to get the full blame? If there were no conspirators, it appears he had no escape plan in mind. A few dollars in his pocket, plus a revolver does not get very far.

But I will admit, that if you consider what is POSSIBLE above (assuming it is), a single shooter is possible. And Oswald could be that shooter. Other than the lack of an escape plan, his reported actions look like what a shooter would have done.

Government Cover-Up

Now comes the problem of the "Cover-Up" by the FBI, and Johnson's government.

I do believe there was a "cover-up"; however, in some cases it may have been from the purest of motives. Katzenbach wrote his famous memo stating that the American public must be convinced that Oswald worked alone, and no further conspirators were at large. If you believe he was not behind it, Johnson could have wanted to protect us from a war. However,

JFK Assassination: Shades From The Fence

I think Hoover had another motive, that is less pure. He wanted to protect the FBI from the exposure of any prior knowledge they had of Oswald, and the idea that they should have known.

Regardless, of the reasons for the "cover-up", there was a cover-up, **and the limits to which the FBI would go to perpetuate this cover-up is an unknown.** I do not put it past the FBI to ignore leads, influence witnesses, intentionally reword witness statements, disrupt the chain of evidence, and even **manufacture** evidence, if it furthered their purposes.

It makes the "evidence" and the "witnesses" testimony all questionable. Many of the people who support the "Lone Nut" side of the issue, do so with this very same *"evidence"*, and analysis and investigation done by the FBI **itself**! How much can we really trust the evidential analysis done by a Bureau with its own agenda on which results are desired?

Problems with Witnesses

I agree that there are problems with human Witnesses. As time passes, they have a tendency to change what they *remember*. They are influenced by other people, official reports, and what they may have *learned* about the events since they experienced them. Because of this, the reports given to officials closest to the event are often the most accurate. Sometimes they may actually *remember* something new, but this can often be attributable to something they have heard or read after the fact. In addition, the skills and intent of the person doing the interview, and the question they ask (or don't ask) can be a major factor. For instance, if you just go by Junior Jarman's statement to the Sheriff / Police, you would not even know that he was on the 5th floor! He talks about his brief visit to the front door of the building, and who was there with him.

JFK Assassination: Shades From The Fence

It seems that whoever was interviewing him was more interested in that information, that where Junior was during the shooting itself. Whenever possible then, I try to look at the initial statements made by witnesses, and take their later statements with a "little grain of salt".

Another problem with humans is that they like to be thought of as "experts". Many will make up stories and put themselves in locations they were not in, and seeing things they did not see. I think a big example of this, was Dean Andrews, who, after Oswald's death, started claiming that he had been Oswald's lawyer concerning his discharge. He also stated that he received a call while he was on drugs in the hospital, from"Clay Bertrand" to represent Oswald. He later claimed that he made it all up, so which version is the questionable one? Did he lie at first? Or did he lie when he claimed it was all a lie?

The flip side of this coin, it that the FBI simply ignored some witnesses, and did not follow leads that some of their accounts may have produced. I suspect that they even went as far as to influence witnesses to say only what they wanted to hear, and even changed some of the testimony when it did not suit their needs. Granted, they too may have felt that some of this was after-the-fact expansion from the witnesses, but they may also have let their own agenda influence them. Again, the FBI lacked objectivity, and thus any evidence or information they gathered may be questionable. They lacked credibility.

Accuracies? By volume?

OK, having said that you cannot always believe witnesses after the fact, I will say that there are some of them I believe. These are the ones that were consistent.

JFK Assassination: Shades From The Fence

For instance, the Newmans never deviated from what they said, both in interviews right after the Assassination, to interviews just this last year. In 1963, the Newmans said the shots came from behind them, however, they do admit that behind them could encompass both the Grassy Knoll (to their right) or the TSBD (to their left). Newman always said he only recalls hearing 2 shots.

But a large number of witnesses immediately believed they saw (or heard) a shooter, smoke, or other activities on the Grassy Knoll. This, plus the films and photos of the event seem to indicate another shooter from that area. Of course, supporters of the Lone Nut theory have explanation for all of these, just as the Conspiracy Theorists have arguments for everything supporting one shooter.

Many of the witnesses that thought something untoward occurred from the direction of the Grassy Knoll included some of the Secret Service, Dallas Police, and other officials within the Motorcade itself. Admittedly, the layout of Dealey Plaza, makes echoes and sounds do strange things, and it is difficult to tell where they are coming from, even from these experienced witnesses. But the volume of these witnesses, along with the films and photos, tend to give credence to a shooter from that location, in addition to a shooter from the TSBD.

I am also greatly bothered by the witnesses stating that there were Secret Service in the Plaza besides the ones in the Motorcade. These witnesses included Dallas Police officers, as well as a few civilians, and are not easily explained.

23. The Smooth and the very Difficult paths...

In one of the early books on the Assassination, William Manchester's "Death of a President", the author introduces an idea that he thinks may explain some people tendencies toward Conspiracies in the Kennedy Assassination. A brief paraphrase is that "A great man like Kennedy, requires a great evil to kill him. People do not want to believe that a nobody such as Lee Oswald could perform such an act." Even today, I have heard Researchers repeat this concept, while others solemnly nod their heads in agreement.

On the flip side, another reason I sometimes hear for those that believe the WC version (white) of events, is that they like the simple answer. They do not like the idea of loose ends, or of unsolved crimes. Again, this is usually a CTer talking about the other side, and accusing them of being Warren Commission apologists.

I have always called both of these the "weak minded" motives. It implies that people are only tending towards a Conspiracy or Lone Nut, for emotional reasons. Additionally, I have never heard anyone apply this reason to *themselves*, but always against the other side. Some of these very people who put this reason out in public, about others, have at some time or the other in their lives, also tended towards a Conspiracy. Especially in 1963, when many believed the Communist forces which Oswald seemed to support where behind the killing.

I am happy with whichever direction the reader wants to believe, but I strongly suggest they not believe either side for simply emotional reasons. I strongly suggest that any Researcher look honestly at both sides, and all arguments, before making up their minds. Do not make a decision based on your "gut feel", emotions, or how you want the world to be.

Smooth Path The so called 'hard evidence' does seem to point to Oswald. He owned a weapon, he went home Thursday night and returned with a long package, he had the access and opportunity to the sniper's nest, he was not seen during the shooting by anyone, he left the building, he went home and got his pistol, he was identified as shooting Tippit, he escaped to the Texas theater, and attempted to shoot Officer MacDonald while resisting arrest.

It would be very easy to simply look at this hard evidence, and believe that Oswald acted. With the lack of hard evidence showing another shooter, or accomplices, it would be very easy to believe that Oswald acted completely on his own. Many Researchers have done this, and I cannot fault them for it.

If the Katzenbach memo was influential in LBJ forming the Warren Commission, it also specifies that the American people must be convinced that Oswald acted completely alone, and there were no co-conspirators still at large after that weekend. It can certainly be argued that the Warren Commission did fulfill that "mission". They came up with a viable argument that Oswald acted completely alone.

The Warren Commission did not really have an investigative arm, although they did perform reenactments and thousands of interviews. Yet, when questions came up, such as trained Dallas Law Enforcement officers seeing people posing as Secret Service, and other discrepancies, the WC examiner would simply ignore the statements. Too often, they also "went off the record" to discuss something.

This and their refusal to allow Oswald legal representation in their examinations and interviews left the door open for skepticism and questions. Without the adversarial interaction that a trial entails, the questions will always be with us.

Having said that, the flip side of the equation is that the ability to ask legitimate questions, does not mean there was a Conspiracy. Like the Davis sisters, standing at the same door and seeing the same man, with very different colored jacket, discrepancies are common. They do not necessarily prove that the WC's version is wrong.

Again, we have the evidence that the Investigators allowed us to have, and see. Some will argue that if there was strong evidence that pointed beyond Oswald, the Investigators would have destroyed it, or concealed it from us. (Maybe they did?)

Unfortunately, many of the LN believers get smug, sanguine, and condescending to those that believe in any Conspiracy. This includes any conspiracy to not investigate fully, or that involves Oswald as a shooter. Most often they will pick the most extreme 'black' theory that Oswald was completely innocent, and try to assign it to anyone that disagrees with them. This is because it is much easier to make fun of the most outlandish theory than any other kind of Conspiracy. Likewise, the CTer will often try to tie the most extreme 'white' theory that Oswald acted completely on his own, because it is easier to make fun of. Low-hanging fruit.

Both sides tend to make blanket statements and insults about the other side. We Fence-sitters simply sit in the middle and shake our heads.

Difficult Path

However, not everyone can simply ignore Oswald's history, and consider it as merely coincidence that has absolutely no bearing on his actions that day. There are many legitimate questions that I have been unable to simply ignore.

The Conspiracy Theorist has the more difficult task. While many will simply take a short-cut and believe since there are unanswered or legitimate questions, their MUST have been a conspiracy. IMO this is a fallacy, and lackadaisical way to believe something. Being able to ask legitimate questions does not prove anything, except that a lack of adversarial trial left the door open.

As we have discussed, there are many varying degrees and shades of Conspiracy. There is only one WC version.

Therefore, if you decide it was a Conspiracy, you must analyze what type of a Conspiracy it was. You will be challenged by others to explain why you believe this way, and what you think actually happened.

This is a very difficult task, and most cannot do it successfully. Some are more cogent than others.

JFK Assassination: Shades From The Fence

Unfortunately, most just resort to insults and ridicule to prove their side. This is done by both sides, far too often. It is easier to make fun of the other view, than it is to analyze and explain your own.

Logistics and Planning

We have all seen Mission Impossible (TV series or movies). Hollywood tells us that almost anything is possible, and planning and logistics can be handles. Whether Jim Phelps, Ethan Hunt, Jason Bourne, or any of the other Hollywood characters, it is quite impressive how elaborate and complicated these plots are. However, that is Hollywood! In real life things have to be planned and logistics handled.

The logistics and planning is the catch-22 for any theory. I have tried to focus on this in many of my writings. IMO, it is not enough to simply say who you think did it, but you have to realize that any conspiracy requires planning and logistics, in addition to doing the actual act. Plots do not simply happen.

Of course, if you do think that Oswald acted completely on his own, the planning and logistics are very simple. On Thursday afternoon Oswald decides he will try one more time to reconcile with Marina. He thinks he will "show the world" he is capable of doing some great act, instead of the "nobody" he seems to be since returning from Russia.

He gets shipping materials to take home, and possible builds a sniper's nest using cartons available on the 6th floor. He may wait until Friday morning, as it would not take long, and if he does it ahead of time someone may discover the 'nest'. He arranges to go to Irving that night with Frazier, and has a curtain rod excuse ready.

The next day, he sneaks his rifle into the building, in the curtain rod bag. Sometime during the morning, he moves some rolling reader boxes to use as a rifle rest, and moves 3 stacks of boxes to create the nest. When nobody is paying attention, he moves the bag and rifle into the nest. Once the floor empties at lunch, he assembles the rifle, and sits quietly in the nest. He shoots 3 shots. He stashes the rifle, leaving the shell casings where they fall. He crosses the 4th floor before Styles and Adams can see him past the mid-wall and boxes. He hears Baker and Truly hollering up the elevator shaft, and so he diverts to the 2nd floor lunchroom. He acts calm for a few seconds while Baker and Truly are with him, and leaves the building by the front stairs, and out the front door.

It takes little planning, if he is the lone shooter, or even the only shooter in the TSBD.

The problems are ones of Motive, and what to do after the act. He seemingly does not have any escape plan.

Now, some Researchers believe that other employees of the TSBD were part of the plot. Some will even name them. These employees also have to same access to the building that Oswald has, so planning is not much a problem for them either. Of course, they have to get Oswald's rifle, to shoot or plant, and must keep Oswald himself from stumbling onto them. The logistics of handling Oswald still apply.

It is the Conspiracy side that has the Logistic and Planning difficulties. Regardless of which Conspiracy you want to look at, there are planning problems with getting other shooters into and out of the Texas School Book Depository. There are 72 or so workers in the building, and you have to get your people into, set up a sniper's nest, and exiting the building, without being seen by any of those 72 employees. Only 1 reported seeing a stranger in the building, although all 73 or so were asked that question.

The outside work crew shown in Oliver Stone's "JFK", are a Hollywood creation. The work was done by normal TSBD employees, and not any outsiders.

Additionally, you have to control Oswald. It certainly would not do to have him standing out on the street next to Roy Truly, or other employees, which would give him an alibi.

Lastly, you have to make sure that Oswald himself does not suspect he is being set up. He cannot see any strangers in the building, and you must give him a reason to wait in some room instead of seeing the President. Some think he is waiting by a phone for a call; however, there are no telephones in either lunch room, and the one he normally is allowed to use is in the middle of the back of the open 1st floor. From there, he can readily see the elevator, stairs and door areas.

You may believe that it is Malcom Wallace and Loy Factor ("The Men on the Sixth Floor" book). But you still have to get them into, and out of the building. That particular book alleged that Oswald was also a shooter on the 6th floor. That being the case, he could have brought the rifle and built the sniper's nest, and then assist them in accessing the building. But why would he not leave with them? He certainly did not seem to "run interference" for anyone. It was only because Baker saw him through a window that the lunchroom encounter happened at all.

If you believe that Oswald was only a "patsy" and was nowhere near the 6th floor, then you have to think through all of the logistics and planning to control Oswald, access the building, build a sniper's nest, do the shooting (or planting weapons) and exit, without being seen by anyone, including Oswald.

There are certainly gaps in time where everyone was working, and the stairs and elevators do not have any use that we know of. I could certainly work out a timeline where the "shooting team" simply stayed on the 6th floor, for a few minutes, before there was a gap in stairs and elevator usage (that we know of) where they could simply walk out. One of the Deputy Sheriffs encountered guys in suits, as he was going into the building. Police Sgt. Harkness encountered men at the back of the building, when he went to seal it off around 12:38.

But how would the Conspirators know that ahead of time?

I have done many articles on the interior of the building, as well as planning and logistics of the Altgen6 and other photos and films. These are not easy obstacles to overcome. It is simply not enough to say "Oswald was in the 2nd floor lunchroom, so someone MUST have been able to handle it." That is a cop-out, IMO.

Any Conspiracy you settle opon, will require evaluation and explanation about the logistics. The planning of any Conspiracy, other than a TSBD employee helping requires it.

So, those of you who believe in the Lone Nut, please be kind to your fellow Conspiracy Theory believers. They have a much harder job supporting their position than you do. Simply try not to be stubborn, and invested in any theory, and understand why others may not exactly agree with you. Be respectful to those who disagree.

24. (Not Much of a) Conclusion

When writing a book, information tends to "pool". You intend to put information in, and every time you go back and read a chapter you want to add to it. But in both my books, it seems that when I get to the end, I have lots of little tidbits of information that I am uncertain I said. It kind of looks like a waterfall: the information throughout the book is regular and consistent, as the water falls evenly. But at the bottom of the waterfall is a pool of water (information) that you did not get into the book, and you still bring it up. I am trying not to do that this time.

Not Covered

For the experienced Researcher, it is apparent that there is enormous amounts of information and controversies that do not appear in this book. This book simply covered the shooting of JFK, and Oswald.

For the new Student/Researcher, or even the casual topic reader, there are many areas that you might want to get into. The reading lists in the back of the book will give you many excellent books on the subjects covered in this book, as well as the many subjects not covered here. I tried to give a general description of what the books listed are about, so you can pick and choose any of these various topics.

Some of the many subjects I did not cover are:
- Oswald's life
- Medical evidence
- Ballistics
- New Orleans
- Mafia connections
- CIA and FBI connections
- LBJ's history and connections
- Military Intelligence and Oswald
- Investigation details

349

JFK Assassination: Shades From The Fence

- Tippit shooting
- Major General Edwin Walker
- Dallas Right-wing extremism
- Evidence details
- Photographs and films
- Jack Ruby
- Cuba and Russia
- JFK Presidency and life
- Witness statements
- Bay of Pigs and anti-Castro groups

And I am certain the above list is missing things!

If you are new to the case, and want to get into the quagmire on information, there are lots of things to get you started on. Try to specialize, as I do not think it is possible to be an expert on everything.

My opinion? (FWIW…)

I am about 99% certain that Oswald killed JD Tippit. This indicates that he was also a shooter of JFK, as there would be no reason to shoot and kill a Dallas police officer, if you had not shot at the President. Likewise, there would be no reason to attempt to shoot Officer McDonald in the Texas Theater. These have often been referred to as the Rosetta Stones of the JFK Assassination.

I am about 85% certain Oswald was a shooter inside the TSBD. This does NOT eliminate a Killing Conspiracy. He could have been encouraged by others, or told to do something by others. They may have promised him an escape and trip to Cuba. (They may have been lying about this, and might have intended to kill him instead, in such a way as to still point to Cuba and Castro.

I am about 80% certain there were Conspiracies to kill Kennedy. Many people hated the Kennedy brothers, and many indicated that they would be 'hit'. Some seem to have prior knowledge of the Assassination, but maybe a lone Oswald got their first. There is no indication that Oswald was a part of these alleged plots. Then again, he could have been.

I am only 75% certain that there were no other shooters, on the Grassy Knoll or Southern Knoll. I am less certain about the DalTex. However, I cannot rule it out completely.

I am about 95% certain there was a 'conspiracy' on the part of the Warren Commission to avoid any direction or indication beyond Oswald. But even if Oswald really was the "Lone Gunman", that does NOT eliminate him being in contact with some Conspiracy, or trying to impress somebody. There is much evidence of pre-knowledge, Oswald sightings, etc., that (unlike the WC), I cannot just chalk up the volume to "coincidence", mistakes and hearsay.

The "WC" came up with a reasonable explanation, and did not follow up on anything that pointed beyond Oswald as a Lone Nut. That was probably their purpose. But just because it was a REASONABLE version, does not mean it is accurate. They simply seemed to avoid or ignore any statement that pointed elsewhere. I cannot simply ignore the information that points elsewhere. Nor can I ignore Oswald's Cuba and Russian history and activity.

Welcome to the Research Community

If this book has given you a "taste" of the most studied crime of the 20th century, it is what I intended. You can join us, and start digging deeper.

I will still be out there in a couple of Facebook Groups. I Administrate Jim Hess' "Fair Play for JFK", which is one of the best groups about the case. There are other groups, but many of them will tell you that they do NOT want you there, if you disagree with them. (Be careful, and hold onto your wallet!)

I also run my own "November 1963: a balanced discussion" group, but there are a lot less members, and more limited discussion.

But there are dozens of other sites, groups, and resources out there.

JFK Assassination: Shades From The Fence

Fair warning: You can get hooked into studying this case, if you are foolhardy enough to press against the "looking glass".

If you are an existing Researcher, you are probably very annoyed at my book, and feel that since I do not agree with you, I am stupid or very naïve. (I will admit that I am probably both.) But I will still be out there, and willing to honestly debate any topic of the case with you.

I wrote in the Acknowledgements that I appreciate every Researcher I have ever encountered. At least down to the Troll level. Maybe a few Trolls have been lightly amusing, but most are not. (House Flies I just don't bother with, and ignore.) Some Trolls have sharpened my knowledge in that I have to think through things to respond. Others... not so much. So, I still Thank You.

The "civil" debate and discussion between Researchers is always welcome in any Group that I moderate. I can think of nothing more boring that a debate group where everyone believes the same stuff! What is the point to that?

But I encourage all of you to believe what you want to believe. I still respect and will engage with you. I do not pick my "friends" based on their beliefs, and whether they disagree or agree with me. But I do expect civility....

Purpose of the book

The purpose of the book was to show that there are simply not "Black" and "White" versions. There are many shades of gray between the extremes.

It always amuses me that when dealing with the Researchers that have already made up their minds about what happened, if you disagree then they Label you as a believer in the opposite extreme. If you do not buy the WC's "Oswald acted alone", then they think you are a CTer. Conversely, if you do not believe in the Researchers particular conspiracy of what happened, then you support the "Warren Commission" and are a LNer. They do not want to think there are middle-of-the-road positions.

Personally, I still have questions that Oswald could have been part of a Conspiracy, based on research, instead of some "book" (and Author's opinion). I am not influenced by any "Author", regardless of how respected they are!

Nor should YOU be...

Sure, use an Author's opinion (such as mine) to get you thinking about different aspects of the case. Most of them will give you detail that you may never stumble across on your own. There is simply too much information out there. But take every opinion with a "grain of salt". (Some Authors you might need an entire "salt lick".)

Use the same skepticism with every documentary, TV show, movie, YouTube, online Forum/Group/Blog, or presentation. Use them as a Resource, and opportunity to see information you might not stumble onto yourself.

The very bottom line

Again, the JFK Assassination is the most studied and debated crime in the 20th century. It is extremely complicated, if you think there might be any form of Conspiracy to either kill, help Oswald, or avoid investigating beyond Oswald.

It is really OK to be undecided about what happened.

At the same time, if you already have your mind made up, I am very happy for you. However, I really hope it is because you researched and came up with what you think happened based on that research. Do not take anyone else's word, including mine. Read. Analyze.

(As if you did not know by now) The main slogan of this book is:

THINK FOR YOURSELF! (as always)

Reading List

Throughout this book I have mentioned a number of book titles, as I quoted or paraphrased what they said. In addition to those, here is the Suggested Reading List I tried to give people when they took my JFK Tour:

Reading List on JFK Assassination Topics

The Kennedy Assassination is a highly complex topic, with over 1,000 books written on the subject. Each author tends to have a particular angle, or theory, which they promote. There is no single book that lists all of the details, and angles. However, I have read all of the following books (among others), and they are all interesting in their subject/theory areas. Inclusion on this list does not mean I believe them, but they will give a fair exposure to the case, from that author's perspective.

Jerry Dealey 2010 NID Presentation "A Shooter in the TSBD?" – JFKLancer.com $10

Warren Commission Report – (A must read) Not the 26 volumes – eBay

D in the Heart of Texas – my book www.dealey.org history of Dealey Plaza and Dallas

Witness Biography
At the Door of Memory – Aubrey Rike (JFKLancer.com)
Steering Truth: My Eternal Connection to JFK and Lee Harvey Oswald – Buell Wesley Frazier (2021) Amazon

Supports the Lone Gunman Theory:
Case Closed – Gerald Posner (Amazon.com) (refuted by about everyone – Case Open below)
Death of a President – William Manchester (most story-like)
Reclaiming History – Vincent Bugliosi – 1600 pages (new) – Prosecutor's point of view. **Killing Kennedy**: The End of Camelot – Amazon – Storylike background history

Criticizes the Warren Report

JFK Assassination: Shades From The Fence

Six Seconds in Dallas – Josiah Thompson (rare)
Cover-Up – Stewart Galanor (used Amazon.com)
Accessories After the Fact – Sylvia Meagher (rare)

Medical Evidence
Best Evidence – David Lifton
JFK: Conspiracy of Silence – Dr. Charles Crenshaw (Parkland Doctor) **In the Eye of History** – William Law (jfklancer.com)

Dallas Policemen
First Day Evidence – Rusty Livingston (DPD Crime Lab)
Retired Dallas Police Chief Jesse Curry Reveals His JFK Assassination File – Jessie Curry (rare)

CIA / Mafia / FBI conspiracies
Bloody Treason – Noel Twyman (probably the largest tome – good)
Oswald and the CIA – John Newman (used Amazon.com)
Legacy of Secrecy – Lamar Waldron (Anti-Castro forces protected from Bobby Kennedy by the existence of
"project Mongoose")

Focus on Oswald's life
Legend: Secret World of Lee Harvey Oswald – Edward J Epstein (rare)
Marina and Lee – Priscilla Johnson McMillan (used) –authorized biography by Marina Oswald

New Orleans DA Jim Garrison
On the Trail of the Assassins – Jim Garrison
False Witness: The Real Story of Jim Garrison's Trial, and Oliver Stone's Film, JFK – Patricia Lambert (antiGarrison)
On the Trail of Delusion – Fred Litwin (eBook)

LBJ and Hoover
Blood, Money and Power: How L.B.J. Killed J.F.K. - Barr McClelland

JFK Assassination: Shades From The Fence

Official and Confidential: The Secret Life of J. Edgar Hoover – Summers **Texas in the Morning** – Madeleine Duncan Brown (LBJ mistress in Dallas)

Political Atmosphere of Dallas in 1963-64
TheKennedyHalfCentury – Larry Sabato – NEW – Kennedy assassination and presidential legacy
Dallas: Public and Private – Warren Leslie (Amazon – Sixth Floor Museum)
Dallas 1963 – Bill Minutaglio and Steven L. Davis (extreme politics of Dallas)
When the News Went Live – Wes Wise, Bob Huffacker, Bill Mercer and George Phenix (Television News)

Pre-Knowledge, Confessions and Miscellaneous
Oswald Talked – Mary and Ray La Fontaine (John Thomas Masen and John Elrod)
Somebody Would Have Talked – Larry Hancock (John Martino and anti-Castro Cubans) (JFKLANCER.COM)
Men on the Sixth Floor - Glen Sample & Mark Collom (shooter Loy Factor, Oswald and Mac Wallace)
No Case to Answer – Ian Griggs (collection of articles from an British ex-Policeman) (JFKLANCER.COM)
The Kennedy Assassination Tapes – Max Holland (11/22 transmissions and phone taping of LBJ)
The Man Who Knew Too Much – Dick Russell (Richard Nagel – has himself arrested to avoid being connected)

The shooting of Officer JD Tippit
With Malice: Lee Harvey Oswald and the killing of Officer J.D. Tippit – Dale K. Myers

JFK: The Book of the Film – Oliver Stone & Zachary Sklar – (footnotes the script of the film)

Appendix – Shadows of the Warren Commission

A few years back, I was a speaker at a Lion's Club meeting and their local TV program. Many of Dallas' elite were at that downtown meeting. I wrote the following notes, with lots of **bold** text for that meeting. (The bold was so that I could present the information verbally while looking at it from the podium.)

This appendix is my notes from that presentation, which I called "Shadows of the Warren Commission". I covered a lot of the issues that have sprung up, which "bothered" me about the official version of the case. Once again it is a repeat of several of the things I have covered in the book, but also includes some Oswald life history, and other information that is not covered. So I decided to put it in an Appendix.

On **November 29, 1963**, President Lyndon Baines Johnson issued **Executive Order No. 11130** to create the <u>President's Commission On The Assassination of President Kennedy</u>, commonly known as the **Warren Commission**.

It was created to stave off a number of investigations which were being discussed:

Texas court of inquiry – before a Magistrate in Texas, by Texas Attorney General Waggoner Carr

Dallas Grand Jury – by Dallas District Attorney Henry Wade

Congressional Hearings – were being discussed by both Houses of the US Congress.

Commission consisted of:

357

JFK Assassination: Shades From The Fence

Chief Justice Earl Warren – Chief Justice of the US Supreme Court, former Governor and Attorney General of California

2 US Senators:
Richard B Russell (D) Senator from Georgia, and chairman of the Senate Armed Services
Committee, former Governor and county attorney in Georgia

John Sherman Cooper (R) Senator from Kentucky, Former County and circuit judge in Kentucky, US Ambassador to India

2 US Representatives:
Hale Boggs – (D) Rep from Louisiana, and majority whip
Gerald R Ford – (R) Rep from Michigan, chairman of the House Republican Conference

2 "private citizens":
Allen W Dulles – Former director of the CIA, fired by Kennedy after Bay of Pigs
John J McCloy – Former president of the International Bank for Reconstruction and Development, former US High Commissioner for Germany, and Assistant Secretary of War during WWII

Purpose:

Cajoled by LBJ to participate, as a committee to "avoid parallel investigations in a body having the broadest national mandate".
LBJ "Treatment"

December 5, 1963 – First meeting the Commission viewed the Executive Order as a "mandate to conduct a thorough and independent investigation. Because of numerous **rumors and theories**, the Commission concluded that the public interest in insuring that the truth was ascertained could not be served by merely accepting the reports or the analysis of Federal or State agencies."

December 13, 1963 Congress enacted **Senate Joint Resolution 137** (public law 88-202) empowering the Commission to **issue subpoenas** requiring the testimony of witnesses and the production of evidence relating to any matter under its investigation, provide the **grant of immunity** to anyone claiming the privilege against self-incrimination under the 5th amendment. (Never used.)

Commission hearings were **closed to the public**, unless the witness appearing before the Commission requested **public** hearings. (Only happened **twice**.)

J. Lee Rankin as General Counsel on December 16 – former Solicitor General of the United States. **14 assistant counsel** from across the US, with varying qualifications, plus **support staff**. Also assisted with various contacts in all Federal Agencies.

Roger E Craig – president of the American Bar Association was asked to "participate in the investigation and to advise the Commission whether in his opinion the proceedings conformed to the basic principles of American Justice." No adversarial proceedings were in place, and no representative for Oswald, Ruby or other participants were used, although some volunteered. (**Mark Lane**)

"Of principle importance was the **5 volume report of the Federal Bureau of Investigation**, submitted on December 9, 1963, which summarized the results of the investigation conducted by the Bureau immediately after the assassination."

"On **December 18, 1963 the Secret Service submitted a detailed report** on security precautions taken before President

JFK Assassination: Shades From The Fence

Kennedy's trip to Texas and a summary of the events of November 22, as witnessed by Secret Service agents."

"A few days later the **Department of State submitted a report** relating to Oswald's defection to the Soviet Union in 1959, and his return to the United State in 1962."

"On January 7 and 11, 1964, the **Attorney General of Texas** submitted an extensive set of investigative materials, **largely Dallas police reports**, on the assassination of President Kennedy and the killing of Oswald."

"Because of the diligence, cooperation, and facilities of Federal investigative agencies, it was unnecessary for the Commission to employ investigators other than the members of the Commission's legal staff. The Commission recognized, however, that special measures were required whenever the fact or rumors called for an appraisal of the acts of the agencies themselves. The staff reviewed in detail the actions of several Federal agencies, particularly the FBI, the Secret Service, the CIA and the Department of State."

FBI: 25,000 interviews, 2,300 reports, 25,400 pages
SS: 1,550 interviews, 800 reports, 4,600 pages
CIA: "Investigative analyses of particular significance and sensitivity in the foreign areas" IRS, State and military intelligence handled additions investigative requests

"Beginning on February 3, 1964, the Commission and its staff has taken the testimony of **552 witnesses**. Of this number, **94** appeared before members of the Commission; **395** were questioned by members of the Commission's legal staff; **61** supplied sworn affidavits; and **2** gave statements."

JFK Assassination: Shades From The Fence

The Commission focused mainly on the Biography of Lee Harvey Oswald, the timeline and physics of Nov 22-24, and the security procedures.

The Commission presented it final report to President Johnson in September 1964, consisting of one volume report, and supported by 26 volumes of testimony and evidence. The summary was that Lee H. Oswald fired all of the 3 shots from the 6th floor window of the TSBD, and there was no conclusive evidence of a conspiracy. Jack Ruby also acted alone.

Time sequence and events:

Lee Harvey Oswald – Biography

Born in New Orleans, October 18, 1939, Lee was the third child of a **Marguerite Claverie Oswald**, and a 2-month deceased father. A half-brother, **John Pic** was the oldest, from a previous marriage, and **Robert Oswald** was 5 years older. Over the years John and Robert were often placed in orphanages, as was Lee from time to time.

At age of **4, Lee was taken out of the orphanage, and he and his mother moved to Dallas**. Edwin A Ekdahl married Marguerite in May of 1945, but they divorced in 1948. Lee went to **1st grade in Covington, LA, in 1947** during a parental separation, but finished the grade in Ft Worth, when parents tried a brief and unsuccessful reconciliation. **Lee attended the next 5 ½ years in Ft Worth**.

In **August of 1952, Lee and his mom moved to New York**, where John Pic was stationed with the Coast Guard. During the next 1 1/2 years, Lee was a constant truant, and eventually ended up at **Youth House**, a institution for truant and law troubled juveniles, where he went under **psychiatric evaluation**. He was diagnosed as an attention starved youngster, quite bright, but with a problem with authority. In **January 1954, with his truant case still pending, his mother moved him back to New Orleans**.

In **10th grade, in October 1955**, 10 days before his birthday, he brought a note from his "mother" (his forgery) saying they were transferring to California, and **dropped out**. He tried to **join the Marine Corps**, military as his brothers had, **but was denied as being too young at 16**. Worked various New Orleans jobs as an office messenger or clerk. During this period he started reading **Communist literature**, after being handed some brochure on Ethel and Julius Rosenberg. He wrote to the Socialist Party of America, professing himself a Marxist. He regaled co-workers about the benefits of Communism.

In **July 1956, he and Marguerite moved back to Ft Worth**. He enrolled in school again, but dropped out in October when he enlisted into the **Marine Corp**. On December 21, 1956, in boot camp Oswald scored a **212** with an M-1 rifle, 2 points over the minimum for a rating of "**sharpshooter**". (He will later shoot for record on May 6, 1959, getting only a **191**, one point over the minimum requirement for "**marksman**".) **Oswald also received training in aviation fundamentals, and radar scanning.**

Known as a loner, Oswald had a continuing problem with authority. He was **court-martialed** once for owning a privately owned weapon (shot himself once in the forearm), and again for using provocative language to a non-commissioned officer.

He served **15 months in Japan** as a **radar operator**. In November 1958, he was stationed in Santa Ana, California. He showed a **marked interest in the Soviet Union and Cuba**, and often expressed politically radical views with a dogmatic

JFK Assassination: Shades From The Fence

conviction. (Allegedly taught himself **Russian, and passed a test**, with 2 more words right than wrong.)

In March 1959, Oswald applied to the Albert Schweitzer College in Switzerland. He requested a **hardship discharge in Sept 11, 1959**, because of his mother's health (from a fall) and financial hardship.

He received an honorable discharge, and stayed with his mother for 3 days, before going through
France, and Finland, into the Soviet Union. There he **requested citizenship**, and went to the American Embassy to verbally **denounce his citizenship and threaten to give Radar secrets to the Russians** (not in WC). He **never processed** the paperwork to denounce, but left his passport with the US Ambassador.

On Oct 21, 1959, he was ordered by the Soviets to leave by 8:00 PM, and he attempted **suicide by cutting his left wrist**, and was hospitalized for 6 weeks. In January of 1960, he was permitted to stay on a "year to year" basis, and moved to **Minsk**. There he worked at a **radio factory**, and was supplemented by the Red Cross and Soviets. He had a nice apartment, and partied at local dances and events.

In **February 1961**, he first wrote the American Embassy requesting to **return** to the US. The following month, he met 19-year old, **Marina Nikolaevna Prusakova**, a pharmacist, whose Uncle was a Colonel in a Soviet security branch. They were **married on April 30, 1961, and had a first child in February 1962**. Their entry to the US was approved in December 25, 1961, but it took a number of months to arrange and execute. The State Department **loaned Oswald $435.71** for travel expenses, and they returned by ship to New York in mid-**June 1962**, and then traveled onto Ft Worth. They lived with Robert Oswald for a few weeks, and also with Oswald's mother for a while. Lee got a job working with **sheet metal on June 16**.

The **FBI interviewed Oswald 2 times** that summer, the first being on **June 26**, and the second on **August 16**. Oswald insisted he never gave the Russians radar secrets, and had never been involved with Soviet intelligence. He agreed to contact the FBI, if he or Marina were approached by the Soviets in any way. **FBI Agent John Fain** deemed Oswald as extremely arrogant, and unwilling to discuss the reasons for going to the USSR.

While in Ft Worth, Oswald and Marina got very involved in the area's **White Russian community**. Marina could speak no English, and Oswald would not, or let others, teach her. (So she would continue to depend solely on him.) The group gave clothing and assistance, whenever Oswald would allow it, or behind his back. Oswald was almost universally disliked by this group, except for **George DeMohrenschildt**, who was a kind of "sophisticated upper-class intellectual".

In **October 1962**, Oswald quit his job, and moved to Dallas. He found an apartment in Oak Cliff, and a "photography job" **(Jaggers-Chiles Stovall)**, which he lost on April 6, 1963. The apartments the Oswalds lived at were on Elsbeth and Neeley Streets in Oak Cliff.

During the winter of 62 / 63, Oswald ordered a **pistol, as well as a Mannlicher Carcano rifle from Klein's Sporting Goods in Chicago, for $12.88**. In February, 1963 Marina was befriended by Ruth Paine of Irving, a member of the group who wished to learn Russian better. The guns arrived to Oswald's PO Box (2915) in Dallas during March and April of 1963. The famous **photographs of Lee holding the weapons** were taken by Marina in the back yard of the Neeley St apartment.

JFK Assassination: Shades From The Fence

On April 10, 1963, Oswald took a shot at **retired Major Gen. Edwin Walker**, at the rear of his Turtle Creek home. He had left a note with Marina explaining what to do if he was caught, and this **note was not discovered until after the JFK Assassination**. At the time, it was an unsolved crime.

After the Walker attempt, **Marina convinced Oswald to move to New Orleans** and try to find work there. Ruth Paine invited Marina to stay with here until Oswald found work in New Orleans. In **May**, Oswald found work greasing the coffee making equipment at **Riley's Coffee Company**. Marina was driven by Ruth Paine to join Oswald at their apartment on Magazine St.

While in New Orleans, Oswald formed a "Chapter" of the **Fair Play for Cuba Committee**, after being in communication with the main offices of the organization. He had Marina sign the membership cards with the name **Alex (Alec) J. Hidell** as President, and it appeared that Oswald was the only member. He handed out Fair Play for Cuba brochures on a number of occasions, with the address **544 Camp St** stamped on some of them. He got into a scuffle with some antiCastro Cubans on August 9, and was **arrested** and held overnight. During the next 2 weeks, Oswald appeared on **2 radio programs**, and even on TV briefly.

On July 19, 1963, Oswald had lost his job at the Riley Coffee Company, and on **September 23, Ruth Paine picked up Marina**, who was expecting a second child, and let her live with her in Irving. Oswald stayed behind, ostensibly to find work in Houston or another city.

Instead, Oswald went to **Mexico City**, arriving on September 27. Lee promptly visited the Cuban Embassy, trying to obtain permission to visit Cuba, and then more on to Russia. The

Cuban Government would not grant the visa, unless approved by the Soviet Embassy first. Oswald made a number of trips and phone calls to both embassies, but was unable to acquire the permission. He then **returned to Dallas on October 3, 1963**.

It was decided that Oswald would rent a room in Dallas, and look for work, while Marina lived with Ruth Paine. Oswald stayed one week with **Mrs. Mary Bledsoe, on Marsalis**, in Oak Cliff. Mrs. Bledsoe refused to extend the stay, because she did not care for Lee speaking Russian on her phone. Lee then found a room at **1026 N Beckley**, on **October 14**. On that same day, Mrs. Paine found out from a neighbor that the **Texas School Book Depository** needed workers, and Oswald acquired a job gathering school books to fill orders. On October 20, 1963, the second daughter was born.

Oswald established a pattern of staying in Dallas during the week, and then going with coworker Buell Wesley Frazier on the weekends to the Paine home in Irving. However, on the **weekend of November 15**, he did not return to Irving, as there was to be a birthday party for one of the Paine children.

On Monday, November 18, Marina tried to call Lee by having Ruth call his rooming house. They found that he was not registered under his real name, but under **O. H. Lee**. (Lee said the landlady made the mistake.) This caused a **fight between Marina and Lee**.

Lee asked Frazier to give him a lift home on **Thursday, Nov 21**. He also told Frazier that he had to pick up some **curtain rods** for his rooming house. Ruth Paine was surprised to see Lee, as this was the only time he had shown up mid-week, without asking first. Marina was still mad at him, and Lee was unable to make up with her. Ruth Paine did recall finding a light left on in her garage that night, which was unusual.

JFK Assassination: Shades From The Fence

Dallas "Hate" Incidents

Spitting Incident – During the 1960 Presidential Campaign, Lyndon Johnson held a rally at the **Baker Hotel** in Dallas. At the same date, the Republicans had a "**Tag Day**", centered at the Adolphus Hotel. Lyndon and his entourage went to lunch in the Adolphus Hotel, which was crowded with anti-LBJ Republicans, and a few "**young men**". A pushing, shouting match ensued, and LBJ and Lady Bird were harassed and spit upon.

Adlai Stevenson – On October 25, 1963, UN Ambassador Adlai Stevenson came to Dallas to celebrate "**UN Day**". The day before was designated "US Day", by Connally, after receiving a number of petitions. Unknown to Connally, the person behind the "**US Day**" was **Edwin Walker**, who held a rally at the Dallas Memorial Coliseum that night. Presumably, Walker rallied others who were against the "United Nations", and Stevenson was jeered and interrupted countless times during his speech. When leaving the function, Stevenson was **struck on the head** and dazed by a lady protestor carrying an anti-UN protestor. (She claimed she was pushed by a black man, but no such individual was present.)

Dallas Citizen Council – Stanley Marcus and others in the DCC actually discussed asking the President not to come to Dallas, but decided there was no graceful way to "**uninvite**" the President.

Mayor Earl Cabell and **Chief of Police Jessie Curry** both called for peace and a warm welcome in the media, and warned that bad behavior would not be tolerated. An ordinance was passed making it illegal to interfere or disrupt any lawful assembly.

JFK Assassination: Shades From The Fence

Planning the Presidential Trip:

In 1962, Kennedy started to consider an Official visit, as he had lost Dallas in 1960, and had not been there since 1960. He wished to resolve the factional differences in the Democratic Party, particularly between LBJ and US Senator Ralph Yarborough. The **decision was made in San Antonio on June 5, 196**2, during a meeting with LBJ and Governor Connally. The original planned called for 1 day, but was extended in September. Connally called the White House on October 4, and it was decided to leave the details in the hands of Governor John Connally. Special assistant Kenneth O'Donnell was to act as coordinator at the White House. Everyone agreed that in Dallas, JFK should be seen by the maximum number of people possible.

Advanced preparations were the primary responsibility of SS Agents **Forrest V Sorrels**, special agent in charge of the Dallas office, and advance Special Agent **Winston G. Lawson**. They were advised of the trip on **Nov 4**. Lawson had responsibility to arrange a timetable, select the luncheon site and motorcade route, and take preventative action against anyone in Dallas considered a threat, by the PRS (Protective Research Section, Dallas police and FBI. On his arrival on **November 12, he worked with these people to ascertain these risks**. He also asked specifically about the Stevenson incident, and agents at the Trade Mart had photos of individuals that were at the Stevenson incident. The Dallas FBI supplied one name, but Oswald was not that individual. 3 sites were evaluated for the luncheon: **Trade Mart, Market Hall, and the Women's Building** in Fair Park. The Women's Building was not large enough, and Market Hall was already booked for the 22nd.

JFK Assassination: Shades From The Fence

Lawson worked with Dallas police in determining the Motorcade Route. Elm St. was briefly considered, but would not expose as many people as would the primary Dallas' parade route of Main St, which had more buildings where the crowds could see the President. (plus would disrupt bus transportation more.) The route was **driven by Lawson and Sorrels**, along with assistant chief Batchelor on **Nov 15**. The police indicated that they felt it was the proper route.

The actual route was **approved on Nov 18**, and given to the White House, and local **newspapers** on that day. It had always included the jog onto Elm St., as this was the only logical way to reach Stemmons. The 2 local papers printed the route in word form, and later in maps for the next several days.

Route: Through fence to avoid Love Field traffic, Mockingbird Lane, Lemmon Ave., right at Turtle Creek, becomes Cedar Springs, Harwood, Main, Houston, Elm, and Stemmons Freeway to Trade Mart.

Other Cities: Left White House Nov 21, 10:45 AM. San Antonio 1:30, with a motorcade through downtown, and a dedication of the US Air Force School of Aerospace Medicine at Brooks, AFB. Late afternoon a flight to Houston, a motorcade and Rice University Stadium at a dinner for US Representative Albert Thomas. Flew late that night to Ft Worth's Carswell, stayed at Texas Hotel.

November 22, 1963 – Event Timelines:

On November 21, there appeared some anonymous handbills, **"Wanted for Treason"**, which was widely distributed. There was also a **"Welcome, Mr. President"** full page ad in the Dallas Morning News. It was highly critical of the President, and was sponsored by the "American Factfinding Committee".

369

JFK Assassination: Shades From The Fence

JFK saw these items, and told Jackie, **"We are going into Nut country, today!"** Per O'Donnell, the President also commented that, **"if anybody really wanted to shoot the President of the United States, it was not a very difficult job – all one had to do was get a high building someday with a telescopic rifle, and there was nothing anybody could do to defend against such an attempt."**

Oswald rode into work with **Wesley Frazier**. Wesley's sister, **Linnie Mae Randall**, spotted Oswald walking up to the car, and placing a long package in the back seat. When Wesley asked what the package was, Oswald said it was the curtain rods they had discussed. Oswald left the car before Frazier, who idled to allow the battery to charge. Frazier said Oswald **cupped the package in his hand and tucked the top under his armpit**. Nobody **else** recalled seeing Oswald with the package.

Kennedy attended a Breakfast at the Texas Hotel, and then made some brief outdoor remarks to a crowd in an open parking lot. They went to **Carswell AFB** for the quick flight over to Dallas.

11:40 AM Air Force One touched down at **Love Field**.

Motorcade Sequence:
DPD Motorcycles – to handle problems and clear traffic as needed
Pilot Car – DPD Officers to report on problems – quarter mile ahead
4 to 6 Motorcycles – to keep the crowd back
Lead Car – Chief of Police Jesse Curry, Sheriff Bill Decker, SS Agents Sorrels and Lawson – rolling command car
Presidential Limousine "SS-100"– 1961 Lincoln Convertible – SS William Greer (driver), SS

JFK Assassination: Shades From The Fence

Roy Kellerman (Agent in Charge) – Governor John Connally, Nellie Connally, President John Kennedy , Jackie Kennedy

4 Motorcycles – to keep crowds back – run beside rear of Limo

SS Follow-Up "Queen Mary" – 1955 Cadillac convertible – 8 passenger – equipped with weapons

Vice President car – Locally obtained Lincoln convertible – SS Rufus Youngblood, Texas

Highway Patrol Hurchel Jacks (driver), LBJ (right), Ladybird (center), US Senator Ralph Yarborough (left)

Vice Presidential Follow-Up Car – DPD officer driving, 3 SS agents, and VP Assistant Cliff Carter

Remaining Vehicles: 5 cars of other dignitaries (Mayor, Congressman, etc., **Admiral George**

Burkley), telephone and Western Union vehicles, White House Communications car, 3 cars for Press Photographers, White House staff bus, 2 Press busses. Dallas Police car and several Motorcycles.

11:50 Working the crowd, they left Love Field and began the **Motorcade**.

Motorcade stopped twice at the President's request: 1 time for a sign **"stop and shake hands"**, and another for a **Catholic nun and a group** of small children. At both times, SS Agents on the follow-up car ran up to the sides of the car. On Main St., SS Agent Clint Hill ran up to the car on 4 occasions, as did SS John D Ready, including chasing back a **15-year old boy who tried to shake hands**. For the Vice President, Youngblood stepped out to keep the crowd back on several occasions.

A man screams and appears to have an **epileptic seizure** in Dealey Plaza on Houston Street, between Main and Elm. Ambulance driver Aubrey Rike comes and picks up the main, and takes him to Parkland Hospital.

JFK Assassination: Shades From The Fence

12:00 – TSBD employees took lunch, and got into positions to see the President. Most were in front of **the building on the porch**, and street, but many took up positions looking out, or filming, out of various open windows on the front.

12:15 to 12:25 – Bonnie Ray Williams eats his chicken lunch on the 6th floor, right by the "sniper's nest". He then proceeds down to the front porch to find his friends. He finds Harold Norman and Junior Jarman, and they go up to the 5th floor to watch the Motorcade. Leaving the elevators on the 5th floor.

12:23 – Witness **Howard Brennan** sits on the wall across Elm St from the TSBD, and notices a man **age 30, 5' 10" in the window** of the 6th floor. He will later give this description to the police a couple of minutes after the shooting.

12:30 – The Assassination – as the Limo rolls down Elm St. 3 shots ring out. The WC does not explain the sequence of the shots, but the single bullet enters JFK's **neck** 5 ½ inches from the point of the right shoulder and 5 ½ inches from the "**bony protuberance behind the right ear**", passes between the strap muscles and exits the **throat** below the adam's apple, in the lower third of the neck. The bullet continued into Governor Connally in the seat in front, and lowers to the left, and entered his **back at a point below his right armpit**. It **shattered his fifth rib**, and exited just below his **right nipple**, it then proceeded through his **right wrist breaking the bone**, and then lodged into his **thigh**.

Another shot **missed the limo, and struck a curb on the south side of Main Street**, about 30' from the triple underpass. A piece of this bullet, or of the curb, then nicked and cut bystander **James Tague**, causing a laceration, and bleeding on his left cheek. The limo's windshield was an obstacle between

Tague and the headshot, so it is doubtful that the curb damage, and wound, could be caused by a head shot fragment.

The fatal shot (at **Zapruder frame 313**), hit the President in the **lower rear of his downward leaning head on the right side**. His head was leaning to the left, as well as forward, and the bullet **exploded out of the upper right** side of the head.

Occupants:

William Greer heard what he thought was a Motorcycle backfire, and when he heard the sound repeated, he turned and saw Connally collapse, and Clint Hill approaching the Limo from behind. He did **not recall seeing** the President, nor braking.

Roy Kellerman testified that he heard the President say "**My God! I am hit**.", turned to see the Governor collapse, and then tell Greer to "Get out of here, fast!". He did say he heard a shot, and then a "**flurry** of shots". He then got onto the radio to tell the Lead car to lead them to the Hospital.

John Connally heard the first shot, and recognized it as a rifle shot. He tried to glance over his right shoulder, but could not see the President. He then started to turn back to his left, when he felt an **impact in his back** right as if he had been hit by a fist. He exclaimed, "My God, they are going to kill us all!"

Nellie Connally heard the first shot to her right, and saw the President having trouble. She heard a **second shot, and pulled her husband into her lap**. She then noticed the blood on his chest. **Both Connallys** insist the he was not hit by the first shot. But they only recall hearing 2 shots.

Jackie Kennedy heard the first shot, and noticed Jack with a strange puzzled look on his face, as he raised his left arm/hand to his throat. She tried to assist him, and saw his **head explode**

with the fatal shot. She has no recollection of **climbing out onto the trunk** of the car.

Follow-Up Car: Many of the **SS Agents felt the first shot was a backfire**, but most of them on the running boards, and in the back seat, **looked back** towards the TSBD / Elm-Houston intersection where the sound came from.

Agent **Clint Hill** (Jackie's agent) jumped from the running board and sprinted to the Limo, arriving in time to **push Jackie back** into the seat from the trunk. The car took off just as he arrived, and after a few stumbling steps, he managed to jump back onto the car. He remained over the President and First Lady on the fast trip to Parkland Hospital.

Jack Youngblood immediately recognized the rifle fire, and jumped over the front seat to push **LBJ down beneath him**. **Ralph Yarborough** noticed the smell of gunpowder, and noticed a **soldier on the grassy knoll dive** to the ground.

Jesse Curry and Bill Decker heard the gunshots, and slowed the Lead car, to allow the Limo to catch up. They then told Greer to follow them, and lead the way to Parkland Hospital. They ordered the dispatcher to send their men, and **Decker's Deputies up to the railroad yards** to see what had happened.

Motorcycle riders were covered with blood, and brain tissue, and **Officer Billy Hargis** (left rear) thought he himself had been hit, based on the impact.

Officer Marion Baker was heading down Houston Street and saw many **birds fly** from the roof of the TSBD in front of him. He then parked his cycle in front of the building, drew his gun and ran in.

Witnesses:

JFK Assassination: Shades From The Fence

Howard Brennan looked up in time to see the last shot, and the rifle being withdrawn into the
6th floor window. 15-year old **Amos Euins** also saw the rifle "pipe thing" being withdrawn, as did **Dallas Times Herald photographer, Robert H Jackson**, from one of the Photo cars. **Mrs. Earl Cabell**, the Mayor's wife, also saw something being withdrawn into the window.

On the 5th floor, **Harold Norman, Bonnie Ray Williams and Junior Jarman** heard the sounds of the rifle from the window above them. Norman also said he heard the **empty shells hit the floor**, and the all noticed **dus**t from above settling in the hair of Norman. They hurried down to the **west windows** of the building, to try to see the Limo as it went to Stemmons. After a minute or two, they left down the **stairs**.

Other witnesses around the Plaza testify that they heard from **3 to 6 shots**.

Abraham Zapruder, and other witnesses line Dealey Plaza anticipating the Motorcade.
Zapruder worked in the Dal-Tex (Dallas Textile) building, and had returned home to get his new
8 MM movie camera. He, and secretary Marilyn Sitzman stood on a concrete plinth next to the Bryan Pergola, and filmed the entire assassination. At exactly **18.3** frames per second, the Zupruder film has become the "timing" device of the entire assassination. **Z1**- When the film starts, with the Motorcycles on Elm St.
Z160- Many believe the first shot, as little Rosemary Willis stops running and looks back towards the intersection. JFK stops waving briefly.
Z166- An Oak tree obscures the Limo from the 6th floor (per WC)
Z186- Passes through an opening in the tree briefly

JFK Assassination: Shades From The Fence

Z205 – President goes behind the Stemmons Freeway sign from Zapruder

Z210 – Emerges from the foliage from the Sniper's Nest

Z223 – Emerges from the sign, on the film

Z225 – President reacts by bringing his arms up to the level of his neck – barely apparent in 225, but very apparent in 226

Z231-Z234 – Connally is convinced he was hit in this time, and reacts – if so, then the rifle, requiring 2.3 second to cycle, would have had to do the first shot by **Z193**

Z238 _ Connally's cheeks puff, and he reacts to obvious pain

Z240-Z312 _ Kennedy continues to react in pain, and leans to his left and forward, with his hands raised in front of him. Jackie reacts by trying to assist him. Connally is pulled back into

Nellie's lap.

Z313 – Head shot causes Kennedy's head to explode

Orville Nix and Mary Muchmore also film parts of the assassination. There are dozens of movie and still photographers in Dealey Plaza. Some films and photos are still missing.

Immediate reactions:

Marion Baker rushes into the building, asking the people on the stairs how to get to the roof. TSBD Supervisor **Roy Truly**, says he will show him, and leads him to the back (north) side. The elevators are on an upper floor, so they proceed up the **stairs** (one-way). Baker sees movement through a door window, as they cross the **2nd floor, and rushes into the lunchroom**. There he encounters **Lee Harvey Oswald**, and holds his pistol on him. Truly comes back to see where Baker went, and Baker asks, **"Who's this man....does he work**

here?" Truly replies, "Yes, he does.", so Baker continues up the stairs to the next level. **90 seconds** after shots.

Motorcycle **Officer Clyde A. Haygood** parks his motorcycle on Elm St. and immediately rushes up the hill to the railroad overpass. He is seen in later films climbing the bridge rail, but sees nobody escaping in the railroad yards. He is quickly speaking with the railroad employees on the bridge, as they move to the grassy knoll and parking area.

Dallas Police communications are hampered because there is a **stuck microphone** open on the primary dispatch channel (1). The Motorcade is using channel 2. This open mike will broadcast for about **3 minutes**.

Officer Joseph M. Smith who was stationed at Elm and Houston to hold traffic, runs down Elm St. extension to search. Other Dallas Police Officers scramble up the grassy knoll, and Sheriff's Deputies spread all over Dealey Plaza from their building east of Houston St.

12:35 After the encounter with Baker, **Oswald is seen with a "Coke"**, and leaves the building out the front door. He gives **directions to a telephone** to a member of the press, as they enter the building. Oswald begins walking east, up Elm St.

The Limo makes it to **Parkland Hospital** some 4 miles away. Curry had called ahead for
Parkland to be ready, and all available officers to converge on Parkland to make it secure. The Lead car, Presidential Limo, Vice President's Limo and all Secret Service follow-up cars go to Parkland, and the **other cars stop at the Trade Mart**.

12:40 Doctor's begin **emergency procedures** on both Connally and Kennedy. Kennedy still has a **pulse and labored**

377

respiration, although his eyes are open and a great wound is in his head.

Oswald boards the Marsalis bus between stops on Elm St. driven by Cecil J. McWatters, between Griffin and Field. On the bus, is former landlady **Mary Bledsoe**, who recognizes Oswald and hopes he does not talk to her.

Inspector J. Herbert Sawyer arrives at the TSBD, takes the west elevator to its top floor (4th) looks around a minute or two. The Texas School Book Depository is **locked down between 12:37 and 12:40** as, and no one is allowed to leave.

12:45 A rough **description** of the shooter is given to police in Dealey Plaza, presumably supplied by **Howard Brennan**. It is broadcast by the DPD Dispatcher:
"…an unknown white male about thirty, slender build, five feet ten inches tall, one hundred sixty-five pounds, armed with what is thought to be a 30-30 rifle."

Cut downs have been made in the President's legs to get him fluid, and his clothing and back brace removed. Steroids are administered for his Atkinson's disease complications, and an emergency tracheotomy is started across an existing wound in his throat. **Connally is rushed into surgery**, and the **Johnsons are being protected** in a secured room in the hospital.

Oswald's bus is stalled in traffic, so he requests a **transfer** (which is later found on him) and starts to walk 3 blocks west to the **Greyhound Bus station**.

Patrol **Officer J.D. Tippit**, who normally patrols south Oak Cliff, is told by the dispatcher to **move into central Oak Cliff**, and cover a wider area while so many Police are focused in downtown and Parkland. Tippit is at Kiest and Bonnie View.

JFK Assassination: Shades From The Fence

12:50 Oswald **catches a taxi**, with driver William W Whaley, after offering it to a older lady at the taxi stop next to the Bus depot. The taxi takes Oswald to Oak Cliff, and leaves him on Beckley, about **5 blocks past his rooming house**.

Captain Will Fritz arrives at TSBD, while Jesse Curry stays at the Hospital.

12:54 Tippit reports that he is at Lancaster and 8th (north Oak Cliff), and is told to be at large for any emergency that comes in. (This will be his **last** transmission.)

1:00 (approx) Oswald's housekeeper, **Earlene Roberts**, sees Oswald come into the house, and rush into his room. She tells him the President has been shot, but he says nothing. She hears a **horn honk** out front, and looks out to see a Dallas Patrol car, but it is not a number she recognizes and she goes back to the Television. Oswald comes rushing out zipping up a jacket, and she last sees him in front of the house "at the bus stop" at **"about 1:00 PM"**.

JFK's pulse has stopped, and after looking at the extent of the head wound, the Doctors **abandon their attempts**, and stop discussing open heart massage. **Father Huber** administers Last Rites of the Catholic church. Death is set at **1:00 PM**, as soon as the last rites are completed.

Police have focused on the TSBD almost exclusively, and are systematically searching the entire building. A number of witnesses, and **3 tramps** are marched into the Dallas Sheriff's offices for questioning. Others are taken to Dallas police station on the east side of town. People fitting the descriptions are being **detained all over the city**, and some even as far away as Ft Worth.

JFK Assassination: Shades From The Fence

1:10 – Johnsons are informed of Kennedy's death.

1:12 – Searching the sixth floor, **Deputy Sheriff Luke Mooney discovers** the wall of boxes blocking off the "sniper's nest". The 3 shell casings, chicken lunch bag, Dr Pepper bottle, and discarded sack are found in the sniper's nest. Photographs are taken of the area, but the **discarded sack** is not photographed.

1:16 A citizens, **Domingo Benavides, uses Tippit's radio** in his car (10), to report that Tippit has been shot at 10th and Patton in Oak Cliff. He is unsuccessful, but a **T F Bowley** arrives and makes the 1st recorded report. He, **Helen Markham** and a cab driver, **William Scoggins**, say that Tippit was cruising slowly east on 10th Street, and **stopped the suspect** (Oswald) facing west on the south side of the street. Tippit talked to Oswald through a **passenger window** of the patrol car, and then got out of the car to walk around. When Tippit was next to his left wheel, Oswald pulled a gun and **shot him 4 times**. Oswald then walked back to the west, and south on Patton, **unloading his revolver** as he walked towards Jefferson. Markham was on her way to work, and standing on the **northwest corner**. Scoggins hid behind his parked cab as Oswald walked by it, muttering "Poor dumb cop." Or "Poor damn cop." Tippit fell on his own drawn revolver, and **Callaway and Benavides took the gun and went driving after him**, for a few minutes.

The **Davis sisters** who lived on the southeast corner of 10th and Patton came out in time to see Oswald walking across the corner of their lawn. They later **found a couple of the shells** and gave them to Police. A local car dealer at Patton and Jefferson (the next block up) **Ted Callaway**, came out after the sounds and yelled at Oswald as he ran past, but did not hear Oswald's response. Oswald continued up Jefferson.

1:22 PM – Deputy Sheriff Eugene Boone finds the rifle in the northwest corner of the building, close to the stairs, under a number of book cases. The rifle is **not touched until photographed, and Lt. J. C. Day** of the police lab grabs it by the strap and removes it. Day decides that the wooden stock and bolt knob contain no fingerprints, so he held it by the stock, while **Fritz ejects a live round**. The rifle contains "C2766" stamp, as well as "MADE ITALY" and "CAL 6.5". Officers just glancing at it think it looks like a 7.65 Mauzer. The rifle is 40" long, but the breakdown length would be about **34"**, of the wooden stock.

1:25 – A **white jacket is found** under a car, a block west of Patton on Jefferson. Description is posted: "**White male, thirty, five feet eight, black hair, slender build, white shirt, black trousers. Going west on Jefferson from the 300 block.**" Tippit is no longer at the shooting site, as **the Dudley Hughes Funeral Home (400 Jefferson) ambulance (602)** has already picked him up and started to Methodist Hospital. By 1:27 NBC was announcing Tippit as DOA, but some confusion on President versus Officer Tippit.

1:29 - Police radio **notes the similarities** in JFK and Tippit shooting suspect's descriptions.

1:33 - DPD checking out a **church basement at 10th & Crawford** (1 block away).

1:34 - Dallas Police surround the **Oak Cliff Library**, where a suspect has run in. Turns out to be an employee. DPD radio log says suspect armed with a 32 automatic pistol. Soon they change it to **automatic .38, based on shells** at scene.

Johnson's leave the hospital for Air Force One in Jesse Curry's car, where they can be more protected. Air Force Two is not used, since One has the better **communications center**.

Curry remains mainly off the air, and asks officers to keep sirens off, so that nobody can easily get their location.

1:37 – Johnsons and entourage arrive at Love Field, and Curry instructs guards to prevent anyone else entering the field.

1:40 – Julia Postal, cashier at the **Texas Theater on Jefferson** phones into the Dallas Police with information that a suspicious person has gone into the Theater without paying. Oswald had ducked in a **Hardy Shoe Store** entrance, a few businesses from the Texas Theater while squad cars speed by. **Manager Johnny Brewer** notices the suspicious act, and follows him. Julia Postal is at the street looking to see why the squad cars are screaming by, and Oswald goes in. **Concession worker Butch Burroughs** does not see him, either. Butch watches the front entrances, Johnny the rear, and Julia Calls in.

1:45 – Police **dispatcher announces that suspect is in Texas Theater**, including that he is hiding in the balcony (incorrect). Many police units converge on that location, 5 squads in rear, and up to 10 in front.

Fritz is also told by Manager Roy Truly that Lee Harvey Oswald is also not in the building. There is also an instruction on the radio log to pick up **Charles Givens**, another TSBD employee that is not at the roll call. After getting the names, and addresses of the missing men, **Fritz returns to DPD** station.

1:48 - Officer N. M. MacDonald and other officers walk up the aisle toward Oswald that is pointed to by Johnny Brewer. Oswald stands up, says "**Well, it's all over now!**". He pulls his pistol with one hand, and hits MacDonald with the other. MacDonald **grabs the gun**, and he and the other officers subdue Oswald. He is injured in the face in the process.

JFK Assassination: Shades From The Fence

1:52 – Oswald is arrested, and enroute to the downtown Dallas Police Station. His wallet is searched, and he has **ids for both Lee Harvey Oswald, and Alex J Hidell**. Oswald is completely uncooperative.

1:55 PM – Parkland employee **Darrell Tomlinson** moves a stretcher in the hallway at Parkland, and hears a bullet hit the floor. He picks it up and gives it to **Parkland Security Director O. P. Wright.** The first Secret Service agent Wright talked to did not seem particularly interested in it, so **Wright carried it in his pocket for about 30 minutes.** Wright later gives it to **Secret Service Agent Richard Johnson**. Johnson gave it to **SS Chief Rowley** back in Washington on the evening of November 22, who turned it over to **FBI Agent Elmer Todd**. Todd gave it to **Robert Frazier of the FBI Crime Lab**.

2:00 – A **Bronze casket** has been delivered to Parkland Hospital, by O'Neal's Funeral Home. Ambulance driver **Aubrey Rike**, who had brought the Epileptic to Parkland, assisted in placing the President's body in the casket. His head had been wrapped in sheets, and a plastic bed cover had been placed in the casket first to protect it. A **shouting and pushing match ensues between Dr. Earl Rose**, stating that Texas law required an Autopsy there, and the Washington party that just wanted to get out of there.

Johnson's aides call **Attorney General Robert Kennedy, and his staff gets the Oath of Office** to be administered to Johnson. Federal Judge Sarah Hughes is summoned to Air Force One.

Fritz, arriving at police headquarters, entered the homicide and robbery bureau office, he saw two detectives standing there with Sgt. Gerald L. Hill, who had driven from the theatre with Oswald. "Hill testified that Fritz told the detective to get a search warrant, go to an address on **Fifth Street in Irving, and**

pick up a man named Lee Oswald. When Hill asked why Oswald was wanted, Fritz replied, "Well, he was employed down at the Book Depository and he had not been present for a roll call of the employees." Hill said, "**Captain, we will save you a trip… there he sits.**"

2:38 – JFK and the Presidential party arrive at Air Force One, and the casket is loaded.
O'Donnell instructs the pilot to take off immediately, but is informed that LBJ is waiting to be sworn in. After the swearing in, they departed for Washington, **arriving at 5:38 PM EST**.

3:00 PM (approx) – **Police arrive at the Paine House**, and ask Marina, through Ruth Paine, if Oswald owned a rifle. Marina took them to the garage and pointed at a **blanket that had the shape of a rifle**, but when police picked it up it is limp.

Throughout the afternoon **Oswald was questioned by Police**, Secret Service, FBI and others. He **denied owning a rifle**, and said he was in the **2nd floor lunchroom when the Motorcade passed by**. He refused to cooperate in any way, and would not explain the multiple id's. He traveled through the **hallways over 16 times**, with **hundreds of reporters jamming** the building. Oswald is allowed to make multiple phone calls, and expresses the desire to be represented by New York's **John Abt**, an attorney known to Oswald as representing Communist related individuals in the past. Throughout the weekend, he arranges no representation.

He also participates in a **number of Line-ups**, and is identified by cab drivers **William Whaley, William Scoggins, Domingo Benavides, and Helen Markham**. Howard Brennan is told that others have identified Oswald, and is personally **unable to identify him as the man**. Oswald **complains bitterly** about the makeup of the other individuals in the line-up, including his being bruised, cut, and his being dressed in a t-shirt.

7:10 PM – Oswald is **formally charged with the murder of Officer J D Tippit**.

Midnight – Responding to pressure from the press, the Dallas Police allow Oswald to stand before the **press in a quick viewing**. The press fires a number of questions at Oswald. Nightclub owner, **Jack Ruby, is filmed on a back table** in the press conference, as well as other times throughout the weekend.

1:30 AM – Saturday – Oswald is **formally charged with the murder of John F. Kennedy.**

11:17 AM Sunday – **Jack Ruby wires some money** to one of his dancers in Ft Worth at the Western Union Office on Main St., 2 blocks away from the Dallas Police Station.

11:20 AM Sunday – **Oswald** is brought out to the DPD basement, to be put into a **Detective's car** and taken to the Dallas County Jail in Dealey Plaza. Ruby had come **down the northern ramp**, on Main St, and is standing among the members of the press at the bottom of the ramp. In a fit of rage, Ruby pulls his snub-nose 38 revolver, **shouts "Oswald", and shoots Oswald** one time in the stomach. The bullet hits most of Oswald's **major organs**, and he collapses to the floor.

11:25 An Ambulance takes LHO to the Hospital, while Ruby is taken upstairs to a holding cell. Ruby considers himself a hero, but Dallas police are shocked, as is most of the nation who sees the **shooting on live television**.

1:07 PM – **Oswald is pronounced dead** at Parkland Hospital's, trauma room 1, having never regained consciousness.

JFK Assassination: Shades From The Fence

November 26, 1963 Ruby is formally charged with the murder of Lee Harvey Oswald.

March 14, 1964 – Ruby is found **guilty** by a jury, and sentenced to death. His lawyers file an appeal, and he remains on the 5th floor of the Dallas County Jail by Dealey Plaza for the next several years. He is interviewed by the Warren Commission and others, and requests **Earl Warren take him back to Washington**, so the "true facts" could come out.

December 7, 1966 – Texas Criminal Court of Appeals **overturns the conviction** on venue considerations, and order a retrial in Wichita Falls, Texas.

December 9, 1966 – Ruby enters Parkland Hospital for a "cold shot", and is diagnosed with Cancer.

January 3, 1967 – **Ruby dies**. Body sent to Chicago for burial.

Benchmarks in the John Kennedy Assassination:

Clay Shaw Trial – New Orleans District Attorney Jim Garrison investigates the assassination due to the links of Oswald in New Orleans. Based on testimony of Perry Russo, Vernon Bundy, and many citizens of Clinton, LA, Garrison believes David Ferrie, and International Trade-Mart founder Clay Shaw knew Oswald. Ferrie dies soon after the investigation starts, but Garrison **charges (March 1, 1967)** and **tries (January 29, 1969)** Shaw on Conspiracy to kill JFK.
Garrison tries to prove a conspiracy involving Shaw, but Shaw is **acquitted on March 1, 1969**. Includes many theories on the assassination.

Ramsey Clark Panel – Because of the questions in the public's mind during the late 60's, and the Garrison investigation, Attorney General Ramsey Clark convened a panel of **4 physicians to review the autopsy, photos, films, x-rays and other materials** in the JFK assassination, on **February 26 and 27, 1968**. The results: **"Examination of the clothing and of the photographs and X- rays taken at autopsy reveal that President Kennedy was struck by two bullets fired from above and behind him, one of which traversed the base of the neck on the right side without striking bone and the other of which entered the skull from behind and exploded its right side. The photographs and X-rays discussed herein support the above-quoted portions of the original Autopsy Report and the above-quoted medical conclusions of the Warren Commission Report."**

Church Committee – After the abuses of Watergate, and the Viet Nam war, **Congress investigated US Intelligence**. The main focuses of investigations were the FBI and the CIA. Although the JFK assassination was not directly investigated, the public's distrust of the FBI and CIA was greatly intensified, thus leaving more doubt of the accuracy of the Warren Commission. In **1975 and 1976** the committee published 14 reports on US intelligence agencies.

House Select Committee on Assassinations – In **1977** the US House of Representatives created a Committee to investigate the JFK, RFK and Martin Luther King assassinations. The committee worked through 1977-78, and published a report in 1979. Their main contribution to the JFK assassination was the study of an audio tape recorded during the event on a **dictabelt,** of a police motorcycle officer's stuck open microphone. They concluded that this officer was one of the

Motorcade motorcycles, and the tape had "impulses" which indicated **4 shots**. This resulted in a **95% certainty that a shot** was attempted from the Grassy Knoll, and thus a conspiracy. It stated that it did not believe the conspiracy was set up by the CIA, nor Organized crime. It further reinforced that **Lee**

JFK Assassination: Shades From The Fence

Harvey Oswald shot the effective bullets from the 6th floor window, and any other shooters missed.

Oliver Stone's Movie: "JFK" – In 1991, Director Oliver Stone released this movie about the trial and investigation of Clay Shaw by New Orleans District Attorney Jim Garrison. The movie used a lot of **"dramatic license"** showing events that did not happen, and glorifying Garrison, played by Kevin Costner. However, it stirred up enough controversy that President Bill Clinton signed into law the "JFK Act" forming the **Assassination Records Review Board**. This board oversaw the release of millions of documents and records held by various intelligence, investigative and the National Archives, to the public. Many of these records have been sealed since the days of the Warren Commission. (Many remain sealed.)

Leaving the door open:

In the book, "Death of a President", by William Manchester, in 1967, the theory of **"Great crimes require Great criminals."**, was asserted. The theory is that a crime as great as the assassination of the leader of the free world, requires a grand conspiracy, or other great criminal to accomplish it. People thus "feel better" if they think there was a grand conspiracy in the act, instead of the inconsequential Lee Harvey Oswald. They assume that if there is not a conspiracy, we will invent one. Personally, I think the above theory is **hogwash**, often used to brush off those

that have legitimate questions about the Warren Commission's version.

The Warren Commission did come up with a logical version of events, where Lee Harvey Oswald could have acted alone and committed the assassination, and Tippit murder. From the government's view the Commission thus fulfilled its purpose, especially if you consider the time and manpower constraints.

There were many major problems with the investigation that left the door wide open for major criticism. Many of the problems were very subjective, such as film interpretation, and the testimony of witnesses, which is usually unreliable. However, there were also very concrete problems as well. It is very unfortunate that the authorities had an opportunity to nail down Lee Harvey Oswald, and did not. I would have preferred a more concrete answer, as I am quite
willing to accept that an inconsequential "Lone Nut" could have done the crime.

For the remainder of this discussion, I will try to highlight some of the problems that were not adequately addressed by the Warren Commission's version.

Sealing of the Records – The Warren Commission "sealed away" their executive meeting minutes, and many other documents, for 75 years. They presumably did this, because many of the documents involved the CIA, FBI and national security. In effect, though, the sealing of these documents itself, fueled much speculation that the government was "holding back" something, and not telling the whole story. It fired the feeling that the government was lying to us, even in this pre-Watergate era.

Lee Oswald's Military and Russian history – indications of connections?

For the sake of national security, some details of Oswald's background were withheld from the public. One such detail was Oswald's area of service in the Marines. Oswald served at our base in **Atsugi,** Japan. This was the base from which our **top-secret U2** spy planes flew out of, when they were making flights over the Soviet Union. As a **radar operator**, Oswald was familiar with these planes, as viewed through the **tracking information** he was seeing.

This was the type of information that Oswald was threatening to give to the Russians, when he expressed his desire to defect in the American Embassy in Moscow, in October 1959. In fact, the military changed many of its codes and procedures when Oswald went to Russia. U2 pilot **Francis Gary Powers** was shot down on **May 1, 1960**, and he later said his being shot down could have been due to information supplied by Oswald.

Oswald is discharged from the Marines, with the type of **Military ID**, which is usually reserved for Dependents of active military, or Military stationed overseas. If he was going home on a discharge, he would have been issued a different type of Military ID, and not one that would continue to let him access the Military Commissary, etc.

Oswald reportedly spent a great deal of time with questionable people while in Japan. He had a 'girlfriend' at the **Queen Bee**, who was reportedly a **Japanese Communist**. He also professed a very pro-Soviet interest, and responded to the name "Oswaldski", and other "red" references. He self-taught himself Russian, one of the worlds hardest languages, and reportedly even took a test on it. During this time he was a **radar operator at one of our most secret U2 installations**?

Oswald spent over **$1500** on his trip to Russia, staying in first class accommodations in Finland and Moscow. There also was **no commercial transportation** into Finland and Moscow, leaving the idea of some kind of assistance given to Oswald. **Ambassador John McVicker**, who spoke to Oswald, said that it appeared that Oswald had been **coached** as to exactly what to say, and the arguments that may be used against him. He also **stopped short** of actually completing the necessary procedures to actually denounce his American citizenship, thus leaving the door open to return.

JFK Assassination: Shades From The Fence

From 1945 to 1959 only 2 US soldiers defect, in **1959-60 7 of them defect, and 6** of them return. (Former assistant to Richard Helms, Victor Machetti, says that ONI had a "defection program" in 59, with plans to train and send 3 dozen defectors to Russia.)

An **FBI memo**, initialed by J Edgar Hoover, discussed the possibility of someone using
Oswald's identity to buy some trucks, in the winter of **1961**. Fred Sewell, manager of Bolton
Ford Truck in New Orleans, said they were buying trucks to send to Cuba, on behalf of the "**Friends of Democratic Cuba**". One of the founders of FDC, was **ex-FBI man Guy Bannister**, who officed on 544 Camp St.

I am bothered by the **ease in which Oswald returned to the US, and managed to get his wife out as well.** I can see where the Soviets did not particularly want Oswald stranded in Minsk, and how bad it would look if they left him there against his will. I can also see where the Soviets may not have trusted Oswald, and may suspect him of being a US Intelligence plant. However, this was a Marine that had threatened to **give radar secrets** to the Soviets, and **OUR government** should have objected to this **traitor** returning to the US.

Oswald back in the states – further connections?

The **CIA** claimed that they had **no information or interest in Oswald before his Mexico trip** in the fall of 1963. This was a Marine who had served as a **radar** operator at one of the most secure air bases, where our most Top Secret **spy planes** flew out of. He had defected to Russia, had stated he wanted to renounce his citizenship, and had **threatened to give radar secrets** to the Soviets. He had spent almost 3 years in Russia, **married a niece of a Russian Intelligence** Colonel, and has

JFK Assassination: Shades From The Fence

lived fairly well by Soviet support. At that time the CIA would often interview tourists who had spent a little time in the Soviet Union.

Oswald got a job upon his return to Dallas with Jagger-Chiles Stovall. They also did the **labeling on the US Spy Plane photographs**. Oswald started there a week or two before the discovery of the missile installation in Cuba, which launched the **Cuban Missile crisis**. It may have been coincidence, as he was not directly involved with that level of secure photography work, but it was a smaller shop and he was in the area. Any **company that handles this type of intelligence should check their employees better**. At the least, the FBI or CIA should have kept track of Oswald better upon his return from the Soviet Union.

Postal regulations require that the form which shows who is authorized to receive mail at a US Post Office box be retained for a number of years. Yet **both of Oswald's Authorization forms for his 2 PO Boxes in Dallas** could not be provided to the Warren Commission. Neither could the receipt for **who picked up the rifle in March, and pistol in April of 63**, and these are also required to be retained by the US Postal regulations. Oswald ordered the rifle, and pistol, through the mails. These weapons could easily have been purchased in many locations in Dallas, many of which would have no record at all. Instead, Oswald orders them through the mail, from **companies which the FBI is already investigating**.

I am bothered by the relationship of Oswald with **George De Mohrenschildt**. Although many years older than Oswald, De Mohrenschildt befriended Oswald. **De Mohrenschildt told researcher Edward Jay Epstein that he had been asked by CIA Agent J. Walton Moore to keep an eye on Oswald**, and find out about his Soviet Union experience. At best, De Mohrenschildt has many suspicious connections to Intelligence and even the Dallas Petroleum group (which many suspect). **De**

392

JFK Assassination: Shades From The Fence

Mohrenschildt committed suicide, on March 29, 1977, the day he received a note from **Gaeton Fonzi, an investigator for the House Select Committee on Assassinations.**

I am bothered by Oswald's time in New Orleans for the **Riley Coffee Company**. Although, this company is not in itself suspicious, it is located in the **heart of the US Intelligence presence in New Orleans.** In addition, the **Crescent City Garage**, where Oswald liked to spend a great deal of his time, was also used by the **Secret Service and other Federal** agencies in the area. The owner of this garage has supposedly stated that on more than one occasion, he had seen Oswald receiving something from some of these agents.

Oswald had many **connections with both pro-Castro and anti-Castro Cubans** while in New Orleans. This includes David Ferrie, and his adversarial connections with **Carlos Bringuier.** The connections with Ferrie are tentative, but there is **photographic evidence of Oswald being in the Civil Air Patrol while Ferrie** was involved with that group. Ferrie himself denied ever knowing Oswald.

I am bothered by the various sightings of Oswald in the company of Dave Ferrie, and/or Guy Bannister. Much of this comes from the investigation of New Orleans District Attorney Jim Garrison for the trial of Clay Shaw. I will readily admit that I think much of Garrison's information was highly questionable at best, but the volume of it leads me to think that some of it was accurate, such as the Clinton sightings.

At one time Oswald's **Fair Play for Cuba pamphlets had the 544 Camp St.** address stamped on them. This was the **same building that housed the offices of Guy Bannister**, which many say was one of the major players in the anti-Castro efforts of the US government in New Orleans. Gerald Posner, among others, has **suggested that Oswald simply selected this address at random** so that his chapter would be more impressive, by having actual offices. However, Oswald **used 3 different addresses** on these pamphlets from time to time. Included with this supposedly pretend address, he also used his **home address and real PO Box** address. The use of these 2 real addresses would **make sense** for anyone trying to **start a chapter and generate interest in the chapter**, as they would give actual places for people to contact for additional information. It would NOT make sense to send them to a fictitious address for more information, as there would be nobody there to respond. It would make **even less sense to send them to a building that is a hub for the ANTI-Castro sentiments,** as Guy Bannister's office was. If someone wants additional information, why would you send them to people that share the OPPOSITE point of view? It will not disrupt these people to have people coming to them for information.

One of the things that bother me about the **Mexico Trip**, is that the person who got a **Passport after Oswald** (time stamps were not part of the log) is reported by many to be an **Intelligence operative**. The trip itself is troublesome, as the **CIA photo is not of Oswald**, and some that have heard the tapes say that Oswald was not the individual making some of the phone calls between the Embassies. The person's **Russian was very, very poor**, and Oswald's was not. The **CIA claimed that they routinely overwrote this tape**, yet there are FBI documents that discuss the **FBI listening to them after the assassination**.

I am bothered by the relationship with the **Paines somewhat, just because Michael was in a high security position**. However, this is not too bothersome, in itself. Coincidentally, the **Texas School Book Depository** was **owned by David Harold Byrd**, who was also a member of the
Dallas Petroleum club, and owner of Temco, which would later be part (the "T" part) of **LTV**

Corporation (Lingco-Temco-Voight). But unless the Dallas Petroleum club, and right-wing of Dallas, was behind the Assassination (as some believe), I am not too much bothered by these coincidences.

Oswald again **opened a PO Box in Dallas** on November 1, 1963. He did pay for 2 month's rental of this PO Box in advance, and they monitored it until it expired after the assassination. Again, the **authorizations on this PO Box were "lost"** by the US Postal Service, or suppressed as many suspect. **Jack Ruby also opened a PO Box on Nov 7, 1963**, at the same post office.

Oswald's constant use of aliases, and modified addresses on official forms, was very common. Of course, this concern affects both a Lone Nut and any Conspiracy theories. He was at the rooming house, using the name "O. H. Lee".

Physical Evidence –

I am bothered about the **general "physics"** of the Assassination, as well as the Motive and lack of Escape Planning. This covers many aspects of the shooting, trajectories, movement downstairs, ability to do it, etc.

Included in the physical evidence is the **rifle and shells in the 6th floor of the TSBD**. These could be tied with Oswald, and included the fingerprints on the trigger guard of the rifle which the DPD said were "most likely" Oswald's. Also included is the **right palm print on the carton**, which were the freshest prints on that carton. There were, however, **other prints on the carton**, one of which has **been attributed to Mac Wallace by some people**. The **palm prints found by the Dallas Police on the barrel, under the stock,** was found on the first day, but **not reported to the FBI until after the evidence was returned to Dallas**, and the DPD heard that they had missed the print. However, the DPD officials said it was probably an **older palm print**, as it had no oils left.

Included in the physical evidence is the **bullet found at the hospital**. There is some question as to **which stretcher** this bullet fell from and, I believe, the **inability of the person who found the bullet to later state that was the exact bullet** found. The alleged path of that bullet is questionable, however these metal jacketed bullets were designed to go through multiple people and still be mainly intact.

The **shell casings** found under the Sniper's Nest window was also subject to a chain of evidence problem. The **receipt for them that was given by the FBI shows 2** shell casings, as a separate receipt for the remaining one was given directly to Fritz by Jim Hosty. However, for the Warren Commission, the 2 was simply **changed to a "3"**, presumably for convenience.

The **clip was also a problem**, as was the **paper bag**. During the search, WFAA-TV
photographer **Tom Alyea** was allowed to stay on the sixth floor and film. He, along with Dallas Police crime lab photographers, took film and photos of the rifle in it hiding place, and immediately after it was pulled out. **No clip can be seen in these films**, yet when Lt Day is photograph outside of the TSBD, there is a clip distinctly shown as being in the rifle. This rifle drops its clip when the last round is loaded, yet the **clip is shown in the rifle in a number of outside photos**. The clip is talked about in Day's testimony, but any discussion on **where it was found**, and how it got back into the rifle is never offered.

The **paper bag** that Oswald allegedly used to carry the rifle into the building, was also controversial. Two police officers stood and guarded the Sniper's Nest until it could be photographed by the crime lab. According to Detective Marvin

Johnson, after the photographers left that corner, his partner, Detective **L. D. Montgomery**, picked up the bag from the corner, and unfolded it to examine it. At that time, the bag had **NOT been photographed, nor brushed for prints**. When questioned, Montgomery appears confused between the rifle bag and the chicken lunch bag, and denies picking up "that bag".

Photographic Evidence –

I am bothered by the Zapruder, other films, and photos that **seem to show that Connally was hit later** than the apparent strike of JFK. This was explained as a difference of reaction time, as Connally seemed to react many frames (**Z238** at 18.3 frames a second) later than does Kennedy (**Z224**). Kennedy had more **pain killers** in him, and should have been the slower of the 2 to react, although he was quite used to them.

The **Connallys have both insisted that John was hit by the second bullet**, and not the first. This could be explained by the **first bullet being the one that missed**, instead of the second. In this case, the **first bullet would have had to be shot while the Limo was at least partially blocked by the Oak tree**. Being the missed bullet, it would have had to be somehow deflected by the tree, and would have been the one to hit the curb by James Tague, and grazed his cheek.
The location of Tague is quite off the mark from that of the Limo at this early location up Elm St. Tague was between Main and Commerce, right by the Triple Underpass. **However, I cannot buy into the Gerald Posner speculation that a twig or branch in the tree shattered this metal jacketed bullet, while the single bullet through Kennedy and Connally remained intact.** Tague could have been hit by a **fragment from the head shot** that went in an arc above the windshield of the limo; however, it is difficult to accept that the same

fragment had enough momentum at this point to do both the curb and his cheek.

I am bothered by the **backward motion of the President's head** in the Zapruder film. This is often explained as a **neuro-muscular reflex** action due to the brain being destroyed by the head shot.

Many have postulated that the Motorcycle cops being sprayed with brains and blood indicates that the **spray was backwards**; however, if the spray were upwards at all, and they were moving forward, they still would have **driven through it on its way back down**, even at those slower speeds. However, Bobby Hargis **said the impact was so great**, that he originally thought he was **hit by a shot**. (This cannot be explained by the material coming back down by gravity, and him driving through it at 11 MPH.)

The films show the Limo slowing to **almost a complete stop**. The driver, **Greer, did hit the brakes** and slow the vehicle while he turned to look at President Kennedy. He then took off when Kellerman told him "let's get out of here". In all **fairness to Greer, some have said that he was mainly a driver in his years with the Secret Service**, for Truman, Eisenhower, and Kennedy, and was not as well trained as many of the other White House Detail. He may also have been **concerned about the people that could be seen atop the Triple Underpass**, so that he would not drive towards the "shooters".

Secret Service

Many of the Secret Service had a particularly slow response. Of course, many of them were **out late the night before**, and some had supposedly been drinking. These actions were both against regulations, and would naturally lead to slower reactions. Of course, **everything happed within 6-10 seconds**, which is a difficult amount of time to react in. The crowds were also **thinned out on Elm St.**, and the Agents may have been **starting to relax** after dealing with the heavy crowds up to that point.

Eyewitness Testimony – TSBD

Many of the co-workers of **Lee Harvey Oswald** saw him down on the **first floor**, and (Carolyn Arnold) on the **second floor lunchroom**, minutes before the arrival of the Motorcade. These seem to indicate that Lee Harvey Oswald was not upstairs getting ready for the Motorcade, which **was running 10 minutes late**! He was either **very nonchalant about shooting the President**, or was actually in the lunch room the whole time, as **he said he was**. His not being on the 6th floor is also supported by **Bonnie Ray Williams, who completed his lunch at 12:25**.

– (First Day Evidence)

The **initial testimony** of **Bonnie Ray Williams**, who was on the fifth floor, directly beneath the sniper's nest during the shooting, was that he heard **2 shots**. He later **changed his story to 3** shots. It would be difficult for someone that close to not hear all 3 shots...although Bonnie Ray could have initially been mistaken.

Junior Jarman was with Bonnie Ray Williams on the fifth floor. In his initial statement to police, he **stops after staying he was in the front entryway to the building**, and does not even mention he went back upstairs and was on the fifth floor. This could be an example of the **interviewing investigator only searching for specific information**, such as the names of the people located on the front entry. He stopped asking questions after he got those names. Later, Junior repeats "Hank said..." in much of his Warren Commission testimony.

JFK Assassination: Shades From The Fence

I am bothered by the testimony of the third man on the fifth floor, **Harold Norman**. **After being on the fifth floor during the re-enactment** done months later by the investigators for the Warren Commission, he **testifies that he could hear the shells hitting the floor between each shot**. The re-enactment did NOT have a rifle firing, but only the shooter stand-in cycling through the bolt action and ejecting the bullets onto the floor. This was not mentioned in his initial affidavit to Dallas police. It would seem that with a **rifle shot echoing through your ears** from the floor above you, **hearing the casings hitting even a plywood floor would be difficult.** Harold did always relate that he heard 3 shots. He said the shots were so loud inside, that pieces of **dust** were knocked down onto his head, which would make it hard to hear the shells hitting the floor with that loud of an echo! He also mentions **only 2 cockings of the rifle**, although all 3 shell casings were supposedly found under the window.

If the **3 men** could hear the shells hitting the board of the floor above them, regardless of the loud reverberations of the rifle, it makes sense that they should have been **able to hear Oswald (or anyone else) run across the floor** to hide the rifle, and escape. Oswald did this, and descended the stairs to the 2nd floor, in less than 90 seconds, according to Patrolman Marion Baker. Yet the TSBD stairs were "**one-way**" stairs, requiring you to go down one "L" shaped flight, then exit onto the **next floor, and cross about 15 feet of it**, to get to the next flight. Yet the men on the 5th floor did not hear, or see him. In addition, 2 other TSBD employees, **Sandra Styles and Victoria Adams**, descended the stairs after the shooting, and did not see him. However, they later testified that it was several minutes after. Of course, if some people other than Oswald shot from any place in the building, these **strangers were not seen by any employees** either.

JFK Assassination: Shades From The Fence

Buell Wesley Frasier, and his sister, **Linnie Mae Randall**, were the only 2 people that saw LHO with **a package** that morning. This, in itself, is not really that bothersome as I can hardly tell you what my own co-workers were carrying when they came into work this morning. However, both of them **insisted that the package was at most "a couple of feet" long**, when LHO's rifle will not break down to that short a size. They even continued to insist this, while **looking at the paper bag** the investigators said the rifle was in.

Eyewitness Testimony: Plaza

I am bothered by the **many people that saw or heard firing from the Grassy Knoll**. These include **Jean Hill, Abraham Zapruder, SM Holland, Ed Hoffman, Gordon Arnold, Malcolm Summers, J.C. Price, Lee Bowers** and many others throughout and surrounding the Plaza. Most of the people **towards Houston thought the shots came from the TSBD**, while most of the people **further down into the Plaza, felt the shots came from the Grassy Knoll**. Granted, Dealey Plaza has many echo causing features with the Triple Underpass, building, and concrete structures. But **many of these witnesses included the Police and Secret Service Agents, who were well trained**. Of course, this does not preclude shots from the sniper's nest, but if true, it does **eliminate a LONE shooter**.

I am bothered by the number of **sightings of Secret Service** and other "Government Agents" in
Dealey Plaza**, before 1:00 PM**, which is officially the first time any SS Agents returned to the
Plaza. These include sightings by **Gordon Arnold**, before the shooting. It also includes **Dallas Police Officers Joseph M. Smith,** and others, who immediately encounter a man who identified himself as **Secret Service**.

JFK Assassination: Shades From The Fence

The **Epileptic seizure**, which occurred on Houston Street at about 12:05 is troubling. Most bothersome about this incident is **the number of "false calls" for an Ambulance to Dealey Plaza** for a couple of weeks prior to the 22nd. An old Dealey family friend, **Aubrey Rike**, has discussed the seizure, as well as the false alarms with me. He was the driver that picked up the seizure victim, and talked to him at Parkland, until the Motorcade arrived. At that time, the seizure victim simply left.

I am bothered by the presence of **"Umbrella Man"** and the gentleman close to him, which appeared to be **speaking into some form of radio**. Also part of this concern is the **vehicles cruising through the Grassy Knoll** parking lots, spotted by Lee Bowers, and also apparently talking into some type of radio.

There were reports of **men with rifles throughout the day**. Many Dallas citizens saw various men with rifles at different locations, and reported them. Of course, in Dallas it was not that unusual to see people with rifles, as they were available at many stores and people did carry them to/from these various locations. Of most concern are the witnesses that saw people with rifles around Dealey Plaza. These include the **pick-up truck seen down on Elm St., by Julia Ann Mercer**, earlier that morning. There were also other sightings at various parts of Dallas that morning.

I am bothered by the reports of the **"Rambler Station Wagon"** reported **by Deputy Sheriff Roger Craig**, and others. Two initial witnesses reported that **3 men came from the back of the TSBD, and got into this station wagon** on Houston St. They left in such a hurry, that one of the doors was still swinging open. Roger Craig reported that this **station wagon picked up a white male that ran down the hill on Elm St.** and got in. **Craig later identified this man as Oswald**, although Fritz insisted that Craig was not in his offices, a claim that is later refuted by press photographs.

402

JFK Assassination: Shades From The Fence

A number of witnesses saw at **least 2 men on the sixth floor**. Some of these could have simply seen the 3 men on the fifth floor and were confused; however, there are a number of people who believe they saw a **"darker complected"** man in the sixth floor, as well as a man who looked similar to Oswald.

Motive and Planning:

Although not required, the Warren Commission discussed a general **lack of motive** by Lee Harvey Oswald. It has been said that he **wanted to be famous, or to make a political statement**; however, he never attempted to do this to the **Dallas Police**, or the many **members of the Press** during his stay in Dallas police headquarters. He simply denied any involvement whatsoever. **Additionally, if he really wanted to be famous, or make a statement, he could have simply stayed at the TSBD, instead of leaving.**

That Oswald did **leave the TSBD, indicates that he either was trying to escape** or simply did not know what had happened, as he said. If he was not aware that the President had been shot from his building, it **could have been during his escape that he realized that he was being framed** for the shooting. This could explain the **"calmness"** that Oswald had when encountered in the 2nd floor lunch room by Officer Marion Baker. This is more attributable to someone who has **NOT just blasted through the head of the President** of the United States. It is especially troublesome in comparison to how Oswald **reacted to being stopped by Tippit, and his lack of calmness when Officer McDonald** reaches him in the Texas Theater! I find it **hard to believe** that being cornered after shooting Tippit was more frightening than seeing the President's head explode in the cross-hairs.

JFK Assassination: Shades From The Fence

I am bothered by the **apparent lack of planning** that Oswald had, if he was the Lone Assassin. He shot the President from his own **place of work**, using his **own rifle**, and **then left the building leaving the shells and rifle there**. He had to **KNOW** that doing all of that would point directly to him! (Unlike the Walker shooting, where he allegedly was firing from a public alley, away from his normal locations, and took the rifle with him and buried it for a few days.)

Oswald seemed to **aimlessly wander** after the Assassination. He seemingly had **no escape plan**, and used a public **bus**, a **taxi**, and later **walking** to make his escape. Not only did he not seem to have an escape plan, but he did **not even have his pistol with him** when he left his rooming house the day before. Again it **indicates that Oswald was NOT a shooter**, but soon realized that he was being set up to take the blame.

Tippit Shooting:

I tend to think that Oswald actually did the Tippit shooting, but there are only a couple of things which are troubling.

I am bothered by the **chain of evidence of the shells** from the Tippit shooting. **Officer Poe** was one of the first officers on the scene, and he clearly states that he marked the shells; however, when shown the shells later by the Warren Commission, **his marks are no longer present**. There were also some discrepancies about the **type of shells**, which were a combination of manufacturer. The **combination of the 4 shells differs** on various reports, as well as the fragments recovered from Tippit's body.

I wonder what Oswald was doing at **10th and Patton in the first place**. If he was going to a movie, he was **a few blocks east of any logical path** from his rooming house to the Texas Theater. He had lived in Oak Cliff for many months at various times, and **certainly knew his way around**. A troublesome fact is that **Jack Ruby's apartment was just a few block east** of where the Tippit shooting occurred, which indicates that Oswald may have been going that direction (if he knew Ruby).

I am bothered by the witnesses that said there was a **second man** involved in the Tippit shooting. One account has that he **drove away**, while another had that he **ran in an opposite direction**. I am also concerned that not enough witnesses were capable of, or asked, to **pick Oswald out of a lineup**. In addition, the lineups may have been unfairly balanced to make Oswald the obvious selection, as Oswald himself complained.

Jack Ruby –

I do tend to think **that Jack Ruby could very well have suddenly decided to shoot** Oswald at the spur of the moment. He did have **a temper**, and was very likely to do something very **compulsive** such as this. Another very minor point in his favor was the **Western Union telegram**, as well as **leaving his favorite dog in the car that morning**. Some say if he was planning on shooting Oswald, he would have made sure the dog was taken care of; however, of the **many times in DPD** headquarters that weekend, he may never have known when the opportunity would present itself. He could have simply gotten lucky that morning after doing the telegram, and the dog just happened to be with him this time. **Western Union Alibi scam.**

Having talked to many people **that knew Jack Ruby**, plus everything I had read about him, I think he is the **last individual in Dallas that I would have made part of a pre-assassination Conspiracy**. He simply talked too much, and liked to be "important", and a **big shot** in everyone's eyes. I therefore would not expect him to keep a secret.

However, if you were part of the **Mafia, and HAD TO** "silence Oswald", Jack Ruby may be the **best last minute choice** you can think of. He did have access, had a gun, a violent temper, and with the proper threat to his family, might be controlled.

I am bothered by **Ruby's access to the Dallas Police Department** all weekend. Of course, the Dallas Police Department was **swarmed by more press** than they were ever prepared to deal with. I have often maintained that under those conditions, with lots of strangers in the building, **ANY familiar face** could be construed as "belonging there", or at the least as "I have checked him before". Once he had gained access, continued access is much less of a problem. But the Dallas Police were **inundated with strangers** from all over the country, and the world, and simply did not do the **diligence** they should have. **General Order**

Seth Kantor's repeatedly insisted that he saw Ruby at Parkland Hospital, although Ruby later denied he was ever there. **Seth knew Ruby**, and would definitely recognize him. Even if Ruby was there, it is doubtful that he would have "planted" the stretcher bullet, as according to Aubrey Rike, the entire **Emergency Room area was "locked down" by the Secret Service** as long as Kennedy and Johnson were there. In fact, Aubrey offered a **cigarette to Jackie** Kennedy by taping the pack, and was **practically taken to the ground** by Secret Service agents. (If looking for someone to plant a bullet shot from Oswald's rifle, I myself would point to the epileptic that was in the area before the President.)

I am bothered by the number of **witnesses that say Oswald knew Ruby**. No evidence has ever been produced, but there were a large number of people that said they saw them at various times together. A few even insist they were **introduced** to Oswald by Jack.

JFK Assassination: Shades From The Fence

I am bothered by the **ties of Jack Ruby to the Mafia**. This includes the increase in long distance phone calls in the period leading up to, and including that weekend. These include **friends and associates that Ruby** had not spoken to in years. Part of this concern is the **panic** reported by Police of Ruby after the shooting, and how that panic seemed to **disappear the second he found out that Oswald had actually died.**

A number of people tie **Jack Ruby to gun running, and events in Cuba**. There are many claims that he was involved with the **Anti-Castro efforts of the Mafia**, and consequently the **Anti-Castro Cubans**. Since, in my opinion, the **Anti-Castro Cubans / CIA elements and Mafia are the most likely candidates for a Conspiracy** to Assassination (**NOT the cover-up**, which may have been a separate conspiracy), this is especially troubling.

Lyndon Johnson and J Edgar Hoover and the Cover Up:

I am bothered by the report of **Madeleine Duncan Brown**, and others of Lyndon Johnson **attending a party at one of the Murchison's** home the night before the Assassination. It was at this party, that Johnson came out after a closed door session and **whispered to Madeleine, "After tomorrow, those $&% Kennedy brothers will never bother me again."** According to Madeleine, when she **asked him about who was behind the Assassination months later, he pointed to the Dallas Petroleum friends of hers.** Other people at the party confirm his presence, but only Madeleine would know what he said to her. **I knew Madeleine**, and she was always a very nice lady to me, and always treated me with respect. I never discussed this story with her, but **share mutual friends that insist she was telling the truth**. I have no basis to state my personal belief in her story and memories, other than I **believe our mutual friends believe her**.

JFK Assassination: Shades From The Fence

If the story is true, it **may indicate that LBJ was first told that night**, that something was going to happen the next day. In this scenario, he **may have been told that they would attempt to blame it on Castro or the Soviets, and that he should just move on and not be tricked into following through with any action against Cuba or Russia.**

I am bothered by the **Cover-Up by Hoover and Johnson**. I tend to believe that this is a **separate cover-up from the Conspiracy itself**, although I have many friends who believe if they were part of the cover-up, then they must be part of the Assassination Conspiracy. Of course, as I stated at the beginning of this page, I do think a **Lone Nut (Oswald) is POSSIBLE**, when I do consider it a Conspiracy, I usually **separate it into 2 separate Conspiracies instead of the "Grand Conspiracy"**. The Assassination could have been the result of a Conspiracy which wanted to blame Castro on the deed; moreover, there were many in the government and elsewhere that did say that Oswald was pro-Castro and pro-Communists, and they suggested Castro was behind it. I usually believe that there was a second Conspiracy to cover-up the first, and point the blame on the Lone Nut, Lee Harvey Oswald. In this case, **the second Conspiracy may have even fouled up the goals of the first**, to place the blame on Castro or the Communists.

The **Autopsy** appears to be a total fiasco. Since I believe there was a **separate Cover-Up to make sure that Lee Harvey Oswald was blamed** as the Lone Assassin, regardless of how the Assassination actually happened, the Autopsy was less of a fiasco as it appears. In this case the government needed to **control the Autopsy, so that no evidence of a second shooter**, nor any information that would contradict the Single Bullet, would be found. But if the Autopsy was to actually determine details of the Assassination, it was done in the worst possible way.

JFK Assassination: Shades From The Fence

A prime example is the **back wound**, which the **Autopsy doctors placed 5 ½ inches below the collar**. In the Warren Report, this is now **5 ½ inches behind the "bony protuberance by the right ear"**. The Autopsy doctors being career military men, and **controlled by the military is suspicious**. Also, although Finck was a pathologist, he was **not a forensic pathologist**, and according to some of the men who worked in Bethesda, these men were basically **administrators** of their departments, and had never been seen in that autopsy room before. **Burning their original autopsy notes** was also a area that automatically raised suspicions.

I am bothered by the **discrepancies between the doctors at Parkland Hospital**, and those at the Autopsy. The Autopsy should have been done here in Dallas, as the law dictated, which would have gone a long way towards eliminating the disconnect between the Doctors. This includes the Bethesda doctors **not even being aware of a throat wound until the next morning**. This brought much of the evidence into question.

Prior Knowledge -

I am bothered by the sheer number of people who **claim**, or were otherwise documented, to **having prior knowledge of the Assassination** of JFK, or of the scheme. Of course, JFK was so despised by many groups, they **may have had wishful thinking and this time it just happened to come true**. I will not list all of the names, as I do not myself assert their claims; however, there are well **over a dozen** that have supposedly **claimed fore-knowledge or involvement in the plot/deed**. These include informants, anti-Castro Cubans, Mafia figures, and others. Naturally, each claim needs to be evaluated on its own merits, but the sheer number is troubling.

JFK Assassination: Shades From The Fence

In Nigel Turner's "The Men Who Killed Kennedy" there is a section that has an **undercover audio tape of a Joseph Milteer**, and FBI informant William Summerset, taken the first week in **November 9, 1963**. This tape talked about how an **"assassination was in the works"**, and it would happen from a **high building with a rifle**. It further talked of having to set up a **Patsy**, to take the blame. The tape was turned into Miami Police on Nov 9, and the November 18 Presidential trip to **Miami was subsequently modified to eliminate a Motorcade**. The FBI filed a report on the incident on November 27, 1962. Some people see a person strongly resembling Milteer in photos of the east side of Houston St. in Dallas.

Actions of the FBI:

Most troubling of all of the events and shortfalls of the Warren Commission was the actions of Hoover's FBI. **Hoover was extremely concerned in protecting the FBI from criticism for knowing about Oswald,** in any way, **before the assassination.** His agency **did a number of things to protect "the Bureau"**, by trying to hide this information. It is true that there would be no trial, so consequently what the FBI did may not be considered "illegal", as it was not the destruction of official "evidence". But if the primary agency responsible for the investigation **shows that it is willing to alter, or suppress, evidence**, it is only natural that the **entire investigation suffers from a credibility** issue.

I am bothered by the **destruction of evidence** done by the FBI, in the form of the **note left to Hosty** by Oswald. Hosty insisted that it was a note telling him to leave his wife alone, while a secretary said it actually threatened the FBI. In either case, its existence would **further the theory that Oswald was a "nut"** capable of violence. Of course, it also showed prior knowledge of Oswald's capabilities.

I am bothered by Oswald **requesting to talk to an FBI Agent DeBrueys** when he was arrested in New Orleans. No **notes were found of this interview** (or they were later destroyed), with **Agent Quigley**. It seems to imply some **involvement between Oswald and the FBI**. This is also after Oswald had ordered 2 weapons from companies under investigation by the FBI for mail-ordered weapons - in Dallas, the previous spring.

I am bothered by the **changes in the evidence gathered** by the Dallas Police Department, once received by the FBI. These changes include the **suppression of Hosty's name in Oswald's address/phone book**, when the FBI transcribed the phone book. It also includes the change of a **Minox Camera** (clearly visible in DPD photos of the evidence) to a **Minox Light Meter** in all descriptions by the FBI. Once the FBI started eliminating evidence, however innocuous that evidence supposedly was, there willingness to cover up and destroy evidence, makes their entire case suspect.

I am bothered by the **statements made to James Revill by James Hosty** on the afternoon of the Assassination. He supposedly stated that the **FBI was aware of Oswald, and that he was capable of shooting the President**. Obviously, Revill was quite angry that the DPD was not informed. This statement was said in the presence of at least one other Policeman, although later denied by Hosty.

The Jim Garrison investigation claimed that there was a **FBI Telex dated November 17, 1963**, warning all FBI offices of the possibility of an attempt on the President in Dallas. This telex was supposedly removed from every FBI office on orders from J. Edgar Hoover. Even the Agent claiming the existence of this telex could not come up with one, but instead re-wrote it from memory.

A number of **witnesses claim that the FBI**, and others, **took their movie film** from them, and these films never surfaced. (**Beverly Oliver** and **Gordon Arnold**) Other witnesses later stated that they were severely 'brow beaten' into keeping quiet, or **changing their testimony to something more acceptable to the FBI** and investigators. Others simply claim the Warren Commission simply changed what they said, and put modified statements into the evidence.

I am bothered by the **chain-of-evidence problems** that arose because the FBI transferred all of the evidence from the Dallas Police Department. Many things were not investigated properly, and much evidence was "suppressed" by the FBI. There was also a great deal of discrepancies in the counts of shells, and other processing problems by transferring the evidence in this way. This includes the Palm Print, and other pertinent information.

Conclusions

These, and other issues, are why **the Conspiracy Theory door was left wide open** by the investigation(s) done in the Kennedy assassination.

All "hard evidence" points to Lee Harvey Oswald. The **supporters** of the Warren Commission can **naturally expect the evidence to point to Oswald, as that is what they believe happened.**

However, **critics** say this is natural, since that is **where the investigators wanted the evidence to point**. It is a form of circular logic, where **the more the evidence points to Oswald, the more the critics can say that the government planted, or**

modified, that evidence. All of the shortcomings of the investigation are simply that.

Generally, you can center your opinion into a number of major classifications:

1. **Lee Harvey Oswald acted totally alone**. Without Oswald himself available, we have to assume many things, and will obviously never have the answer.

2. **Lee Harvey Oswald acted in coordination** with other "conspirators", and possibly other shooters. However, he was completely aware of what he was doing, and **actively participated**.

3. There was a Conspiracy, and Oswald was set up as the "Patsy". The planners and shooters manipulated **Oswald to be the fall guy, and he did not actively participate in the shooting**. However, he quickly became aware of his precarious position as the Patsy, and panicked, killing Tippit and resisting MacDonald.

4. There was a Grand Conspiracy, and **Oswald was completely innocent**. He did not shoot at Kennedy, or at Tippit. He was completely set up as a Patsy for the crime, and would have been railroaded as guilty, or eliminated.

There is also the consideration as to how far any Conspiracy goes: Was **Johnson involved in the conspiracy**, or did he simply try to **cover up to protect the public** from World War 3, involving the Russians and Cubans? If involved in the Conspiracy, was he involved in the "Grand Conspiracy", knowing about the event **before hand**? How much did he know, and how far before hand? **Jack Ruby**?

Printed in Dunstable, United Kingdom

64499969R00238